All Abraham's Children

All Abraham's Children

Changing Mormon Conceptions
of Race and Lineage

ARMAND L. MAUSS

University of Illinois Press

URBANA AND CHICAGO

Library of Congress Cataloging-in-Publication Data
Mauss, Armand L.
All Abraham's children : changing Mormon conceptions of race
and lineage / Armand L. Mauss.
p.   cm.
Includes bibliographical references and index.
ISBN 0-252-02803-1 (alk. paper)
1. Ethnic relations—Religious aspects—Church of Jesus Christ of
Latter-day Saints—History of doctrines.
2. Race relations—Religious aspects—Church of Jesus Christ of
Latter-day Saints—History of doctrines.
3. Ethnicity—Religious aspects—Church of Jesus Christ of Latter-day
Saints—History of doctrines.
4. Race—Religious aspects—Church of Jesus Christ of Latter-day
Saints—History of doctrines.
I. Title.
BX8643.E85M38   2003
261.8'348'008823—dc21   2002009722

To Charles Y. Glock,
mentor, colleague, and cherished friend,
who graciously waited, wondered, and finally
outlived my procrastination

Know ye therefore that they which are of faith, the same are the children of Abraham. . . . And if ye be Christ's, then are ye Abraham's seed and heirs according to the promise.

—Galatians, 3:7, 29

Contents

Preface

THIS BOOK IS the product of four decades of intermittent thought and work. The project has been interrupted often, sometimes by unavoidable career contingencies and sometimes by regrettable digressions that I could have prevented. Now, however, in the twilight of my academic career, I am anxious to see the work published, lest all those decades and their cumulative work go to waste. The years between the germination of this project in my youth and its fruition now have naturally brought some refinements and insights. Some things stand out even more clearly in the softened twilight than in the glare of midday.

As a young man starting graduate work at the University of California at Berkeley in 1955, I had originally hoped to draw on nearly five years of experience in Japan and earn a doctorate in Japanese history or Asian studies. I did earn a master's degree in history, with an Asia emphasis; but a doctorate in those fields was eventually pushed beyond my reach by the demand of my academic mentors that I learn to read a second Asian language (in addition to Japanese and to the two European languages routinely required for doctorates in those days). Instead, I was encouraged by the faculty in the Department of Sociology (which had only recently been established) to pursue my doctoral studies in that discipline, with such continuing focus on Asian studies as time would permit. Since the new department needed students, I was made very welcome as a promising doctoral prospect in sociology, even though, as a full-time public schoolteacher, I could make only a part-time commitment to my graduate studies. By the time I finally earned the doctorate, I was past forty, and my sociological studies, while deeply enriching and fulfilling, had taken me far away from my original interests in Asia.

Once in sociology, I contemplated two possible topics for a doctoral dissertation. The first, which I tentatively entitled "Mormonism and Urbanism," grew out of my youthful experiences in California, starting from the depression era (when Mormons outside Utah were rare and mainly of the working class) to midcentury and the postwar maturation of Mormon institutions along the urban, cosmopolitan coast. As I reflected on those experiences, I realized that I had been living through a struggle in which Mormons were daily constrained to express their religious commitments and traditions in an environment that was increasingly secularized and sometimes hostile. The vaunted Age of Aquarius in the 1960s only increased the pressure on traditional Mormon values, not just in California but everywhere. In the ensuing struggle, Mormon institutions were at first partly assimilated and then reacted against that assimilation in some surprising ways. Such was the story I told in *The Angel and the Beehive: The Mormon Struggle with Assimilation* (1994), which was the incarnation of my original "Mormonism and Urbanism" project.

My doctoral dissertation, entitled "Mormonism and Minorities," came out of the second topic I had considered as a graduate student. This topic was the natural product of a convergence between two developments in the early 1960s that proved very important for my academic career: (1) the rising crescendo of the national civil rights movement, especially in such places as the Berkeley campus; and (2) the funding received by Professor Charles Y. Glock, of the Department of Sociology and the Survey Research Center at Berkeley, for a comprehensive study of the Christian roots of anti-Semitism (Glock and Stark 1966). As a practicing Mormon in urban California, I had become acutely aware of the growing conflict over racial politics between my denomination and most of the rest of the country. I was particularly struck by the anomaly, as I had experienced it, of a Mormon religious heritage that combined an explicitly negative perspective on blacks (or "Negroes," as they were then called) with an explicitly positive characterization of Jews.

As I learned about Glock's project, I became aware that his surveys were to include samples of only Protestants and Roman Catholics in northern California. There were no plans to collect any data from Mormons. Accordingly, I approached Glock with the proposition that my dissertation could be a useful supplement and satellite for his project in at least two ways: I could model my study and my questionnaire after his, thereby producing Mormon data for comparison with his Catholic and Protestant data; and the Mormon data would permit an especially interesting test of his theory about the origin of various kinds of prejudice from different kinds of religious indoctrination (given the contrasting Mormon teachings about blacks and Jews).

Glock became my chief mentor at Berkeley and a lifelong friend. At length I finished the dissertation (Mauss 1970) and published a number of articles along the way on the connection between religion and prejudice among Mormons (Mauss 1966, 1967, 1968, 1972a, 1981, and 1999). My survey data could not, alas, be collected in time to be useful to Glock because my research had to await church approval and personal funding arrangements. His questionnaire, mentorship, and data did, however, prove extremely valuable to me in guiding my project. The dissertation itself, to Glock's disappointment, was never published, but major portions of it are subsumed in my other publications and in the present book, which is the culmination of an even more comprehensive project on religious belief and racial conceptions. Furthermore, I am happy to say, it is being published in time for Glock to see this latest installment in his rich legacy (he was an active eighty-three-year-old in October 2002).

The Nature and Scope of the Present Book

This book is, however, not simply a belated version of another dissertation that was never published. It is not only very different from the dissertation but also much richer in social theory and history. Like the dissertation, this book analyzes the origin and nature of traditional Mormon attitudes and behavior toward Jews, Native Americans, and people of black African origin. Also like the dissertation, the book employs survey data on Mormons that I and others collected, and it compares "racial" attitudes of Mormons with those in certain other religious denominations for which survey data were available. That is where the similarity ends between the two works.

The book offers a theoretical framework going well beyond the straightforward and additive one borrowed from Glock for my dissertation. Glock had employed a basically Weberian perspective in which ideas have attitudinal and behavioral consequences. Specifically, his study postulated a cognitive process in which religious beliefs and feelings accumulated in linear fashion to produce anti-Semitic intentions and behavior. The decades of religious change that have intervened since Glock's study have permitted me to add historical to cognitive processes in the theory that guides this presentation. The theory guiding this book is derived partly from the social psychology of *identity formation and attribution,* for Mormons first had to construct an identity for themselves as a people before they could construct identities for others across the boundaries between "them" and "us." The process of constructing and reconstructing these collective identities through time is one of the theoretical underpinnings of this work. For this theoretical strand, I am also indebted to the later work of Glock on the construction of worldviews as a source of racial attitudes, particularly worldviews based on supernatural beliefs (Apostle et al. 1983; Glock 1989). One thing I had not recognized at the beginning was that for Mormons the constructions of these various identities all took place as part of the same historical and ideological development. They were all "of a piece" and combined to provide Mormons with a coherent explanation of the place of each people, Israelite and otherwise, in the divine plan. A general theory of identity construction thus seemed necessary.

At another level, I found myself dealing with still a different Weberian problem: the relation between *ideas and organizational change.* Do organizations change under the influence of new ideas, or do ideas change in response to organizational developments and imperatives? Weber's theoretical reasoning had endorsed both causal directions, seeing them as part of the same circular process. In my 1994 book, I showed both directions at work in Mormon organizational developments during the second half of the twentieth century. In this present book, I show again how an organizational imperative—namely, the church's worldwide missionizing commitment—was driven by its fundamental theological ideas, but I also demonstrate how those ideas, in turn, were changed by more than a century of global proselyting encounters.

Beyond enhanced theoretical richness, the book differs from the dissertation in the degrees of attention and emphasis given to the various "racial" relationships in the Mormon experience. An early chapter of the book traces the construction and deconstruction of the Mormon identity itself as a divinely chosen one of Israelite origin, a topic not addressed at all in the dissertation. Then the book devotes three long chapters to a century and a half of Mormon relationships with the so-called Indians or aboriginal peoples of this hemisphere, particularly in North America. This topic, too, received only scant attention in the dissertation. The inclusion of all this new material has necessitated giving far less attention to the earlier surveys of Mormon relationships with Jews and African Americans and much more to the history. There is room here only to summarize the analysis of the survey data. The entire dissertation is, in effect, condensed here into only two chapters. However, such an allocation of space and effort in this book seems appropriate in the light of the work that has been published elsewhere since the dissertation. When considered together with that earlier work, the treatment here, I trust, does justice to the topics of Mormon relationships with all these peoples. Readers wanting more details on the survey data and methodology will find them in my other works, especially Mauss (1970, 1985, and 1994, 33–45, 215–228), and in the American Religion Data Archive at Pennsylvania State University, where my data sets on Mormons are deposited and documented. The appendixes to the present book have still more such information.

Acknowledgments

All authors know that intellectual debts are difficult to identify, much less to repay. Like so many others, I have almost certainly forgotten some of these debts and will thus overlook acknowledgments that truly are owed. I have already mentioned Charles Glock as my chief mentor and model. To his name should be added that of Rodney Stark, also a student of Glock and his collaborator in much of their early work. Although a bit behind me in age, Stark was well ahead of me in graduate school and functioned very much as both mentor and colleague. He was always generous with his time and guidance during our graduate school days; since then, as one of the world's luminaries in the sociology of religion, Stark has truly been an inspiration, not only because of his intellectual creativity but also because of his astonishing productivity in the scholarly literature. He has also maintained a particular interest and competence in Mormon studies from graduate school days, which has further distinguished him from other non-Mormon scholars in this field. I have discussed my own debt to Stark in greater detail elsewhere (Mauss 1990b).

Besides Glock and Stark, credit is due many others who have provided expert guidance and assistance during my career since graduate school. For the present book in particular (and for much else in my research on Mormons), I am especially grateful to Professor Gary Shepherd, of Oakland University, Rochester, Michigan, and to Professor Ronald W. Walker, of Brigham Young University, both of whom meticulously read and criticized an earlier and longer version of this manuscript. Many others did the same with portions of it. In particular, Robert H. Briggs and Professors Lawrence G. Coates, Edward L. Kimball, V. Con Osborne, and John W. Welch, of Brigham Young University, as well as Thomas W. Murphy, of Edmonds Community College (Washington), all generously contributed their time and expertise in criticizing one or more of my chapters. Their efforts particularly strengthened my treatment of Latter-day Saints' relationships with the aboriginal inhabitants of this hemisphere. Professor Newell G. Bringhurst, of the College of the Sequoias in California, himself a pioneering historian of Mormon relationships with blacks, offered several helpful suggestions on my chapters dealing with that topic.

Still other colleagues gave me crucial guidance and assistance in the quantitative and statistical portions of this manuscript and some of my earlier work. As a special consultant in such matters, my longtime friend and colleague Professor Michael Patrick Allen, of Washington State University, was particularly helpful. Julie C. Nelson, while she was a graduate student of mine at Washington State University in the 1970s, did most of the organizing, formatting, and processing of the data from my early surveys of Mormons in Utah and California. More recently, my friend and colleague Manfred Heim, of Pullman, Washington, updated this work and then created an additional data set from the annual General Social Surveys of the 1970s, 1980s, and 1990s, so that I could compare these national data with my own data from the 1960s. In all of this, we received regular and generous guidance from Zoltan Porga, who heads the Social Science Data Processing Center at Washington State University. Additional staff time and consultation were donated by expert personnel at the Social and Economic Sciences Research Center at Washington State.

In the final preparation of my manuscript, I received valuable and time-consuming library assistance from my colleague Devery Anderson, and when the book was finally completed, Dynette Ivie Reynolds prepared the index under great time constraint. To all of these acknowledgments must be added my deepest appreciation for the constant encouragement and guidance of other interested colleagues, not least the editors at the University of Illinois Press.

Finally, for reasons going far beyond mere author convention, I must express my intellectual, spiritual, and emotional debt to my family, starting with my late parents and my two siblings and including my eight children, all of whom sacrificed involuntarily some of the paternal companionship to which they were entitled during my work on this project, in particular, and in my academic career more generally. In these respects, of course, my debt is greatest of all to Ruth, my beloved wife and partner of half a century, who has endured much on my account from our earliest days together and who has become an increasingly important intellectual companion in my mature years.

All Abraham's Children

1. The Mormon Missionary Impulse and the Negotiation of Identity

Even if politically imbalanced, conversion encounters are always two-sided, and the social and intellectual dynamics of each camp affect the outcome.
—Robert W. Hefner, 1993

SEVERAL STORY LINES are intertwined in this book. At the most abstract level, one story illustrates the power of religious ideas and human behavior on each other, indeed on the operational definition of reality itself.[1] It is an oft-told story, but this version shows how the followers of the nineteenth-century American prophet Joseph Smith created a spiritual and ideological world within which they encountered and attempted to convert various peoples. In the process, these ideas and the ongoing reconsiderations of their meaning changed both the Mormons and their converts. Another story line implicates religious ideas in the creation of racial prejudice and invidious ethnic distinctions. This, too, is an old story, but the Mormon version is much more complex than most, and it reveals some profound unintended consequences. Still a third story explores the construction and reconstruction of various peoples' identities. Ethnic, religious, and even family identities are not created in a vacuum but are the products of negotiations across time between peoples—often peoples of unequal power, sometimes mutually hostile peoples. The identities at stake here are not only that of the Mormons themselves but also those of certain other peoples with special definitions in traditional Mormon religious teachings.

I ardently hope that the facts, figures, and details in this book will not obscure these underlying stories that I am trying to tell. They are important stories, quite apart from the academic trappings that occasionally encumber them here. Stories about human beings and their institutions always involve the discovery of paradoxes and contradictions. One of the contradictions in the Mormon case is found in the juxtaposition of two general historical realities: Mormonism has traditionally taught particularistic doctrines favoring some ethnic groups over others, yet the church has always had an extensive proselyting program with a focus intended for all peoples every-where.[2] These two tendencies have remained in dialectical tension through-out Mormon history, and each has affected and modified the other. Most ob-servers seem to have noticed only the impact of the *first* on the *second*—that is, how (until recently) traditional doctrines have channeled Mormon mis-sionary efforts *toward* some societies (those in northwestern Europe, Latin America, Polynesia, or the North American aboriginal peoples) and *away* from others (for example, societies with large populations of blacks).

While these two general tendencies are, of course, always acting on each other, this book gives more attention than most to the impact of the *second* on the *first*—namely, the universalistic missionary program's impact on tra-ditional doctrines. This is the reciprocal relationship between ideas and be-havior to which I referred at the beginning: If religious doctrines and other ideas are expressions of the cultural settings from which they emerge, they also reflect back on those cultures—though perhaps only selectively—to influence the religious, social, and political *behavior* of the people. In this story line, the reader will see the overarching intellectual presence of Max Weber, whose extensive works on the connections between religious ideolo-gy and behavior have influenced a century of scholarship.[3] In the chapters to follow, there is more than one illustration of Weber's underlying theme of the reciprocal influences of ideas and experience in human history.

Of special interest here is the account of the development of religious ideas in response to *proselyting* experience—the unintended consequences, in particular, of the ambitious Mormon missionary program, which gradually transformed the Latter-day Saints from a "peculiar people," preoccupied with invidious divine distinctions among lineages, into a worldwide movement embracing all humankind as "Abraham's children." The moral and spiritu-al concomitant of this ideological transformation was the refinement of the Latter-day Saints' own understanding of universal kinship in the gospel of Jesus Christ. We are thus presented with the inspiring irony that a modern, universalistic vision of the spiritual potential in *all* peoples should emerge from the parochial nineteenth-century Mormons' vision of themselves as a chosen lineage.[4]

Although not well known to non-Mormons, traditional Latter-day Saint (LDS) doctrine defined most of today's Mormons as literal descendants of one of the ancient twelve tribes of Israel, primarily the tribe of Ephraim. This designation was part of an implied arrangement of various contemporary peoples, by divine plan, into ancient lineages from most favored to least fa-vored. Descendants of Ephraim stood at the top, as most favored, while de-scendants of Cain were least favored, having been singled out for a special curse that prevented them from holding the priesthood until very recent times. American Indian peoples, as descendants of both Manasseh and

Ephraim, stood near the top in favored status, as did the Jews (descendants of Judah), who provided the lineage for the Messiah himself. Descendants of the remaining Israelite tribes, some of whom are scattered throughout the world, were apparently yet to be identified or to come forth as a distinct people before the return of the Messiah; nevertheless, they had been understood as enjoying favored lineages by virtue of sharing in the special covenant that God made with their ancestors Abraham, Isaac, and Jacob. Standing in a kind of neutral zone, somewhere below the Israelites but well above the descendants of Cain, have been the "Gentiles," whom God has been able to use for his purposes throughout history and who might, through their acceptance of the Messiah, eventually be "grafted into" the covenant people of Israel.[5]

Paradoxically, these ideas have always coexisted in Mormonism with the much more general Christian teaching that the Abrahamic covenant since Christ has its efficacy no longer in lineage per se but rather in acceptance of the true gospel. Through faithful adherence to that gospel, anyone of any lineage is spiritually incorporated into the family of Abraham and given both the blessings and the responsibilities of the "chosen people." With the passage of time, especially in recent decades, authoritative Mormon discourse has placed less emphasis on the salience of literal lineage and more emphasis on the potentially universal inclusiveness of God's ancient covenant with Abraham. As this change of emphasis continues, the logical paradox is on the way to resolution. After all, if embracing the gospel of Christ is all that really matters for full participation in the Abrahamic covenant, why should one's *genetic* lineage be given any salience whatsoever? Yet the earlier focus on the importance of literal Israelite lineage has remained influential in the thinking of many Mormons, even into the twenty-first century, seemingly as a residue of the racialist interpretations of history once so common in America as well as in Europe. How and when did such ideas arise in early Mormonism? What was the course of their development? What purposes did they serve?[6]

Within weeks of its formal founding in the spring of 1830, the Church of Jesus Christ of Latter-day Saints began to dispatch missionaries in all directions. They saw themselves as heralds of a new dispensation of the gospel of Christ, a new restoration of the ancient gospel and church, sent to preach that gospel "to every creature," as in ancient times. Despite the most discouraging obstacles and opposition, these missionaries within a generation had visited every continent and nearly every major nation on earth. As of this writing, some sixty thousand LDS missionaries are now at work in 150 nations. Their numbers and methods have varied with time and place, but their message has always included a "call to repentance," a challenge to the inhabitants of the earth to forsake all other religions and to embrace instead the "only true gospel" as taught by the latter-day prophets and apostles of Jesus Christ.

Such a message would not be considered by most peoples as an expression of universal tolerance and appreciation for the world's varied races and cultures—any more than it was so considered by the Roman world to which the emissaries of Jesus preached two thousand years ago. Yet the apostle Paul envisioned a world outside Jerusalem, where all humankind could become "the children of Abraham," without regard to original race, lineage, or culture. This Pauline vision has only gradually taken hold in Mormonism and displaced the racial exclusivism that had earlier been absorbed from the Anglo-American heritage of most Mormons. Of course, Christianity in general has always struggled with invidious comparisons among racial or ethnic groups in the world. Paul and his followers had already encountered this struggle in their own disagreements with the early Christian Judaizers of ancient Palestine. Even at the end of the twentieth century, Christianity was still trying to purge itself of a pervasive, inherited anti-Semitism and from a great many other mutual ethnic hostilities among Christian peoples themselves.

While such racialist thinking is clearly apparent also in early Mormonism, as in early America more generally, I argue that the full-fledged racialist framework of modern Mormonism arose primarily during the century after the arrival of the Saints in Utah.[7] It was the product not of any particular revelation but of a social and intellectual movement among some of Mormonism's most powerful and articulate leaders. The public discourse of these leaders demonstrates that they synthesized or combined certain interpretations of LDS scripture with two important influences from *outside* Mormonism: British Israelism and Anglo-Saxon triumphalism. In doing so, they contributed greatly to the emergent ethnic consciousness that Thomas F. O'Dea discovered in his study of the Mormons at midcentury (O'Dea 1954).[8] Their retrospective construction of a "chosen" lineage identity also enabled them to resist the growing national and international definition of Mormons as a despicable people.

As will be seen later, although the specific *content* of this retrospective reconstruction of lineage has much that is unique to the Mormons, the *process* is far from unique. Many peoples, indeed entire nations, have constructed idealized ancestries for themselves, with or without much empirical, genealogical evidence, as part of a larger mythological history. It is important for all peoples, but especially scholars, to understand that these constructed histories and lineages carry their own truths and have their own purposes totally apart from historical reality. One of these purposes typically is the creation and vindication of a favorable national or ethnic identity in which all members, particularly the youth, can be taught to take personal pride and find personal honor. Another common purpose is more political: a means of resistance against *outside* powers threatening domination, colonialization, assimilation, or all three. Such purposes are all apparent at different times in Mormon history.

Two different aspects of lineage identity are considered in this study. One is the reciprocal relationship in Mormon history between lineage identities and proselyting programs—that is, how the selection of certain peoples for proselyting has been influenced by Mormon preconceptions about their lineages and how, reciprocally, these preconceptions have been modified by the church's actual proselyting experience. A second and related aspect is the discourse and the processes involved in the *social construction and uses* of lineage, both by missionaries and by the converted peoples. It is important to emphasize at the outset that what follows is *not* intended as a *general history* of the processes, relationships, or periods under discussion. Such a history of Mormon relationships with the various ethnic groups would take far more space than one volume could provide, and anyway I make no pretense of expertise as a historian.

What I attempt instead is a certain *sociological interpretation* of historical materials provided mostly by other scholars, supplemented by documentary and survey data from my own original research. For my theoretical frameworks, as well as for any interpretations of specific episodes, my presentation therefore draws only selectively on historical materials, though I have tried to avoid undue bias. With this strategy, I feel no need to cite every source, primary or secondary, bearing on a given assertion or interpretation, for that only lengthens endnotes and often results in "overkill" in trying to establish a given point. Finally, let me be clear that my focus is intentionally limited to the Western Hemisphere, where lineage constructions and negotiations among Mormons have principally occurred. I begin, however, with some comparative examples of identity construction and then return to the Mormon case.

Lineage and Ethnicity as Social Constructions

Lineage and ethnicity, whether of an individual or of an entire people, are popularly understood as matters of objective "fact." When one thinks of his or her lineage, one tends to think in simple genealogical terms: One is or is not a descendant of a given ancestor; it is a matter of finding out from reliable records who were one's parents, grandparents, great-grandparents, and so on back, as far as the records will go. Similarly, whether in ordinary conversation or in our mass media, one tends to regard "ethnic group" as given in nature: One simply is or is not Anglo-American, African American, Hispanic American, and so on.

Yet scholars and scientists who work with such concepts have long recognized the inadequacies and ambiguities of such popular understandings. Where lineage is concerned, very few people in any society have any idea who their ancestors were more than four or five generations back, to say nothing of five hundred or a thousand years ago. Reliable records simply have not survived, if they ever existed. As for ethnicity, the many migrations and invasions that have occurred in human history have rendered such categories as "ethnic group" and especially "race" increasingly imprecise and suspect. This is particularly the case in such highly assimilative societies as ancient Rome and the United States, as is well attested by the recent quandary in the United States over how to classify and count the many citizens of mixed ethnic background in the official census. To be sure, various scholarly definitions for *ethnicity* or *ethnic group* have continued to be proposed and have proved more or less satisfactory for some purposes; but much imprecision and uncertainty remain in actual cases.[9]

In the face of all this ambiguity, social scientists have come increasingly to understand that the collective *construction* by a people of their own ethnic and genealogical past is probably more important than the historical and empirical realities, even if these could be scientifically determined. After all, people act on what they *believe* to be true and real, about themselves and about others, rather than on what science has "shown" to be real. This principle of behavior applies at the collective level of the nation, the society, or the *ethnos,* just as it does at the level of the individual or the family. The "historical record" itself, as constructed across time by the scribes or oral custodians of that record, is at least as likely to be the *product* as the *source* of a people's collective understanding of themselves and their ethnic or genealogical heritage. Furthermore, as often as not, the popular and especially the official record of the past is a retrospective reconstruction produced in the service of the religious or political objectives of a powerful interest group in a particular era.[10]

This process has been discovered repeatedly in the analysis, deconstruction, and critiques of the great recorded sagas of many different cultures. An important recent example is the work of E. Theodore Mullen Jr. on the origins of the Hebrew Pentateuch and the Deuteronomistic history of Israel (1997, 82).[11] Setting aside the long scholarly dialogues and disputations over historicity and the so-called documentary hypothesis, Mullen argues that these books, in their received form, date back only to the mid-sixth century B.C.E., for they bespeak the concerns and preoccupations of the post-exile scribes during the period of the Second Temple and the Persian hegemony. Although these scribes (e.g., Ezra and Nehemiah) doubtless had some earlier records, record fragments, and oral histories at their disposal, the Pentateuch and derivative books of the Hebrew Bible familiar to us (i.e., translated into modern languages) were products of this post-exile period (Mullen 1997, 80).

Mullen adduces a great variety of evidence and reasons for his thesis and identifies numerous post-exile concerns and Persian interests presumably guiding the scribes. However, my interests here are limited to what he has to say about the post-exile struggle to reformulate and retain Israelite identity through claims about lineage and efforts to resist assimilation; for the biblical discourse on these issues has its analogues, as will be seen, in the Mormon discourse of much more recent times. In the case of the ancient Hebrews, *Israel* had referred to different entities at different times. In patriarchal times, it was the new name God gave to Jacob on renewal of the Abrahamic covenant; later, it referred also to a territory and then, in the time of the monarchy, to a nation-state. The conquest and exile at the hands of the Babylonians, however, effectively rendered all those meanings obsolete, along with their associated identities. When the Israelites (now mostly Judaic, or "Jews") were returned to Jerusalem and environs under the new hegemony of the Persians, the task of reconstructing an identity for Israel, according to Mullen, fell to the scribes who were associated with the Second Temple, which then became the symbol of that new identity.[12]

Given the new circumstances, the new identity would be that of a *people* (or "ethnic group") recognized by lineage, a special covenant and relationship with God, and certain cultural and religious boundaries against assimilation by politically and culturally dominant neighbors (Mullen 1993 and 1997, 156, 196). Mullen contends that "a new set of boundaries that defined the people was created and, once it had been accepted by the Persian authorities and implemented by their administrative officials, a new sense of the ideal of 'Israel' as a distinct ethnic community came into being" (1997, 73). Since the return from exile took place after two generations of Babylonian assimilation and was in any case controlled by the Persians, it is by no means certain that the refugees from exile were necessarily all of Israelite lineage, for the Persians had their own political reasons for wanting a viable colony in Palestine (Mullen 1997, 77–80). Mullen maintains that "it was through the [temple scribes'] composition of a variety of mythic accounts of their ancestral past that this 'Israel' developed its claims to being the genealogical descendants of the original 'exiles' from the area of ancient Judah" (1997, 77).[13]

Of course, the mythological foundations of nations and peoples commonly include myths of origin in time and space, specifications of ancestry, and accounts of migration. For the returned exiles and their descendants, "Israel," Mullen argues, now became "both a distinctive people with an exclusive divine claim to a particular land and [individuals] who could trace [their] claim back to the 'original' ancestor, Abram. The myths of origins and migration created a specific lineage that would stand over against any 'indigenous' claims to the right to the lands promised to Abram and his offspring" (1997, 156).[14] From whatever written or oral records might have survived to that point, the temple scribes created a whole new work, a "primary history" of this people's whole existence from the Creation to the exile. This ac-

count of the past contained also the divinely established normative boundaries by which Israel was to maintain its identity among the nations against
various threats to its ethnic and religious distinctiveness. Selected narratives
from this literature could be read aloud by the scribes at festivals or on other public occasions to "re-create" Israel and reformulate the associated ethnic identity again and again.[15]

Mormon Identity Construction and the Search for Boundaries

The analogues to all of this in Mormon history are easy to find, although
obviously there are also enough differences that one should not reach too far
for such parallels. Thomas F. O'Dea (1954) found in nineteenth-century
Mormon history an ethnic consciousness and sense of peoplehood that approached nationalism in its intensity and boundary maintenance. Although
the Mormons did not, of course, go on to enjoy several centuries of their own
nation-state, as ancient Israel had done, they came close to the beginnings
of one in Nauvoo and in early Utah with their devotion to a political kingdom of God. In any case, Mormons always gathered in politically separate
enclaves. Like ancient Israelites, Mormons were given by their God a "Zion"
of their own in Missouri, which was to be theirs until the coming of the
Messiah, but they were exiled by superior military force to Illinois, then to
Iowa and Nebraska, and finally to remote Utah. Nor were they long left at
peace even in Utah. They soon became not only an exiled people but also a
pariah people to the rest of the world.

The century of Mormon history after the 1847 exile to Utah is a much truncated counterpart of the history of ancient Israel, though the Mormon exile
was an expulsion, not a captivity. No doubt there are other important differences as well. Yet the Mormons, like the ancient Israelites, suffered a loss
of their promised land, despite divine covenants. During the chaos following the end of their "Kingdom on the Mississippi" and the assassination of
their prophet-king, they came perilously close to complete fragmentation and
thus annihilation as a separate people, again despite divine protection and
promises to them as God's own people. All of these setbacks required explanation through a new narrative history.[16]

Apart from the extraordinary spiritual and material suffering entailed in
these setbacks, their resettlement in Utah (like the Jewish resettlement during the Second Temple era) brought together religious refugees of varied
origins, not only from the considerably different regions on either side of the
Mason-Dixon line in the United States but also from the British Isles, Scandinavia, Germany, and other European countries. Against this background,
the scribes and prophets of Mormonism faced much the same task as had

their ancient Jewish counterparts—namely, the creation of a new people, a new *ethnos,* unified by a common understanding, explanation, and vindication of their past; by renewed covenants with their God; and by the retrospective creation or discovery of a common ancestry, particularly an ancestry in which they could share pride or even chauvinism as a defense against the calumny and denigration increasingly heaped on them from the outside.[17]

It is not my purpose to offer the kind of comprehensive historiography and analysis of ethnic identity construction for the Mormons that Mullen has provided for the ancient Hebrews. Rather, I propose to focus on only one aspect of that ethnic identity formation: the retrospective construction of Mormon *lineage* and the part it played in the creation of Mormon ethnicity from roughly the mid-nineteenth century to the mid-twentieth. By linking themselves in a literal, genealogical way to ancient Israel, particularly to the tribe of Ephraim, the Mormons were able simultaneously to carve out for themselves a special niche and a special connection to the whole redemptive history and destiny of God's chosen people and to claim a favored identity that would belie the identity imposed on them by their enemies. As they later synthesized their Ephraimite doctrines with the philosophies of British Israelism and Anglo-Saxon triumphalism coming from outside Utah, their identity as a people of destiny seemed all the more vindicated. Like the Deuteronomistic narratives of the Second Temple period in ancient Israel, the narratives of modern Israel in Utah created this new lineage and new ethnic identity again and again in the sermons and writings of the most popular and influential church leaders.

A key element, of course, in the construction of ethnicity is *boundaries,* particularly the issue of where the boundaries are drawn and who has the power to draw them. Boundaries might be asserted from the inside by a "peculiar" people, as was historically the case with Anglo-American Mormons. Boundaries might also be imposed from the outside, politically, socially, or through other institutions, which, again, the early Mormons experienced. Throughout American history, contests over ethnic boundaries have been recurrent and so have the differential *attributions* constructed on either side of each boundary. Contests over boundaries become especially acrimonious when access to power and resources is at stake, as in the case of the controversy over ethnic declarations in the U.S. census of recent decades.

Mormon doctrines about race and lineage have never been involved, of course, in national policy-making about the census or anything else, but in the late twentieth century these doctrines were heavily implicated in Mormon relationships with other Americans, especially black Americans. Two chapters are devoted to this issue; for now, the point is that the nineteenth-century Mormon attributions of differential spiritual merit by lineage, originally constructed to maintain a special Mormon status in the divine scheme of things, eventually came to function as a *boundary-maintenance* device against a powerfully assimilative American culture. As the rapidly assimilating Mormons found it increasingly difficult to identify culture traits truly distinguishing them as a "peculiar people," the internal boundaries against full ecclesiastical citizenship for the "lineage of Cain" came to seem all the more salient.[18]

If the ongoing construction of a special Mormon identity seemed to require boundaries excluding black African lineage, the same process required inclusion of Jews as part of the divinely favored lineage. Like many Protestants in the nineteenth century, Mormons embraced the Old Testament attributions of divine favor for Israelite lineage: Jacob (Israel) and his descendants had inherited the divine birthright and covenant from his father, Isaac, who, in turn, had inherited the same from his father, Abraham. Mormons could hardly claim Israelite lineage for themselves while denying the same to their "cousins" the Jews. The Mormon claim to a divinely favored lineage gained credibility only to the extent that the boundary between Israelites and Gentiles could be successfully drawn to include *as Israelites* both Mormons (whose lineage claims were problematic) and Jews (whose claims were not). As later chapters reveal, variations across time in Mormon understandings about Jews have carried differential implications for Mormon policies, but almost from the beginning Mormons have drawn the Israelite boundary to include themselves with the Jews.

Boundary definitions have proved somewhat more difficult with regard to the aboriginal inhabitants of the Western Hemisphere, or "Lamanites," as they have been designated in Mormon literature. The Book of Mormon (1830) seemed to define Euroamericans, including the Mormon converts themselves, as "Gentiles" charged with the special responsibility of taking that book (and the gospel more generally) to the literal descendants of Israel who had inhabited this hemisphere since 600 B.C.E.. However, as the Lamanites among the various "Indians" of North America proved generally resistant to proselyting efforts and hostile to the white occupation of their ancestral lands, Mormons became increasingly ambivalent about the status of the Indians in the divine plan. Furthermore, as will be seen in the next chapter, Mormons came to understand themselves increasingly as literal Israelites rather than as the Gentiles of the Book of Mormon. As such, they could claim inclusion with the newly discovered Lamanites within the boundary between Israelites and Gentiles.

As will be seen in later chapters, this boundary gradually expanded in Mormon lore, eventually including all the aboriginal peoples of the hemisphere, south and north, as well as many Polynesian and other Pacific island peoples.[19] Boundary expansion seemed to occur with missionary success. However, by about 1980, these boundaries had become much more porous and therefore much less salient. In some cases, they seemed to have been rather too hastily drawn, as in the case of the North American aboriginal peoples, long considered Israelites (Lamanites). When a sustained investment of Mormon energy and resources in thousands of these Indians after World War II produced only a dubious cost-benefit ratio in terms of durable converts, these investments were redirected to Mexico and South America, where about a third of all Mormons now reside. Concomitantly, many Mormon scholars and others began to redefine the boundaries of the Lamanites as limited to a relatively small part of the hemisphere (Sorenson 1985).

Shifting conceptions among Mormons about the boundaries between themselves, as a divinely favored Israelite people, and other peoples, such as black Africans, Jews, or American Indians, tended to reflect the shifts also occurring in Mormon relationships with those peoples and with the American nation more generally. Nineteenth-century Mormons had produced an emergent ethnic consciousness and self-definition as separate from other Americans—not just in religion but in culture more broadly, beginning with their claim to literal Israelite ancestry. Their lineage was carefully distinguished, furthermore, from those others who at first had shared with Mormons a culturally denigrated status but who increasingly also laid claim to a legitimate place in the American mosaic. This Mormon struggle to find and maintain a "chosen" identity over against all others might have been partly a reaction to external pressures, as noted earlier, but it was also reinforced by external boundaries and attributions from American society generally. At the beginning of the twentieth century, Mormons began an assimilation campaign aimed at recovering an identity as essentially loyal, mainstream Americans, but they met considerable external resistance for much of the century.

In this regard, the Mormon experience paralleled somewhat that of the later Japanese Americans, who in 1942 found the cultural boundary officially redrawn in such a way that their identity became essentially Japanese rather than American, as they had always claimed to be.[20] Happily, after World War II, the boundary was redrawn again, not only to include them as true Americans but now (like many other Asian Americans) with new ethnic traits more favorable than ever (Nagel 1986). The identity of Mormons as an accepted category of patriotic Americans (or Canadians) is no longer contested to any appreciable extent in North America, but a comfortable identity for Mormons elsewhere in the world remains problematic.

Identity in the Theories of Social Psychology

Contests over the construction of a favorable identity, especially by a people under political and cultural attack from a dominant surrounding society, are fairly common in human history.[21] Identity construction has many counterparts around the world even today, including the Afrocentrism movement among black intellectuals in the United States since the 1960s.[22] Social psychologists postulate an innate human preference for a favorable self-concept. Our self-concepts are typically derived from, shared with, and validated by our most salient reference groups. We therefore seek favorable definitions, not only of ourselves as individuals within our reference groups but also for our own reference groups vis-à-vis outside groups. Laboratory research on group formation has demonstrated that even when individuals are arbitrarily assigned to groups of total strangers, they soon begin making invidious comparisons between "their" respective groups and the other ones.[23] This "we versus they" consciousness is, of course, greatly strengthened to the extent that between or among groups we see competition, power differentials, conflict, persecution, and the like.[24] This same principle largely explains intergroup religious prejudice, especially among those whose religious commitment and group identity are very strong (L. Jackson and Hunsberger 1999).[25]

In an essay on "ethnogenesis," Jonathan Hill makes an observation that certainly would seem applicable to Utah in the nineteenth century: "To successfully resist ongoing systems of domination, racial or ethnic stereotyping, and cultural hegemony, the first necessity of disempowered peoples, or of marginalized subcultural groups within a national society, is that of constructing a shared understanding of the historical past that enables them to understand their present conditions as a result of their own ways of making history" (1996, 17). Max Weber had already noted a century ago that ethnic groups can "entertain a subjective belief in their common descent because of similarities of physical type or of customs or both, or because of memories of colonization and migration . . . [I]t does not matter whether or not an objective blood relationship exists" (quoted in Alba 1990, 16). Or, as a contemporary anthropologist states, "The ethnic 'past' is always a subjective reconstruction," adding that "strong ethnic feelings need not be based on a strong 'objective' cultural continuity" (Roosens 1989, 17, 152).

The greater the number of roles or institutions through which a people can express the same identity (e.g., family, church, politics), the more durable and motivating that identity is for the individual. External pressure, denigration, or persecution of such a group might make members of the group feel insecure, both individually and as a group, but the result will likely be increased mutual dependence within the group and a determination to prevail. Since, in Stephen Reicher's words, "group members desire a positive social identity, then a tension arises when they discover themselves to be negatively defined in relation to other groups. It is this tension which provides the dynamic for change" (1996, 322–23). The "dynamic for change" here would include, for the Mormon community, missionizing and mobilizing in the common interest.

This process of collective construction of lineage or ethnic identity involves what is sometimes called "identity work," including, in Michael Schwalbe's words, "mythopoetic discourse" and "all the acts of signification and interpretation used to shape the meaning of an identity shared by members of a group. In other words, when a group of people who share an identity collaborate to preserve or change the meaning of that identity, they are doing . . . identity work" (1996, 105). Discourse is an important form of such identity work, for, as Margaret Wetherell writes:

> Talk and writing are not merely *about* actions, events, and situations; they are *creative of* those actions, events, and situations. . . . In talking, people are constituting their social realities and collective cultures, manufacturing and constructing their lives, and are themselves manufactured as personalities and subjects in the process. Through this negotiation, the social world becomes populated with characters which are given certain attributes. . . . Social life in this way is in no sense separate from the words. . . . Discourse comes to constitute social life as we know it. (1996, 281, emphases added; see also Ng [1996] on the importance of discourse in identity construction)

The following chapters are rich with examples of such "identity work," not only among the Anglo-Mormon Ephraimites but also among the various peoples with whom the Mormons have been negotiating during the past century or more for a satisfactory mutual understanding of the identity of such peoples as the Lamanites, Jews, and African Americans. Much identity work is also involved, of course, as modern Mormons strive to understand whether, why, and how ethnic lineages of any kind retain any meaning or utility in an increasingly universal religion.

Notes

1. The epigraph is from Hefner (1993, 23). I am grateful to Professor Thomas W. Murphy for acquainting me with this quotation and the book in which it is found.

2. The "church" usually refers to the Church of Jesus Christ of Latter-day Saints. Alternate terms, such as Latter-day Saint(s), LDS, Mormon, and Mormonism, all have the same referent. These terms have been chosen for their presumed familiarity to most readers. It should be acknowledged, however, that LDS leaders announced in 2001 their officially preferred reference as simply "The Church of Jesus Christ" for use in publications and in the mass media.

3. I have in mind particularly Weber (1930 and 1963), both originally published in German near the turn of the twentieth century. For an interesting study of Weber's work by a well-known Mormon scholar, see the published doctoral dissertation by Lowell L. Bennion (1933) and a discussion of Bennion's work by Laurie DiPadova and Ralph Brower (1992). More recently, Pierre Bourdieu has adapted and applied an essentially Weberian framework to the relationship between ideas and behavior, with special reference to the reproduction of culture and of "cultural capital" (e.g., Bourdieu and Passeron 1977).

4. To a limited extent, this process in Mormon history is parallel to the historical im-

pact that missionary work in China and the Far East had on the mainline Protestant denominations. In these denominations, a century of missionary confrontation with the ancient Eastern religious cultures undermined the Calvinist and other forms of fundamentalism brought to China by the earliest missionaries. An eventual result, after two or three generations, was the increasing embrace by many missionaries of the more universalistic and syncretic spirit of these exotic cultures, which contributed, in turn, to the rise of modernism in the mainline Protestant denominations and to the schism between modernists and fundamentalists. A thorough treatment of this process is in Xi (1997). No comparable schism or even wholesale intellectual movement occurred in Mormonism, of course. I am grateful to Professor Philip L. Barlow for calling my attention to this book.

5. Actually, *Gentile* has had somewhat different meanings in Mormon history and remains rather ambiguous. See the brief explanation in Underwood (1993, 30).

6. These questions are explored in the next chapter of this book, which is based on my more detailed treatment in the *Journal of Mormon History* (Mauss 1999), with thanks to the editors of that journal.

7. I use the term *racialist* here in contrast to *racist*. By *racialist* I mean a perspective that emphasizes the salient or even determinative role played by race in human nature and destiny. *Racist* goes beyond such a general framework, referring to explicit, invidious distinctions, prejudice, and discrimination based on attributions of race or racial characteristics. Of course, in practice the distinction between the two terms might be moot, despite the "neutral" intentions of the racialist. In any case, both terms beg the question of how *race* should be defined, a very complicated or even futile matter in the history of the social sciences. A colleague has rightly questioned whether it is fair to use either term in reference to the early Mormonism of Joseph Smith's time, which (like much of the Old Testament) focused on lineage, not on race per se. Yet given the general cultural and intellectual context, even of the early nineteenth century, with its spreading Anglo-Saxon triumphalism and denigration of dark-skinned peoples, it does not seem inappropriate to consider the earliest Mormon focus on lineage as at least "proto-racialist," whether intended or not.

8. Elsewhere I have argued that Mormon "ethnic" consciousness had largely disappeared by the end of the twentieth century, though it might have retained certain strategic uses (1990a and 1994, 60–74). For an alternative view, see May (1980).

9. Even though such scholars as Fredrik Barth (1969a) and A. P. Royce (1982) have proposed useful definitions and criteria for distinguishing ethnic groups, the ultimate ambiguity and arbitrariness in the concept are apparent from the examples and essays in the *Harvard Encyclopedia of American Ethnic Groups* (Thernstrom 1980).

10. In this connection see, for example, B. Anderson (1991); Berger and Luckmann (1967); Lewis (1975); and Van Seters (1983).

11. See particularly Mullen (1993 and 1997). I am grateful to Professor Jan Shipps for calling to my attention this impressive work by her colleague at Indiana University–Purdue University, Indianapolis.

12. On the loss of the earlier or traditional Israelite identities, see Mullen (1993, 12–15, 55–62); and Neil (1975, 203–12).

13. William Neil also emphasizes the renewed importance in post-exilic Israel of establishing and maintaining purity of lineage, as per the teachings of Ezra and Nehemiah, who forbade marriage to non-Israelites and even to Samaritans in the North, who were largely of Israelite descent (1975, 212–15).

14. On this same page and in his earlier work, Mullen (1993, 10) cites A. D. Smith (1986, 24–25) on eight typical foundational myths. Smith points to a "common myth of descent" as an especially important aspect of ethnic community identification.

15. Much of this is simply rephrased from Mullen (1997, 328–31). On the importance of public narratives in the social construction of ethnic reality, see also Mullen (1993, 15–18).

16. There are plenty of examples of such apologetic, narrative history in the official and semi-official histories of the Mormons published in Utah. B. H. Roberts wrote some of the earliest and most scholarly works of this genre (e.g., 1930). More recently, the one-volume history by James B. Allen and Glen M. Leonard (1992) is an example of the much more sophisticated "new Mormon history," but it, too, would probably be considered apologetic by many non-Mormons.

17. The American political context and process in which Mormons came to be persecuted as a pariah people is laid out clearly and convincingly by Terryl Givens (1997), among others.

18. The case for this concern with permeable boundaries is made in Mauss (1994, 123–40, 196–214). The Mormon restrictions against members of black African origin were all dropped in 1978.

19. Passing references to the Polynesians are made in this book from time to time, but no effort is made to assess their general place in the Mormon lineage scheme. Various Polynesian peoples have proved extraordinarily receptive to the Mormon message since the middle of the nineteenth century, and they are widely regarded in Mormon lore as having originated in ancient America among the Nephites of the Book of Mormon and thus as Israelite peoples. Polynesians would probably be regarded by most Mormons (at least in the United States) as sharing a divinely favored lineage with American aborigines. See Loveland (1976).

20. Givens (1997) sees the nineteenth-century propaganda against the Mormons as partly inspired, ironically, by a popular distaste for their putative "orientalism."

21. The theoretical perspective reflected in this section is based primarily on the following works in social psychology: Alba (1990); B. Anderson (1991); Barth (1969b); Berger and Luckmann (1967); A. Cohen (1985); Hechter (1987); Hill (1996); Nagel (1986, 1994); Nielsen (1985); Olzak (1983 and 1992); W. Robinson (1996); Roosens (1989); Rosenberg (1979); Tajfel (1981); and Waters (1990). I am especially grateful to Viktor Gecas, my colleague at Washington State University, for his consultation and guidance in my exploration of this literature.

22. On this variety, see Roosens (1989), which discusses the construction of ethnic identity among, for example, the American Indians and the Quebecois in Canada; the Aymara of Bolivia; the whites in Zaire; and various groups in Belgium. On Afrocentrism in the United States, see Asante (1987 and 1988); and T. Anderson (1990).

23. See the description by John C. Turner (1996) of the research on Henri Tajfel's "minimal group paradigm."

24. Such thinking can also be carried to pernicious extremes, as can be seen in the "terrorist" movements of the late twentieth century and early twenty-first, exemplified especially by the September 11, 2001, attacks in New York City and Washington, D.C.

25. Here again the attribution process analyzed by Glock and his colleagues is relevant. Even though their analysis arises out of a framework that is somewhat different from the so-called identity theory applied here, their work reveals that a "supernatural mode" of

explanation for racial differences has a mildly conservative effect on support for ameliorative public policies to resolve racial conflicts. This effect derives from the tendency of "supernaturalists" to bypass both characterological and social structural explanations for perceived "racial" traits in favor of divine explanations (Apostle et al. 1983, 100–102, 126–35, 143–47).

2. Mormons and Israelite Lineage

The sons of Ephraim are wild and uncultivated. . . . The spirit in
them is turbulent and resolute; they are the Anglo-Saxon race . . .
bearing the spirit of rule and dictation.
—Brigham Young, 1863

[We] are a branch of the house of Israel . . . a portion of that
martyred nation, chosen of God and sent upon the earth to suffer
and endure for His sake . . . a preexistent race, ordained before the
world was, to perform [a] great and important mission, the
gathered children of Ephraim.
—Orson F. Whitney, 1905

I have learned to admire, respect, and love the good people from
every race, culture, and nation . . . no race or class seems superior
to any other in spirituality and faithfulness.
—James E. Faust, 1995

THE WAXING AND WANING of the Israelite identity, which the Mormons
once constructed for themselves, is capsulized in the declarations of the three
apostles in these epigraphs.[1] By the middle of the nineteenth century, official Mormon discourse had constructed a synthesis of Israelite and Anglo-
Saxon identity, partly to establish a Mormon continuity with ancient Israel
and partly in response to the calumny coming from the outside world. By
the early twentieth century, official discourse had traced this special identity
back to premortal times and attributed it to a divine plan. By the end of the
century, however, the highest ranking church leaders had left such tribal
teachings to languish in disuse, displacing them with the original universalist teachings of the apostle Paul.[2]

The Religious and Intellectual Environment of
Early Mormonism

The earliest teachings of Joseph Smith, founding prophet of the Mormons,
had much in common with the religious environment of his time and place.
The ecclesiastical hegemony of Puritanism had broken down, and even its

theological heritage had been considerably attenuated by Smith's time (Bush-man 1984, 4–8). Quite apart from the Second Great Awakening usually men-tioned in discussing Mormon origins, the evangelical Protestantism of the time in both England and the United States had long been preoccupied with signs and expectations of the coming millennium (Harrison 1979; Sandeen 1970; Toon 1970; Underwood 1982 and 1993). "America in the early nineteenth century was drunk on the millennium," declared the historian Ernest San-deen (1970, 30). An integral part of any preparation for the Lord's return was, of course, the gathering of Israel, which Smith (like many others) believed was already beginning to take place. The Jews would be gathered back to Palestine, but the gathering of the rest of the scattered Israelites, or "lost ten tribes," presented many unresolved questions: Where were they? Were they all in one location or scattered around the world? Would they gather direct-ly to Palestine or to some other location? (Bushman 1984, 135–39; R. Sanders 1978; Ethan Smith [1825] 1996, 42–52). Eventually, of course, the ten tribes, sometimes called collectively by the name Ephraim, would join the Jews in the same location.[3] Meanwhile, the "Gentiles," custodians of the true gospel since its rejection by Israel in the time of Christ, were charged by the Lord with the responsibility for finding and converting all of gathering Israel.[4]

The Mormons and British Israelism

Beyond this general Protestant outlook on the "last days," various other the-ories about the lost tribes were advanced by imaginative thinkers of the peri-od. Some prominent scholars and clergy identified the American Indians as consisting partly of these tribes (Bushman 1984, 133–37; Ethan Smith [1825] 1996), an idea that went back at least as far as Cotton Mather (Hansen 1972, 380). Others hypothesized that some of these lost Israelites (often generically called "Jews") were simply mixed among the rest of the inhabitants of Europe and elsewhere and thus "invisible," without known genealogies. Advocates of one or another version of this "Christian Israelism" included Joanna South-cott, Richard Brothers, and John Wroe, all of whom garnered followings and published books in England before and after 1800. Among their most com-mon ideas were that the British Isles were inhabited mainly by Israelites of various tribes, especially Ephraim and Manasseh, and that England was intend-ed as one of the gathering places for the "lost" or invisible tribes. By the mid-dle of the nineteenth century, some fifty different societies of Christian Isra-elites had appeared in England and were periodically encountered by Mormon missionaries there. Even before those encounters, early Mormons had proba-bly heard of a derivative New England sect called New Israelites, which had been established briefly in Vermont near where the Smiths happened to be living early in the nineteenth century (Brooke 1996, 57–58, 99–102).[5]

While these early exponents of British Israelism could not truly be considered mainstream thinkers in their time, neither were their ideas regarded as particularly far-fetched. Biblical origins had been claimed by British royals since medieval times, sometimes starting with the patriarch Noah and coming down through King David of Israel and King Arthur of Camelot. Such ideas were often disseminated in popular English literature, including the poetry of William Blake (Mauss 1999, 138–39). A synthesis and in many ways a culmination of this emergent British Israelism appeared just as the Mormon missionary effort was beginning to thrive in England. John F. Wilson, having popularized such ideas on the lecture circuit during the 1830s, published *Our Israelite Origin* in 1840, which was extraordinarily popular on both sides of the Atlantic. Wilson integrated many of the ideas espoused earlier by Southcott, Brothers, and Wroe in claiming that the British (and perhaps other Europeans) were a people of mixed Gentile and Ephraimite descent, destined to bring about "the fulness of the Gentiles" and lead the gathering of Israel (Mauss 1999, 139; J. Wilson [1840] 1844).

Anglo-Saxon Triumphalism

If British Israelism could be considered a religious movement, given its derivation from the Bible, then Anglo-Saxon triumphalism was its secular counterpart and emerged during the same period (Mauss 1999, 139–43). Unlike British Israelism, however, the Anglo-Saxon ideology was not merely the preoccupation of a relatively few sectarian enthusiasts; it was championed by many of the most influential intellectuals of the time. Although in some of its versions it recognized the hand of Providence in Anglo-Saxon destiny, it found its evidence for that destiny mainly in contemporaneous science. It was as though the intellectuals of the time, having spurned the myths and superstitions of religion, constructed their own racialist myths instead, for few of their "scientific" judgments have withstood the scrutiny of scholars in later generations (Horsman 1981; Snyder 1962; Tuveson 1968; Wood 1990).

A romantic view of the ancient Anglo-Saxons and other Germanic peoples actually had become quite widespread in Europe during the eighteenth and nineteenth centuries, extending to the ancient Scandinavians, as well as the English. Scholars of the time were proposing schemes to classify humankind into "races," such as white (Caucasian, Aryan), black (Hamitic), and yellow (Turkic, Mongol). To Joseph de Gobineau and other early exponents of such racialism, the Aryan was superior, and "blood" accounted for the main differences in civilization (Snyder 1962, 46–53).[6] Not all racial triumphalists in England, however, were willing to share this general Nordic mystique with their Continental cousins. A glorification of the Anglo-Saxon heritage in particular was popularized in four volumes by Sharon Turner

(1799–1805) at the turn of the nineteenth century. His work provided the raw material for many romantics of the time, especially Sir Walter Scott, whose *Ivanhoe* and other novels glorified, in Reginald Horsman's words, "the virtuous flaxen-haired maidens and sturdy, blue-eyed yeomen" of England (Horsman 1981, 40–41; see also 160–61).[7] Several of Scott's works, incidentally, were available in the Manchester, New York, lending library during the Smith family's stay in nearby Palmyra (Paul 1982).

Yet this literary romanticism was but a repackaging of the "scientific" racialism of the time, which was expounded by scientists and intellectuals of all kinds and found its way into elite periodicals and widely published monographs in history and philosophy. Among the best-known exponents in the United States were the prominent historians Francis Parkman and George Bancroft (Horsman 1981, 182–86). The Reverend Josiah Priest produced widely published works explaining the origins and inherent inferiority of both the "African race" and the "ancient peoples" of America. Earlier scholarship had tended to emphasize cultural differences among peoples, but by the middle of the nineteenth century, the importance of "blood" and other physical traits "was assumed in a manner quite unlike that of a hundred years before," according to Horsman (1981, 27, 60). Of course, the appeal of such ideas can be understood partly as a function of the intense encounters that Americans had been having with seemingly "inferior" native "Indians" and black slaves (Hansen 1972; Horsman 1981, 99–105; Snyder 1962; Wood 1990).

Although Anglo-Saxon triumphalism had champions different from those of British Israelism and was far more pervasive than the latter in its cultural impact, the two philosophies have an obvious affinity. It is therefore not surprising that in time they came to be combined in popular thinking. Of course, they were also pressed into the service of British imperialism, on one side of the Atlantic, and American Manifest Destiny, on the other (Horsman 1981; Tuveson 1968). The elite clergy of the mid-nineteenth century were especially influential in synthesizing and propagating the two philosophical streams. Among the most prominent of these in the United States were Lyman Beecher, Horace Bushnell, Theodore Parker, Timothy Dwight, and Josiah Strong (Tuveson 1968, 138; Hansen 1972, 376–78).

To Parker, the New Englanders, in particular, were "the most spiritual part of the old Anglo-Saxons which came over, the least materialistic, the most ideal, the most devout . . . [and] . . . fired too with . . . duty to God and the destination before man" (quoted in Tuveson 1968, 155). In their synthesis of biblical and Anglo-Saxon racialism, these early American theologians not only found justification for Manifest Destiny but also were able to explain the rise of Protestantism itself as evidence of both Nordic superiority and divine commission. Their doctrine represented, as Ernest Tuveson put it, "the climax of the Protestant millennialist interpretation of the prophecies, combined with certain ethnic theories which seemed, providentially, to support it" (1968, 138)—a vision, that is, of a "racially infused millennium," to borrow a phrase from Klaus Hansen (1972, 378).

Early Latter-day Saint Conceptions about Lineage

Ideas of the kind just reviewed not only were contemporaneous with the rise of Mormonism on both sides of the Atlantic but also had been around in Joseph Smith's own social environment both before and during his ministry. We cannot be sure whether or how much his revelations and teachings were stimulated by, influenced by, or totally independent of this environment.[8] We can at least say, however, that his teachings had much in common with those found in American Protestantism more generally. Of course, there were different schools of thought among Christian theologians and preachers of the time, but many LDS teachings converged with one or another of these perspectives (Bushman 1984, 179–92). In some respects, however, Smith's teachings, even if not entirely new, went beyond those generally accepted. One of these stressed the importance of divinely "chosen" lineages in human destiny. In the beginning, this idea was not particularly racialist, since its salience was more theological than social. In time, however, the contrast with the "non-chosen" lineages became increasingly invidious.[9]

Early LDS Families as Israelites

References to modern Israelites in the LDS discourse of the early 1830s characterized them as "elect" and "chosen" in the traditional Protestant sense that the time had come for them to be gathered and restored as a mighty people (Mauss 1999, 144*n*44; Moench 1979). The young prophet Joseph Smith apparently recognized himself in a Book of Mormon passage, where the ancient biblical Joseph prophesied of a descendant of the same name, who would have the special mission of bringing God's word to others of the same lineage as part of the restoration of Israel promised in the last days (2 Nephi 3:6–15). Yet the title page of the Book of Mormon presented it as having come forth "by way of the Gentile," in line with the general Protestant understanding of the time about the role of the Gentiles in the gathering process (Mauss 1999, 144*n*45). It is therefore not clear whether, as early as 1830, young Joseph would have seen his own specific lineage as simply giving him a unique personal tie to Book of Mormon peoples in an otherwise Gentile nation, or if he would have generalized that Israelite lineage to his entire family.

In November 1831, Joseph Smith received a revelation that seemed to refer to him and his associates in the church as descendants of Ephraim, around whom all the tribes of Israel would soon gather (Doctrine and Covenants

133:7, 12, 21, 26, 30–34). Yet the language of this revelation did not actually depart much from one of the Protestant ideas of the time, which recognized the primacy of Ephraim over the other "lost" tribes and sometimes referred to them collectively by that name (e.g., Ethan Smith [1825] 1996, citing Ezekiel 37 and Jeremiah 31). Nor does it appear that LDS discourse or preaching at this early time gave much attention to the literal lineage of the Saints—at least if we judge by the journals of William McLellin.[10] There is little else in the earliest LDS scriptures or discourse that would tie either specific individuals or the Saints in general to *literal* Israelite lineage, though "Israel" as a symbol or type was already common in both Protestant and Mormon usage.

The earliest and most explicit tie of LDS families to literal Israelite lineage occurs in patriarchal blessings.[11] The patriarchal office was established in late 1833, and during the following year only a few blessings were given, mainly to members of the immediate Smith and Young families. Beginning early in 1835, however, Patriarch Joseph Smith Sr. began giving many more, and by the end of the Nauvoo period (1846) thousands of such blessings had been given by Father Smith and his successors (Bates 1991 and 1993; Bates and Smith 1996). Few of these early blessings are available for public scrutiny, but there are samples of the very earliest and most revealing. To judge from some several hundred of them, identification of lineage was not a particularly common feature of the blessings; references to lineage occurred only about a third of the time through 1836 and about half of the time through 1844.[12]

However, when Father Smith gave official blessings to members of his own extended family, he was explicit in tying their lineage to the ancient biblical patriarch Joseph or at least to the latter's son Ephraim. Attributions of Israelite lineage increasingly appeared also in the blessings given to members of other early Mormon families, which would be a natural development since so many were cousins or other Smith relatives anyway. Blessings to non-Smiths were somewhat less likely to specify the lineage of Ephraim, referring instead to other patriarchs of ancient Israel. However, after the mid-1830s, whenever lineage was cited, Ephraim began to predominate, and eventually the Saints were in general described as literal descendants of Ephraim, called by the Holy Spirit out from among the Gentiles of America and the British Isles. There is reason to suspect that such beliefs were important in Joseph Smith's decision to send missionaries to England in 1837, bringing a bounteous harvest of new converts during the next few decades.[13]

Believing Blood

As early as 1833, W. W. Phelps, an early Mormon publicist and leader, used the phrase "blood of Israel" to refer to those who were ready for the Lord's coming (1833, 77). It is not clear whether he intended "blood" in a literal sense or even in reference to any particular historical lineage. Without a modern understanding of genetics, people in the nineteenth century and even the twentieth often spoke of inherited traits as coming "in the blood," even traits of a spiritual kind. Anglo-Saxon triumphalists were especially likely to attribute a special mystique to blood. The Mormon prophet Joseph Smith was among those who took literally the relationship between lineage and blood, declaring in a 1839 sermon that converts from Gentile lineages would miraculously undergo an actual change of blood, making their conversion a somewhat more physical experience than would be the case for those converts of literal Israelite descent. The converted Gentile, Smith declared, must have "a new creation by the Holy Ghost . . . to purge out the old blood and make him actually the seed of Abraham." By contrast, when the "Holy Ghost falls upon one of the literal seed of Abraham, it is calm and serene, and his whole soul and body are only exercised by the pure spirit of intelligence . . ." (Joseph Smith 1902–32, 3:380).[14]

Smith's successor, Brigham Young, was even more graphic, referring to the "fits" and "spasms" that would accompany the "grafting" from the wild to the tame "olive tree" (1855, 2:268–69).[15] Later Mormon apostles, such as the scientist John A. Widtsoe, using somewhat less dramatic language, would describe this "grafting" process as a "subtle change . . . in the very physical system of the man, which makes him indeed one who belongs to the family of Abraham" (1950, 36). Though all who accepted the universal gospel of Christ could become children of Abraham, as Paul had promised, apparently some of them would have to undergo physical as well as spiritual changes. If the Smiths, Youngs, and other founding families of Mormonism had come to identify the favored Ephraimite (or Israelite) "blood" primarily with Anglo-Saxon ancestry, it is not clear how widespread such an idea would have been among the early Saints generally, but certainly it was present in official discourse by 1840.

Lineage Salience versus Universalism in Early Mormon Thought

For the early Mormon apostle Parley P. Pratt, the favored "blood" or literal lineage was so important that it was a prerequisite for the highest ecclesiastical offices: "no man can hold the keys of the Priesthood or of Apostleship . . . unless he is a literal descendant of Abraham, Isaac, and Jacob" (1853, 1:261). Yet such a preoccupation with lineage was more an Old Testament idea than a New Testament one, for such an emphasis is at odds with the universalism in the writings of the apostle Paul and others, for example, to the Romans (4:12–13), Galatians (3:7–9, 27–29), and Ephesians (2:11–20). New Testament universalism had also been prominent in the earliest Mormon discourse, starting in the Book of Mormon itself, where we are assured that "all [are invited] to come unto him, black and white, bond and free, male and female; and he remembereth the heathen; and all are alike unto God" (2 Nephi 26:33). Sidney Rigdon, another early leader, regularly declared in church publications that "all the families of the earth [will] be blessed; . . . all who are in Christ Jesus . . . will have redemption [and] forgiveness of sins" (1835, 73; see also 1840, 245–46). As the focus on favored lineages became more common, it simply existed in tension with this original universalism. (A much fuller examination of this tension is in A. Green [1999]).

As for the lineage of the Smiths themselves and other founding families, the Book of Mormon declares that it was preserved to come forth in the last days "by way of the Gentile," implying that the early Mormons were actually Gentiles. The early apostle and pamphleteer Orson Pratt, while acknowledging that "there may be many of the blood of Israel among us," referred to the Latter-day Saints throughout his life as "numbered with the Gentile nations" and "a people identified with the Gentiles" but given a special commission to take the gospel to the Israelites, beginning with the "Lamanites," or American Indians (1855a, 2:295; see also Underwood 1993).[16] No early Mormon questioned that the gospel was to go forth to the entire world in the new dispensation. It was not always clear, however, what priority, if any, should be given to which peoples with which lineages.

Premortal Origins and Nordic Lineages

By the time of the move to Utah, intimations of a special priority for the descendants of Ephraim had become prominent in both authoritative and popular discourse. From that point on, an expanded understanding about the origins and destinies of various lineages continued to develop among the Saints well into the twentieth century. One new element in this evolving doctrinal complex was a linkage of mortal lineage to premortal developments. By the 1850s, the Saints were beginning to learn that they had been identified and set aside in premortal life to enter mortality through Israelite (especially Ephraimite) lineage as a people of "royal" blood. A second element, now more fully articulated than earlier, was that this royal Israelite blood, by divine design, had been frequently distributed especially in the British Isles and in northwestern Europe. All of this helped to account for the success of the Mormon missionaries in converting thousands from those countries and to explain the persecution increasingly experienced by these converts. To the apostle Wilford Woodruff, such persecution was "the strongest evidence that this is the work of God. Why? Because we have been chosen out of the world and therefore the world hates us. . . . We are [but] a handful of people chosen . . . before we were born . . . to come forth in this day and generation to do [God's work]" (1880, 21:193).[17]

Israel in the Preexistence

A distinguishing tenet of Mormonism from its early days has been the doctrine that all of God's sons and daughters had a conscious "preexistence" as spirits in God's presence before their mortal birth. In the very beginning, the Mormon understanding of this premortal phase was close to the conventional Protestant one, namely, that such terms as *predestined* and *foreordained* referred to plans in the mind of God, not to any conscious premortal existence of spirits (Harrell 1988; Ostler 1982).[18] However, after his work on the Book of Abraham in the late 1830s, Joseph Smith understood that conscious spirits or "intelligences," with individual identities and personal qualities, had existed in the presence of God before mortal existence.[19] It is not clear how widely Smith disseminated this doctrine prior to the serialized publication of the Book of Abraham in 1842. By then, he had begun explicitly to invoke the language of that book to refer to the preexistence as a time when the spirits were "organized"; accepted the divine plan for their mortal existence within certain (geographical) "limits and bounds"; and were, in some cases, ordained to minister to the earth in key roles (Harrell 1988, 86–88).

Yet it is not clear from the record whether the prophet himself saw the preexistence as a time for divine assignment to mortal roles only on an *individual* basis, or if he believed that entire *categories* of spirits were set apart for specified mortal *lineages.* Clearly some of Smith's successors, however, did come to infer from the Book of Abraham a collective foreordination to lineages and to other mortal circumstances. A sermon by the apostle Orson Pratt gave this idea a somewhat racial connotation when he declared that some of God's children, who were more noble and intelligent than others in the preexistence, had been held back for special missions on earth as "Prophets, Priests, and Kings to the Most High God" in the last days and that they "had not been kept waiting . . . to send them among the Hottentots, the African negroes, the idolatrous Hindoos, or any other of the fallen nations that dwell upon the face of this earth" (1852, 1:62–63). In the same vein, of course, was the quotation from Brigham Young, with which this chapter opened (1863a, 10:188; see also 1863b, 10:232), and the apostle Erastus Snow's assurances that "the entire lineage of Ephraim" had been called, chosen, and foreordained in the preexistence "to perform a certain work at a certain time of the world's history" (1882, 23:184–85).

The doctrine that the Saints were a royal, Israelite people, chosen and foreordained in the preexistence, was developed most fully, however, by a later generation of LDS leaders, who brought the church into the twentieth century. The apostle Orson Whitney, also quoted at the beginning of this chapter, exemplified this generation (1905, 91). So did the apostles Melvin J. Ballard and Rulon S. Wells, whose general conference sermons continued to assure the Saints that they were descendants of Abraham, Isaac, Jacob, Joseph, and Ephraim, chosen before birth to come to earth at the right time, by divine plan, to "carry the gospel to all the inhabitants of the earth" (Ballard 1924, 28) and to convert "the honest in heart among every nation" (Wells 1924, 41–42). However, it was not until such doctrines about premortal divine plans had been synthesized with certain ideas about specific mortal ancestries that the Mormon framework took on a more overtly racialist cast.

Israel in Britain and the Nordic Countries

Given the circulation of theories about the significance of Israelite, Aryan, or Anglo-Saxon ancestry, it is not surprising that early Mormon publications reflect such ideas.[20] It was only near the end of Joseph Smith's life, however, and after the publication of John Wilson's *Our Israelitish Origin* that LDS discourse began to recognize the common destiny of the northern Europeans and the Latter-day Saints. The early successes of the missionaries in England probably encouraged such a recognition, and it was eventually made explicit in a series of articles, written by George Reynolds, which appeared in each issue of the *Millennial Star* during 1878. Eventually the series was collected into a single booklet and published into the middle of the twentieth century (G. Reynolds [1883] [ca. 1950]).[21]

In these articles, Reynolds combines the British Israelist and the Anglo-Saxonist strains of racialist triumphalism discussed above. He cites various familiar prophecies from the Old Testament and the Book of Mormon about the future destiny of Israel, especially the tribe of Ephraim. Among Reynolds's other noteworthy citations are John Wilson, chief codifier of British Israelism, mentioned earlier; Edward Hine, a prominent Wilson disciple; and Sharon Turner, author of the *History of the Anglo-Saxons*, also mentioned earlier (G. Reynolds [1883] [ca. 1950], 28, 37–49). From these sources and others of an apocryphal, mythological, and scientific nature, Reynolds makes several specific claims: (1) the wanderings of the lost ten tribes can be traced from Assyria to Europe; (2) the exact identity of these tribes in modern times cannot yet be established, but numerous parallels in language and customs suggest that the Anglo-Saxons and related peoples are Israelites; (3) descendants of the vanguard tribe of Ephraim, in particular, constitute perhaps the majority of the populations of the British Isles and the Nordic countries; (4) wherever descendants of Israel are found, they are especially responsive to the teachings of the gospel; (5) the same peoples show a natural penchant for superior cultural traits, such as enterprise, vitality, and representative government; and (6) LDS missionary success in the British Isles and Scandinavia is a natural consequence of these historic developments ([1883] [ca. 1950], 11–15, 19–24, 32–36, 43–49).[22]

Official discourse periodically echoed such claims well into the twentieth century. Erastus Snow recounted the same migration of Israelites to Europe, where they "mingl[ed] their seed with the Anglo-Saxon race" to become "first and foremost in everything noble among men in the various nations," including the founding of American republic, "thus preparing the way for the coming forth of the fulness of the everlasting gospel" (1882, 23:185–86). In an 1890 discourse, George Q. Cannon found evidence of Israelite origins in the "readiness to receive the Gospel" not only among the indigenous peoples of the United States and Polynesia but also "throughout Great Britain and Ireland . . . the Scandinavian nations . . . and the Germanic races" ([1890] 1988, 2:4–5). B. H. Roberts expressed disappointment in the lack of Mormon missionary success "among the Latin races of southern Europe" and attributed the notably greater success in northern Europe to the descendants of the tribe of Ephraim in the British Isles, Scandinavia, and Germany (1907–12, 2:483). After the outbreak of World War I, the mission president Serge F. Ballif felt it necessary to reassure the Saints that the German people still had "the blood of Israel in their veins" (1917, 119). He offered similar assurances in later years, as well (1920, 90; and 1923, 96).

From Nordic Racialism to Modern American Racism

Like much of the world, the United States had come to think of the past and the future in racialist terms by the turn of the twentieth century. A strong nativist movement and even some elements of the Progressive movement had injected various forms of racism into the mainstream of American politics. The more overt and pernicious expressions were not only discriminatory against black and Asian Americans but anti-Semitic as well. A thriving Ku Klux Klan gained increasing respectability and infiltrated powerful centers of politics during the 1920s. In films and popular literature, it was, of course, the age of the popular film *Birth of a Nation* and cowboy "westerns," in which "the only good Indian [was] a dead Indian." One of the legacies of this period was a powerful eugenics movement aimed at preventing the dilution of the superior American "breed." One aspect of this movement was the restrictive legislation during the 1920s intended to limit immigration from places outside northern Europe and to prevent naturalization of immigrants from Asia (Myers [1943] 1960).

Such, then, was the environment in which Mormonism entered its powerful "Americanization" phase. It is not surprising to see a certain "elective affinity" in Utah with the racialist thinking that permeated the nation as a whole. Mormon racialism, however, had some distinctive features. On the one hand, the doctrine of divine "lineage assignment" in a premortal life seemed to add special justification, not available to other Americans, for a racialist understanding of history and destiny. On the other hand, Mormons had little sympathy with the anti-Semitism common in the nation during this period, and they still had optimistic expectations for the future of the American Indians. Apart from these few uniquely Mormon ideas, authoritative church pronouncements during the early decades of the twentieth century generally reflected a widespread popular and official support for linking the Latter-day Saints to Israelite origins through their Anglo-Saxon and Nordic ancestries (Jenson 1913, 80–81; Penrose 1922, 30; N. Pratt 1906, 104; S. Young 1906, 93).[23]

Certain institutional centers of the church were particularly active in disseminating these racialist ideas. One of these was the office of church historian, whose chief spokesman for many years was Andrew Jenson, assistant historian. In several sermons during these years, he spoke on themes that linked the Saints to an Israelite and Anglo-Saxon heritage. "[W]e are of Israel," he once declared, "and . . . when our genealogy is revealed in detail, it will lead us back . . . to England [and thence] to Scandinavia and Germany, and from there to . . . that part of Asia where the Ten Tribes were lost . . ." (1913, 80–81). Unfortunately, Jenson explained, the church had not had much missionary success "among Latin or Oriental races" because of a paucity of "the blood of Israel among them" (1913, 81; see also 1925, 111; and 1930, 151).

Another influential center of British-Israelist thinking was the Genealogical Society of Utah, whose director during the 1920s and early 1930s was Anthony W. Ivins, first counselor in the First Presidency of the church.[24] In both 1926 and 1929 general conferences, Ivins spoke approvingly of "the British-Israel movement . . . sponsored by many of the great scholars and statesmen of Great Britain," and he cited various kinds of folklore to the effect that the "British race" was actually Hebrew in origin (1926, 17–18; see also 1929, 99). Archibald F. Bennett, long prominent in the Genealogical Society and eventually its executive secretary, was an influential advocate for similar ideas in the pages of the *Utah Genealogical and Historical Magazine* (e.g., "Ephraimites are the Anglo-Saxon race" [Bennett 1930, 67]) and later in his widely used book *Saviors on Mount Zion* (1950, 15–17, 57, 144, 200–203). The *Utah Genealogical and Historical Magazine* also carried regular articles by Andrew Jenson and Joseph Fielding Smith on similar themes.

The executive secretary of the Genealogical Society for its first forty years (1894–1934) was James H. Anderson. Neither a general authority of the church nor as well remembered as Andrew Jenson or Archibald Bennett, Anderson was nevertheless featured regularly in LDS periodicals, at events in the Tabernacle, and in LDS radio broadcasts. His books were popular enough to enjoy publication by the church press during the 1930s (J. Anderson 1933 and 1937; Van Orden 1981, 15–20). Anderson embraced British Israelism comprehensively, including ideas he found in *Destiny*, a periodical of the Anglo-Israel Federation of America—an organization that was both anti-Semitic and anti-

Catholic and that called for criminal sanctions against "miscegenation" to preserve the "racial purity" of the Anglo-Saxons. Among the most prominent of Anderson's disciples was Earl W. Harmer, who also borrowed from the pages of *Destiny* and argued that Joseph Smith, "racially an Anglo-Saxon," was also a rightful "claimant to the leadership" through his Ephraimite birthright (quoted in A. Green 1999, 213).

There can be little doubt that such thinking represented the explicit outside influence of the British-Israelist and Anglo-Saxonist movements. Certain specific ideas from those movements were clearly reflected in the discourse and teachings of LDS leaders; furthermore, starting at least with George Reynolds in the 1870s, these movements and their spokesmen were explicitly cited from time to time. Later general authorities continued to do the same until the middle of the twentieth century. As late as 1939, the apostle John A. Widtsoe was still crediting the "notable British-Israel movement" for ideas that helped explain the "ready acceptance of the gospel by the British, Scandinavian, and German peoples" (1960, 406–7; see also Ballard 1938, 43). It would be fair to say that British-Israelist and Anglo-Saxonist ideas were common and familiar elements in official and unofficial LDS literature for several decades prior to World War II, if we judge by statements in the *Journal of Discourses,* the *Millennial Star, Conference Report,* the *Utah Genealogical and Historical Magazine,* the *Deseret News,* and various authoritative books.[25]

The influence of Joseph Fielding Smith (1876–1972) on racialist thinking among Mormons was especially important from the time he became an apostle in 1910 until approximately midcentury. Even before his apostolic calling, he served with Andrew Jenson as an assistant historian and then held the role of church historian (and apostle) from 1921 to 1970. He was widely regarded as the ultimate authority on doctrinal and historical questions during much of his life, which culminated in a brief tenure as church president in his midnineties. His 1931 *Way to Perfection* continued to be published as a church classic even into the twenty-first century.[26] While President Smith expressed approval for certain ideas in British Israelism (e.g., [1931] 1951, 138–39; and 1957–66, 2:55), his influence is most clearly seen in the general rationalization and codification that he provided for the rather disparate Mormon racialist teachings that had accumulated up to his time.

A comprehensive summary of his teachings would go something like this (Joseph Fielding Smith [1931] 1951, 42–51, 129–30; see also 1954–56, 3:246–53; and 1957–66, 1:141, 2:55, 3:62–63, 4:40, and 5:138–39). In premortal life, we, as God's spirit children, had our agency to follow him in varying degrees of obedience, just as in mortal life. Also, as in mortality, we acquired and developed certain premortal talents and aptitudes, including intelligence, spirituality, leadership ability, artistic and scientific talents, and other traits. Eventually God assigned each of us (with our concurrence) to come into mortal life at specific times and places, partly on the basis of his own strategy and partly on the basis of our own individual premortal merits and talents. These assignments were made not only to key individuals (such as prophets) designated to appear on earth at certain points in history but also to entire *mortal lineages,* based again on premortal merit. The most meritorious, all things considered, have come into mortality through the lineage of Ephraim, although other Israelite lineages indicate similar premortal merit. The least meritorious have entered mortal life through the lineage of Cain and Ham. These different lineages have had different roles and destinies in history. The destiny of the "chosen" people (Israelites), particularly the "birthright tribe" of Ephraim, is to lead the world to a higher spiritual threshold through conversion to Christ and administration of the saving and exalting ordinances of the priesthood—the modern manifestation of the covenant between God and Abraham's descendants.

Since God had scattered Abraham's descendants throughout the earth, people of Ephraimite and other Israelite lineages could potentially be found and converted elsewhere than in Anglo-Saxon and Nordic populations. Still others around the world could be converted with or without Israelite lineage. However, those without the literal "blood of Israel" would be only adopted or "grafted" onto the Israelite "olive tree," and their conversion would entail physical as well as spiritual changes. Their blood would literally be changed, and if they were very dark (like the Lamanites, or American Indians), their skin color would actually become lighter. Thus, although the gospel and the Abrahamic covenant are ultimately for everyone, the lineage of Abraham, especially Ephraim, will always enjoy a special primacy or "birthright" as the lineage on which God depends to lead his work on earth.

Probably only a fraction of today's Mormons are aware of such traditional teachings by President Joseph Fielding Smith and others. When modern readers do become aware of them, they often find them quite disturbing, especially when expressed in concrete, earthly terms. For example, it is difficult to avoid the gratuitous racism in President Smith's claims that God selects the "choice spirits to come through the better grade of nations, [which would] account, in very large part, for the various grades of color and degrees of intelligence we find in the earth" or his declaration that the "chosen lineage" was a "special race [with] peculiar covenants and obligations, which other nations would not keep," with the consequence that this race was divinely "segregat[ed] from other races" ([1931] 1951, 41, 48, 129–30). It was within this general racialist context, of course, that President Smith also formulated his rationale for denying the priesthood to people of black African ancestry ("the lineage of Cain and Ham"). Here again, however, he was a codifier and systematizer rather than an innovator, for diverse LDS attitudes and policies toward blacks had been evolving since the 1830s. Yet it was precisely during the period in question here, the late nineteenth century and early twentieth, that the traditional church restrictions on the priesthood for blacks, along with the supporting doctrinal rationale, took final form (L. Bush 1973; Joseph Fielding Smith [1931] 1951, 42–49, 97–111).

Whatever the extent of Joseph Fielding Smith's doctrinal influence by mid-century, his teachings could hardly be regarded as heterodox, for nearly all of his colleagues in the church leadership and most of the general membership embraced similar ideas. Smith simply synthesized in coherent fashion a major theological stream that had been developing in Mormonism since at least 1850. His successor as president of the church, Harold B. Lee, espoused similar ideas (1955, 170–72; and 1973, 167–68), as did Alvin R. Dyer, once a member of the First Presidency (1966, 541). No one, however, disseminated President Smith's ideas about race as fully, widely, forcefully, and recently as his son-in-law, the late apostle Bruce R. McConkie (1966a, 2:274–84, 3:330–31; 1966b, 23, 81, 114, 305, 457; 1979–81, 1:23; 1982, 182–83, 191, 196, 203, 320; and 1985, 510–21).

The teachings in McConkie's 1966 books seem especially anomalous and anachronistic in the Mormonism of the twenty-first century, for they perpetuate such nineteenth-century notions as "believing blood"; northern Europe as the main locus of the descendants of Ephraim; a literal change in the blood of non-Israelite converts; selection to "chosen" lineages through premortal "merit"; and an endorsement of racial and ethnic segregation, including caste systems, for the spiritual protection of favored lineages from contamination through mixture with the cursed lineages.[27] During the 1970s and 1980s, McConkie modified some of his ideas in line with evolving church policies on the gathering of Israel (1982, 191, 196, 203, 320; and 1985, 519–21, 565–69). Another important change in church policy also required him to drop his long-standing prediction that blacks would not be given the priesthood during mortality, for in 1978 the priesthood was finally extended to all black males. Yet McConkie never recanted any of his other racialist ideas.[28] In authoritative books published even during the final years of his life, McConkie continued to teach that merit earned in a premortal life determined the races and lineages through which all God's children were to be born as mortals (1979–81, 1:23; 1982, 182–83, 191, 196, 203, 320; and 1985, 510–21).

With the turn of the twenty-first century, such a racialist understanding of history and destiny had virtually disappeared from official and authoritative church discourse. However, a residue has remained in McConkie's books, still very much in print, and in the work of some of his disciples well into the 1990s (e.g., Millet and McConkie 1993; Blodgett 1994; and Thomas 1996). These publications offer explanations for mortal lineages and circumstances that still rely on divine decisions made in the preexistence favoring lineages located mainly in northwestern Europe and emphasizing to some extent the importance of maintaining the purity of certain lines (Millet and McConkie 1993, 17–19,

40–55). Even in the quasi-official *Encyclopedia of Mormonism* (Ludlow 1992), there survives the idea that non-Israelite converts undergo a literal change of blood; and, more generally, the encyclopedia reveals an engaging ambivalence in which Christian universalism and premortal lineage birthright are espoused simultaneously but never really reconciled (compare G. Brown 1992; S. Brown 1992; Ostergar 1992; B. Smith 1992; and Top 1992, 522).

As late as 1998, the president of the Netherlands Mission was circulating a discourse he had written on the "prophesied growth" of the church in Western Europe. In his optimistic projections on this topic, he not only reviewed the earlier McConkie claims (1966b, 81) about the power of "believing blood" but also quoted a contemporary apostle as preaching in 1995 that "Europe [still has] the richest composition of the blood of Israel we've known" (Brewster 1998, 13, 3). Clearly, the concept of favored lineages and special "blood" remained salient to some important church leaders at least to the end of the century.

The Waning of Lineage Identity and the Resurgence of Universalism

Despite this residual racialist legacy, official discourse since the middle of the twentieth century has reflected a diminishing concern with literal Israelite or Nordic ancestry for Latter-day Saints anywhere. Especially in the United States, Mormons are no longer a people seeking to escape pariah status by claiming their rightful place in a divine rank-ordering of the world's civilizations. The church is now far less concerned with its Hebraic past and far more concerned with establishing its contemporary Christian legitimacy before the world. In its general conferences and publications, the church now emphasizes more than ever the traditional Christian inclusiveness and universalism of the apostle Paul. Today the world is called not to "the mountains of Ephraim to dwell" (as in a traditional Mormon hymn) but to "come unto Christ." All who do so are "Abraham's children," whether by lineage or adoption. For modern Mormons, the blood of Christ has far more theological significance than the blood of Israel. Such a change did not, of course, occur over night. It was both a consequence of and concomitant with the spread of the Mormon missionaries and membership to increasingly "exotic" parts of the world. The change occurred almost imperceptively on ritual occasions as Mormons gradually came to redefine the scope and significance of Israelite lineage.

Proselyting and Lineage Advocacy

During the second half of the nineteenth century, the blood of Israel, especially of Ephraim, seemed particularly abundant in those parts of the world to which most Mormons could trace their own ancestors, as well as among those aboriginal peoples whose ancestors were featured in the Book of Mormon. As that century wound down, however, the bounteous harvest of new converts in such locations had been reduced to a laborious gleaning effort. Apostles began to lament publicly the drastic decline in conversions from the British Isles and Europe, as both economic and political conditions made the Mormon message seem less appealing in those countries once so important to church growth (F. Richards 1898, 33; Buchanan 1987; Thorp 1975). With the turn of the twentieth century, however, the varied missionary outreach of the church began to produce evidence of the blood of Israel in other parts of the world, where the gospel was starting to be well received. These included Latin America, southern and eastern Europe, Russia, Asia, New Zealand, and various Pacific islands.

Mormons had originally identified the "Lamanites" of the Book of Mormon primarily with the North American tribes, but Mormon leaders had always recognized that the other aboriginal peoples of the hemisphere were probably Lamanites also. After a couple of abortive attempts, a mission was finally established in Mexico in 1901 and one for the rest of Latin America in 1925. Jurisdiction for Latin America was divided in 1935 between missions headquartered in Brazil and in Argentina. Thereafter, missionary work in those two countries focused mainly on recent immigrants from Europe (*Deseret News Church Almanac* 1975, D-13, 14). Yet hopes remained high for responsiveness to the gospel message from the estimated "hundred million" pure Lamanites between Mexico and Cape Horn whose blood had "not been contaminated by admixture with any other race," as Anthony Ivins put it (1901, 58). An early and regular advocate for the abundance of the blood of Israel in Mexico was Rey L. Pratt, a longtime mission leader there who identified the Mexicans as from the tribe of "Manasseh principally, also with a sprinkling of the blood of Ephraim" (1916a, 122).[29] The church patriarch Hyrum G. Smith extended the Manasseh designation to all the "Indians of North and South America," while still emphasizing the primacy of Anglo-Ephraim in North America (1927, 79; and 1929, 123).

Serge F. Ballif, the president of the Swiss-German Mission during three different terms, periodically returned to affirm in general conferences that the "blood of Israel" was present in Germany, Switzerland, Austria, Hungary, Poland, and Russia. The apostle Melvin J. Ballard and Roy A. Welker, a mission president in Germany and Austria, found "believing blood" in Lithuania, Germany, Poland, Russia, Spain, and Italy. Reinhold Stoof, a mission president in South America, proposed that the Spanish and Italian settlers in Argentina had Israelite blood, if only because of the invasions of southern Europe by northern tribes during late Roman times.[30]

A mission to Turkey had been opened in 1884, with a focus mainly on

Armenian and Coptic Christian peoples in that part of the world. Having had only limited success, the mission closed in 1909 but periodically reopened and closed in a number of neighboring locations during the first half of the twentieth century (*Deseret News Church Almanac* 1975, D-10). As the apostles contemplated opening a mission in Japan, they discussed the likelihood of finding Israelite blood even in that country. Seeing in many of the Japanese people "the features and manners of the American Indians," the apostle Heber J. Grant, in his dedicatory prayer opening the Japan Mission in September 1901, petitioned God to remember the "promises made unto [the ancestors of the Japanese]" in the Book of Mormon (quoted in Gibbons 1979, 118, and in Nielson 2001, 48–49; see also Grant 1902, 48). Even after this mission was closed in 1924, with minimal results, the returning mission president Lloyd O. Ivie testified in a general conference to his "firm belief . . . that there is the blood of Israel" among the Japanese people, whose "probable" origins could be found in Asia Minor or the eastern Mediterranean (1926, 96).

These and other LDS mission leaders and missionaries thus became advocates, as it were, for extending literal Israelite identity to a great variety of peoples, some of them quite exotic by comparison with the Anglo-Ephraim-ites of Utah.[31] In the process, "believing blood" came to be found almost everywhere the missionaries went, and gradually the proselyting role came to be understood less as searching for Ephraim or Israel and more as simply carrying the gospel to all the world, as the apostles had originally been charged to do in the New Testament (Matthew 28:19; Mark 16:15).

Universalizing Israelite Identity through Patriarchal Blessings

Earlier in this chapter, I explained how the unique LDS institution of the "patriarchal blessing" began among the founding families of Mormonism and was gradually extended to the general church membership. With the dispersion of missionary efforts during the twentieth century, references to lineage came to acquire a certain degree of ambiguity. Even by midcentury, these references were not understood in quite the same way by all patriarchs, leaders, or members. No doubt many, even down to the present, still regard the "declaration of lineage" in one's blessing as referring to literal genealogical descent, or "blood." Yet others take a less literal view and use alternative terms for "declaring" lineage—such terms as *assign, identify, specify,* or even simply *give.* In my own recent questioning of at least two dozen stake patriarchs about their understandings on this point, I found that their explanations ranged across a continuum from literal to functional. Some patriarchs regarded "Ephraim" as simply the designation given those most responsible for the Lord's kingdom in these latter days. Others simply mentioned Ephraim routinely unless inspired to specify an unusual lineage (perhaps for obvious "racial" reasons). Still others sidestepped the question by explaining that while lineage assignment occurs by divine inspiration, it has nothing necessarily to do with actual ancestry.[32]

Already in the 1950s, the church patriarch Eldred G. Smith spoke of the "declaration" of lineage as referring simply to "the tribe through which the promises of inheritance shall come" (1952, 39). Patriarchal blessings, he explained "do not always need to declare genealogy. . . . It is the blessings that are declared" (1960, 66). Later he explained that he did not interpret his declarations of lineage to refer to literal descent and was trying to turn the attention of those whom he blessed away from a preoccupation with lineage and toward the content of the blessing itself (Bates 1993, 5). Current instructions to patriarchs "contemplate an inspired declaration of . . . lineage" without specifying the meaning of that phrase (Allred 1997, 27–28).

The quasi-official *Encyclopedia of Mormonism* is somewhat ambiguous on all this. On the one hand, it acknowledges that the patriarch "seeks inspiration to specify the dominant family line" of the person, leading back to Abraham; on the other, it explains that whether "this is a pronouncement of inheritance or of adoption does not matter, [for it is] the line and legacy through which one's blessings are transmitted" (Mortimer 1992, 1066–67; see also A. Ballif). The main point here is that the very ambiguity in this variety of understandings about "lineage" in patriarchal blessings serves to deemphasize, intentionally or not, the importance of *literal* lineage. This recent tendency might or might not have been derived from the expansion of Israelite lineage in missionary discourse, as described above, but the two developments at least occurred in parallel.

Conclusion

During the life and ministry of Joseph Smith, Mormonism shared several millennial expectations with its Protestant American environment. These included the gathering of both the Jews and the "lost tribes" of Israel, with a special vanguard role for the tribe of Ephraim in that gathering. The early Mormons increasingly came to see themselves in the role and lineage of Ephraim. Like many other Americans, they also identified the American Indians as descendants of the lost tribes. With the exodus to Utah in the middle of the nineteenth century, Mormon conceptions about lineage evolved into a fuller racialist explanation of history generally and of the Saints' own destiny in particular. This racialist framework synthesized three elements: (1) an emerging and expanded understanding about premortal life; (2) British Israelism; and (3) Anglo-Saxon triumphalism. Anglo-Saxon triumphalism and, to a lesser extent, British Israelism had gained widespread popularity among intellectual elites in America, as well as in parts of Europe.

By the early decades of the twentieth century, a racialist historical narrative had developed in which some lineages were favored over others by deity or destiny or both. The Mormon version of this narrative provided a rank-ordering of lineages that maintained the preeminent position of Mormons as mainly Anglo-Saxon descendants of Ephraim, charged with the responsibility of building and ruling the eventual kingdom of God on earth. As this scenario was refined and codified, it eclipsed for several decades the more universalistic Christian scenario that had also been present in Mormonism from the beginning. As the twentieth-century dispersion of Mormonism brought missionary encounters with increasingly exotic parts of the world, however, the favored Israelite lineage was discovered in converts everywhere. Accordingly, the focus on lineage distinctions began to fade from Mormon discourse and thinking, so that once again the simpler and more inclusive understanding of the Christian heritage reasserted itself, and all peoples were recognized as "Abraham's children" once they accepted Christ. The 1978 change in church policy toward people of black African lineage removed the final official encumbrance to a full resurgence of this original Christian impulse.

By the end of the twentieth century, official discourse was virtually ignoring all the earlier ideas about favored (or disfavored) lineages. Howard W. Hunter, president of the church from 1994 to 1995, declared that race, color, or nationality made no difference, for "we are all of one blood" and children of the same God (1979, 72). The gospel message, he said, stands "squarely against all stifling traditions based on race, language, and economic or political standing . . . or cultural background" (1991, 18). His colleagues in the leadership increasingly made similar declarations (e.g., Faust 1995, 61–63; and Hinckley 2001, 125). An article in the *Encyclopedia of Mormonism* described the "Abrahamic covenant" as a "divine archetype" rather than lineage-specific favoritism, for all who accept Christ "become Abraham's seed spiritually and receive the same blessings as his biological descendants" (E. Rasmussen 1992, 9–10).[33] A similarly inclusive definition of the Abrahamic covenant has been emphasized in the official church magazine (Wilcox 1998). Although Mormonism had entered the twentieth century with preoccupations about lineage, it had largely worked itself free of these as the century ended. The Christian universalism, which Paul had taught the Galatians, was now restored to its original preeminence in Mormonism as well.

Notes

1. The opening quotation is from Young (1863, 10:188). For the others, see Whitney (1909, 91); and Faust (1995, 61). During the presidency of Gordon B. Hinckley (1995–), universalistic comments like those of Faust became especially common in general conferences. General conferences occur twice a year. The annual general conference always occurs on

or around April 6 to commemorate the organization of the church in 1830, and the semi-annual general conference takes place during the corresponding week each October. Called and conducted by the "general authorities" of the church (the topmost leaders), general conferences are regarded by most Mormons as the sources of the latest divine guidance for the faithful. Typically lasting two days (a Saturday and a Sunday), the conferences consist mainly of a series of discourses by apostles and other leaders. Traditionally held in the nineteenth-century tabernacle on Temple Square in Salt Lake City, the conferences in recent years have been moved to a new and spacious conference center just north of Temple Square. They are also broadcast by radio and television to numerous sites throughout the world and are carried in the official magazine, *Ensign*.

2. I have already traced this process at some length in an earlier publication (Mauss 1999). This chapter is mainly a condensation of that article, where details, documentation, and footnotes are considerably more thorough than space permits here.

3. Many Christians of the early nineteenth century understood Old Testament history as bestowing divine primacy on the tribe of Ephraim over the other tribes in the "Kingdom of Israel," as northern Palestine became known at the division of Solomon's kingdom. The two "sticks" in Ezekiel, chapter 37, were identified with the two resulting kingdoms, Judah (the Jews) and Israel (Ephraim). See Ethan Smith ([1825] 1996, 34, 47, 178–82, 191). Mormons extended that basic distinction to the scriptures by identifying the stick of Judah with the Bible and the stick of Ephraim with the Book of Mormon.

4. On early Protestant dispensationalism (the gospel first to Israel, then to the Gentiles, then back to Israel), see Sandeen (1970, 68–69); and Ethan Smith ([1825] 1996, 192). For the LDS version, see Bushman (1984, 136–39); O. Pratt (1872, 15:190–91; and 1874, 16:352–53); and Woodruff (1863, 10:220). On the eventual conversion of the Jews, see Sandeen (1970, 9–13, 55–56); and Ethan Smith ([1825] 1996, 43–46).

5. For further details, see Mauss (1999, 136–39). As those pages make clear, I am relying mainly on expert secondary sources for my description of British Israelism. I also benefited greatly from the research of Donald Bradley (1997), who shared with me his unpublished work on key primary sources from the period.

6. Snyder's book (1962) is especially valuable for its compilation (in the second half of the book) of primary source essays, such as that of Gobineau. Snyder also discusses Gobineau's connections with later racialism exponents, such as Richard Wagner and Houston Stewart Chamberlain. See also Horsman (1981, 29–41).

7. Even in the late twentieth century, somewhat more pernicious uses were found for Turner's ideas in the work of the so-called Christian Identity Movement (Aho 1990; Barkun 1994; Ogilvie 2001).

8. This is always an issue in studying new religious movements. See Stark (1996); and, for the Mormon case in particular, Bushman (1997–98).

9. The racialist significance grew with the development of the "Hebraic layer" that Jan Shipps (1998) described in the evolution of Joseph Smith's teachings. See also Bringhurst (1981b, 95–97, 129). Such ideas apparently did not take hold, however, in the later rise of the Reorganized Church of Jesus Christ of Latter Day Saints (Madison 1992).

10. McLellin, who eventually broke with Joseph Smith and the church, had a missionary ministry for six years, during which he emphasized the gathering of Israel as harbinger of the millennium, but he did not focus on the primacy of the tribe of Ephraim or the lineage of the Latter-day Saints. His journals, edited and published in 1994, provide descriptions, sometimes quite cursory, of his ministry. See Shipps and Welch, eds. (1994).

11. These are blessings given to individuals by divine guidance under the hands of "patriarchs" especially designated and ordained for that function. The first LDS patriarch was Joseph Smith Sr., the prophet's father, and originally the patriarchal office was to be passed by primogeniture from one generation to the next. After the arrival of the church in Utah, however, patriarchs were also designated in each stake (diocese), and eventually the churchwide patriarchal office was phased out (Allred 1997; Bates and Smith 1996; A. Ballif 1992; Mortimer 1992).

12. A disk containing a sample of 131 early blessings was graciously made available to me by Gregory Prince. Some of these had been obtained from E. Gary Smith and Irene Bates, who, in turn, had examined several hundred more for their book (Bates and Smith 1996). See the analysis and discussion of these blessings in that book and of the 744 examined for the article by Bates (1993).

13. See Mauss (1999, 147) for evidence on this point. The ambient Anglo-Israelism might also have focused the prophet's attention on missionary prospects in England. Of course, in a reciprocal way, early missionary successes in England could well have fostered Anglo-Israelism among the Mormons. Regardless of which came first, the circular dynamic, once established, had unquestioned energy.

14. Quoted in Joseph Fielding Smith, comp. and ed. (1938, 149–50). See additional information on this quotation in Mauss (1999, 148n55).

15. Reference to the grafting from the wild to the tame olive tree evokes the long parable in Jacob, chapter 5 (Book of Mormon), in which the wild olive tree symbolizes the Gentiles and the tame one Israel. See also Romans 11:13–21 in the New Testament.

16. Many similar statements by Orson Pratt appeared in the *Journal of Discourses* (1854–86) during his lifetime. See, for example, 9:177 (July 15, 1855); 17:300–302 (February 7, 1875); 18:64–65, 166 (July 18, 1875); and 18:225–26 (August 26, 1876). Later the apostle George Q. Cannon offered similar explanations for how the Saints might be both Israelite and Gentile, based on his own reading of 2 Nephi 30 in the Book of Mormon (1880, 130; [1890] 1988, 4–5).

17. Such observations about the connection between persecution and the divinely chosen status were made by other church leaders during the same general period. See examples in Mauss (1999, 150n58). President Joseph F. Smith once made an explicit comparison between Mormons and Jews in this connection (1919, 340).

18. Such was the general LDS understanding at first of such New Testament passages as Ephesians 1:4; and I Peter 1:2; as well as Alma 13:3 (Book of Mormon) and Doctrine and Covenants 93:23–33 (May 1833). Neither Harrell nor Ostler sees such passages as referring to the kind of premortal existence with agency described later in the Book of Abraham. The earliest LDS discourse relied heavily on conventional Protestant understandings of most biblical passages, according to Gordon Irving (1973). As late as 1835, the apostle Sidney Rigdon referred to converts as "chosen to be sons of God in Christ" in accordance with "what *God had purposed in Himself*" (1835, 73, emphasis added), pointing to God's intentions rather than to an individual, premortal existence.

19. His 1839 statement that the Latter-day Saints had been "called and chosen of God, according to the purposes of His will, from before the foundation of the world" might have been intended as an allusion to premortal life, but it reverts to the earlier Protestant language (Joseph Fielding Smith, comp. and ed., 1938, 137).

20. Early LDS leaders' explicit references to other sects espousing such ideas (e.g., Aitkenites, Irvingites, and Southcottians) can be found in P. Pratt (1836); and H. Kimball (1840).

21. The *Latter-day Saints' Millennial Star,* published in England from 1840 through 1970 (with periodic interruptions), was the official voice of the LDS Church in England and North America during times of turmoil when no other official publications could be issued. The citations that follow here, however, come from the seventh reprint of the booklet *Are We of Israel?* (n.d. but apparently about 1950, bound with a treatise by Reynolds on the authenticity of the Book of Abraham). By the time Reynolds was actually made a general authority of the church in 1890 (as a member of the First Council of Seventy), he was already a person of great influence in the church as an author, the erstwhile personal secretary for many years to Brigham Young, and the "sacrificial lamb" in the 1879 Supreme Court case of *U.S. v. Reynolds.*

22. The missionaries going to Scandinavia in the 1850s and later shared the belief that, in William Mulder's words, "the blood of dispersed Israel was [running] thick" in that region especially ([1957] 2000, 30).

23. As Bruce Van Orden pointed out, many important church leaders (e.g., James E. Talmage, Joseph Fielding Smith, and Bruce R. McConkie) continued to quote approvingly from Reynolds's version of Anglo-Israelism well past the middle of the twentieth century (1981, 12). This view of Nordic peoples as Israelites has been accompanied by a complementary tendency to see Israelites as Nordic, if we are to judge by popular LDS pictorial art, in which scriptural figures look more like Vikings than Mediterranean Semites.

24. The LDS Church is headed by the president, also often called "the prophet." He serves with counselors (usually only two), all of whom collectively constitute the First Presidency.

25. For numerous examples involving several prominent leaders, see A. Green (1999, 207–14, especially 211–13nn45–50).

26. The quotations from that book appearing here come from the ninth edition (1951). Another influential work by the same Smith (1957–66) was a five-volume collection of the articles from his column "Answers to Gospel Questions," which had appeared in the *Improvement Era* (the official church magazine through 1970).

27. McConkie (1966b, 23, 81, 114, 305, 457), as well as topics headed Adoption, Believing, Birthright, Caste System, Election, Foreordination, Gathering of Israel, Gentiles, Lost Tribes of Israel, and Pre-existence. Although McConkie refers here to "believing blood" as a "figurative expression," it is clear from his explanation that he regards the term as figurative *only* in the sense that *blood* cannot really "believe"; but he still holds that *people* with the "right kind" of blood are more likely to believe.

28. In August 1978, a couple of months after the change in policy toward blacks, McConkie gave a speech in which he called on his hearers to "forget everything I and others have said" on the denial of the priesthood to blacks (1981, 126–27). Nevertheless, he never recanted anything else he had taught about racial differences, even in a paperback reissue in 1979 of his *Mormon Doctrine* (1966b). Furthermore, in the 1978 speech, he continued to refer to blacks as descendants of Cain, though now eligible for the priesthood.

29. Rey L. Pratt, whose father had been a pioneer missionary to Mexico, was an early mission president there, starting in 1911, and became a general authority in 1925 as a member of the First Council of Seventy. For similar and related declarations about the lineage of Mexicans, see R. Pratt (1916b, 148; 1918, 81; 1924, 144; 1925, 170; and 1928, 22).

30. All these declarations were made during official general conferences of the church and were published in the *Conference Report.* See S. Ballif (1909, 80; 1917, 119; 1920, 90; and 1923, 96); Ballard (1926, 40; and 1930, 157); Welker (1937, 59); and Stoof (1936, 87).

31. This advocacy constitutes a good if inadvertent example of the "identity work" discussed in chapter 1.

32. See Bates (1993, 3–5), for the variety of understandings that she discovered in her research on this point. On the ambiguity in lineage assignment arising from "racial" characteristics, one of my informants recounted a conversation he had overheard during 1994 in Johannesburg, South Africa, in which an area president instructed a stake patriarch that black church members seeking blessings were to be assigned to the lineage of Ephraim as a matter of church policy (A. Clark 1995; see also A. Clark 1994).

33. Similar universalistic declarations can also be found in E. Clark (1992); Mayfield (1992); B. Smith (1992); Top (1992); S. Brown (1992); and Ostergar (1992), all of which appeared in the *Encyclopedia of Mormonism*. The inclusive treatment of the Abrahamic covenant by S. Michael Wilcox (1998) seems especially significant, since it appeared in the official church magazine and was clearly intended to supplement the official Sunday school curriculum on the Old Testament.

3. From Lamanites to Indians

> What says the Book of Mormon in relation to the building up of
> the New Jerusalem on this continent . . . ? Does not that book say
> that the Lamanites are to be the principal operators in that
> important work, and that those who embrace the Gospel from
> among the Gentiles are to have the privilege of assisting the
> Lamanites to build up the city called the New Jerusalem?
> —Orson Pratt, 1855

> An occasional whiff of nonsense goes around the Church
> acclaiming that the Lamanites will build the temple in the New
> Jerusalem and that Ephraim and others will come to their
> assistance. This illusion is born of an inordinate love for Father
> Lehi's children. . . . The temple in Jackson County will be built by
> Ephraim, meaning the Church as it is now constituted . . . and it
> will be to this Ephraim that all the other tribes will come in due
> course to receive their temple blessings.
> —Bruce R. McConkie, 1985

THE JUXTAPOSITION of these two apostolic statements, separated by more
than a century, illustrates well the transformation across time in the early
Mormons' understanding of their relation to the American Indians.[1] For
Orson Pratt and others of the founding generation of Mormonism, the "Lamanites" (as they called the Indians) were at the forefront of the eschatological drama then unfolding in preparation for the millennium. The Church
of Jesus Christ of Latter-day Saints, just established among the Gentiles, was
to play a supporting role in this drama by bringing to the Lamanites and all
other remnants of Israel the lost knowledge of the true Messiah and his gospel. The church was also to assist politically and materially in the gathering
of Israel to the divinely designated Zions—Jerusalem in Palestine for the Jews
and the New Jerusalem in America for the Lamanites and the rest of scattered Israel. Once the "day of the Gentiles" was thus "fulfilled," the divine
destiny would again belong to God's chosen Israel, as promised in scripture
and sacred history.[2]

After a century of acting on such an understanding, however, the Mormons
had found little Lamanite receptivity to their religion and even less endur-

ing attachment. The understandable consequence was that the "Lamanite" identity of these native peoples came to seem less salient to Mormons than their identity simply as "Indians." In this respect, the Mormon experience simply replicated that of other American religious denominations (Deloria 1969 and 1992; Tinker 1993). The resistance of the Indians to the continuing efforts of whites to "civilize" them (and to usurp their lands) was often violent. The manifest futility of transforming the continent's aboriginal peoples, either spiritually or culturally, eventually brought a transformation in white aspirations and policies toward them. Changing Mormon views across the century, then, came to correspond to those of other Americans, even if with some lag in time. Of course, Mormons continued to envision an eventual divine destiny for the Lamanites, but now (like the millennium itself) at a much later and more indefinite time. Meanwhile, the Mormons had acquired a new understanding of themselves as literal Israelites, as explained in the previous chapter, and had taken over the responsibility for building the New Jerusalem. The original romantic scenario for the Lamanites had become, in Bruce McConkie's words, a "whiff of nonsense," based on an "inordinate love" for them.[3] Religious idealism had thus become a casualty of practical experience—and not for the first time in human history.

The convergence between the Mormon and the general American outlook on the Indians was apparent as early as 1845, when the *Proclamation of the Twelve Apostles of the Church of Jesus Christ of Latter-day Saints* was issued in Nauvoo laying out LDS plans for proselyting in the world. That proclamation read, in part, that Mormons would "soon be required to devote a portion of their time in instructing the children of the forest; for they must be educated and instructed in all the arts of civil life, as well as in the gospel. They must be clothed, fed, and instructed in the principles and practice of virtue, modesty, temperance, cleanliness, industry, mechanical arts, manners, customs, dress, music, and all other things which are calculated in their nature to refine, purify, exalt, and glorify them as the sons and daughters of the royal house of Israel and of Joseph . . ." (in James Clark 1965–70, 1:256). Brigham Young's philosophy expressed periodically thereafter in Utah remained consistent with that declaration: "We have found it cheaper to feed than to fight [the Indians]. [A]t the same time, we do not believe in descending to their degraded level to do them good, but to raise them up to our standard, and little by little teach them to be industrious, orderly, honest, and peacable" (quoted in Coates 1976, 118).

This philosophy bore a strong resemblance, of course, to the one articulated about the same time by the U.S. Indian Commission, which in 1869 declared the Indians to be "wards of the government," whose duty it would be to "protect them, to educate them in industry, the arts of civilization, and the principles of Christianity" (quoted in Getches, Wilkinson, and Williams 1993, 177).

As time went on, the policies of the Mormons toward the Indians did not differ much from those of the government itself. Both policies were benignly condescending in intention, motivated partly by religious impulses, and aimed at the eventual destruction of Indian cultures in favor of "civilization."

To be sure, the Mormons never repudiated the special identity and spiritual status they had ascribed to the Indians, and these attributions moderated their attitudes and behavior to some extent. Yet, as will be seen in this chapter, the ethnoreligious boundary between the chosen and the others was gradually moved. At first, the Mormons placed the Lamanites on the side of the chosen, along with themselves, especially as their own Israelite identity began to develop. Before the end of the nineteenth century, however, a rapprochement was underway between the Mormons and the others in the rest of America, while the seeming intransigence of the Lamanites had transformed them into simply "Indians" in the experience of most Mormons. In that process, the Indians came to seem increasingly other or at least to occupy a kind of "no man's land" along the eroding boundary with Gentile America.[4]

Perhaps the Mormons could not, in any case, have entirely escaped their Anglo-American cultural biases, for their attitudes toward Indians, like those of other Americans, were always somewhat ambivalent, if not confused—or, in the more charitable assessment of one scholarly observer, "cyclic . . . a product of the tension between two conflicting forces—separatism and assimilation . . ." (Charles F. Wilkinson quoted in Getches, Wilkinson, and Williams 1993, 31). To understand this larger American context more fully, let us briefly review federal Indian policy as it evolved up to the twentieth century.[5]

U.S. Indian Policy as a Context for Mormon-Indian Relations

Even the earliest European attributions about the American Indians presented a mixture of romantic admiration, condescension, and downright disdain (Pagden 1993). Romantic attributions took various forms, including recurrent stories about remnants of the lost tribes of Israel found among the native peoples. Some of these peoples had allegedly been recognized as Israelites by *conversos* (converted Jews) among the conquistadores (including perhaps Columbus himself). Rumors about these lost Israelites spread from Spain through the Netherlands to England, there to mix with romantic if exaggerated stories, such as those about Pocahontas and Squanto (Pagden 1993; R. Sanders 1978). Such romantic images and attributions proved surprising durable, at least among some Europeans, but the difficult experience the native and the colonizing peoples had with each other inevitably brought increasing ambivalence and mutual hostility.

In North America, where the Mormon story would eventually take place, the native peoples found themselves not only pushed westward but also set against one another by military alliances, first in a war between the French and the English and then in a war between the English and their own colonials.[6] In the century after the American Revolution, U.S. government policies toward the Indians were a patchwork, a contradictory record of treaties first broken and then "extinguished": first, the creation of "reservations" within native ancestral territories; then forced removal from those territories altogether (in the 1820s and 1830s) to new territories farther west; then confinement again, even within those new territories, to still more reservations under direct federal control and dependency (in the 1860s and 1870s); and so on.

The earliest American legal doctrines relating to the aboriginal peoples, like those of England and most of Europe, derived from the medieval legal tradition of Christian crusades and conquests, capsulized in the "Doctrine of Discovery," which denied the rights of "infidel" peoples. For U.S. law, this tradition was first formalized in a trilogy of Supreme Court decisions in 1823 under Chief Justice John Marshall, the underlying effect of which was to claim for the United States the right to eliminate the Indian title of occupancy through purchase or conquest. The three broad principles deriving, in turn, from this doctrine were (1) the plenary power of Congress over Indian affairs; (2) Indians' limited sovereignty over their own affairs and reservations; and (3) the trust responsibility of the U.S. government for the Indian tribes (Getches, Wilkinson, and Williams 1993, 36–37, citing Robert A. Williams).

In applying these principles, the federal government, during the earliest decades of the Republic, sought to protect the rights of Indians within their treaty territories and to bring all commercial and political intercourse with the Indians under its control, in effect dealing with them as though they were a collection of foreign governments. Yet individual states, contrary to federal law, continued to enter into relationships and treaties with the tribes inside their state boundaries, while lawless white Americans all across the frontiers frequently violated Indian territories and rights. The inability of the federal government to assert and maintain its legal controls during those early days created a nightmare of illegitimate white acquisitions and usurpations of Indian property that have continued to provide the grist for litigation even to the present (Getches, Wilkinson, and Williams 1993, 99–104, 118–19, citing Francis Paul Prucha and Charles F. Wilkinson).

As more states were created and white settlers continued their westward encroachment on Indian lands, the federal government found itself under increasing pressure from states and private parties to open those lands for settlement. The Louisiana Purchase seemed to provide a relatively easy and conscience-saving way for the federal government to accommodate the white expansion while still acquitting its fiduciary responsibility toward the hapless Indians. Accordingly, after two decades of argumentation and negotiation involving federal and state governments and political parties, and despite opposition from the Indian tribes and their allied Christian missionaries,[7] the Indian Removal Act of 1830 was passed by Congress and signed by President Andrew Jackson (himself long an advocate for removal). That legislation permitted the removal of various Indian tribes (by force, if necessary) from the east side of the Mississippi River to the new lands of the Louisiana Purchase on the west side of the river.

By the mid-nineteenth century, large expanses of land in the western plains had been set aside as "Indian territory" for the removed tribes, with a plan eventually for at least one separate Indian state in the Oklahoma Territory. What followed was a long and cruel process of forced migration, a process especially senseless for the Cherokee and the other so-called civilized tribes, which had already demonstrated an aptitude for constitutional government, settled agriculture, industry, commerce, and peaceful cohabitation with white neighbors in their shrinking ancestral lands in the East (Getches, Wilkinson, and Williams 1993, 120–30, citing Francis Paul Prucha).[8] In exchange for the territories relinquished in the East, the various tribes were given new western lands in perpetuity, with the boundaries to be guaranteed by the federal government itself. Yet as white settlers continued to press westward, these designated areas in Indian territory increasingly gave way to "reservations," shrinking islands within the larger areas that had been given to them. In the process, the original federal hopes for some kind of assimilation of the Indians gave way to a policy of separatism.

However, in the 1850s and 1860s, as the western Indian lands were increasingly surrounded by whites, government policy again began to emphasize assimilation on the shrinking reservations. The cruelty and ineffectiveness of the reservation system were recognized and explicitly articulated as early as 1869 by the federal Board of Indian Commissioners itself:

> While . . . the government of the United States . . . has evinced a desire to deal generously with the Indians, . . . [their] actual treatment . . . has been unjust and iniquitous beyond the power of words to express. . . . The benevolent measures attempted by the government . . . have been almost uniformly thwarted by the agencies employed to carry them out. . . . Whatever may have been the original character of the aborigines, many of them are now precisely what the course of treatment received from the whites must necessarily have made them—suspicious, revengeful, and cruel in their retaliation. (Quoted in Getches, Wilkinson, and Williams 1993, 176)

While the army's role was to make sure the Indians moved to reservations and stayed there, the chief responsibility for assimilation was given to Christian teachers and missionaries sent to the reservations.[9] Naturally, Indian outrage and hostility over these cultural and territorial encroachments made for regular and hostile resistance, but the army nearly always prevailed. Since separatism had proved futile, the new order of the day became forced assimilation on reservations.

The large role that had always been implicit for the agents of religion in this assimilation was now explicitly assigned by the Board of Indian Commissioners (itself made up largely of Protestant clergymen), which called for, among other things, government schools to be established for every tribe, the English language to be taught, and Christian missions and schools to be encouraged and fostered: "The religion of our blessed Savior is believed to be the most effective agent for the civilization of any people" (S. Lyman Tyler quoted in Getches, Wilkinson, and Williams 1993, 170). Beginning with Ulysses S. Grant's administration, federal policy called for "civilizing" and "Christianizing" the Indians, under the supervision of these Protestant commissioners (which greatly curtailed both Catholic and Mormon missionizing on most reservations). Government-sponsored schools then imposed a radical and sometimes violent assimilation process on the Indian students, ranging from control over hairstyles, clothing, and language to religious and political indoctrination (Utley 1984, 203–26).

An even more radical vehicle of assimilation was introduced by the General Allotment Act (or Dawes Act) in 1887. In the belief that reservations were actually retarding the assimilation process by keeping the Indians too close to their traditions, the government now invoked a vision of future Indians as individual, independent, landowning citizens. Assimilation could take place much more efficiently on an individual basis than on a tribal one. Reservation lands would be broken up and distributed in allotments to individual Indian owners to use as they might see fit (the allotment concept had actually been introduced in several treaties prior to the Dawes Act). Individual Indians would also be eligible to receive nonreservation lands under federal homesteading laws. Not all reservations were broken up by the time this policy had run its course, but some 41 million acres of formerly tribal lands were allotted to individuals, often in great haste.

In retrospect and no doubt to the Indian tribes of the time, this policy had all the appearances of a radical renunciation of solemn treaties and a process for scattering the Indians and grabbing their lands. To the federal government, the policy change was simply a matter of accepting the new reality: The Indians were doomed by Manifest Destiny to be surrounded on all sides in any case. New lands acquired through treaties with Mexico and England had become available with the completion of the transcontinental railroad in 1869. Of course, the government claimed more altruistic motives, as well: As landowners, individual Indians would have personal security that tribal life could not afford them; by learning to stand on their own two feet, the Indians would gain new self-respect, while simultaneously relieving the federal government of their support; and as "regular Americans," they would now have access to all the institutions and opportunities to acquire the "benefits of civilization" (Getches, Wilkinson, and Williams 1993, 190–93).

At least some in Congress, however, could see the Indian viewpoint: "[I]f the people who are clamoring [for this kind of legislation] understood Indian character, Indian laws, . . . Indian morals, and Indian religion," declared a U.S. senator in 1880, "they would not be here clamoring for this [allotment policy] at all." In the same year, a minority report from the House Indian Affairs Committee asserted, "The real aim of this [allotment] bill is to get the Indian lands and open them up to settlement. The provisions for the apparent benefit of the Indian are but the pretext to get at his lands and occupy them. . . . If this were done in the name of greed, it would be bad enough; but to do it in the name of humanity, and . . . to mak[e] him like ourselves, whether he will or not, is infinitely worse . . ." (both declarations quoted in Getches, Wilkinson, and Williams [1993, 193], with consequences graphically described in H. Jackson [1881]). Nevertheless, the allotment policy proceeded apace and reduced reservation lands by millions of acres before the turn of the century, when its failures began to become conspicuous. This radical effort to atomize Indian communal life and the establishment of government boarding schools to assimilate Indian children contributed to widespread Indian destitution and social disintegration (Getches, Wilkinson, and Williams 1993, 168–214).

As one might expect, the allotment policy proved faithful to the "law of unintended consequences." Many of the land parcels allotted were not suitable for agriculture, at least not without considerable technological intervention. The distribution of the parcels proceeded at a pace far greater than that at which individual Indians could be trained to use them. Lacking experience or interest in the whites' economic or agricultural ways, many Indians also lacked the inclination to use the land in the ways envisioned by the government. Accordingly, many Indians were only too glad to lease their land to whites (under the Dawes Act, they could not actually sell it) and to live on the income from the lease. Lacking a culture of capitalism, with its emphasis on budgeting, saving, and investing, most Indian lessors quickly squandered their income and found themselves dependent on public welfare in greater numbers than ever. With each new generation of heirs, of course, the allotments were divided into ever smaller parcels, thus greatly reducing the per capita income even from leasing.

Meanwhile, under the new Bureau of Indian Affairs (BIA), Indian children from homes on or off the reservations were to be placed in the boarding schools for eight years without personal contacts from parents or relatives. Indian language, religion, and culture were prohibited (D. Adams 1995; Benedek 1995, 99–

117). The idea was to purge the Indian youth of their cultural heritage. The result, again seemingly so predictable in retrospect, has been summarized: "Ostensibly educated, articulate in the English language, . . . with their hair short and their emotionalism toned down, the boarding-school graduates were sent out either to make their way in a White world that did not want them, or to return to reservations to which they were now foreign" (Francis Paul Prucha quoted in Getches, Wilkinson, and Williams 1993, 208–9).

Such, then, was the federal policy of "assimilation" and the concomitant plight of most of America's native peoples, in "Mormon country" and elsewhere, as the late nineteenth century merged into the twentieth: increasing invisibility and poverty, whether by "allotments" or on deteriorating reservations, and boarding schools for the force-feeding of the American way of life. On the rare occasions when Mormons or other Americans had firsthand experience with actual Indian life in the twentieth century, they were likely to see reservations that were heart-wrenching enclaves of misery or encounter individual Indians displaced to urban slums by the federal allotment policy. Ironically, this "syndrome of forced dependence and resulting social and economic decline became the rationale for even greater government domination of Indian life," as David Getches, Charles Wilkinson, and Robert Williams pointed out (1993, 168). This was, of course, a far cry from the destiny envisioned for the Lamanites by the early Mormons—or probably by any Americans for the Indians.

Early Mormon Conceptions and Definitions of the American Indians

While early Mormons differed somewhat from other Americans in their conceptions and policies toward Indians, they also shared in the general political ambivalence and selective romanticism of most other Americans. In the early nineteenth century, as Joseph Smith was reaching maturity and starting his ministry, theories and rumors about the so-called Indians abounded, not only in England and America but in much of the rest of Europe as well (Pagden 1993; R. Sanders 1978; Ethan Smith 1996; Vogel 1986).[10] According best with the popular millenarianism of the period were those theories that defined the Indians as constituting one or more of the lost ten tribes. Biblical prophecies, after all, had long promised that these lost tribes of Israel would be led from some unidentified northern regions of the earth back to their historic homeland in Palestine, there to be reunited with the Jews in preparation for the millennial reign of the Messiah. The story in the Book of Mormon made no attempt to account for all the lost tribes (though their continuing existence was clearly acknowledged). Rather, the book was linked to the popular genre by its account of certain Israelite "stragglers" (as they might be called), who found their way to the Western Hemisphere before the Babylonian captivity of 589 B.C.E. brought a final end to the Davidic dynasty in Israel.

The main protagonists of the Book of Mormon story are descendants of only two families of Israelites, mainly of the house of Joseph through his sons Manasseh and Ephraim. These families had been living in Jerusalem as subjects of the Kingdom of Judah before it was finally overwhelmed by the Babylonians. Their leader was Lehi, a descendant of Manasseh (Alma 10:3) and a prophet and patriarch contemporaneous with Jeremiah (though not mentioned in the Bible).[11] By divine guidance, Lehi led these families out of Jerusalem a few years before its captivity and across the Arabian Peninsula. There they built a ship on the Persian Gulf and crossed the Pacific Ocean, eventually landing at an unspecified site somewhere in the Western Hemisphere.[12]

During the next thousand years, this colony grew in numbers and worldly sophistication, with alternating periods and episodes of repentance and spiritual retrenchment in the Old Testament pattern. Early in its history, the colony broke into two factions, called Nephites, after one of Lehi's sons, and Lamanites, after another (somewhat rebellious) son. The Nephites kept the records that eventually became the Book of Mormon, and they portrayed themselves as the righteous faction, led by their own prophets and attempting to follow the true religion most of the time. By contrast, they portrayed the Lamanites as a fallen and degraded people who had rejected God and regularly waged war against God's people. This fallen condition was signified by a divine curse and mark on the Lamanites, according to which they became a "filthy," "loathsome," and dark-skinned people, despite sharing an identical Israelite ancestry with the Nephites (1 Nephi 12:23; Jacob 3:5, 8, 9; Alma 3:6–19).

The religion of the Nephites at first was a combination of Hebrew and proto-Christian, in which they were led by prophets of their own in anticipation of the coming of a messiah.[13] At the meridian of time, some six centuries after their departure from Jerusalem, the Messiah did appear in the person of the resurrected Jesus Christ, after he had finished his Palestine ministry. Christ's establishment of a full-fledged Christian church among the Nephites brought a golden age of peace and prosperity, during which the Lamanites were converted. Thereafter a complete assimilation of the Nephites and Lamanites took place, so that there were no more "Lamanites, nor any manner of -ites" (4 Nephi 1:17). After a couple of centuries, however, the usual cyclical drift into apostasy and corruption began again, culminating in a civil war about 400 C.E. This time, however, the Nephite and Lamanite antagonists were distinguished only by their differential spiritual condition rather than by skin color or other "racial" characteristics.

The earliest understanding by Joseph Smith and his associates of the appropriate Mormon relationship with the Indians was based, of course, on this Book of Mormon story. As literal descendants of Israel, these so-called Indians were actually among God's chosen people, with both a heritage and a destiny of high civilization.[14] Once they could be made aware of their true origins, through the Book of Mormon, surely they would embrace both that book and the true (original) religion, now being promulgated by the prophet Joseph Smith and the "Gentile" missionaries whom he would send to bring them the good news: "And then shall they rejoice; for they shall know that it is a blessing unto them from the hand of God; and their scales of darkness shall begin to fall from their eyes; and many generations shall not pass away among them, save they shall be a pure and a delightsome people" (2 Nephi 30:6). The Book of Mormon introduced itself as a Nephite record divinely preserved to "come forth in due time by way of the Gentile . . . to the Lamanites, who are a remnant of the house of Israel, and also to the Jew and Gentile . . . ," an important Gentile role reiterated in a number of other Book of Mormon prophecies about the latter days (quoted from frontispiece; also 1 Nephi 15:13).

Here Gentiles apparently included the white LDS custodians of the Book of Mormon (see also Doctrine and Covenants 42:39, 109:60; and Underwood 1984, 44–47). Later in the nineteenth century, such passages were reinterpreted to mean that white Mormons, though part of a Gentile nation, were actually Ephraimites. As indicated in chapter 2, the Book of Mormon contained a passage seeming to identify its translator, the prophet Joseph Smith, as a descendant of the biblical patriarch Joseph, but an awareness that Mormons more generally could be literal Israelites seems to have developed only gradually. The original understanding seems to have been that all whites or Euroamericans were Gentiles, but those who joined the LDS Church were *repentant* Gentiles who could then be "grafted" into the house of Israel and become fully "Abraham's seed" in accordance with the Pauline explanation in Galatians 3. Oliver Cowdery, one of Joseph Smith's scribes in preparing the Book of Mormon, seems to have shared the idea that the Latter-day Saints were basically Gentiles charged with a divine mission to the Israelites (especially the Indians): "[W]hen it [the Book of Mormon] shall be brought forth by the power of God it shall be carried to the Gentiles, of whom many will receive it, and after [that] will the seed of Israel be brought into the fold of their Redeemer by obeying it also" (1835, 198). Early Mormon discourse thus continued to include white Mormons in the "Gentile" category for many years.

Later on, Latter-day Saints came to understand themselves as *literal* remnants of Israel (especially of Ephraim) who had been recovered by Mormon missionaries *from among Gentile nations* (including the United States). For example, Orson Pratt spoke of the Saints as "numbered with the Gentile nations [though] there may be many of the blood of Israel among us" (1855a, 2:295). This process was spelled out in greater detail near the end of the century by George Q. Cannon, though his explanation (like those of many of his colleagues in the leadership) does not entirely clear up the confusion over whether the Saints were literally (genealogically) Israelites or Gentiles in their *ultimate* origins:

> We are designated Gentiles in . . . the Book of Mormon. And it is predicted in that book that [some of] the Gentiles would receive the Gospel . . . and . . . would be the means in the hands of God for carrying this record . . . to the descendants of . . . Israel. . . . Though of Gentile descent, . . . through our obedience to the Gospel . . . we become incorporated, so to speak, among His covenant people. . . . We frequently say that we are descendants of the house of Israel. This is undoubtedly true. It is clear to any close observer that this people are Hebraic in their character. . . . Our ancestors were of the house of Israel but they mingled with the Gentiles and became lost. . . . ([1890] 1988, 2)[15]

In any case, these "Mormon Gentiles" were charged not only with bringing the Christian gospel and the Book of Mormon containing it to the benighted Lamanites but also with providing for their care and nurture. Isaiah had already prophesied the day when the Gentiles "shall bring thy [Israel's] sons in their arms, and thy daughters shall be carried upon their shoulders. And [Gentile] kings shall be thy nursing fathers and their queens thy nursing mothers" (Isaiah 49:22–23). The prophets in the Book of Mormon expanded the Isaiah prophecy (G. Davis 1998, 54–60) and applied it directly to the relationship between white Gentiles and Lamanites (1 Nephi 21:22–23, 22:6–9; 2 Nephi 10:9–19). The Mormons thus understood themselves as these nursing fathers and mothers among the Gentiles, and they saw the Indians as "Lamanites," with all the connotations implied in that term. Like the early American image of Indians, the early Mormon image was ambivalent, even if on somewhat different theological grounds.[16] On the one hand, the Lamanites were remnants of Israel, God's chosen people, to be redeemed and gathered in preparation for the Lord's return, and the Mormons were the nurturing and saving agents assigned the responsibility for this redemption. On the other hand, the Lamanites were a fallen people, degraded by centuries of spiritual apostasy and cultural corruption. All such attributions, of course, were part of the same process, discussed earlier, by which Mormons constructed and reconstructed ethnic identities for themselves and others—a common human process (Nagel 1994, 155).

That is, the Mormons began by defining themselves as Gentile agents chosen to redeem the Indians, thereby serving God as Israelites in a figurative or symbolic sense. However, led by the Smith family, Mormons soon came to regard themselves as literal Israelites (from Ephraim), thereby eroding somewhat the ethnic boundary between themselves and the Indians (at least at the theological level). They envisioned the day that together with the Lamanites they would build a common civilization, called Zion, in preparation for the return of the Messiah (as implied by Orson Pratt in the epigraph that opened this chapter). At times, even intermarriage with Indians was envisioned within such a common ethnic boundary (Walker 1993, 10). Later on, as part of the Utah experience, this theologically inclusive ethnic definition became increasingly theoretical and futuristic, like the millennium itself, as Mormons again came to identify more with white Americans and relegated Indians to the category of "other."

Of course, the native peoples themselves experienced shifts in ethnic boundaries across time, often imposed from the outside. The very designation "Indian"—or even "Native American"—lumps together a variety of peoples, cultures, and languages not very meaningful on the "Indian" side of the boundary—except perhaps as a vehicle, more recently, for asserting collective claims to power and resources against the larger white society. Among the Indians, too, boundaries have been drawn and redrawn between nations, tribes, clans, or other categories. In relationships with the Mormons, some tribes in the West actually identified for a time with the "Mormonee" against other whites ("Mericats") out of a sense of shared subordination. In a few cases, whole tribes or bands, including their chiefs, actually joined the Mormons through baptism, which apparently did not, however, involve any recognition of common ethnicity by the converts (Arrington and Bitton 1992, 148–52, 157). In whatever ways the reciprocal identities of Mormons and Indians were evolving, their relationships were increasingly complicated by a third party with its own varied interests and attributions, namely the "Gentiles," especially government agents and Christian missionaries. This third presence intruded into the Mormon consciousness well before Utah, of course.

Mormons, Gentiles, and Lamanites: A Triangular Relationship

It is not surprising that the Mormon rivalry with the Christian establishment and its allies should extend to relationships with the Indians. Nor was this a clear-cut triangular relationship, since each of the three parties had more than one faction, often with contrasting agendas. Besides the obvious divisions among Indian tribes or nations, each with a somewhat different posture toward the Mormons, the divisions among white Gentiles included the army, the federal Indian agents, Christian missionaries, and westward migrants, each with its own ideas about Indians and Mormons. As for the Mormons, most tended to follow the relatively conciliatory policies of Brigham Young, but others were hotheaded, vengeful, or simply greedy and exploitative (R. Bennett 1987 and 1997; Coates 1969; and J. Peterson 1998).

Like most other nineteenth-century Americans, Mormons also tended toward literal interpretations of the scriptures, whether from the Bible or the Book of Mormon. Key Mormon beliefs in the 1830s included the gathering of Israel; the establishment of Zion in America; the restoration of the Lamanites as a great and civilized Israelite nation in their own right (2 Nephi 6:6–14, 9:1–7, 10:18, 26:1–15); and the millennial reign of Jesus the Messiah as the climax to all these developments (1 Nephi 15:18–20, 22:1–12). Also like other religious Americans of the time, Mormons tended to interpret national and world developments in the light of scriptural prophecies. Thus Mormons saw the hand of Providence in the Indian relocation policies of the U.S. government, which moved many of the aboriginal peoples from the east side to the west side of the Mississippi River, just as the Book of Mormon was being published. Less than a year later, the Mormons were divinely directed to Zion, a new homeland in Missouri, "unto the borders of the Lamanites" (Doctrine and Covenants 54:8). To the prophet Joseph Smith and his followers, these were no mere coincidences, given their special divine charge to carry to the Lamanites the newly translated Christian scripture, with its history of their very own forebears, in preparation for building the new Zion (Joseph Smith 1902–32, *History of the Church* 2:358–62; Phelps 1835, 193; Phelps 1836, 245).

Joseph Smith did not wait long to act on this understanding. The new church was organized in April 1830 in Fayette, upstate New York. After only a few months of missionary work and a few dozen converts in the same general vicinity, the first real missionary expedition was dispatched by Smith in October to travel "into the wilderness among the Lamanites" (Doctrine and Covenants 32:2). The party of four missionaries made brief stops among tribes near Buffalo, New York, and in western Ohio, before hurrying on to visits with the Delaware, the Shawnee, and the Potawatomi in Indian territory west of the Mississippi. The expedition did not last long and produced no converts, not because of any particular apathy or hostility among the Indians but mainly because of the hostility of the Gentiles encountered in the form of U.S. government agents and missionaries from other denominations. Thus began the triangular relationship that was to complicate the Mormon program from then on: The Gentile establishment always stood between the Mormons and the Indians (Parry 1985, 73–77).

Later historians have usually mentioned this 1830 mission simply in passing, almost as an isolated incident in a history otherwise preoccupied with Mormon-Gentile relationships during the 1830s and 1840s (Walker 1993, 1–3, 9). In particular, the Lamanite focus of this missionary expedition tends to get short shrift compared with its principal unintended consequence, which occurred en route to its wilderness destination—namely, the discovery and conversion in Kirtland, Ohio, of Sidney Rigdon and his Campbellite congregation. With at least a hundred souls, this congregation more than doubled the total membership of the fledgling Mormon movement (J. Allen and Leonard 1992, 63–66; Arrington and Bitton 1992, 145–46; Parry 1985, 72–73).

Ronald Walker, however, has reconstructed Mormon-Indian relationships during this period to show how much more extensive those relationships really were (Walker 1993). It is clear from Walker's thorough and insightful research that the earliest Mormons spoke and acted regularly on their understanding from the Book of Mormon about their responsibilities to the Indians, and they did so at some cost: Mormon discourse and initiatives with these native peoples proved to be a pervasive and continuous source of suspicion among non-Mormons and contributed significantly to the persecution of the Mormons in Missouri and elsewhere.

Furthermore, lest anyone assume that the Mormons first thought of the Rocky Mountains only in a desperate search for refuge in the late 1840s, Walker identifies a preoccupation with the Rockies and the West in Mormon discourse from the earliest times. One sees in this discourse an aspiration for a Mormon-Lamanite partnership that would build a new Israel, preparatory to the millennium, extending from the Mississippi River to the Rockies and even beyond. Such a new civilization, to be made possible somehow by divine sponsorship, would have a culture based on the true gospel of Christ and would be governed as the kingdom of God on earth. In pursuit of these aspirations, but with one eye always on the Gentiles, Joseph Smith had several contacts during his lifetime, direct or indirect, with the leaders of various Indian tribes and nations. Some of these tribes were apparently interested in cultivating a relationship with the Mormons as a kind of buffer or counterbalance to white America more generally, perhaps in the belief that Mormons and Indians shared a common sense of grievance toward the rest of the nation.[17] Similar considerations seem to have motivated the Mormons at times, but always in the larger context of the Mormon spiritual program. In pursuit of that program, as we have already observed, the prophet Joseph Smith was divinely instructed to establish the headquarters of Zion, this new civilization, in western Missouri, on "the borders of the Lamanites," for the Ohio sojourn was to be only temporary (Doctrine and Covenants 54:8 and all of 57).

Besides the initial contacts with various Indian tribes during the first missionary expedition of 1830–31, the Mormons seem to have quietly cultivated other Indian relationships from their Missouri headquarters during the 1830s, sometimes ostensibly for trading (Walker 1993, 10). A few of these contacts did result in the conversion of at least a small, mixed band of Sac, Fox, and Kickapoo Indians, probably contacted first in Ohio or Indiana but who eventually moved to the Kansas Territory. After the Mormons' flight from Missouri and their settlement in Nauvoo during the 1840s, various contacts and relationships with Indians continued. Missionary specialists in proselyting among Indians were periodically sent, starting as early as 1840, in both easterly and westerly directions, visiting such peoples as the Oneida, Stockbridge, and Onandaga in the East, as well as the Sioux, Kickapoo, and Delaware in Indian territory in the West. A few Indians from these expeditions even joined the LDS Church and moved to Nauvoo. Various tribal delegations also came to visit Joseph Smith in Nauvoo during the 1840s, including the Sauk, Fox, and Potawatomi, the last of whom came seeking moral and other kinds of support in their grievances against the U.S. government (Coates 1978, 429; Walker 1993, 18–27).

In assessing the significance of Mormon relationships with the Indians during the lifetime of Joseph Smith, one must concede the part that these relationships played in inciting the hostility of other Americans against the Mormons, especially in Missouri (Arrington and Bitton 1992, 48–50). Although Joseph Smith and other leaders attempted periodically to rein in the excesses of Mormon public rhetoric on this relationship, that rhetoric all too often provided the basis for Gentile and government suspicions that the Mormons were cultivating alliances with the Indians against their fellow Americans. Prophecies in the unique Mormon scriptures, as well as some Mormon commentary on those prophecies, seemed to justify such suspicions. When the Book of Mormon has Christ promising that the "remnant of Jacob" (i.e., Indians) shall go among the unrepentant Gentiles "as a young lion among the flocks of sheep" (3 Nephi 21:12–13), it would make the Gentiles wonder. Nor would they likely be reassured by public proclamations warning the unrepentant Gentiles that God is about to sweep them off the land because of the "cries of the red men, whom ye and your fathers have dispossessed and driven from their lands" (quoted in Underwood 1984, 43–44; see also Walker 1993, 13–20).

Yet as much as the Mormons' experience with their neighbors in Missouri was complicated by their understanding of a mutual destiny with the Indians, this early millennial preoccupation with the Lamanites had a formative and productive impact on the Mormons themselves for the next several decades. Mention has already been made of the valuable and important but unintended discovery of Sidney Rigdon and his Kirtland, Ohio, flock during the first missionary expedition to the Indians.[18] Perhaps even more important in the long run, the Mormon preoccupation with Indians came to extend, early on, to a much more general focus on the mystique of the West (Walker 1993, 20–33). As part of an emerging separate ethnic identity, the Mormons began to define their destined homeland as extending from Wisconsin down to Texas and from Missouri across to the Rockies and even beyond, with the Indians as partners in building Zion throughout that entire region.

When, in 1846, the Mormons were finally chased out of Nauvoo, their last refuge in the United States proper, their main question was to what part of their western homeland they should gather next. They felt that they "belonged" anywhere in the region (Walker 1993, 20, 29–31). In that sense, the Mormons considered the entire West as "sacred space," dedicated for occupancy by Lamanite Israel and all others, including any white Gentiles who would embrace this gospel and kingdom—a Mormon version of Manifest Destiny, as it were. Wilford Woodruff, in late 1847, had even seen the Mormon expulsion from Illinois and the rejection of the gospel by the United States as marking the end of the "day of the Gentiles" and the beginning of the "day of the Lamanites," which would bring the wholesale conversion of the Lamanites and their tribal leaders. Brigham Young, however, did not resume missionary work among these Lamanites until after the exodus to Utah (R. Bennett 1987, 92–93).

At this point, the Lamanites, or Indians, were far too preoccupied with the consequences of their own forced removal to the new Indian territory to be receptive to another religion from white people (R. Bennett 1997, 96–114).[19] The Plains Indians, consisting of a dozen or so tribes and tribal remnants, numbered more than 50,000, according to a War Department tally in 1843, and most of these had been removed from ancestral lands east of the Mississippi River (R. Bennett 1997, 113–14). Apart from their understandable indignation toward the government, the various tribes were in something of an uproar with one another because they were forced to compete for new territory and resources. Naturally the larger tribes, such as the Sioux, had the advantage over the smaller ones, which sometimes in their desperation sought refuge among the Mormons, despite the Mormons' efforts to remain aloof from all intertribal conflicts (R. Bennett 1997, 57, 101, 108–9).

The Mormons and the Plains Indians

Against the backdrop of all this chaos among the Indians themselves was the sudden increase in whites migrating across the plains to the West during the 1840s. The number of such immigrants per year during 1845–47 doubled and then tripled by comparison with the immediate three or four previous years, reaching a high of almost 4,500 during 1847, the very year of the main Mormon exodus to Utah. Those years, however, were kept relatively quiet by a combination of skillful government diplomacy among the Plains Indians and the dispatch of several hundred army troops in 1845 (R. Bennett 1997, 110–12). The tensions were probably as high between the Mormons and other white immigrants as between the whites and Indians, as rumors ran rampant along the Oregon trail of threatened Mormon depredations or alliances with Indians—with a reciprocal wariness about the Gentiles among the Mormons themselves (R. Bennett 1997, 103–7; see also R. Bennett 1987, 20–21). Given all the potential for violence from these various quarters, it seems truly remarkable that during the 1840s so many immigrants made so many crossings among so many Indians with as little bloodshed as there was.

Prior to the massive 1846 Mormon exodus from Illinois, at least as early as the summer of 1845, Brigham Young had begun a process of private diplomacy with Indian tribes in the Iowa Territory in preparation for the Mormon removal across their lands en route to Utah. While actually crossing these lands in 1846, Young continued his negotiations with the various tribes along the way, offering both goods and services in exchange for permission to make ongoing use of the lands for hunting, grazing, and cutting timber. Strictly speaking, such private negotiations were illegal under federal law, but enforcement was often rather casual, and Young at one point got temporary and retroactive permission to settle on Potawatomi land (at present-day Omaha) from Captain James Allen, who had arrived in mid-1846 to recruit the Mormon Battalion for the war with Mexico (R. Bennett, 1987, 63–7, 72, 103).[20]

Since some of the tribes in the Iowa Territory had rather contentious relationships with one another, the Mormons were sometimes regarded by one tribe as potential allies (or at least buffers) against another tribe. Mormon-Indian relationships in Iowa were not without their tense moments, particularly when tribal elders had difficulty restraining the predatory inclinations of their renegade youths. In general, however, many of the tribes in the Iowa and Nebraska territories had already formed favorable impressions of the Mormons from the earlier visits of Mormon missionaries and emissaries, so a relatively peaceful sojourn in those territories was achieved (Coates 1978, 429–33; Walker 1993, 25–29). Such Indian predations as occurred usually took the form of stealing cattle or horses, with an occasional attempt to kidnap Mormon women. Yet there was very little fear of the Indians; hundreds of Mormon diaries surviving from this migration reveal instead a generally favorable characterization of Indians (Stanley Kimball 1985). As the Mormons eventually traveled farther west, however, they experienced considerably more tension with the Pawnee and Sioux, requiring much more military readiness and painstaking negotiation than ever (R. Bennett 1987, 120–27, 150–53).

Such peace as the Mormons enjoyed in Indian territory had less to do with religion than with Brigham Young's "rules of engagement." Well aware of Gentile suspicions about Mormon plans and motives and the complex relationships among the various Indian tribes themselves, Young devised policies aimed at getting the Mormons to their final destination in the Rockies with a minimum of entanglements along the way—with either Indians or federal agents. Even proselyting among Indians was put on hold for the time being. One of Young's policies was to give the Indians as many hints as pos-

sible of Mormon military strength, without ever actually using it or revealing its true extent. Another policy was to avoid taking sides—or even appearing to do so—with one tribe against another. A third was to avoid economic
or close social contact (especially sexual) with Indians. Federal law greatly
restricted economic relations between whites and Indians (beyond a certain
amount of barter), and Young did not wish to run afoul of the U.S. Indian
agents any more than absolutely necessary. Finally, bloodshed was to be
avoided, even at the cost of tolerating a certain amount of stealing by the
Indians. Of course, such policies were not always followed to the letter, and
there were a few tense confrontations over the thefts of Mormon cattle by
desperate and hungry Indians, the Mormon cutting of scarce timber, and so
on. In general, however, Young's policies kept the Mormons out of trouble
with the various Indian tribes (R. Bennett 1987, 46–50, 93–97).

Yet the Mormons could never forget the third side of the "triangular relationship." As Richard Bennett summarized the matter, "If patience and diplomacy characterized Mormon relations with the Indians, a spirit of suspicion dominated negotiations with representatives of the Office of Indian
Affairs" (1987, 91). From the Mormon viewpoint, the Indian agents sent by
the U.S. Office of Indian Affairs were acting largely out of religious prejudice and deliberately turning the Omaha, Oto, and other Plains Indians
against them in an effort to get them out of Indian territory as soon as possible, despite the permission that the Mormons thought they had obtained
from the Indians and the army to remain for two years on either side of the
Missouri River. From the viewpoint of the Indian agents, however, they were
only reminding the various Indian tribes of their rights in the face of the
Mormon incursion and occupation of their lands.

The agents' suspicions about ultimate Mormon intentions were increasingly aroused with the passage of time, particularly after the Mormons
changed their departure dates and plans and built durable Mormon homes
and communities in the area, apparently in contravention of federal law. Even
more disconcerting to the agents was Brigham Young's strategy of deliberately keeping them guessing about long-standing rumors of Mormon alliances with Indians against the government (and an opposite strategy in his
confrontations with the Indians). Young was usually able to minimize misunderstanding and acrimony when he was personally on the scene, but some
of his lieutenants were not so careful in their dealings with government agents
(R. Bennett 1987, 91, 98–111).

The Utah Experience

In their westward migrations across the plains to the Rockies during 1846 and
1847, the Mormon pioneers had only a few threatening encounters with Indi-

an tribes along the way. Once they got to Utah, however, they found they had settled among native peoples somewhat less accommodating than those whom they had known in the East or on the plains.[21] By this time, federal policy was beginning to favor the confinement of Indians to reservations, rather than the earlier Jacksonian policy of generally leaving both the indigenous and the "removed" tribes to their own devices in Indian territory west of the Mississippi River. Brigham Young was appointed both territorial governor of Utah and federal superintendent of Indian affairs early in 1851. At least from that point, Young and the Mormons came to favor the new "reservation" policy, although this policy was not really implemented in Utah until after the Civil War (K. Carter 1964, 76; Coates 1978, 450–52; Cristy 1978, 228–29).

Until that time—that is, for about the first twenty years of Mormon life in Utah—the Saints and the Indians lived literally as neighbors. Newly established Mormon villages and settlements were interspersed with Indian villages and encampments, mostly of various Ute peoples. As John Peterson put it, the Mormon-Indian relationships during this period were generally not only symbiotic but also peaceful and even intimate, at least until the increasing Mormon settlement began to destroy the ecosystems on which the Indians had traditionally relied (1998, 6). Of course, the Indian bands often came and went in accordance with their own seasonal subsistence patterns, but they usually returned periodically to the same general vicinities, so that white settlers came to know these same bands and even individuals (Van Hoak 1999). As food became scarcer for the Indians, interaction with the Mormon settlements came to include begging, which perhaps increased mutual familiarity but also probably a degree of mutual contempt.

Besides the Ute throughout Utah, the major tribes encountered by the Mormons between the Great Salt Lake and the Colorado River, totaling perhaps some 20,000 people, were the Shoshone to the north and east, the Paiute and Gosiute to the west and southwest, and the Navaho, Apache, and Hopi to the far south.[22] These different peoples had somewhat different economies, ranging from the settled agriculture of the Hopi to the hunting and gathering of the Paiute, the nomadic sheep and goat herds of the Navaho, and the modified buffalo culture of the Ute and the Shoshone. Partly for pragmatic reasons and partly because of a continuing belief that these new neighbors were still Lamanites to be missionized and redeemed for building Zion, the Mormon policy under Brigham Young was generous and enlightened, especially compared with the policies of other whites in and out of government. Even after two decades in Utah, Young still exhorted his followers to "feed and clothe [the Indians] so far as it lies in your power. Never turn them away hungry from your door, teach them the arts of husbandry, bear with them in all patience and long suffering, and never consider their lives as equivalent for petty stealing" (1866a, 11:263).

In addition to such instructions for ad hoc encounters with Indians, Young devised and endeavored to enforce several major policies for the church as a whole and its scattered communities. One of these was to negotiate an agreement with the relevant Indian tribe before establishing a Mormon settlement in its territory. Sometimes, of course, this required substantial gifts to the tribe. Another policy was to centralize and coordinate all Mormon trading with the Indians, so that transactions were conducted only by Mormon spokesmen in each community or area who were acquainted with the Indian languages and customs and so that trade would not be subject to individual competitive bargaining, exploitation, or intimidation. This policy, in turn, required that a portion of the goods and labor donated as "tithing" to each community's storehouse be allocated to an "Indian account" for use in trade and for occasional gifts. The women's Relief Society also regularly sewed and donated articles of women's and children's clothing and bedding to the storehouse. Benevolent as such policies might have been, the Mormons were under no illusions about their need to be prepared for unexpected hostilities. Most early settlements were surrounded by fortlike walls and had trained local militias for guard duty, defense, and occasional recovery of stolen livestock from marauding Indian bands (Arrington and Bitton 1992, 148–50; K. Carter 1964, 77; Coates 1978, 435, 441–45). John Peterson characterized this general policy as one of armed vigilance, especially after the earliest skirmishes (1998, 256–59, 342–47).

Some policies were guided less by diplomatic or pragmatic considerations than by the Mormon understanding of their divinely bestowed responsibilities for the spiritual welfare of the Indians as Lamanites. One of the great ironies resulting from this understanding was the territorial legislature's 1852 act permitting slavery in the Utah Territory. This act was partly designed to permit Mormon converts from the Old South to bring with them their black slaves, few though these were. An even stronger motivation for the act, however, was to permit Mormon families to buy Indian children who had already been enslaved by a long-standing slave trade between various Indian tribes and with Mexican slavers (S. Jones 2000). Since selling children stolen from other tribes was an important source of revenue for the Ute and others, simple persuasion or suppression of the practice was not feasible. The Mormon leaders reasoned that Indian children bought by Mormon families would be removed from the slave trade and could be brought up as civilized Mormons by families with the resources to buy them. Scores of such children were adopted in that manner, and some eventually even married into white families. Not all such adoptions turned out well; some of the children were never able to adjust to the ways or the diseases of the white Mormons (Arrington and Bitton 1992, 11–13; Brooks 1944; B. Cannon 1999; Coates 1978, 435–36; Dutson 1964).

For almost two decades after the 1847 Mormon arrival in Utah, experiences with their Native American predecessors were more peaceful than might have been expected considering the number of people involved on both sides. Yet this period was also laced with many skirmishes and eventually with considerable disillusionment. Moreover, the Mormons had to depend on their own Nauvoo Legion for protection, since the federal army offered none, even after it was stationed in Utah in 1858. Until the Black Hawk War, starting in 1865, there were only a few serious outbreaks of hostility, all fortunately rather brief, involving small numbers and losses on each side and often instigated by hotheaded young Indian renegades (or their white counterparts) rather than by the tribal leadership. (Several of the earliest incidents are described in Coates [1978, 442–50].)

The first major skirmish occurred in the Provo area in 1849. The Mormons had established a fort there and were grazing cattle in the vicinity. The local Ute felt entitled periodically to take some of the cattle, much to the irritation and consternation of the settlers. The killing of a prominent Indian by the Mormons provoked several weeks of hostilities and casualties on both sides (J. Peterson 1998, 49–58). One band of these Ute from the Provo area even raided some northerly ranges west of Salt Lake City (K. Carter 1964, 109–11; Coates 1978, 446–50). A militia of only forty Mormons was able quickly to rout and scatter the band. An 1853 raid by the Gosiute and the Shoshone on the same ranges was put down by a posse led by Jacob Hamblin under circumstances that to Hamblin demonstrated divine protection for both sides and a divinely sponsored reconciliation between the hostile parties. This incident seems to have played a part in Hamblin's later decision (discussed below) to devote his life to the Southern Indian Mission (C. Peterson 1975). Also in 1853, a more serious incident eventually implicated the powerful Ute Chief Wakara ("Chief Walker") in hostilities that cost the Mormons four hundred head of livestock but few human casualties. Wakara, however, was quick to respond to Brigham Young's peace overtures and actually rounded up a number of other chiefs for a large peace powwow with the Mormons near Nephi in central Utah.[23]

The most serious episode of all and the first extended period of hostilities was the Black Hawk War, which began just as the Civil War was ending (Arrington and Bitton 1992, 156–57; K. Carter 1964, 106–7; J. Peterson 1998). While the Black Hawk War was precipitated by specific instances of hostile interaction, its actual causes lay in the entire previous history of the tripartite relations among Mormons, Indians, and Gentiles. The war started in 1865, after the major chieftains in Utah had signed a treaty at Spanish Fork with the United States in which they conveyed title to the areas settled by whites in exchange for a large cash settlement and agreed to remove themselves to the new Uintah Reservation. Not all of the Indian parties were reconciled to the treaty, however, and eventually one of the more prominent chieftains, named Black Hawk (originally Antonga), put together a coalition of some three hundred who rejected the treaty and decided on all-out guerrilla war. Intense and organized hostilities between the Indians and the Mormons' Nauvoo Legion lasted about three years before Black Hawk finally led a peace delegation into the town of Mt. Pleasant in central Utah. Although a large contingent of the U.S. Army under Colonel Patrick Edward Connor had been stationed in Utah all that time, it took no part in the war because Connor had a rather jaundiced view of the Mormons and preferred to let them deal with the hostilities with their own resources. After Black Hawk made peace, however, the army took over pacification of the remaining Indian parties not yet reconciled to Black Hawk's treaty. The Mormon losses in this war were relatively light—only seventy human lives, two thousand livestock, and the forced abandonment of twenty-five settlements.

Brigham Young's efforts to end the hostilities and prevent vengeful white reactions produced a reconciliation with Black Hawk and his people so complete that the Mormon prophet himself preached at Black Hawk's funeral in 1870, after old wounds and a long illness had finally claimed the warrior's life. By that time, in line with federal policy, most tribal peoples had vacated the Mormon-occupied territory for their reservations in the Uintah Basin of eastern Utah, as provided in the 1865 treaty (Arrington and Bitton 1992, 165). Thus ended two decades of a Mormon-Indian relationship fraught with tension, ambivalence, and brutality on both sides. The Mormon pioneer population, which had numbered 12,000–15,000 around 1850 (a number far smaller than that of the surrounding Indians), had at least quadrupled in twenty years (Arrington and Bitton 1992, 156–57), while the Indians were being decimated by warfare and disease. In the context of the times and whites' turbulent and genocidal dealings with Indians in North America generally, Mormon-Indian relations must nevertheless be considered relatively peaceful.[24] As the century wore on, furthermore, the Mormons in general had less and less to do with the Indians.

As federal policy during these years began to favor individual Indian "allotments" over reservations, the Mormons sought to help occasional bands of Indians who were rejecting reservation life and opting instead to learn and live by whites' ways. The largest and most enduring of these was a wandering Shoshone band baptized in 1873 and resettled a little later in northern Utah (K. Carter 1964; S. Christensen 1999; Coates 1969, 315–21). In an ambitious campaign of Indian education and assimilation, the Mormons sent scores of farmers, craftsmen, and teachers to work with these natives in clearing and irrigating land and building local industries, houses, a school, and a church. By 1889, some seven thousand acres of land had been cleared for farming and living, though the Indians never really internalized the whites' work ethic. Eventually they were formed into the Washakie Ward, with a regular church program of auxiliaries and activities, which, by 1892, had more than two hundred members with their own Indian leaders. By then, too, most of the children could read and write in English. This project endured to the middle of the twentieth century and served as a model for a few other (less successful) Indian agricultural settlements.

In general, however, the nineteenth-century Mormon experience with the American Indians was somewhat disillusioning. There can be little doubt that in the beginning the Mormon leaders and the great majority of the white converts took very seriously the portrayal of the Indians in the Book of Mormon as Lamanites—that is, as literal Israelites, people destined to recover the spiritual and cultural greatness of God's chosen people. Mormon discourse also reveals an attitude of condescension and superiority, but in this respect Mormons were much like other white Americans. The difference was that Mormon condescension was qualified and provisional. That is, early Mormons fully expected that Indians could be "civilized" fairly quickly and thereby converted into the cultural and spiritual equals of whites. The earliest Mormons actually expected Indians to become full partners—perhaps even leading partners—in the preparations for the Lord's millennial reign over his gathered people and the rest of the earth (e.g., see the Orson Pratt epigraph at the beginning of this chapter).

Rhetoric to this effect continued, from Missouri to Utah, to feed the suspicions of the nation generally and government agents in particular about Mormon machinations and alliances with Indians. One historian saw this triangular relationship among Mormons, Gentiles, and Indians as a major cause of the "Utah War" of 1857–58, when the U.S. Army was dispatched to Utah to put down a nonexistent Mormon rebellion (Furniss 1960, 28–51, 159–70). This debacle was a response to periodic reports from federal agents and other American visitors to Utah calling for preemptive action to prevent the Mormons from "tampering" with the Indians and turning them against army outposts and other whites in the area. The same complicated triangular relationship provided a background for the tragedy of the Mountain Meadows massacre in September of 1857, when a company of midwestern migrants en route to California were murdered in southern Utah by a band of local Mormons and collaborating Indians (Brooks 1962). Brigham Young's intervention came too late to prevent the massacre. Though his attempt was sincere, he had invited the suspicion of complicity by his overheated rhetoric earlier that year when he warned the army that he might turn the Indians loose to prevent further white migration westward.[25] The mutual suspicion and criticism between the Mormons and the federal officials over dealings with the Indians continued to the end of the century. As late as 1890, Mormons were still being blamed, without credible evidence, for aiding and abetting the ghost dance movement led by the Paiute prophet Wovoka, which eventually ended in the infamous army massacre of Sioux believers at Wounded Knee, South Dakota (Coates 1985; Smoak 1986; Utley 1984, 227–72).

Mormon Missions among Indians in Nineteenth-Century Utah

Despite the general context of three-way conflict, the Mormons never abandoned their efforts on behalf of Indian spiritual welfare. Naturally enough, these took the form of missions and missionary expeditions, even beyond the periphery of Mormon country. This missionary work did not begin immediately, for Brigham Young had apparently decided on a two-stage strategy in which the Indians would first be "civilized," so that they might more readily be able to understand the significance of the Mormon religion. The Lamanite "curse" would first have to be removed by, in Charles Peterson's words, "instilling cleanliness, industry, morality, and other virtues prerequisite to redemption" (1975, 24).[26] Wilford Woodruff apparently understood Young's original philosophy similarly, for within days of the 1847 Mormon arrival in Utah, he recorded in his journal, "Brigham Young spoke to the Saints. He told them, among other things, that . . . our people would be connected with every tribe of Indians throughout America, and that our people would yet take their squaws, wash and dress them up, teach them our language, and learn them . . . the gospel of there forefathers, and raise up children by them, and teach the children; and not many generations hence they will become a white and delightsome people, and in no other way will it be done; and that the time was nigh at hand when the gospel must go to that people" (1985, 3:241, journal entry of July 28, 1847).

If Young's envisioned miscegenation included reciprocal intermarriage, not merely concubinage, it might be seen as reflecting a less fundamental form of white racism—a view that Mormons and Lamanites literally shared a common Israelite ancestry and that the divine "curse" manifest racially on the Lamanites was temporary and accidental rather than essential. Yet, in actual practice, white Mormons proved unwilling to see their daughters marry Indians (Arrington 1970, 17; Coates 1972, 5), and very little intermarriage actually occurred, suggesting that ordinary white racism probably trumped any theologically constructed affinity in Mormon thinking. In any case, since the Indians resisted the various "civilizing" efforts, it is easy to see why these efforts did not last (Coates [1987] offers a revealing case study).

When the first Indian missions were finally begun in 1853, some of them lasted for decades and produced Mormon experts trained in Indian languages and cultures. Some thirty or forty men were sent to each mission outpost.

Those who did not bring wives were permitted, even encouraged, to marry Indian women, although few actually did so. Their main function was spiritual, in both the formal proselyting sense and the broader sense of "civilizing" the Indians by teaching them the arts and crafts of the whites. Accordingly, all the missions attempted to train and assist Indians in agriculture and in livestock husbandry. Leonard Arrington identified eight different missions established by the Mormons during 1854 and 1855, from Shoshone country in the north to Navaho country in the south and from the Washoe Indians of western Nevada, to the west, all the way to the Creek and Cherokee on the plains to the east (1970, 16–21; see also Coates 1969, 99–115, 315–21). Most of these missions survived only a few years, because of the Utah War of 1857–58 and the general hostility of federal Indian agents.

While ideally all these missions had as their principal purpose the conversion of Lamanites, other purposes were apparent as well. As Charles Peterson explained, some missions were set up on the major travel routes to counter Gentile influence and control trade (1973; and 1975, 26–27). Others were more expeditionary and temporary in nature, such as those along the southern route to California or those sent throughout Arizona and into Mexico in the 1870s. Peterson found it significant that the two periods most productive of missions occurred right after the two most significant Indian wars, the so-called Walker War of 1853 and the Black Hawk War of the 1860s. These were times when Mormon leaders, distressed that the failure of their diplomacy had led to Lamanite bloodshed rather than redemption, redoubled their spiritual efforts, both rhetorically and operationally (see also Coates 1969, 116–69).

Naturally the various wars with Indians in the 1850s and 1860s, as well as the Utah War in 1857–58, were enormously disruptive of Mormon missionary efforts. However, after all of those had ended, the 1870s and 1880s saw a new emphasis on missionary work among the Indians, with many new proselyting expeditions and baptisms. As Peterson put it, "[T]he day of the Lamanite seemed again at hand" (1975, 28). Missions were established again from Shoshone country in the north to Navaho, Hopi, and Apache country in the south. In addition to the Washakie settlement mentioned earlier, missionaries sent to the Shoshone remaining on the reservation at Wind River succeeded in converting Chief Washakie himself and 422 others there as early as 1880. Reservation Shoshone during the 1880s did not respond as favorably as those who had left the reservation to Mormon efforts at teaching them to live like whites; so by the end of the century, these efforts had been largely abandoned in favor of simply proselyting (Coates 1969, 284–92; Coates 1972, 6–8; S. Christensen 1999; C. Peterson 1975, 29).

Meanwhile, as the missionary efforts began to reach south toward Mexico, church leaders began to remark on the promising prospects represented by the five million Lamanites located in that country (C. Peterson 1975, 29). Actually, the earlier expeditions into Arizona had originally been intended largely as the first phase of a more ambitious missionary program for Mexico and Latin America in general. Minutes of meetings held by the Quorum of the Twelve Apostles with the Presiding Bishopric in January 1876 record the instructions of John Taylor (then president of the Twelve) as lamenting the failure of colonizing efforts in Arizona and calling for two hundred Saints to be sent back there immediately "to get in an early crop in the spring . . . [lest] others from the East and West may slip in and occupy the land before us, . . . [for] it is the intention . . . of Prest. Young to have settlements . . . in a direct chain as far as Mexico . . . into the midst of the different tribes of Indians, [spreading] not only the Gospel but all kinds of Industrial and Manufacturing labor." Taylor further anticipated that railroads would be built in "those southern countries and be a mighty engine toward gathering . . . the various tribes of the house of Israel."[27]

Once again in the 1880s a renewed emphasis on missionizing the Lamanites was prompted by an 1882 revelation to John Taylor, who had become president of the church in 1880, in which the Seventy (a special missionary corps) were to be given the main responsibility for "introducing and maintaining the Gospel among the Lamanites throughout the land" (quoted in Hartley 1983, 67). In a letter sent a few days later to the LDS mission president in England, Taylor elaborated on the meaning of this revelation: "The work of the Lord amongst the Lamanites must not be postponed if we desire to retain the approval of God. Thus far we have been content to simply baptize them and then let them run wild again; but this must continue no longer; the same devoted effort; the same care in instructing; the same organization of the Priesthood, must be introduced and maintained among the house of Lehi as amongst those of Israel gathered from among the Gentile nations . . . ; [that is] treat them exactly, in these respects, as we . . . treat our white brethren (1882, 733).[28] An additional meaning of this revelation to George Reynolds, one of the leaders of the Seventy, was that "the fulness of the Gentiles long looked for has come in, and that henceforth the burden of our labors will be directed to the House of Israel commencing with the Lamanites by whom we are surrounded . . ." (quoted in Hartley 1983, 67). Wilford Woodruff, head of the Quorum of the Twelve Apostles, was subsequently quoted to similar purport (Hartley 1983, 67).

In diary entries during the first ten months of 1883, the apostle Franklin D. Richards traced the operational significance of Taylor's revelation. During that year, the Indian Territory Mission was opened again in the Oklahoma Territory, and various apostles were assigned to the Cherokee and others among the "Five Civilized Nations"; to the "Northern Tribes"; to the "Uintah Basin" (where reservations had been established for the tribes once roaming Utah); to the Wind River Reservation of the Shoshone in Wyoming; to the Shoshone, Bannock, and Nez Perce tribes in Idaho; and to the Crow reservation (Hartley 1983, 68; see also Arrington 1987; and G. Wright 1981). Yet, as in the 1870s, this initial enthusiasm seems to have died out. The Committee on Indian Affairs was still functioning in 1888, but very few of the Seventy had been sent on regular missions in accordance with Taylor's 1882 revelation (Hartley 1983, 68).

Apparently as part of the contemplated missionary outreach to the more "civilized" tribes, one missionary effort was surprisingly successful during the 1880s, but that was well outside of Mormon country: The entire surviving tribe of Catawba Indians was converted in South Carolina. Having numbered some ten thousand in 1750, the Catawba had been reduced to fewer than two hundred when the Mormon missionaries arrived in 1883 (D. Brown 1966; Hudson 1970; Merrell 1984). The church invested heavily in education and infrastructure for this tribe, helping to free its economy from dependence on federal aid and its people from alcohol and drug addiction, suicide, and illiteracy. By 1975, its numbers were back up to three thousand, the only Indian tribe in North America to convert to Mormonism (or perhaps to any Christian religion) in toto (G. Hicks 1977; J. Lee 1976). Actually, well before the first visits by Mormon missionaries, the Catawba had become highly assimilated to the white American identity, even to the point of sharing to some extent the general American disdain for blacks and other "Indians" (G. Hicks 1977; Merrell 1984).

Best known among all the missions and missionaries in nineteenth-century Utah was probably the Southern Indian Mission, based in Santa Clara, Utah, begun in 1853 under Jacob Hamblin, who was given by Brigham Young the irregular but meaningful title of "apostle to the Indians" (Arrington and Bitton 1992, 153–55; K. Carter 1964, 114–17; C. Peterson 1975). Like many other well-meaning Americans of his time, Hamblin assumed a posture of benevolent condescension toward Indians, but he clearly felt a deep personal and divine call to his work. By his death in 1886, he had spent the last three decades of his life living among the Paiute, Navaho, and Hopi. There were only a few enduring converts from this mission, but many had been taught how to improve their farms, fields, and physical circumstances in general. His reputation for honesty, fairness, and benevolence was apparently legendary among the native peoples.

Hamblin is doubtless the most often and fully chronicled Mormon missionary to the Indians, but he was actually only one of a whole class of such rough-hewn men who were never part of the church leadership per se but contributed enormously to improving the material condition of various Indian tribes or bands and enhancing Mormon relationships with them. The motives of these Mormon "Leatherstockings" ranged from the almost pure missionary altruism of a James S. Brown, a George Washington Hill, or a Dimick B. Huntington (S. Christensen 1999) to the more adventurous and "pacifying" outlook of a Porter Rockwell or a George W. Bean (O'Neil 1985), with Hamblin somewhere in between (see C. Peterson [1975] and his numerous sources). Such Mormon missionary types were, of course, the counterparts of the many better-known Catholic and Protestant missionaries to the Indians, such as Junipero Serra, Pierre-Jean De Smet, John Eliot, and Marcus Whitman, and shared with them the mixture of zeal, condescension, and unintended cruelty that has so often characterized all missionary efforts among the aboriginal peoples of the world (Tinker 1993).

Few of these missions survived the nineteenth century (see C. Peterson [1973] for details). One that did survive was based at Ramah in western New Mexico.[29] The Ramah Mission was first opened in 1876 and produced about 150 Navaho and Zuni converts before a smallpox epidemic in the area forced the mission to close temporarily until 1884. After about 1880, however, the main focus of the church in Arizona and New Mexico gradually changed from missionary work to colonization, based on irrigated agriculture, and all those who had been sent on formal missions there were released to follow their own inclinations (C. Peterson 1973). Released missionaries often stayed on to form regular stakes and wards of the church, and these became the organizational basis for continued work with the Indians, in both proselytization and education (Coates 1969, 244–79). In general, the Mormons apparently maintained good relations with the three Lamanite groups in the area (Navaho, Zuni, and Spanish American), proving especially helpful as technical advisers in agriculture to the Zuni and Spanish Americans. Relations with the more nomadic Navaho, however, grew strained as Mormon settlements encroached on traditional Navaho herding lands, a strain that was only somewhat relieved by the federal allotments eventually given to the Navaho in the 1920s. The Mormon missionary impulse in Ramah remained largely dormant until the 1950s, when it was revived again on a local stake basis, with some success among the Navaho but little among the Zuni (Vogt 1966, 55–58, 69–72).

Conclusion

The various Mormon missionary enterprises to the Indians cannot be considered very successful if measured by the sheer number of converts or their retention in the faith. The more secular accomplishments of the missionaries as church emissaries, pacifiers, and technical advisers seem to have been more extensive and more enduring (O'Neil 1985; C. Peterson 1975). The few decades of regular and intense Mormon experience with the various Indian peoples of the Utah Territory proved frustrating, rarely if ever according with the inspiring and optimistic prophecies of the Book of Mormon. As time went on, those prophecies, like the millennial reign itself, came to seem to white Mormons as increasingly theoretical and remote.

By the early twentieth century, sermons in the official general conferences mentioned the millennium and the gathering of Israel much less frequently and the Lamanites scarcely at all (Shepherd and Shepherd 1984, 239–45). A review of an index to the *Conference Report* from the 1890s through 1959 (Butt 1960) reveals that references to Indians or Lamanites were very rare during this seventy-year period, and those few references can be found almost entirely in the sermons of a very small number of general authorities who had always championed the causes of the Lamanites (e.g., Anthony W. Ivins, Rey L. Pratt, Milton R. Hunter, and Spencer W. Kimball). These conference addresses, furthermore, increasingly referred to them as "Indians" rather than by the scriptural term *Lamanites*. With the passage of time, these conference speakers also focused more on claims of various archaeological "proofs" for the Book of Mormon and its Lamanites rather than on the contemporary Indians.

In the weekly *Church News,* articles on Indians appeared only four or five times a year up to the mid-1950s. In the monthly official magazine, *Improvement Era,* the subject of Indians was largely ignored until the mid-1940s, when a sudden proliferation of articles appeared on archaeological research. Thereafter, the topic of Indians, too, whether in the northern or southern part of the hemisphere, became much more common in the pages of the *Improvement Era* (Harold B. Lee Library 1957 and 1961).[30] Yet special missions, missionaries, or other programs for Indian peoples all but ceased for several decades until 1943. Occasionally in Mormon Sunday schools and sermons, lessons were drawn from the Book of Mormon about the divine curse on the Lamanites and about the awful fate befalling any of God's people when they reject him—the message of the Old Testament, too, of course. In all, however, only five lessons focusing on Indians, or Lamanites, appeared in the teaching manuals during some seven decades, all of which were historical in nature (Harold B. Lee Library 1967).

Once the native peoples of Utah had been "pacified" and moved to reservations, as in the rest of the continent, they were rarely seen by most white Mormons, even in Utah. During and after World War I, Mormons began migrating out of Utah in large numbers to the urban areas of the two American coasts, and their grandparents' encounters with the Indians became a distant memory. Succeeding generations of Mormons in the twentieth century, like other Americans, came to know Indians largely through the distorted and demeaning portrayals in cowboy westerns on film or in print. As Mormons were assimilated into the American way of life more generally, they increasingly embraced the images most Americans had about Indians. These images included the pathetic indigent Indian begging from farm to farm or, increasingly, in the urban areas of major cities (but see S. Smith [2000] for a countervailing trend in some American literary circles). When white-Indian hostilities occurred in the remote areas of Utah near reservations, white Mormons tended to see them as plain old-fashioned "Indian uprisings," just as other Americans did (e.g., McPherson 1985; and R. Salmon and McPherson 2001). The nineteenth-century Mormon ambivalence about Indian identity, as between "Lamanites" and "Indians," was thus gradually resolved in favor of the latter, with the Lamanites of the Book of Mormon remaining significant in a remote theological or spiritual sense but as irrelevant—or even nonexistent—in any operational sense. And so they were to remain until the middle of the twentieth century.

Notes

1. See appendix A for a note on the basic sources I have used in reviewing the nineteenth-century relations between Mormons and Native Americans.

2. This "dispensationalist" understanding of sacred history was a common Protestant theme at the time and was shared (with some variations) by early Mormon leaders. The contemporary Mormon doctrinal commentator Avraham Gileadi revisits the same theme in various ways (1991, 113–76).

3. The effusive William W. Phelps expressed the romantic strain in early Mormon aspirations for the Indians through his poem "O Stop and Tell Me Red Man," put to music and found in Mormon hymn books well into the twentieth century (1834, 34).

4. This process of drawing and redrawing ethnic and cultural boundaries in response to changing historical experience is treated in Barth (1969b) and Nagel (1994), among other places in the sociological literature.

5. The following section and others on federal Indian policy in this chapter are taken primarily from Getches, Wilkinson, and Williams (1993), which is not merely a secondary source in the usual sense but also a rich collection of excerpts from case law and other *primary* sources, along with commentary from such distinguished scholars as Charles F. Wilkinson and Francis Paul Prucha.

6. To be sure, the Indian nations were not necessarily passive victims in these wars among Europeans but sometimes sought such alliances in their own perceived strategic interests. See, for example, R. White (1991).

7. The government's removal efforts were opposed by most Protestant denominations on the grounds that such efforts would disrupt the successes that the missionaries had achieved in their efforts to "civilize," Christianize, and assimilate many of the eastern tribes. I am grateful to Lawrence G. Coates for sharing with me the results (yet unpublished) of his research in the 1826–38 issues of the Protestant publication the *Missionary Herald*, which strenuously opposed removal.

8. The five so-called civilized tribes were the Cherokee, Choctaw, Chickasaw, Creek, and Seminole.

9. Among the most strident criticisms of the role of Christian missionaries in this process are those of the Native American scholar Vine Deloria Jr. (1969 and 1992).

10. For a contemporaneous review of eighteenth- and nineteenth-century theories in America, see Ethan Smith ([1825] 1996). It is clear enough from Dan Vogel's work (1986) that the early Mormons had been exposed to many of the theories and legends about

Indian origins then circulating in America and Europe. For an example from a Mormon primary source, see H. Kimball (1845).

11. Later Mormon writers also attributed descent from Ephraim to the family of Ishmael, which accompanied Lehi's family on the migration, but this is not indicated in the Book of Mormon and seems to be an afterthought identifying the Book of Mormon more closely with the "stick of Ephraim" prophesied in Ezekiel 37:15–19 (see *Journal of Discourses* 1854–86, 23:184).

12. It was once widely believed by Mormons that Joseph Smith himself had identified the coast of Chile as the area where Lehi's party had first landed, but B. H. Roberts, early in the twentieth century, discovered that such a belief was based on an editor's comment, not on anything Joseph Smith had actually said (Bitton 1999, 68; Godfrey 1999, 76).

13. Scholars outside the LDS fold have analyzed the Book of Mormon as a nineteenth-century American document reflecting the religious and political beliefs and issues common in Joseph Smith's own time and place (e.g., Brodie 1972; and O'Dea 1957). For a rebuttal and an analysis more in line with traditional LDS views, see Bushman (1976 and 1984).

14. Deloria made the interesting point that many of the aboriginal peoples already had names for themselves indicating "the fundamental belief that the tribe is a chosen people distinct from other peoples of mankind . . . [i.e.] chosen for particular religious knowledge and experiences" (1973, 217).

15. To add to the confusion, Brigham Young sometimes used the term *Gentile* in rather different ways, depending on the context. At one point, Young declared that the term referred only to "those who reject the gospel," which, he pointed out, could include the Jews (1868a, 12:269), but only a few months later, he defined the Gentile as "one who has none of the blood of Israel within him" (1868b, 12:311). For modern Mormon commentary, see Gileadi (1991, 113–76), which still does not entirely clarify matters.

16. Following Thomas O'Dea (1957, 256), Keith Parry used the terms *missionary* and *pioneer* to designate the ambivalent Mormon outlook on the Indians, which would, of course, have applied equally well to the contemporaneous American outlook more generally (1985, 71–75).

17. Parry also noted, citing Robert Flanders, that some of the Indian tribes during the Nauvoo period were by no means helpless but actually rather adept at playing the Mormons off against the Gentiles to their own advantage (1985, 73).

18. The importance in Mormon history of Kirtland and Rigdon has been explored in J. Allen and Leonard (1992, 63–74); Backman (1983); and Van Wagoner (1994).

19. Most of the account in the next section is based on R. Bennett (1987 and 1997).

20. Allen probably exceeded his governmental authority in granting such permission. To avoid trouble with the federal agents, Young eventually gave up the settlements on the west side of the Missouri River and moved his followers across the river to the east side in present-day Council Bluffs, Iowa. The Oto, Potawatomi, and Omaha tribes, on whose lands the Mormons were staying, also had to give permission, of course, which they did in exchange for Mormon help in blacksmithing and other skills. The Mormon welcome was enhanced by the favorable business relationships they established with Peter Sarpy, a local trader and entrepreneur, at least one Gentile for whom apparently "business was business," whether with Mormons or not.

21. In this section, I rely heavily on the following secondary sources: Arrington and Bitton (1992, 145–60); K. Carter (1964); Coates (1969 and 1978); and J. Peterson (1998).

22. Population estimates for Indians during this period are dubious, at best, but the Daughters of the Utah Pioneers' publication compiled by Kate Carter (1964, 81–82) credited the Utah historian Andrew Neff with figures adding up to approximately 20,000, though they could go as high as 35,000, depending on the manner of counting (A. Neff 1940, 369). John Peterson quoted estimates ranging from 10,000 to 23,000 for Utah Indians of various tribal combinations as of about 1865 (1998, 81–82). In a prepublication review of this manuscript, Ronald W. Walker maintained that these are all underestimates of the actual population. See also Cuch (2000) and the Carter publication for descriptions, compiled from various sources, of the varied lifestyles and economies of the different native peoples in and around Utah.

23. An 1849 agreement between Young and Wakara and his confederates had apparently broken down, necessitating the 1853 gathering. In early 1850, Wakara was actually baptized into the LDS Church and urged other Ute leaders to do the same (Coates 1978, 439–46). Mormon incursions in traditional Ute lands were a continuing source of tensions (Van Hoak 1999), but apparently a major factor in provoking the hostilities of the 1850s was the ongoing Mormon effort to stamp out the slave trade in Indian women and children (J. Peterson 1998, 64–71).

24. The most serious and bloody battle in Mormon country was the Bear River massacre of 1863, in which the Mormons themselves played no part. Certainly the increasing Mormon incursions to the north, especially in Cache Valley after 1856, had increased the hostile feelings of the Shoshone, as they watched Mormon cattle and agriculture displace their food staples of wild grasses, roots, and game. (Brigham Young had at first deliberately avoided colonizing both Cache Valley and Utah Valley for this reason—see Coates 1978, 434.) Yet the Bear River massacre itself was the product of a U.S. Army campaign led by Colonel Connor, whose rowdy and brutal troops had been spoiling for a fight because of their disappointment at being sent west instead of south during the Civil War. Connor justified the massacre as necessary for the safety of travelers along the Oregon Trail, and for the protection of the Soda Springs settlement of the Morrisite schismatic group fleeing north from Brigham Young. On the massacre and events leading up to it, see Madsen (1985). On Colonel Connors's protection of the Morrisites, see C. Anderson (1981, 165–68).

25. Young's ominous declaration that he would no longer "hold the Indian by the wrist" partly reflected his frustration, in his role as local superintendent of Indian affairs, at having so often been caught in the middle of disputes between the government and the Indians over supplies and provisions (quoted in K. Carter 1964, 78).

26. In line with Young's apparent hopes to "civilize" the Indians before trying to missionize them, he sent a kind of "peace corps" to the Manti area in central Utah as early as 1849 to teach the Indians agriculture (K. Carter 1964, 105–06; Coates 1978, 440–41).

27. These quotations are taken from the General Bishop's Minutes, Presiding Bishopric, January 8 and 13, 1876. I am grateful to William G. Hartley for providing me these excerpts from the LDS Church Archives. Of course, church leaders had explored the possibilities of expanding missionary work to the "southern countries" all the way to South America at least as early as 1851–52, when Parley P. Pratt spent a hard and unproductive year in Chile (A. Palmer and Grover 1999). No more missions were opened on that continent until 1925.

28. The recurrent problem of "baptiz[ing] them and then let[ting] them run wild again" points to the drastically different understandings of "conversion" that were apparent between the two cultures involved.

29. This community (with the pseudonym "Rimrock") eventually became part of the Harvard research project "Comparative Study of Five Cultures," which started in 1949 (see, e.g., Vogt and Albert 1966). The five cultures in the area were Mormon, Anglo-Texan, Spanish American, Navaho, and Zuni. Many prominent social scientists began their careers as advanced students on this project, including Thomas F. O'Dea, who was first introduced to Mormons while working on this project.

30. During the 1940s through 1955, more than a hundred articles (of varying lengths) appeared on Indian/Lamanite topics in the *Improvement Era,* fully half of which were on some aspect or another of Indian archaeology or anthropology. Most of them were written by Charles E. Dibble, with others by Dewey Farnsworth and M. Wells Jakeman, all of whom were associated with the new Department of Archaeology and the New World Archaeological Foundation, both established at BYU in the mid-1940s. These were the first rays of a new "day of the Lamanite" about to dawn at midcentury.

4. The Return of the Lamanites

We have a definite responsibility to the Lamanites. . . . It is my conviction that the end will not come, . . . that the Lord himself will not come in His Glory, until a substantial part of the Lamanites have had the gospel preached to them. . . . [W]e have hardly scratched the surface in . . . converting the Lamanites.
—Spencer W. Kimball, 1957

You're Indians. You're Lamanites . . . a covenant people, a chosen race, a people of destiny. . . .
—Boyd K. Packer, 1979

AS THE TWENTIETH century arrived, historians and pundits pronounced the western frontier of the United States "closed" (F. Turner 1911). Americans came to know Indians mainly through popular fiction and films, which triumphantly glorified the "winning of the West" by the white pioneers and portrayed Indians simply as backward and savage obstacles to the progress of civilization. Mormons generally came to share in this construction of the American past. By 1896, when Utah was brought into the Union as a state, its Indians had long been confined to reservations in a few remote corners. Except for those few whites living in small towns and villages near reservations, Mormons only rarely had personal encounters with Indians in Utah or neighboring states. Furthermore, in the early decades of the century, Mormons began to leave Utah in increasing numbers to live in cities elsewhere, especially in California, where Indian survivors were even rarer. In adopting the general American image of the Indians, Mormons came to think of them less often as "Lamanites," for the Lamanites had already receded back into the pages of the Book of Mormon, just as the Indians were rapidly vanishing into reservations and into the dim recesses of the national memory.

Yet the theological legacy of the Lamanites remained in Mormonism, as this chapter's opening epigraph from Spencer W. Kimball clearly indicates (quoted in Wilkinson and Arrington 1976, 505–6). In particular, the destiny of Mormons and Lamanites was interwoven with the culmination of history in the end times. By midcentury, as will be seen later, it was time for the Lamanites to return again to center stage in the Mormon eschatological drama, once again to have their day in the divine sun, perhaps this time for good. This return of the Lamanites, however, occurred in two phases. The first phase, which is the main focus of this chapter, took the form of still another outreach by the church to those tribes and nations in North America that had been the original object of the Mormon missionary effort. By about 1980, however, this effort had also met with the usual frustrating results, and the second phase (discussed in the next chapter) was underway in the form of considerable missionary success in Mexico and Latin America. All of this played out against the usual chaotic background of shifting U.S. federal policy (Getches, Wilkinson, and Williams 1993; Philp 1995; Wilkins 1997).

The Continuing Cycles of Federal Policy toward the Indians

Until the 1930s, U.S. relations with the tribal peoples were ostensibly governed by the 1887 Dawes Act, with its provisions for individual "allotments" and eventual assimilation of the Indians.[1] Nevertheless, tribal identity survived, partly because not all reservations had been allotted even by the 1930s and partly because many tribal communities went "underground" with their tribal languages, customs, and kinship systems, out of sight of the Bureau of Indian Affairs (BIA) and the missionaries. Then the Indian Reorganization Act (IRA) of 1934 reversed federal policy by recognizing and encouraging these tribal identities and cultures, including religious freedom and pluralism; the teaching of Native American languages; opportunities for vocational and even college education; the reacquisition (with government funds) of some of the land lost earlier through the allotment regime; and elected tribal governments' control over their respective lands and internal commerce. Tribes were required to vote on the new IRA framework, and most voted for it, which further renewed and strengthened tribal identity (Gibson 1980, 529–44; Getches, Wilkinson, and Williams 1993, 215–29). Yet the pendulum of federal policy was to swing back again.

With the end of World War II, the federal government was able to turn its attention again to such domestic concerns as its Indian policy and to evaluate the impact of the IRA. In general, the government did not like what it saw. This was particularly the case in the new Republican regime, which took over both the executive and legislative branches of government in 1953 with a call for less citizen dependency on government programs. The burgeoning federal debt from the recent world war and subsequent recovery effort required more economies in social welfare spending. Under the IRA, tribal organization and identity might have been enhanced, but Indian dependency on the government had certainly not been reduced. Furthermore, the nation was just entering the era of "civil rights," which translated into a federal policy of racial integration and assimilation for black Americans. Why, some politicians wondered, should federal policy be different for the Indians? Senator Arthur V. Watkins of Utah was among many in Congress who wondered why the American tradition of assimilation had failed in the case of the Indians. Already in 1949, the Hoover Commission on Government Reorganization had recommended "complete integration . . . [of Indians] into the mass of the population as full, taxpaying citizens" (quoted in Getches, Wilkinson, and Williams 1993, 229–30).

The emerging federal policy came to be known as "Termination," expressed in House Concurrent Resolution 108 (1953) and in a number of other legislative and executive acts during the rest of the decade. The response of most Indians to Termination was not only opposition but also alarm, yet the new policy met with surprisingly little opposition, or even interest, in any branch of the federal government. Taken together, the various governmental acts constituting Termination were intended effectively to end tribal sovereignty and the federal trust responsibility over Indian lands. Federal jurisdiction over tribes and individuals was to be replaced by state jurisdiction, which meant an end to all special federal programs for Indians and to exemption from state taxes. It also meant easier access to the natural resources on Indian lands now required for the postwar economic expansion. The government, for its part, proposed to compensate, or "buy out," individual Indians by sending each one a check for the value of the share of the confiscated land, amounting to very little in most cases. Of course, there was no way to compensate a tribal government for the loss of its sovereignty over a traditional territory (however small that might have been) or to compensate an individual for the loss of an Indian identity (Getches, Wilkinson, and Williams 1993, 234–37; Philp 1999).

Fortunately for the survival of tribal identity and self-government, however, several years were required in the Department of the Interior for the planning and actual implementation of Termination. As late as 1962, only about 3 percent of Indian trust land and a similar percentage of all federally recognized Indian individuals had been affected. By that time, federal policy was changing yet again; as the 1960s progressed, a return to tribal self-determination was under discussion. However, an unintended consequence of Termination was the creation of a new "Indian nationalism," a supratribal consciousness or "Pan-Indianism"—that is, a solidifying realization that a national alliance of all the tribes would be necessary to resist successfully the total destruction of the Indian ways of life and the reservation territories on which those ways were based (Hertzberg 1971).[2] State governments, too, began to protest against Termination as they came increasingly to see the policy as simply a federal effort to dump the "Indian problems" on the states.

By the early 1960s, the momentum of Termination had definitely slowed. The administrations of Presidents Kennedy and Johnson not only took no actions under the inherited Termination policy but actually began to invest substantial federal funding in social programs and infrastructures on the reservations, partly in response to a new political activism that Indians had been learning from the successful black civil rights movement. The Indian Civil Rights Act was passed in 1968 (Cornell 1988).[3]

It was a 1970 message to the U.S. Congress from President Richard M. Nixon, however, that marked the formal end of Termination and the beginning of a new policy, sometimes identified as Indian "self-determination." In this speech, Nixon decried, among other things, the dismantling of the tribes in the assimilation process; the loss of the special standing the tribes had historically enjoyed under federal law; and the loss of federal responsibility for Indian social and economic well-being. Instead of Termination, Nixon called for "a new era in which the Indian future is determined by Indian acts and Indian decisions," in which "the Indian can assume control of his own life without being separated involuntarily from the tribal group" (quoted in Getches, Wilkinson, and Williams 1993, 253–54).

President Nixon went on to spell out a number of legislative proposals covering Indian control over federal programs, Indian economic development, Indian education, and many other aspects of tribal life. Congress correspondingly passed a variety of acts that expressed Nixon's general philosophy (Getches, Wilkinson, and Williams 1993, 255–60). Probably the most comprehensive of these was the Indian Self-Determination and Education Assistance Act of 1975, which was followed shortly by, in the words of David Getches, Charles Wilkinson, and Robert Williams, "an unprecedented volume of Indian legislation, most of it favorable to Indian interests, and all of it enacted at the behest of the tribes, or at least with their participation" (1993, 256). Much of this legislation has been resisted by countervailing interests and has had to be tested in the courts, often all the way to the U.S. Supreme Court. The Court has quite consistently upheld tribal rights and self-determination, including even the federal policy of giving preference to Indian candidates for appointment and employment in the BIA. Yet the recurring changes in federal policy across time left a wake of ambiguities and litigations for state and federal courts lasting well into the twenty-first century.[4]

As the twentieth century closed, citizens and politicians were sometimes criticizing the latest federal policy of Indian self-determination as anachronistic or even un-American in a society supposedly committed to the goal of the great American "melting pot." However, the Indians have not been the only ethnic group to point out the conspicuously mythical nature of the melting pot ideal, for some minority peoples have proved especially difficult to assimilate. It was precisely this gap between the mythic ideal and the political realities that gave rise during the 1960s and 1970s to somewhat radical self-determination movements for black and Hispanic minorities. The same occurred among the American Indians in the form of, for example, the American Indian Movement (AIM). One of the effects of such movements is always to make the less radical activists seem moderate by comparison. As Indians learned to play the American political game, they became increasingly effective as organizers, campaigners, and lobbyists. This development largely explains why no federal legislation dealing with Indians had been passed over Indian opposition for several decades by the century's end (Getches, Wilkinson, and Williams 1993, 259, 276–78).

With the dawn of the twenty-first century, prospects for the survival of Indian populations, identities, and self-determination were greater than at any time since the founding of the American republic. Of course, these various changes in the *structural* relationships between Indians and the government, however desirable in their own right, have not always brought improvements in the *material* situation of Indian citizens at the grassroots. For at least the past twenty years, investigative reporters have been revealing outrageous negligence, incompetence, and dishonesty in the administration of Indian affairs, even after Indians themselves were given prominent positions in such agencies as the BIA.[5] Furthermore, some "Indians" with questionable motives and dubious genealogical pedigrees have pressed their claims of tribal prerogatives successfully enough to establish some thriving casino businesses on disputed lands as far east as Connecticut (Benedict 2000).

Nevertheless, many tribes and tribal federations have gained the political experience, power, and resources that enable them to deal with both federal and state governments from a position of strength. Several general factors have made this relatively favorable situation possible, including the great increases in educational attainment and political sophistication of a new generation of Indian leaders. Many of these are now prominent as officeholders at various levels of government. The BIA, furthermore, has been, in effect, transformed into primarily an Indian agency, and federal legislation has increasingly delegated to Indian tribes authority once retained by the government.

Especially important have been the recovery through litigation of traditional treaty rights and the extension of tribal jurisdictions, usually at the expense of state jurisdictions, over revenue raising (taxation), over criminal and civil court proceedings, over child and family law, over natural resources, and over commercial enterprises, including gambling casinos. Tribes and their subdivisions are often the largest employers on reservations—and not only in gambling enterprises, although these have often proved extremely lucrative for some tribes (Getches, Wilkinson, and Williams 1993, 284–85). If their success in all these ways is to continue, however, the tribes, despite a legal kind of self-determination, will likely experience the fuller assimilation into the "American way of life" that they have tried so hard to resist for hundreds of years. For all other peoples, success in modern industrial systems has historically required increasing levels of education and economic sophistication, which, in turn, have brought political, social, and finally cultural assimilation. If this process is repeated, the newly visible American Indians will, despite themselves, simply achieve the traditional American form of invisibility after all, as part of the larger "melting pot."

Midcentury Resumption of Mormon Missionary Work

During the period of the Dawes Act, when allotment, assimilation, and Indian invisibility were the order of the day, the Mormon posture toward the Indians was not very different from the general American one. The "day of the Lamanite" had appeared on the Mormon horizon three or four different times since 1830, but each of the periodic missionary campaigns had proved somewhat anticlimactic, with only a few enduring converts to show for the efforts. After half a century, President John Taylor still complained of the recurrent tendency to baptize Indian converts and then "let them run wild again" (1882, 733). The dispatch of several different missionary delegations to various Indian peoples in the 1880s (mentioned in the previous chapter) seems in retrospect to have been one final effort to realize the "day of the Lamanite" before the century ended.

From that last thrust in the 1880s until the 1940s, there were no new Mormon initiatives on behalf of the Indians. The general neglect that characterized federal policy, at least in operational terms, also characterized Mormon policy. During this period, of course, there were many crises, both in the church and in Utah, that would have diverted energy and resources away from enterprises with such poor cost-benefit ratios as missions among the Indians. The 1880s, for example, brought the final federal assault on polygamy and other Mormon institutions. Having capitulated (at least ostensibly) on the polygamy issue in 1890, the church narrowly avoided federal receivership of all its assets and an occupation of Utah by the U.S. Army. After all that, the next few decades were taken up with struggling for Utah statehood and respectability, mobilizing Utah's people for participation in three wars (the Spanish-American War and two world wars), and dealing with the Great Depression of the 1930s.

It is thus understandable that during these decades new missionary work was not often initiated among American Indians or other "exotic" peoples. Short-lived missions were attempted in Turkey (1884–1909) and Japan (1901–24), but otherwise Mormon proselyting before 1925 remained confined largely to the whites of North America (mainly in the West) and to the peoples of northwestern Europe, where it had traditionally yielded at least satisfactory results. New missions were, however, opened in Mexico (1901) and in various parts of Polynesia (1888–1916), apparently in response to the successes of early exploratory efforts indicating that the "blood of Israel" was abundant in those areas. In effect, the LDS commitment to Lamanites was to be focused not only on the Indians of North America but also on the *other* Lamanites of Mexico and Polynesia (*Deseret News Church Almanac* 1990, 225–42; A. Palmer and Grover 1999).

The so-called Indian Territory Mission, periodically opened and closed after 1855, had been reopened in 1883 under Andrew Kimball (father of Spencer W. Kimball), until it was renamed the Southwestern States Mission in 1898 and then the Central States Mission in 1904, indicating a change of emphasis from Indians to Euroamericans in those regions, as in the rest of the United States (*Deseret News Church Almanac* 1990, 226–67). A few missionaries remained to work with Indian converts and potential converts in those missions, but these were mostly older married couples on short-term missions or else long-term resident Mormons engaged in the Indian trade or other enterprises appropriate to the territory (exemplified by the Bloomfields in G. Lee [1987, 93–102]). A survey of the church presence among the Indians revealed that in 1932 only five small Indian branches of the LDS Church remained organized from the last major missionary campaign in the 1880s, although a few unorganized bands of Mormon Indians could still be found scattered throughout Utah, Arizona, and Idaho (Julina Smith 1932, 68–69). Echoing the 1882 lament of President John Taylor noted above, the apostle Delbert L. Stapley expressed his distress, as late as 1956, that the church's efforts on behalf of the Indians (Lamanites) had not been sustained "but intermittent, and each stoppage of activity causes us to lose ground. . . . We truly cannot afford to neglect them. . . . We must regain through devoted service to the Indian God's approval and blessing . . ." (1956, 417). The Indian presence in the Mormon consciousness had obviously receded about as fully as it had for the rest of the United States.

When the Indian Reorganization Act of 1934 ended individual allotments and attempted to renew Indian reservation life, the church began to look again at the feasibility of special missions to Indian territory (for its own purposes, of course, not as part of the IRA's objectives). Early and substantial backing for the renewal of missionary work among the Indians of the Southwest in the 1930s and 1940s came from George Albert Smith, a senior apostle who soon became church president. The Navaho-Zuni Mission, organized in 1943, was the product of initiatives by local Mormon missionaries and leaders in certain stakes of Arizona and New Mexico, starting in the 1930s.[6] The earliest missionaries in the new Navaho-Zuni Mission were, again, married couples who had lived in the region for some time. The first mission president was Ralph W. Evans who, like the Bloomfields mentioned earlier, was also a trader by occupation. Church leaders intended that the new mission would oversee and coordinate missionary work to the Indian peoples of the southwestern states. The name was changed in 1949 to Southwest Indian Mission, and in 1964 missionary work to the Indians was further expanded by the creation of the Northern Indian Mission, headquartered in Rapid City, South Dakota (Flake 1965, 112–24; D. Green 1955, 233; Whittaker 1985, 38–40).

The renewed missionary focus on Indians at midcentury can also be seen in numerical terms. By 1965, there were more than three hundred missionaries and perhaps as many as fifteen thousand Indian LDS members in those two missions, plus many portions of other missions focused on local Indian bands or communities. Once again "the day of the Lamanite" seemed to be dawning. By 1970, more than fifty branches of the church had been organized among LDS Indians in the Southwest and elsewhere, although many of them had leadership that was at least partly white. The number of American Indian LDS members in all these branches probably exceeded fifteen thousand, but it is not clear by how much. Under the Indian Committee, the church also attempted to "translate" the organization, ecclesiastical procedures, and other complications of the normal church program into a simplified "basic unit program" for the Indian branches and wards (Durrant 1983, 1–10, 20–26, and appendixes A, B, and C). Somewhat ironically, this simplified structure proved more successful among new Mormon branches in the Third World and newer mission fields than among the American Indians (Livingstone 2000).

Estimates of the LDS Indian population and the number and strength of Indian branches at their height can vary greatly depending on how much of North America is included and whether the count includes branches in stakes, as well as in missions (Embry 1990a; Larsen 1965, 9–10; LDS Indian Committee 1965a).[7] In the mid-1970s, a church brochure offered the following statistical dimensions of the programs for Indians: 500 full-time missionaries serving Indian people; an Indian church membership of more than 35,000 in 152 Indian wards and branches; more than 15,000 Indian high school seminary students; more than 5,000 students in the Indian Student Placement Program; more than 400 enrolled at Brigham Young University (BYU); and more than 30 agricultural extension projects for Indians supervised by BYU experts.[8]

During the 1960s through the 1990s, the church and BYU had a constantly changing policy toward separate Lamanite branches or wards. Indian students at BYU who preferred regular "geographic" wards were always free to attend them. Special "Lamanite" wards were sometimes promoted by church leaders but at other times closed down in an effort to integrate their members into the "mainstream" of the university and the church. These changes in policy seemed to reflect changes in the preferences of specific church leaders involved at different times, as well as variations in the preferences of Indian students. Each time the policy changed, there were casualties in church participation. Those Indians who preferred separate wards and branches were especially likely to drop out when the policy switched to integration (Embry 1990a and 1992b).[9]

Sunrise on a New Day of the Lamanite

Spencer W. Kimball and the Renewal of the LDS Commitment to American Indians

Much of the expansion in efforts on behalf of the Indians can be attributed to the initiative of Spencer W. Kimball, who became an apostle in 1943 and was shortly placed in charge of Indian affairs for the church. Even during periods when official LDS missionary work among American Indians had lapsed, as during the first half of the twentieth century, many individual church members and leaders had been unrelenting champions of the cause of Lamanite conversion.[10] For the most part, however, their effectiveness had been local and limited, with the conspicuous exception of Kimball. Having been reared in "Indian Country," Kimball, like his parents (Jenson 1901–36, 1:365–66), had had considerable association with various native peoples, especially the Navaho in Arizona, and had developed a profound sympathy and admiration for them (E. Kimball and Kimball 1977, 236–346; G. Lee 1987, 116–18, 198–205, 258–61, 331–44). With his new calling as an apostle and head of the Indian Committee, Kimball was in a position to launch and support several important church programs on behalf of Lamanites during the next four decades, even after assuming the duties of church president at the end of 1973. The rise and decline of these programs follow a track that corresponds closely with the waxing and waning of Kimball's own career as apostle and president.[11]

While obviously the various Indian programs were not the accomplishments of Kimball alone, his leadership and sustained commitment were crucial. Fortuitous also was the increasing transformation in the political and social climate of the United States with regard to racial and ethnic minorities, starting with the civil rights movement in the early 1950s. Later, in the 1960s and 1970s, the total federal abandonment of Termination in favor of the new self-determination policy for Indians was accompanied by a more general proliferation of federal and state programs to relieve discrimination and disadvantage for various ethnic minorities, including Indians. Although the governmental objectives during the civil rights era tended to foster Indian self-determination and multiculturalism, the LDS and other mission-minded churches were working toward de facto assimilation. Nevertheless, for some purposes, the forces of cultural change both inside and outside the church converged to create a highly favorable historical period for improving the economic and political conditions of the Indians, especially those living in the traditional Mormon homeland.

We can see in retrospect an interesting parallel between the humanitarian initiatives of the Mormons in their traditional western "backyard" and those of other religious denominations in their more urban environments. That is, just as the Catholic and certain Protestant denominations became champions of the black populations in urban "ghettos," so the Mormons reached into the Indian reservations to offer support and relief to "their" minorities (Barnhill 1986). In both these instances, of course, the intended beneficiaries or clients of such religious magnanimity found plenty of reasons to complain about the presumptuousness and condescension of their benefactors, but that is another issue.

In any case, after again initiating missionary work among the Indians in the 1940s, the church began in the 1950s, with Kimball's leadership, to institute a number of special programs that would aid in the *retention* of the new converts, especially the youth, lest they slip back into their non-Christian "Indian ways." These programs were coordinated by a committee known by various names throughout its history, but usually by Indian Committee or Lamanite Committee, which was placed administratively under the Social Services Department in 1971 (Durrant 1975 and 1983, preface and 1–10; LDS Indian Committee 1968). The educational programs were, roughly in order of their creation, the Indian Seminary Program, the Indian Student Placement Program, the Indian Studies Program at BYU, and the Institute of American Indian Services and Research, also operating out of BYU (all described in a special issue of the *Ensign*, December 1975; see also Callister 1970; Felt 1964; and Larsen 1965). While these four might be considered aspects of a single program, they did differ to some extent in drawing on Indian clienteles of different ages, locations, and circumstances. Yet for some of the clients, the four aspects constituted a continuum of services, starting with small children in federal boarding schools and ending with graduates from BYU or reservation extension programs.

This continuum functioned as a kind of "conveyor belt" for those who entered church sponsorship as children in one of the "seminaries" (LDS catechism classes) established at federal boarding schools or near regular public schools (R. Clark 1967, 146–85). From the seminaries (or directly from the reservations), students could be recruited (with parents' permission) into white LDS foster homes under the Indian Student Placement Program; from that program, the most promising were recruited to BYU, under whose auspices and scholarships they might receive college degrees, technical training, or jobs in off-campus extension projects. After all that, the young Indians

would be expected to serve as missionaries themselves and then establish
stable LDS families to start the cycle all over again. Such, at least, was the ideal.
By 1975, the main staff administrator of the Lamanite Committee was optimistic that the eventual result of all these programs would be the preparation of young Indians to assume major roles as leaders and teachers, not only
in the programs themselves but also in the church more generally, a process
he saw as already underway (Durrant 1975). A highly idealized portrayal of
these programs—ironically just as the church was starting to phase them
out—was provided by the apostle Mark E. Petersen (1981).

In actual operation, these programs struggled with all the practical realities that one might imagine (and many others unimaginable) when a culturally and politically dominant people undertakes to assimilate another (well
exemplified in Tinker [1993] and Treat [1996]). Like the Catholic and many
of the Protestant denominations, the Mormons had had extensive historical
experience with the Indians. Yet, unlike the other denominations, most
Mormons continued to understand Indians as "Lamanites" and therefore
looked at them through the prism of the Book of Mormon story. Such a view
combined the negative attribution of a fallen and degraded people with the
positive expectation of a people ready and willing to be redeemed and restored to greatness. In that general sense, the Mormon approach to the Indians was doomed by a tendency to aim either too low or too high. There is
little doubt about the religious commitment, the benign intentions, or the
human and material resources the church and its members devoted to the
redemption of the Indians, and many individual success stories could be told.
However, the review of these various programs, which follows, suggests that
on the whole they produced ambiguous cost-benefit ratios in both spiritual
and material terms.

The Indian Seminary Program

Seminary for Mormons refers to a supplemental religious education program
for LDS school children, usually at the secondary level. (Since Mormons do
not have a professional clergy, they do not have seminaries in the usual sense.)
The Indian Seminary Program began in the 1950s primarily for the hundreds
of students starting to arrive at the federal Indian boarding school in Brigham
City, Utah. The Intermountain School and many other boarding schools like
it had been established in 1949 by the federal government as a rather belated
expression of its "allotment" and detribalization policies from earlier in the
century. Such policies required the federal government to provide off-reser-
vation education, which eventually brought some three thousand students
per year (mostly Navaho) to the Intermountain School. Seminary instruction for LDS students at this school began as early as 1955, though the offi-

cial resolution authorizing the program churchwide was not issued by the church's board of education until September 1958 (Carver 1971). At that time, the seminary program embraced the elementary grades as well as the secondary, and three-fourths of the instructors were full-time missionaries, rather than professional educators of the Church Education System (C. Jones 1975; LDS Church Education System 1971).

By the end of 1975, the LDS seminary program had served some seventeen thousand Indian children, kindergarten through high school, LDS and non-LDS, from forty tribes in twenty states and five Canadian provinces. Federal policy provided time in boarding school curricula for religious instruction at least weekly, and at some schools the LDS Church succeeded also in providing daily seminary instruction in early morning classes before the start of regular instruction. Eventually these special Indian seminary classes were established in several hundred different locations, from Riverside, California, to Lawrence, Kansas, mainly at the secondary level. They were established not only in the federal boarding schools (on and off reservations) but also in day schools (Hales 1963; Larsen 1965, 1–4; LDS Church Education System 1960, 3; Packer 1962). As the LDS Indian students graduated or dropped out of school and, in many cases, went to live in urban areas, the church launched a "follow-up" program to maintain contact with its seminary graduates in various locations.

As the proportion of American Indians living in urban areas approached half of the national total, the LDS Church adapted the seminary program for urban Indians specifically. A special manual instructed local church leaders and seminary teachers in the procedures and curriculum to be followed in organizing and implementing a seminary program for Indians in urban areas. While assuming a generally sympathetic stance toward the special values, needs, and difficulties of urban Indians, the manual still envisioned a seminary program emphasizing structure, organization, punctuality, and other formal features (Baird 1968). Since the merging of religious instruction with an assimilative "Americanization" process has always characterized the LDS approach to Indians, it is not surprising that the seminary curriculum included instruction in such practical skills as reading, oral communication, and money management. Even instruction in certain LDS "lifestyle" norms against tobacco, alcohol, and nonmarital sex served an assimilation function (Hales 1963; Preece 1967).

An early evaluation of the seminary program revealed that it seemed to have had a greater impact on the graduates who had gone to urban areas (50 percent of the total) than on those who had returned to reservation life. Those in urban areas showed some evidence of having experienced greater assimilation than had the reservation returnees. The urban graduates had much higher rates of employment, home ownership, and LDS friends. Despite their

LDS seminary instruction, many of the graduates, urban or not, revealed a rather casual approach to formal marriage, indicating that their church assimilation was far from complete (L. Smith 1962).

Though the Indian seminaries might not originally have been conceived as the beginning of the "conveyor belt" of the Mormon education and socialization process, they served that purpose for more than two decades. Thousands of LDS Indian children were recruited from seminary classes to the Indian Student Placement Program and BYU (Hall 1970). It was perhaps inevitable that these special seminaries would not survive the church's policy changes that eventually phased out the Indian Student Placement Program and BYU's programs. Beginning in 1980, the Indian Seminary Program lost its separate status when it was integrated with the general high school religious education program of the church.

The Indian Student Placement Program

Begun on a small scale with local LDS initiative in southern Utah, this program was formally adopted by the church in 1954.[12] By 1972, it had grown to involve as many as 5,000 LDS Indian students per year in "placement" in white LDS foster homes during the school year. Enrolled from both primary and secondary levels, the students came from sixty-three tribes in twenty-one states and provinces. About half of them were Navaho (the largest single category of aboriginal peoples in the country as a whole, but especially in the West). More than 10,000 white LDS families in the western states and provinces volunteered, at their own expense, to take in children from the reservations; and by the 1975–76 school year, more than 20,000 Indian students had been placed with these families. During the school year, these children attended regular public schools and local LDS churches with their white "siblings" in their respective foster families.

In the beginning, Indian children were selected by missionaries and local church leaders, but eventually the selection was turned over to professional LDS social service personnel, under the authority of state departments of public welfare and children's services. Full consultation was sought with local church leaders (often themselves Indians) and with the "natural" families of the children on the reservations. Each summer the children would return to life on the reservation with their natural families. A series of church manuals and directives defined carefully the roles and responsibilities for all the parties involved in this program (LDS Indian Committee 1965b; 1967; LDS Social Services 1970 and 1973). With professional social workers involved, the program gained legitimacy from both federal and tribal governments (Durrant 1975).

By 1980, however, the program had been cut approximately in half, to about 2,500 Indian students per year. Beginning in the 1985–86 school year, it was cut still again (D. Albrecht 1985; G. De Hoyos 1992). By then, more than 70,000 Indian students had participated in the program (Pavlik 1992, 25). Yet by 1996, the program had been all but terminated. The first cuts were made by gradually dropping students younger than high school level and by raising the academic entrance standards for the older ones. There were many reasons for this drastic reduction from the levels of the 1970s. One was the growing criticism of the program from Indian activists and even some tribal leaders, who rightly or wrongly saw the program as another white assimilation campaign. Many feared that Indian families were being pressured to give up their children and cut them off from their cultural heritage, resulting in harmful psychological confusion about their identity (J. Allen 1998, 106–8; "The Latest in the 'Social Genocide' Field" 1972, 11; Keane 1982; Pavlik 1992, 25; H. Rainer 1976, 126). It is during the winter when most of the lore, legends, and cultural legacy are passed from tribal elders to the youth on reservations, experiences that would obviously not be shared by those spending the school year in white foster homes (Mitchell-Green 1987). Such concerns were eventually neutralized somewhat by careful church negotiations with Indian leaders, by surveys of LDS Indian parents, and even by a favorable verdict from a federal government commission; but the church was stung in the process. Other reasons for reducing the program so drastically included a rapid improvement after 1970 in the quality and quantity of educational opportunities on reservations themselves and the ambivalent outcomes of various evaluations of the program by both inside and outside researchers.

There were actually quite a few professional evaluations on different aspects of the program at various times, many of these in the form of graduate theses or dissertations. Some studies focused on the academic and other secular impacts of the program on the Indian children, while others concentrated on the outcomes of the religious indoctrination they received during their placement in white LDS homes and schools. Still others examined the feelings and assessments of the white foster parents, the natural Indian parents, or the teaching and social service professionals who handled the children (Barklay et al. 1972; Bishop 1960; LDS Indian Committee 1966; G. Lee 1975; Lindquist 1974; Schimmelpfennig 1971; R. Smith 1968; G. Taylor 1981; Topper 1979; Willson 1973). The most thorough evaluation, conducted by church researchers themselves, was published in part after appropriate peer review. The published versions (Chadwick and Albrecht 1994; Chadwick, Albrecht, and Bahr 1986) offered emphases and nuances somewhat less critical than the unpublished in-house version (LDS Research Information Division 1982). Since these studies represented many different auspices, objectives, measures, samples, sample sizes, control groups, and research methods, they are difficult to compare. Accordingly, the contrasting conclusions they reach make unambiguous generalizations very difficult.

The various researchers tended to find a more favorable impact of the program on Indian students and on their natural families to the extent that the studies were (1) based on large samples; (2) conducted in the program's later years—1970s and 1980s; (3) done under church or BYU auspices; and (4) focused on behavioral outcomes of a secular kind, such as education and acculturation, rather than on religious outcomes. The most ambiguous findings of the various program evaluations had to do with the realm of religion. One reason for this ambiguity might have been a "placement conversion" factor. That is, although the Indian children almost always had the concurrence of both natural parents for entering the program, a fairly large proportion of the students joined the church right at the time of their placement, suggesting that their families might have had mixed motivations. By the early 1970s, about two-thirds of the recruits to the program had been baptized only in the immediate past (G. De Hoyos and De Hoyos 1973; Pavlik 1992, 24–26). Long-term religious change would thus have been difficult to effect under the circumstances. Whatever the reasons, the program did not seem nearly as effective in making and keeping the students observant Mormons as it did in enhancing their prospects for successful adult lives in the white world.[13] Nonetheless, neither did the studies yield appreciable evidence of damage to the students' psychological or emotional well-being (J. Allen 1998, 104–6; G. De Hoyos 1973 and 1992; G. Taylor 1981). The program seems simply to have died a natural death as greatly improved opportunities for public education became available to Indians on and off the reservations and as the church's own cost-benefit assessments became ambiguous (J. Allen 1998, 107–10).

At the individual level, the impact of the placement experience on the Indian children seems to have varied considerably. All of them found it difficult to adjust, first to the drastically different cultural and material circumstances of their white foster homes and then to the recurrent cultural and emotional shifts back and forth between life during the school year (in foster homes) and reservation life during the summer. Much depended on whether they came from LDS convert families, as contrasted with other reservation origins, and on how reluctant their families of origin were to let them return to school each fall. Of course, many individual factors also affected the children's reactions, including age, aptitudes, and general temperament. These variations in the long- and short-term effects can be seen from a number of retrospective assessments by LDS and other Indians who passed through the program. Most accounts, including the oral histories of LDS Indians in the BYU Redd Center repository (see appendix A; and Embry 1992d), credit the program and the foster families with benign and kind intentions, and many regard the experience as having had a positive and formative influence in their lives (J. Allen 1998, 96–100; Benedek 1995, 118–31; Birch 1985; Hangen 1997; G. Lee 1987, 103–16, 203–24, 250–55).

Brigham Young University Programs: College Education for Indians

Students taking the "conveyor belt" from the placement program or Indian seminaries to BYU were at least more fully prepared than were Indian students who went to college directly from the reservations or from federal boarding schools.[14] In recognition of the large attrition among the nation's Indian college students before graduation, the church and BYU launched a major program to bring promising Indian students to BYU on full scholarships. Furthermore, for Indians and others who might wish to specialize in Indian studies, a minor in that field was established in 1975 as part of the BYU baccalaureate curriculum (Gowans 1999). The university recognized from the beginning that some degree of assimilation in academic and other values of the general American culture would be crucial to success at BYU, and students who had as children taken part in church education programs would obviously have an advantage in gaining university admission (Steele 1968). A report to the BYU president indicated that during the 1971–72 school year half of the Indian students on campus had come from the placement program (almost all of whom had originated on reservations) and another 43 percent from the church's Indian seminaries. A retrospective look two decades later estimated that altogether some 35 percent of the Indian students at BYU had come out of the placement program (Osborne 1993, 282; Webb 1972, 6).

The original idea for the BYU program seems to have been presented in a 1951 proposal to the First Presidency from the Indian Committee, headed by Spencer W. Kimball, but very few Indian students were actually enrolled before 1965, and most of them failed to graduate, despite considerable financial and academic support. From about 1965 on, however, the program was greatly revised, expanded, and more fully supported from various sources. The LDS Church itself generally budgeted about $700,000 annually for the Indian scholarships alone, and increasingly scholarship funds came also from private, public, and tribal sources. On admission, each student received a full-tuition grant, contingent on maintaining acceptable grades.[15] In a 1975 publication, BYU claimed to be devoting more of its operating budget per student to Indian education than to any other undergraduate program and contributing more of its own funds to Indian scholarships than were all other universities in the country combined (Warner 1975, 20).

Sustained recruiting drives brought Indian enrollments at BYU from 43 in the 1963–64 school year to triple that number by 1968 and then to 500 or more throughout the 1970s, giving BYU the largest Indian enrollments of any university in the country. As part of the recruiting campaign, several appealing pamphlets and brochures were issued by the Indian Education Department at BYU (1976, 1977a, 1977b, 1978a, 1978b, 1981). As the recruiting program became more elaborate, it not only drew on LDS placement and seminary students but also reached into various public, reservation, and BIA high schools. Most of the time, about half of all the Indian students recruited were from the Navaho nation (Osborne 1975, 6, 41, 61). Once recruited, the students were then put through an extensive preenrollment summer orientation program lasting several weeks (Osborne 1993, 57–60, 97–104, 165–77).

Admission requirements for Indian students were somewhat relaxed compared with the general campus standards but not drastically so. Their ACT scores were relatively low, but once actually enrolled at BYU, they earned grades higher than would have been predicted by the usual entrance data. Their grades averaged around 2.00 in the required academic courses, while the non-Indians at BYU averaged around 3.00. The Indian students found special difficulty with course work in reading, composition, and mathematics, which is understandable given their deficient preparation in these subjects and in study skills. Accordingly, they took an average of about a year longer to finish their degrees than white students did. In general, average grades for Indian students differed little on the basis of background (reservation, nonreservation, urban, etc.), but reservation students who had gone through the placement program got appreciably better grades than did those who came to BYU directly from reservations (Osborne 1993, 17; Warner 1975, 5, 9; Webb 1972, 12, 36–40).

While academic difficulties obviously contributed to a relatively high Indian dropout rate at BYU, other important reasons were job opportunities, marriage, military service, and (at least temporarily) LDS mission calls. Extraordinary efforts were made by the university to prevent or delay their dropping out. Besides the financial support, the Department of Indian Education at BYU provided many other kinds of cultural, social, and academic supports for the Indian students. Many of their courses were provided in special classes with normal academic content but small class sizes. These classes were not racially segregated, for they maintained an approximately equal proportion of Indian to white students (actually, 40:60). Yet the classes did employ specially skilled teachers using modified methods, extra-class tutorials, and other devices calculated to enhance student retention and success.

In cooperation with a local state trade-technical college, BYU offered the Indian students four different "tracks" to graduation with either two-year or four-year degrees, depending on their career plans (Osborne 1993, 14–31, 108–17; Webb 1972, 23–29). Graduation rates of Indian students at BYU reached five times the national average for Indians (though still only 20 percent of those enrolled); and by 1980, hundreds had graduated from at least seventy-five different tribes in North America. The extensive lists compiled by V. Con Osborne indicate that more than 500 Indians from various tribes graduated from BYU between 1950 and 1985. If graduate degrees are included, the number is closer to 600 (Osborne 1993, 18–19, 150–61, 249–54). By 1992, BYU records listed more than 1,500 Indian alumni (not just graduates) over a forty-year period. A survey that year of all alumni who could be located (over 300) indicated that a large number had entered modern professions, such as law, education, and engineering. Comments volunteered on the questionnaires also provided a rich variety of candid observations, both appreciative and critical, on the BYU experiences of these alumni. Half of the respondents reported continuing church activity in significant roles (Osborne 1993, 255–56).

Beyond academic outreach, Indian students on the campus also had their own wards (congregations) of the church for at least two decades. There were three "Lamanite wards" on the BYU campus by the mid-1970s, attended and staffed almost entirely by Indian students (Osborne 1993, 39–40, 85). Other social supports included the Tribe of Many Feathers, which organized social and cultural activities of special interest to Indians. Begun in 1950 by a small number of Indian students and white supporters, this organization eventually grew to a membership of several hundred on the campus. The club sponsored all kinds of activities, on and off the campus, including the annual Indian Week, which featured prominent and successful Indian "role models" (LDS and non-LDS), and the annual "contest" for the selection of "Miss Indian BYU" (who would go on to compete in the "Miss Indian America" contest).[16] Under a faculty adviser in the Department of Indian Education, students published their own newspaper, the *Eagle's Eye*. The Lamanite Generation was a traveling troupe of dozens of students from various tribes and Polynesian islands that provided musical, dramatic, and other kinds of entertainment on the BYU campus and elsewhere during periodic travels (Warner 1975, 8–12). The BYU Intertribal Choir, organized in 1974, also enjoyed success in the region but survived for barely a decade.

Indian student publications had started as early as 1957 with the *Liahona, Thunderbird,* and *United Israel* as predecessors to the *Eagle's Eye,* which began publication irregularly in 1971 (for a list of student editors and faculty advisers from 1970 to 1985, see Osborne [1993, 162–64]). It carried news especially of Indian-related events in the LDS Church and periodically featured short articles on "model" Indian youth with noteworthy achievements. The *Eagle's Eye* was sometimes published monthly between 1976 and 1982 but usually much less frequently. After 1985, as part of the general transformation of the entire "Indian" education program to a new "multicultural" focus, the *Eagle's Eye* was also transformed. The auspices announced on the masthead changed from Native American Studies Center to Multicultural Programs or Student Life and eventually (in 1997) to Official Journal of Multicultural Student Services. Contents of the issues in the 1980s and 1990s

increasingly included material and features on non-Indian student categories, such as Polynesian, African American, and even Southeast Asian.

The Lamanite Generation was begun in 1971 by a white BYU student and
his Maori wife. He had been a missionary in the Southwest Indian Mission
and conceived the troupe originally as a vehicle for cultivating pride in the
Indian/Lamanite identity among its Indian performers (D. Sanders 1985). In
time, however, the Lamanite Generation began to romanticize the Indian
cultures and increasingly became largely a professionalized public relations
showcase for BYU. It eventually came under the auspices of the BYU School
of Music. After the mid-1970s, it included various kinds of "Lamanite" elements and performers from Latin America and Polynesia and thus was no
longer strictly "Indian." Eventually it traveled all over the United States and
the world presenting Lamanite talent in all its many varieties and expressions.
The number of performances varied from year to year but reached a high of
forty-five during 1977. As time went on, the original purpose of the Lamanite Generation came to be subordinated to other church purposes, such as
expanding the public definition of *Lamanite* to include other ethnic groups
and giving worldwide attention to the part played by all these groups in the
work of the church. As one of its presumably unintended functions, this
troupe also promoted romances and marriages among the performers, often across ethnic lines, despite regular countervailing admonitions from
church leaders (Osborne 1993, 124–28, 220–47; D. Sanders 1985).

The special BYU program for educating American Indians, despite its
apparent success, did not long survive the 1970s. During 1978 and 1979, the
BYU administration began a process of downsizing and refocusing, a process explained below in greater detail.

Brigham Young University Programs: Off-Campus Indian Services

Besides the on-campus programs for Indian students, the university and the
church during the 1960s and 1970s launched initiatives intended to upgrade
native peoples economically, technologically, and physically (LDS Indian
Committee 1973; Toscano 1975b). Most of these projects were developed
under the auspices of the Institute of American Indian Services and Research,
inaugurated as early as 1958 (under a slightly different name). This institute
depended heavily on private (nonchurch) funds; little or no funding came
from the university itself, except in the form of office space and one or two
staff salaries. Accordingly, fund-raising efforts occupied a major share of staff
time. Such efforts are illustrated by a ten-page brochure (Institute of American Indian Services and Research 1972), in which specified amounts were
solicited for leadership development, small business development, alcohol-

ism education, teacher training, counseling, and scholarships. A somewhat later booklet ends with an impressive list of the various corporate donors that had responded, including General Mills, the Kellogg Foundation, Weyerhaeuser Foundation, oil companies, and airlines (Warner 1975, 15–24).

By the mid-1970s, this institute had served thirty-eight different tribes with seventy-two different projects. These projects involved water reclamation, agriculture, horticulture, and the like. More than eighty agricultural projects among forty-three different tribes, from Arizona and New Mexico to Saskatchewan, had brought under cultivation thousands of new acres supporting eleven thousand Indian families. From 1978 on, the institute published a periodic newsletter, *Buffalo Hide,* which provided details on its many projects (see also Lyman 1985, 194–242). The institute also offered support services in literacy, employment, career planning, small business development, housing, alcoholism counseling, and other social needs. These BYU services sometimes seemed to duplicate or even compete with those being offered by other social service agencies, one of which moved its headquarters to Denver after only a year in Salt Lake City.[17] The institute also offered postsecondary training for Indian students in various crafts, trades, merchandising, and other occupations. In addition to these services, the work of the institute included gathering and disseminating reliable information on Lamanite cultures and teaching about the connections between these cultures and their ultimate Israelite heritage (Institute of American Indian Services and Research 1966 and 1978–85; LDS Indian Committee 1968, 16–17; Osborne 1993, 33–37, 86–89; Webb 1972, 63; Wilkinson and Arrington 1976, 530–33). Eventually, the work of this institute was apparently transferred to a non-BYU foundation (Chadwick and Albrecht 1994, 291; Clemmer 1999).[18]

Through its Office of Continuing Education, the BYU campus itself, during the mid-1970s and early 1980s, also carried on very successful extension and teacher-training programs among the Ute and the Navaho, funded with both federal and tribal grants (Osborne 1986). In the same period, LDS Welfare Services sent several hundred so-called health and welfare missionaries to Lamanite communities in North America, South America, and Polynesia. These were usually older missionary couples, often retired, who were given brief periods of special training at BYU before departing for their assignments (defined in "Economic Restoration of Lamanite Israel" 1970, 4; Janice Clark 1975). Major literacy programs were instituted on reservations and even more prominently in several countries of South and Central America, under the auspices of BYU education experts. The church built and staffed scores of elementary schools in Mexico and various Polynesian countries (L. Johnson 1975; Toscano 1975a). For North American Lamanites, however, all such special programs were left to other auspices after the 1980s.

Private Initiatives by Mormons for Indians

Among such "other auspices" were the many private programs undertaken by individual Latter-day Saints, acting on their own religious beliefs about the special obligations that Euroamerican Mormons have to "redeem" the Lamanites. Examples of such programs include American Indian Services in Provo, Utah; Utah/Bolivia Partners in Alpine, Utah; AYUDA in Delta, Utah; and the Foundation for Indian Development (FID) in Provo, Utah. Some of these initiatives, especially AYUDA, and their accomplishments are recounted in detail in a privately published 1985 book by Dr. Melvin A. Lyman (161–93; see also Lyman 1982). Dr. Lyman, of Delta, Utah, was one of the founders of AYUDA, created in 1969 to bring together various professionals who could provide medical and other life-sustaining services to aboriginal peoples throughout the hemisphere. Originally inspired by a Seventh-Day Adventist medical mission and hospital in Monument Valley, Utah, AYUDA eventually grew into a major vehicle for coordinating and delivering medical and other services (Litt 1980). FID, supported by an annual budget of only about fifty thousand dollars during the 1990s, provides free educational and economic development services to native populations (Foundation for Indian Development 1993; Böhmann 2000).

Both AYUDA and FID have come to focus their efforts mainly on Guatemala and other Latin American populations rather than on the North American tribal peoples. Enterprise Mentors, based in St. Louis, Missouri, is of more recent origin. Its two dozen officers and board members consist mainly of Mormon and non-Mormon professionals from BYU and the corporate world, chaired by Marion D. Hanks, an emeritus general authority of the LDS Church. This foundation specializes in providing expert consultation and micro-loans for small businesses in Latin America and the Philippines. The literature of all these foundations, especially AYUDA and FID, explains their work with rationales drawn from the Christian religious heritage in general and from the Book of Mormon in particular (Foundation for Indian Development 1993; Böhmann 2000; Enterprise Mentors 1994; Litt 1980). The legal services of Wilkinson, Cragun, and Barker in Washington, D.C., including many on a pro bono basis, also contributed to various Indian causes (Deem and Bird 1992).

Beyond these organizational examples, there are many private efforts by individual Mormons, often through their enterprise in obtaining special grants. For example, in the early 1970s, Howard Bahr and Bruce Chadwick, then professors at Washington State University (and later at BYU), established a paralegal program in Seattle for training urban Indians in the acquisition of social and legal services (Clinton, Chadwick, and Bahr 1973). In 1971, Rex A. Skidmore, a prominent LDS dean of the School of Social Work at the

University of Utah, obtained a large grant from a consortium of federal and other agencies to establish at the university a seven-year program to train Indians as professional social workers ("Social Work Awarded $1 Million— Five Agencies OK Indian Program" 1971). Another example is the training program established by J. Richard Franks, an LDS professor at Washington State University during the 1980s and 1990s, in speech and hearing therapy for promising Indian students at the master's level, in the expectation that they would then serve their respective native populations. Many other examples could be cited of altruistic initiatives on behalf of aboriginal populations by Latter-day Saints motivated explicitly or implicitly by their special Mormon religious commitments.

The Day of the Lamanite in Seeming Eclipse

When the observer steps back and reviews the half-century of Mormon commitments to the North American Indians after World War II, a remarkable panorama emerges in general terms, whatever controversies there might be over the details. This panorama reveals, first, a catechism or seminary program at both grade school and high school levels for the systematic inculcation of an alien religion into youth with little grasp of English; second, a foster placement program for the same grades (but increasingly mostly secondary) involving thousands of children and their natural Indian families and many more thousands of white foster parents who devoted time and treasure to the education of these children, sometimes for as long as eight years. Then there were the extensive BYU programs, both on and off campus, with several hundreds of full scholarships for two-year and four-year degrees, even if only about a fifth of the recipients earned degrees (a comparatively high proportion for Indian youth). Add to that the hundreds of young college-trained Indian men and women who either went out into the white world as role models or returned to their own tribal homelands as civic leaders and church leaders.[19] The off-campus programs trained probably hundreds more Indians and their families in agriculture, trades, and entrepreneurship. Why did the church "pull the plug" on such a seemingly successful and comprehensive enterprise?

The answer seems to hinge on the definition of *success*. The education and assimilation of thousands of Indian youth during one entire generation would be considered success by most government officials and educators and was so considered by the LDS professional social workers, faculty, and staff of BYU, who administered these programs. However, the church is not in the business of education and assimilation for its own sake. It is in the business of "making Mormons"—or, in church terms, saving souls and bringing them to Christ. For the church and its leaders, therefore, success is not achieved without sustained growth in church membership *and retention.* In these terms, the outcome must have seemed disappointing to late-twentieth-century church leaders, as it had seemed to their predecessors a century earlier. Even President Kimball, generally so hopeful on Indian matters, periodically expressed disappointment in the spiritual progress of Indian converts, a situation that he tended to attribute as much to the prejudices and failings of white Mormon members and leaders as to any lack of faithfulness among the Indians themselves (E. Kimball and Kimball 1977, 273–74, 296–97, 340–42, 366–67). Yet, in time, the invidious comparisons in spiritual growth between North American Indians and their presumptive counterparts in Latin America and Polynesia became too compelling for church leaders to ignore. Accordingly, resources that had gone for decades exclusively to American Indian converts and prospects were reallocated to the support of other "minority" peoples coming to BYU and joining other church programs, as well as to the support of the burgeoning church populations in other Lamanite sectors of the world.

The Death Knell

The change in direction was duly if starkly announced early in 1979 by Boyd K. Packer, then the senior apostle over Lamanite affairs for the church.[20] Read in retrospect, the apostle's remarks seem to be sounding the official death knell of the special LDS focus on North American Indians. It is unlikely that his audience recognized the full significance of the occasion, for ironically his remarks were delivered during the proceedings of the annual Indian Week on the BYU campus (Packer 1979). Replacing a scheduled speaker at his own insistence (Osborne 1993, 132), Packer began by reminding his listeners of his long-standing commitment to the various church programs for Indians and his originally high hopes for what the Indians might become as they worked to fulfill their divine destiny as Lamanites. Yet he then ventured the admonition that when he looked to the south, he saw "millions who have an equal claim on that destiny spoken of in the revelations." In contrast to the relatively few in North America who could claim Lamanite lineage (1.3 million), Packer pointed to the many millions in Mexico, Yucatan, Guatemala, and throughout South America: "In all . . . there are seventy-five million six hundred thousand who share in your birthright, of whom thirty-one million nine hundred ninety thousand are pure Indians."

Packer went on to express his disappointment in the accomplishments of the North American Indians converted to the church in recent decades, declaring that "if it sounds like I'm scolding you just a little, it will be because I am." The church leaders had had high expectations that the converted Lamanites of North America would take the lead in converting their fellow

Lamanites farther south, but they had not done so: "[T]he Lord has said, 'Where much is given much is expected'. . . . Those millions to the south are waiting for redemption. They're waiting for you. You can do more to redeem them than I can do. . . . [Y]ou have so much power that I do not have, and so much affiliation and affinity with these people that I could never have, that it pains me to see [all of that] being wasted." It was all well and good, said Packer, for the Indian students to achieve something in worldly terms, but "if all you come away with is a degree, and the ability to make a living, if all you have come here for is to get, then you may well have failed."

In rejecting a worldly definition of success, Packer was revealing just how wide the gap was between the expectations of the church leaders, on the one hand, and the educators and government leaders, on the other, whose assessments were much more upbeat: "[T]he impact of BYU's Indian graduates in Indian communities, schools, other professions, and in LDS wards and branches was unprecedented. Leaders emerged in federal, state, tribal, and Church organizations. Educators filled desperately needed positions in reservation and community schools. . . . Certainly not all returned to the reservation or Indian community . . . [which] too often . . . did not offer employment in the skills possessed by the graduates. Too often, the dream of 'returning to help my people' was unrealistic" (Osborne 1993, 107). This assessment was supported in the impressive compilation by Terry Warner (1975) and in the "Fact Sheet" distributed by the Indian Education Department at BYU (1976), which claimed that the federal Government Accounting Office had just issued a glowing report on the BYU Indian programs.

Even though most Indian applicants to BYU had always been relatively ill prepared for college work and their graduation rates were low compared with those of white students, their graduation rates at BYU had been three or four times those of Indian students elsewhere. The Indian students had also faced something of a moving target, for admission and graduation requirements in general had continued to rise, especially at BYU, which, according to a report to the dean of the College of Student Life at BYU, "was fast becoming an elite school, where the under-prepared, less academically gifted student had little chance," although "BYU had gained an enviable reputation throughout the Indian world as a model of higher education for Native Americans. Many other colleges and universities sent representatives to visit its program and study its operations" (Osborne 1993, 107, 131).

Clearly the church professionals serving the cause of Indian education were using criteria somewhat different from those used by Packer and other church leaders, who apparently had envisioned a different kind of yield from their investment in Indian education. Their ultimate objective was clearly more spiritual than simply "a degree and the ability to make a living," desirable as these might be. As Packer made clear, he and his ecclesiastical colleagues were looking instead for converted Indian youth who would attend their church meetings regularly and participate fully in church service, so that they would be prepared to take the gospel to the "countless millions of your people waiting for your ministry. Now, you may say, 'Well I don't feel comfortable. I'm a little reticent to speak. I feel backward.' And I ask the question: Are you ashamed to be an Indian? Are you? If not, why are you not there? . . . We're not interested in [your] being comfortable. We're interested in your being of service" (Packer 1979).[21]

Implementing the New Policy

To his assembled audience, Packer's pronouncements might have seemed spontaneous, if strangely stern, but it is clear in retrospect that he was only making public what had already been determined by officials of BYU and the church: namely, that they could no longer justify such a heavy investment of resources in special programs for North American Indians. To some extent, perhaps, this determination was a logical extension of the "reduce and simplify" theme running through the "correlation movement" of the church since the 1960s.[22] Yet the Indian programs had never suffered or caused budget shortages. As these programs were closed down, the funds and the two dozen faculty involved were simply reallocated to other departments and to similar programs serving *various* students with "special needs"—no longer just Indians (Osborne 1986 and 1993, 132–44). Not long after the Packer speech, the enfeebled President Kimball was further incapacitated and could no longer be the strong Indian advocate that he had once been in church councils. His decline and eventual demise in 1985 was thus a metaphor for the parallel fate of the church's Indian program.

Just how the new policy was implemented operationally, and who were the principals delegated to carry it out at BYU and elsewhere, can be only inferred from information publicly available and from those church leaders and professionals directly involved in the policy changes. At the top ecclesiastical level, the Indian or Lamanite coordinating committee was eventually renamed the Committee for Lamanite and Minority Affairs, and by 1980 it had been relocated administratively from the Social Services Department to the Missionary Department. Its chief administrator, Stewart A. Durrant, continued to serve until 1983, reporting regularly to Carlos Asay of the Seventy, who in turn reported to the apostles through Packer (Durrant 1975 and 1983; Osborne 1993, 137–38). In the light of Packer's concerns, this committee advanced a number of ideas for strengthening the church's effectiveness with Indians and other minorities, including the trimmed-down "basic unit program," mentioned above (Durrant 1983, 20–26; Livingstone 2000). Yet Packer and other leaders continued to express their misgivings about the resources being allocated to Indian church members despite their relatively low levels of religious participation and activity.[23]

One can certainly sympathize with all of the parties involved in implementing the policy changes. On the one hand were the many educators and social service workers whose altruism and long-standing accomplishments with Indians were seemingly discredited and whose careers were seriously disrupted by the change of direction. On the other hand were the administrators at BYU and in the church bureaucracy more generally, who had the unenviable responsibility of dismantling or greatly reducing the Indian programs over the resistance of those educators and social service workers. From 1979 through 1983, the BYU administration called for a series of seemingly redundant self-studies, audits, and reports by the chairman of the Indian (later Multicultural) Education Department and his colleagues. In view of the comments that had been made in Packer's 1979 speech and the sequence of events thereafter, it is understandable that all this paper work could be seen in retrospect as an exercise in futility, for the church (and therefore the university), in Osborne's words, "had already determined [its] course of action" in closing down its special Indian programs (1993, 133). Most of the dislocated professionals were absorbed into other church employment, but many were deeply demoralized by the process, and some resigned and went elsewhere (S. Adams 1987; Osborne 1986 and 1999).

It is important to understand, however, that these changes in policies and programs for the Indians at BYU did not take place in an organizational vacuum. They were contemporaneous with certain other administrative and curricular changes in the university having little to do with LDS Indians themselves. In this context, cause and effect relationships in programmatic changes would be hard to disentangle. The Indian education enterprise had already been involved in more general administrative reconfigurations between 1965 and 1978 (Osborne 1993, 1–89). After it became a separate entity in 1972, the Indian Education Department soon became the main administrative home for the matriculation of other "Lamanite" students, as well. By 1977, more than a thousand of these from outside the United States, mainly from Latin America and Polynesia, had enrolled on various public and university grants (Osborne 1993, 71–73). The next year, the Multicultural Education Program was created for all such minorities, so that the Indian Education Department could focus on its traditional clientele. Nevertheless, a clear tendency was underway to replace "Indian" references with "Lamanite" wherever possible.

Meanwhile, out of other considerations, the university disbanded the College of General Studies, where both the Indian and the multicultural programs had been administered, and placed them in the new College of Student Life, along with a miscellany of programs, including ROTC. Since

Student Life was not considered an *academic* unit, neither were its component programs, such as Indian Education. Always academically suspect and widely perceived as "coddling" its students, the Indian Education Department came to be defined as a student support group rather than as an academically legitimate department (Clemmer 1999; Osborne 1993, 90–93, 134–35). The special Indian focus was lost altogether in 1982 when the Indian Education Department was merged with the Multicultural Education Program to form the Department of Multicultural Studies, which was itself gradually disbanded by 1985 (Osborne 1993, 92–93, 115; Osborne 1999). All that remained of the once-thriving Indian enterprise of the university was a minor in Native American studies, serving mainly non-Indians by 1998, and administered by the Department of History (Gowans 1999).

The number of BYU students from the North American tribes dropped steadily from a high of about 500 per year in 1978 to fewer than half that number in 1986. By the 1998–99 school year, scarcely 150 remained, most as simply minors in Native American studies and not all on BYU scholarships (Clemmer 1999; Gowans 1999; Osborne 1993, 136). This decline in BYU Indians was the inevitable outcome of the more general change in church posture toward the North American aboriginal peoples by the time of President Kimball's passing. Special missions to these peoples had been closed or subsumed; Indian youth seminaries had been abolished; and the Indian Student Placement Program had been reduced to a mere handful of high school youth. All these had been conduits, now closed, for recruitment to the BYU programs, both on and off the campus.

This rapid demise of church programs for Indians left a certain degree of ambivalence and anguish in its wake, especially at BYU. Indian alumni were no longer so willing to continue contributing to a multicultural program largely purged of its erstwhile Indian focus (Osborne 1993, 92–93, 115; Osborne 1999). By 1995, the university president had constituted two different ad hoc committees, one to reconsider the needs and prospects for Indian students and the other to devise ways of increasing enrollments and support for other minority students. The first of these committees comprised members with a variety of interests and motives, so that any consensus would have been problematic. In any case, this committee produced no final report, at least none that was made public (Clemmer 1999; Osborne 1999). The report of the second committee, however, can be found in the BYU archives (Wade and Tanner 1995). As if to highlight the growing multicultural focus at Student Life, at the expense of the strictly Indian focus, the performing troupe Lamanite Generation had been renamed Living Legend by the mid-1990s, performing an ethnically varied program on a much reduced schedule. Lamanite Week (once Indian Week) was renamed Heritage Week. The Indian student publication *Eagle's Eye* was still being published, somewhat irregularly, but it now covered the interests and activities of various minority groups, not just Indians. The transformation of this publication caused considerable consternation and "murmuring" from the traditional American Indian clientele, which the new director of Multicultural Student Services felt obliged to address in a 1998 issue (Heperi 1998).

The Changing Political Environment

All these changes did not, of course, occur suddenly. As in most complex organizations, a period of transition occurred during which newer policy emphases overlapped with residual elements of the older policy direction. Many church leaders were reluctant to relinquish a campaign for Indian conversion that had been half a century in the making. In that interim, however, political realities both inside and outside the church had changed. As for the outside, criticism and resistance from such militant partisans as the American Indian Movement (AIM) had become especially strong during the 1970s (Deloria 1992). Among other tactics, AIM held a demonstration at Temple Square in Salt Lake City during the April 1973 general conference and periodically demanded a million dollars from the church to help "rehabilitate" suffering Indians ("Locked Gates Meet March on Temple" 1973; E. Kimball and Kimball 1977, 404–5).

The church felt obliged to respond, both with rejections of the militants' more damaging claims and with publicity about the benefits and progress enjoyed by Indian participants in the various LDS programs (Clemens 1972, 1; "Miss Indian American Warns Youth against Militants" 1971, 17). The official church magazine *Ensign* in 1975 carried important articles in its January and December issues highlighting these programs and, in the November issue, the recent appointment of George P. Lee, a Navaho, to general authority status as a member of the Seventy ("News of the Church: George Patrick Lee of the First Quorum of the Seventy" 1975). The *Church News* carried shorter articles of the same kind several times a year during 1974, 1975, and 1976. The church's protestations, however, could do little to stem the external resistance to its religious and assimilative efforts even from the intended beneficiaries themselves (or at least from their putative spokespeople).

Partly in response to political protest, federal policy itself had been moving toward greater cultural and political autonomy for the tribal peoples. As the national posture became more humane, enlightened, and respectful toward Indian relationships later in the twentieth century, Indians were able to garner more resources, education, and political power and expertise. They were also able to sustain movements and pressure groups in pursuit of their own interests, just as so many other ethnic groups had done in American history. As this new and more sophisticated generation of Native Americans became increasingly aware of what they had lost, both materially and culturally, through even the best-intentioned policies of the U.S. government and its agents, they were scarcely inclined to see the Mormon variants of such policies in a favorable light. However, in representing various Indian claims and causes, the new leaders came to seem somewhat less unique, and increasingly their claims were simply placed on the national agenda along with the competing claims and causes of other hyphenated-American interest groups. The national equivalent of the Mormon "day of the Lamanite" had become "the day of the minority."

Like other minority groups, American Indians (by 1980 called Native Americans in politically proper parlance) began to enjoy the patronage represented by important appointments in public agencies of special interest to them. Eventually the BIA was turned over largely to bureaucrats and functionaries from among the various tribal peoples. Both the political and economic power of tribal peoples and institutions grew significantly from the federal and tribal funding that was increasingly directed toward those institutions. From the 1970s on, new federal, state, and tribal funding programs began to build schools and colleges on or near traditional Indian lands, so that the Indian youth were much less dependent on educational opportunities of the kind offered by the Mormon church. Interestingly enough, many of these new institutions have been staffed largely by Mormon graduates of BYU, both white and Indian (Ainsworth 1986). Especially prominent was George P. Lee, who, before his church call, served as president of the College of Ganado, Arizona ("News of the Church: George Patrick Lee of the First Quorum of the Seventy" 1975). The tribal governments understandably began giving priority to their own institutions in allocating scholarships and other educational funds, with commensurate reductions in the proportions of such funds made available for the support of Indian students at such private colleges as BYU (Clemmer 1999; Getches, Wilkinson, and Williams 1993, 215–29, 255–60).

The environment within BYU and the church had also been changing. BYU increasingly found itself in competition with other major universities, which had been changing their recruiting goals in line with emerging political fashions, not only in multicultural outreach more generally but also specifically in rivalry with BYU's Indian emphasis. BYU recruiters, accustomed to having the field to themselves, began running into their counterparts from dozens of other institutions as they made their annual recruiting visits to high schools with large Indian populations. The gradual increase in academic requirements for Indian and other students entering BYU also reduced the eligible recruiting pool, as did the decision by the church itself, of course, to close down its separate Indian missions, its Indian seminaries, and the Indian Student Placement Program, all of which had been conduits into BYU (S. Adams 1987, 16; Osborne 1993, 134–37).

However, the church has certainly not turned its back on those North American Indian members who have continued strong in the faith. Efforts continue to be made through the normal ecclesiastical channels and programs to reach Indian members and potential members with occasional conferences and training efforts. On July 25, 1997, as part of the general sesquicentennial celebrations of the first Mormon arrivals in Utah, a one-day conference was held at BYU especially for LDS Indians. Conducted by the politically prominent LDS Indian Larry Echohawk, who now teaches at the BYU law school, the conference featured various activities and workshops for both children and adults. According to the news coverage, as might be expected, special attention was given to speeches by general authorities of the church, as well as to workshops in leadership, genealogical research, and other activities designed to acculturate the Indians more fully in LDS teachings and practices (E. Carter 1997; *Church News,* August 2, 1997, 5).

A talk by one of the Native American Mormon women emphasized traditional values that Indians shared with (and could benefit) other Latter-day Saints, and some of the speakers commented on the traditional Mormon conception of Indians as Israelite peoples of destiny. Interestingly enough, however, Jeffrey Holland of the Quorum of the Twelve Apostles predicted the imminent end of all tribal, racial, or cultural distinctions in the church instead of emphasizing an enduring Lamanite heritage. M. Russell Ballard, another apostle, to the extent that he mentioned Lamanites, referred primarily to church growth in Latin America and all the "Lamanite stake presidents [there] who have come out of the world and embraced the gospel" (quoted in "News of the Church: Native American Conference" 1997, 76).

To be sure, inside the church there have also remained strong partisans of the cause of the American-Indian-as-Lamanite, both among church leaders and among the educators and social service professionals (many now retired), who had devoted their careers to the various Indian programs after midcentury. Inspired originally by President Spencer W. Kimball, these church leaders and professionals, both white and Indian, tried desperately to keep a strong official focus on the needs and development of the church's Indians. Yet their main champion, President Kimball, had neither the stamina nor the internal political clout to continue his crusading for the Lamanites of the world. In 1985, he died at the age of ninety. Perhaps the most tragic exemplar of this lost cause, however, was George P. Lee, a prominent Navaho product of the LDS Indian programs. With the sponsorship of President Kimball, Lee rose to the highest ranks of church leadership (as a member of the Seventy) but then fell out with the other general authorities over the importance of Indians in LDS theology and policy.

In particular, he insisted that the Book of Mormon and the earliest church leaders had defined the Lamanites as Israelites by birthright and descent, whereas white Mormons were the Gentiles destined to bring the Book of Mormon to the Lamanites and to give them help and sustenance, but not to rule over them. White Mormons, he claimed, could become part of the house of Israel by adoption or "grafting," just as other non-Israelites could. This would seem to have been a defensible position for Lee to take, and it would probably have been supported by some early leaders, to judge from the Orson Pratt epigraph that opened chapter 3. In pressing his point, however, Lee went so far as to accuse contemporary church leaders of usurpation, arrogance, and racism, which eventuated in his excommunication from the church in 1989—inadvertently providing another metaphorical comment on the fading Indian emphasis in the church (G. Lee 1989).[24]

Conclusion

The church's *Lamanite Handbook* listed eight major objectives of the various programs for Lamanites described in this chapter (LDS Indian Committee 1968, 5). These included helping Indians compensate for economic, linguistic, and cultural "handicaps"; training them as potential church leaders for their own people; and educating them so that they could "compete successfully" in the white world. The subtext here is unmistakably assimilation to white ways. Even the Mormon family model, with a patriarchal focus largely alien to Navaho culture, was spelled out about the same time by a well-meaning Mormon educator: "The Navaho man must learn the meaning of Priesthood authority and how to use it properly. Through magnifying his priesthood, he could bless his children, heal the sick, and thus eliminate the need for sings, sand paintings, and the medicine man. He must become the priesthood leader in the home, where he can . . . [direct] the affairs of the family" (Mathews 1968, 76).

This advocate of such goals for Mormon Indians was no novice in experience with the Navaho. He had extensive service among them as a missionary and teacher and was sincerely devoted to seeking their spiritual and material improvement. His statement is from his master's thesis, which is rife with both sympathy and ambivalence. On the one hand, he recognizes that acceptance of the gospel should not require the world's peoples to give up their cultural traditions altogether; on the other hand, he regards some of those traditions as seriously in conflict with the church's standards and teachings. Indian converts can thus never become fully acceptable to the Lord and his church unless they give up their "superstitions," their casual attitude toward "sexual morality," their debased music, their frenetic dances, and even their seeming diffidence in family and public encounters (Mathews 1968, 39–49).[25]

Similarly, the chief administrator of the church's Lamanite Committee explained that although he was sympathetic to "preserving native cultures" of Indians, Polynesians, and others, the church could not tolerate clear and direct violations of gospel principles in native cultures (Durrant 1975 and 1983, 12–15). Conflicts sometimes arose, for example, when tribal dances held under church auspices deteriorated into frenzy and abandon or when the dances became so commercialized and so much a preoccupation in themselves that the gospel faded into the background. One of my most knowledgeable white Mormon informants, married to an Indian wife, expressed deep sympathy for the historic plight of the native peoples and roundly condemned the prejudice and discrimination so often practiced against them in white LDS settings. However, he went on to add that the only hope of the tribal peoples for a viable future lay in abandoning their "degenerate" traditional cultures, which were "not worth saving," and assimilating to white ways (D. Sanders 1985). He also deplored the "pernicious" power that traditional Indian groups and organizations had exerted to draw Mormon converts back to their old ways.

Such ambivalence has been common among white Mormon leaders, teachers, and missionaries working with Indians. Certainly Mormons attempting to serve their Indian clients and charges have always differed considerably among themselves in the extent of their sophistication and understanding about Indian cultures, but the potential for serious cross-cultural misunderstandings has been a constant. Despite the benign intentions behind Indian programs and the sincere belief that Indians, in their own right, are literal Israelites and thus people of divine destiny, neither the white nor the Indian Mormons have ultimately been able to escape the fundamentally assimilationist implications of these programs. The Mormon religious conceptions have been so intertwined with common American ethnocentrism that it is hard to tell which predominated by the end of the twentieth century. For their part, the Indian converts had their own kind of ambivalence. They saw their white Mormon leaders, teachers, and friends as benefactors (in economic, cultural, and religious terms) and yet also as conventional white oppressors who denigrated their culture and wanted to destroy their ancestral way of life.

In trying to implement their Indian programs, then, the Mormons had to struggle with the same quandaries that have always faced Christian missionary endeavors, whatever the denomination: How can reservation Indians be converted and retained without the simultaneous imposition of white Christian culture? Like other Christians, Mormons can (and do) envision their gospel as a worldwide religion linking a diversity of peoples with all the known varieties of culture. However, as soon as this ideal vision is reduced to practical proselyting and church organization, it tends to get translated into the social and cultural practices and institutions most familiar to the missionaries and their leaders. Thus, Mormons familiar with Indian peoples and cultures often expressed sympathy and admiration for those cultures and even a desire to see them preserved, but they nevertheless expected Indian Mormons somehow to adapt to "normal" LDS ways and to carry out ecclesiastical roles and duties in the same ways that white Mormons do.[26] This point was emphasized by Jessie Embry, who attributed to her Navaho, Hopi, and Sioux informants the observation that "a leadership style and behavior based on an Anglo model constricts those cultural groups that are less gregarious" (1992d, 104–5).

Many Indians seemed willing to make certain adaptations, especially in such realms as entrepreneurship and technological improvements, and a certain amount of the whites' education seemed useful for such purposes. However, a wholesale abandonment of traditional Indian lands, religions, and values was something else again. In the nineteenth century, this had meant war. In the twentieth, war was replaced by various kinds of active and passive resistance, which fed the white stereotype of Indians as backward, lazy, dishonest, and opportunistic. For Mormons, all this simply reflected the darker side of the Lamanite character. What proved especially difficult was getting Indians to adapt their traditional etiquette and comportment to Mormon organizational roles and expectations. The dashing of those expectations on the rocks of cross-cultural differences is the theme of a wonderfully engaging short story by Michael Fillerup, a white Mormon teacher and church leader who lived in Chinle on the Navaho reservation with his wife and several children for six years.

Fillerup's account, autobiographical in content but fictional in details, portrays graphically the frustration, disappointment, and despair of well-meaning Anglo-Mormons as the Navaho converts never seemed to take hold of their new religion but instead constantly slipped back into the ways of the reservation: "Ten years. In that time [Max, the Anglo-Mormon branch president] had seen dozens of Navajo families join the church; none had remained active. Hundreds of Navajo kids had been baptized and bussed off on Placement; hundreds more had been bussed back home. Some graduated, then fell away. A few went on to BYU, and fewer still managed a temple marriage. Of these, a handful had forsaken the reservation. The others had returned and, in time, had sought out the peyote meetings, the squaw dances, the bootleggers. . . . Two steps back for every one forward" (1985, 154–55).

The backsliding by the converts was matched by the demoralization of the branch president. "Initially [I'd] been optimistic, positive. [I'd] tried to learn all [I] could about the land and the people. [I] took night classes in Navajo language and culture. . . . At church, in talks and testimonies, [I] constantly stressed unity and the similarities, rather than the differences, between the Anglo and Navajo members. . . . We are literally brothers and sisters, sealed to one another by the blood of Jesus Christ . . ." (1985, 164–65). But he confessed, "Somewhere along the line I lost my innocence. I came here a man of faith and planted what I thought was a good seed. But the soil, and this ten-year drought . . . I couldn't get a bud, let alone a blossom" (1985, 171). A parallel but entirely nonfictional account was told by a Mormon teacher and leader based for three years at the Navaho Community College in Tsaile, who commented on the constant intercultural misunderstandings, the desultory religious participation even by Navaho church leaders, and the serious organizational failures and neglect by supervising Anglo-Mormon leaders (Ainsworth 1986).

So why did the Mormon effort among Indians not yield more enduring church growth? Perhaps the impression left in this chapter is unduly pessimistic. As an author with no firsthand experience in living or working with Native American peoples, I have had to depend on the experience and expertise found in the firsthand accounts of others, plus a few secondary sources. Yet even my primary sources might have focused disproportionately on the problems and setbacks they had experienced, for they responded to my questions more fully when explaining their struggles than when identifying their successes. For that reason, my portrayal might well convey a pessimistic bias unintended by other authors or informants.

One of my most important informants, after reading an earlier draft of this chapter, took me somewhat to task exactly on that point (Osborne 2000). While admitting that he might be feeling somewhat defensive, he nevertheless insisted that his years of experience in working with LDS Indian programs refuted any verdict of a wholesale defection of Indian converts. He continued to believe that in general these programs had achieved much more positive results in religious terms than a reader might believe from the account I have given here. Even while conceding that these programs were not judged cost-effective by the church leaders and administrators in charge of them, he had seen enough constructive consequences in the lives of his clients and converts to remain generally positive about what had been accomplished.[27]

There seems little doubt that literally hundreds (perhaps thousands) of the Indian youth who passed through the various Mormon programs benefited from them enormously in the material and cultural terms of Euroamerican assimilation. Such is a recurrent message in the survey of BYU Indian alumni (Osborne 1993, 248–68) and the Embry interviews (1992d). Yet the spiritual transformation understood as "conversion" by Euroamerican Mormons, whether that transformation is considered cognitive, emotional, or something else, is quite a different matter from material and cultural assimilation. It is hard to know how widespread that transformation has been among Mormon Indians, as long as the church continues to measure it by such organizational indicators as attendance, church activity, temple marriage, tithe-paying, and other forms of behavioral conformity. In those terms, Packer, at least, did not seem to see a satisfactory level of durable conversion among the Indian youth. Unquestionably there have been individual cases of such conversion. All things considered, however, it is difficult to escape the realization that the idealistic LDS hopes for such transformative conversions on a large scale had been doomed from the start, despite the unique and relatively benign church theology and policies toward these Lamanites.

Ultimately, the church could never fully extricate itself in the Indian mind from the complex of Anglo-American churches, government agencies, armies, and other institutions that had for three centuries seized ancestral Indian lands (some with great religious significance), broken scores of solemn treaties, spread devastating epidemics, denigrated cherished Indian cultures, and generally waged an extensive campaign of both physical and cultural genocide. Whatever differences the Mormons saw between their vision of the Indian future and that of America more generally, the Indians saw these two visions as a lot alike, for both meant eventual "integration" into American society and an end to aboriginal cultures (Tinker 1993, 1–20; Weaver 1998a, 1–6).

Such an integration, of course, would involve a change of religion, as well, which, for tribal peoples, would entail something far more fundamental than changing churches. While there is religious variety, to be sure, among these tribal peoples, they tend to share a general worldview about life, death, nature, and the cosmos that is drastically different from that of Christianity. This difference in worldview is certainly apparent from many accounts, and it looms large in the struggles of generations of individual Indians to come to terms with Christian teachings, whether these teachings are embraced, modified, or rejected. My own understanding of these differences in worldview is based mainly on a careful perusal of Deloria (1992), McPherson (1992), Treat (1996), and Weaver (1998c). It is not difficult to see why the Mormons, as well as the missionaries of other denominations, found it so difficult to bridge the gap between the Christian and the traditional Native American understandings of "conversion" or what was entailed in the "converted" condition.

For Christianity and its cousin monotheistic traditions, conversion has usually included a fundamental change in *identity*. Baptism and similar initiatory rites (at least for the mature initiates) imply leaving behind one's earlier life and self for a new life and self. It is difficult for the tribal peoples (and for many other non-European peoples) to understand how such a fundamental change can be achieved or expected. Whatever the differences among the various American Indian religious traditions, they all share an understanding that one's identity is given by nature and the cosmos through birth into a given people. Compared with that essence, one's connections or affiliations with political, religious, or other social institutions, however important for some purposes, are ultimately utilitarian and not necessarily permanent in the way that kinship is permanent. (The struggle with identity for LDS Indians is addressed at greater length in the next chapter.)

The entire way that social life operates among most tribal peoples is fundamentally at odds with the organizational assumptions on which the LDS Church is based. In most Native American societies, a person's relationship with others is determined by an elaborate kinship structure. A person's rights and duties toward others in various categories are determined by blood and marriage, some of which are matrilineal and some patrilineal. Those rights and prerogatives that are matrilineal in origin naturally clash with the patrilineal and patriarchal traditions of governance in white LDS society. Furthermore, the traditional definition of "family" in Native American cultures is much more extensive than the nuclear family considered the basic unit in Euroamerican cultures, and the decision making is correspondingly more diffuse. In such an organizational complex, the top-down, centralized decision making by a single leader or a small leadership cadre (the usual LDS model) seems alien.

In the light of such differences, Indian participation in the LDS Church or in any other Christian church, though entirely sincere during a certain phase of a person's life course, can never replace the permanent Indian essence, and it can never take priority over the individual's obligations to the family and people given in life and in nature. Nor do even multiple church affiliations, whether serially or simultaneously, imply any lack of sincerity, since they are all peripheral to that essence. It should therefore not be surprising that changes in types or levels of church participation might have been defined as defection or "falling away" by Anglo-Mormon leaders while considered as fairly natural comings and goings by many LDS Indians. Against such contrasting cultural assumptions about membership, conversion, and retention, it is certainly difficult to decide definitively how one would measure the success of the LDS missionary enterprise among the Native American peoples from an outside perspective (Deloria 1992).[28]

Yet from inside the LDS Church, the leaders and members almost always looked upon the tribal peoples first and foremost as divinely destined objects of missionary endeavor rather than as peoples with a cherished history, culture, and future of their own. In using the term *Lamanite,* Mormons seemed to assume that all they needed to know about these peoples was implied by that term, which linked the contemporary Indians to the Book of Mormon (Mitchell-Green 1987). From any non-Mormon viewpoint, this linkage totally bypassed hundreds of years of the history and culture of a diversity of North American peoples to construct a dubious pre-Columbian identity for them. Ironically, even this Mormon viewpoint implied a future of assimilation to Anglo-American civilization rather than to the ideal culture described in the Book of Mormon, whether that culture is conceived as literally historic or only as religio-mythic. Since few Indian converts retained much enthusiasm about either Mormon vision of their future, church leaders gradually and reluctantly came to the conclusion that nearly half a century of special programs and resources for Indians in the North American West had done little more to bring "the day of the Lamanite" by the end of the twentieth century than had the earlier missionary efforts by the end of the nineteenth.

This disappointing eclipse of the day of the Lamanite in North America, however, occurred as the sun emerged to shine brightly on the Lamanite lands farther south. The burgeoning growth there presented a compelling contrast, and the cost-benefit implications of this contrast could hardly be ignored by such pragmatic prophets as the leaders of the Church of Jesus Christ of Latter-day Saints. Yet a shift in focus from north to south would require some redefinition and reconstruction of the Lamanite identity and its mythic legacy.

Notes

1. As in the previous chapter, I am relying mainly on an edited collection of primary source materials with expert commentary (Getches, Wilkinson, and Williams 1993) and, to a lesser extent, Wilkins (1997). Philp (1995) is valuable in providing a less legalistic and more qualitative texturing of government-Indian relations.

2. I am grateful to Thomas W. Murphy for calling my attention to the Hertzberg book and many other useful sources. Not the least of the changes contributing to Pan-Indianism was the growing urban Indian population that had resulted from the earlier policies of allotment and termination.

3. My colleague Lawrence Coates (2000) pointed also to additional indications of an aroused and effective Indian activism during this period: the 1961 American Indian Conference in Chicago, convened by the anthropologist Sol Tax; the 1968 organization of the American Indian Movement (AIM); the takeover by Indian activists in 1969 of Alcatraz Island and the Navajo Community College; the "Broken Treaty March" on Washington in 1972; the confrontation and bloodshed at Wounded Knee in 1973; and the walk from Alcatraz to Washington, D.C., in 1978.

4. The major federal case in Mormon country was the "Big Ute Case" of 1946–50 (*Confederated Bands of Ute Indians v. the United States* [1950]), which eventually brought a judgment in the U.S. Court of Claims for $32 million in favor of the Ute (Deem and Bird 1982, 237n1, 240n118). Details of this case and several later ones involving Indians are provided in Deem and Bird (1982, 102–269). The fees received in these cases by the Mormon law firm of Wilkinson, Cragun, and Barker were substantial and sometimes controversial, but much of its work was done on a pro bono basis, partly out of a sincere belief in traditional LDS teachings about Indians.

5. See the exposé in a series of articles in the *Arizona Republic* during September 1987, dealing with inefficiency, incompetence, and fraud in the BIA and other federal agencies and programs for Indians.

6. The church had organized the Spanish-American Mission in 1936, but the work there

focused mainly on Mexican Lamanites living on either side of the Texas-Mexico border (*Deseret News Church Almanac* 1990, 229).

7. Documents providing these estimates and furnishing much of the other information for this chapter can be found in the archives of the LDS Church or Brigham Young University. Figures provided me in 1975 (personal files) by the staff of the Minority Affairs Committee (which replaced the Indian Committee) estimated the Lamanite population of the church in the United States and Canada (i.e., *not* including Latin America or Polynesia) at 61,000, or 4.5 percent of the total Native American population. A 1981 estimate put the Mormon membership among the Navaho alone at 40,000, or about 20 percent of that nation's people (Pavlik 1992, 21).

8. This summary comes from a four-page brochure issued by the Indian (Lamanite) Program of the LDS Church (BYU Archives). No publication date is indicated, but the enlarged membership and missionary figures, compared with those in earlier documents, indicate the mid-1970s. Brief historical accounts of the establishment and growth of Indian wards and branches after the midcentury renewal of missionary work are in Flake (1965); Embry (1990a); and Lyman (1985, 133–60). Until about 1970, Mormon efforts to organize congregations and build chapels among Indian members were often hampered by opposition from tribal leaders and other religious denominations.

9. Stewart Durrant, who administered the coordinating committee for minorities (earlier called the Indian Committee), expressed the ambivalence about separate ethnic branches that characterized the church leaders themselves (1983, 16–18). He cited (and joined) Spencer W. Kimball and Gordon B. Hinckley in favoring a temporary policy of separate church units on the way to eventual integration. Whenever separate units had been disbanded, according to Durrant, the Indian members were "lost almost totally." By 1983, church participation in separate ethnic units had been made "optional" (1983, 18).

10. Although the main focus in this chapter is on LDS programs for North American Indians, it is important to remember that the church has for many decades had schools, literacy programs, and various other humanitarian efforts in Polynesia and in Latin America, whose populations are also considered Lamanites in Mormon teachings. See Oakes (1971); and Cummings (1961).

11. This waxing and waning can be tracked in the official publications of the church from about 1950. Indian topics had been almost totally absent from twentieth-century general conference sermons until an upsurge in the 1950s (Shepherd and Shepherd 1984, 241). My tabulations from the "Index to Periodicals of the Church of Jesus Christ of Latter-day Saints" (LDS Historical Department 1961–90) and its predecessor indexes reveal that about ten articles a year on Indians (or Lamanites) appeared during the 1950s in the two main church organs combined (*Improvement Era* and *Church News*), rising to about double that number by 1965. That level obtained through the 1970s (about twenty per year) in the *Ensign, Church News, New Era* (for youth), and *Friend* (for children) combined. The peak years seem to have been 1977–79 for entries under "Lamanites" or "Indians," but already the Lamanite listings were referring increasingly to Latin America. See also the LDS Historical Department's *Index to Mormonism in Periodical Literature*, especially vol. 5 (1976–80).

12. I have taken the information for this section from J. Allen (1998); Birch (1985); Bishop (1967); W. Bush (1970); G. De Hoyos and De Hoyos (1973); G. De Hoyos (1992); Gottlieb and Wiley (1984, 163–66); Hangen (1997); LDS Indian Committee (1967); G. Lee (1980 and 1987, 111–35, 147, 168–69, 177, 203–7, 223–24, 250–55, 264); and Pavlik (1992).

13. This seems a fair summary of the findings of Chadwick and colleagues (1986 and 1994) and G. Taylor (1981). James B. Allen (1998, 100–108) summarizes the accumulated evaluations similarly if slightly more optimistically, emphasizing the relatively high graduation rates of these students compared with other Indian youth (102–3) and the maintenance of relatively high rates of expressed religious belief, even if their religious behavior did not endure (106, 110).

14. This section is based mainly on Ainsworth (1986); Clemmer (1999); Durrant (1975 and 1983); Larsen (1965, 7–8); Osborne (1975, 1981, 1986, 1993, and 1999); D. Sanders (1985); Toscano (1975c); Wade and Tanner (1995); Warner (1975); Webb (1972); and Wilkinson and Arrington (1976, 503–35).

15. V. Con Osborne provided a 1981 "audit" and general description of the BYU program from 1965 onward (1993, 69–74, 269–79). L. Robert Webb indicated that BYU provided between six and nine hundred dollars per Indian student during the 1971–72 school year, matched by BIA or tribal grants (1972, 16–18). As time went on, the BYU scholarships were increasingly replaced or supplemented by tribal or federal grants.

16. Osborne provided extensive information on the Tribe of Many Feathers, including its constitution, its officers for 1970 through 1985, its Indian Week activities and speakers during the same period, and the Miss Indian BYU contest and winners from 1966 to 1986 (1993, 178–219). Indian Week was usually commemorated in special brochures. Whether exceptional or typical for such annual brochures, the 1978 version was elaborate, with photos of each Miss Indian BYU back to 1967 and pages covering various Indian student leaders, the summer orientation program, the Tribe of Many Feathers, the Intertribal Choir, the Lamanite Generation, and the various Indian Week activities (Indian Education Department 1978a).

17. This was the American Indian Commission on Alcoholism and Drug Abuse. Its complaints were described in "Indian Alcoholism Board Claims Cooperation Lack" (1972).

18. The foundation in question was sometimes called the Lehi Foundation (Chadwick and Garrow 1992, 985). It is not clear whether this was the same as the Lehi Symposium, a coordinating umbrella for church and private programs for Native Americans. Based in Richfield, Utah, according to its stationery (copy in personal files), this symposium brought its constituent members together a few times in the mid-1980s, but it had apparently become defunct by the time I tried to locate it in December 2000.

19. Steve Pavlik pointed to the increasingly important political influence of Mormon Indians in Navaho politics by 1990 (1992, 28). V. Con Osborne (1986) claimed that eleven of the department heads in the Navaho tribal government were Mormons, nearly all of them BYU graduates.

20. Packer had replaced Kimball as head of the Indian Committee by the time Kimball became president of the church in late 1973. Already by 1971, "much of the Indian work had been taken over by others," according to Edward L. Kimball and Andrew E. Kimball Jr. (1977, 404).

21. This difference in priorities between the ecclesiastical leaders and those with more mundane responsibilities in Indian communities often came to the fore, even when the community leaders were LDS Indians. See, for example, "Summary" (1967), which describes a Sioux leaders' meeting with two LDS apostles.

22. The "correlation movement" (also simply "correlation") refers to a policy to centralize control over all church programs, auxiliaries, and curriculum and to tighten the coordination among various organizational and geographic units. Although under dis-

cussion for many years, it was implemented in earnest beginning about 1960 to help manage the mushrooming growth of the church (Mauss 1994, 82, 100, 164–67).

23. V. Con Osborne recalled attending an important 1980 meeting of the Lamanite and Minority Affairs Committee, which was chaired by the committee staff head Stewart Durrant and included a number of general authorities but *not* George P. Lee, the only Indian who was a general authority. The ostensible purpose of the meeting was to review and assess all church programs for Indians, but in retrospect the meeting appears to have initiated the dismantling of all such programs (Osborne 1986 and 1999).

24. This excommunication occurred only two years after the publication of Lee's autobiography (1987), in which his conflicts with church leaders and policies could already be detected, though heavily muted. In his interview for the James M. Moyle Oral History Collection in the LDS Church Archives (see appendix A), Lee had been considerably more candid about the alienation and frustration he felt over the abandonment of the programs for Indians and the insistence of his superiors that he think of himself as a "general" authority, not as the spokesman for LDS Indians (Hartley 1981 and 1985).

25. On Mormon leaders' general ambivalence toward Indian and other native music and dance, see the revealing account in M. Hicks (1989, 209–27). A sophisticated Indian perspective is offered by P. Jane Hafen (1984 and 1985). For some reason, the same folk arts encountered in Hawaii and elsewhere in Polynesia have been more acceptable and (somewhat ironically) even promoted in a church commercial project, the Polynesian Cultural Center, in Oahu (M. Hicks 1989, 217–18). Yet native musical expressions among converts in West Africa have not been tolerated (M. Hicks 1989, 219–22).

26. Among the more perceptive treatments of the fundamental cultural differences between Anglo and Indian Mormons are those of Hall (1970); Schimmelpfennig (1971); and R. Smith (1968).

27. Support for Osborne's perceptions about the many LDS Indians who had retained their church activity and reared their children as devout Mormons can be found in his final report to the dean of the College of Student Life, where he reported the results of a survey showing half of the BYU Indian alumni (over forty years old) still active in the church (1993, 255–56). This encouraging tabulation must, however, be considered against the reality that less that 20 percent of these alumni could be found for the survey.

28. The tendency for native peoples to identify sometimes with several religious traditions simultaneously is illustrated in Oshley (2000), a tendency difficult to understand for LDS missionaries and leaders striving for the retention of Indian converts. I am grateful to Thomas W. Murphy for calling my attention specifically to the issue of cultural variations in the meanings of such terms as *conversion* and *retention*.

5. Old Lamanites, New Lamanites, and the Negotiation of Identity

[Through the Book of Mormon] I have become acquainted with my ancestry, the dealings of the Lord with them, and the glorious promises to them in the near future.
—Margarito Bautista, 1920

Mexico will be the principal place and Mexicans the principal people playing the most important role in these the last days.
—Margarito Bautista, 1935

You're Lamanites . . . a covenant people, a chosen race, a people of destiny. . . . [M]illions have an equal claim on that destiny. . . . Those millions to the south are waiting for redemption.
—Boyd K. Packer, 1979

WHEN SPENCER W. KIMBALL took up his mantle as president of the church at the end of 1973, he had championed the cause of the American Indians as an apostle for at least three decades. He had much to show for his efforts and for those of his associates who had served during those years on the church's Lamanite Committee, or Indian Committee, as it was variously called. Yet these leaders were becoming increasingly aware of a paradox in the progress of the church among the tribal peoples of North America. On the one hand, these Kimball decades had brought more native peoples into the church than ever before, especially from the arid surrounding homeland of the Mormons in Utah, Arizona, and New Mexico. As the 1970s drew to a close, thousands of Indian youth had graduated from urban and suburban high schools with the foster care and support of white Mormon families; hundreds had attended Brigham Young University on full scholarships; and scores had become religious and civic leaders among the Navaho and other tribal peoples. On the other hand, increasing membership figures had not been translating into durable church growth. Even BYU graduates had not adequately embraced the LDS lifestyle or participated in church life in the proportions expected by church leaders, nor had they accepted calls to missions or positions in the lay priesthood as expected.

This paradox was heightened by striking contrasts with church growth elsewhere in the hemisphere. As the twentieth century neared its end, LDS membership in Mexico alone had reached almost a million, with another three million in the countries farther south (*Deseret News Church Almanac* 1996, 355). Whole new Mormon congregations were being created almost on a weekly basis in Mexico and Latin America—and even in West Africa, where the church had finally begun in 1978 to extend the lay priesthood to its black members. Also in 1978, the first Mormon temple for South America was dedicated in Brazil, the most racially mixed country in the hemisphere. Since the very founding of the church in 1830, Mormons had believed that North American Indians were Lamanites, described by the Book of Mormon as literal Israelites, the seed of Abraham, who would flock to the church as lost sheep responding to the voice of the true Shepherd of Israel and would actually take the initiative in building a New Jerusalem on the American continent.

Mormons had looked for this "day of the Lamanite" for a century and a half. It had seemed to be on the horizon several times during the nineteenth century but never more so than during the Kimball decades of the late twentieth century. For a time, it appeared that a new generation of Lamanite converts in North America might provide the many missionaries and church leaders increasingly needed among the Lamanites farther south. Despite the impressive accomplishments of the church programs in enhancing the lives of these Indian Lamanites materially and culturally, their parallel spiritual and intellectual development had lagged. It is not surprising that as the 1970s ended, church leaders began to look elsewhere for a new day of the Lamanite—indeed, for a new kind of Lamanite—for Mormons and their leaders were beginning to conceive of "the Lamanites" differently late in the twentieth century. How had those conceptions been changing since the Book of Mormon was published in 1830?

Traditional Mormon Constructions of Identity for Native American Peoples

Aside from the claims and counterclaims about the authenticity and historicity of the Book of Mormon itself, our interest here is in the *uses* made of that book by nineteenth- and twentieth-century Mormons in their characterizations of the Lamanites. As is clear from the preceding chapters, Joseph Smith and the entire founding generation of Mormonism believed that the descendants of the Lamanites were first and foremost the tribal aborigines of North America (Whittaker 1985, 34–44, 64n).[1] The Book of Mormon was their authentic ancient history, and the attributions and prophecies therein about the Lamanites, both positive and negative, referred to the destiny of the American Indians. If the Book of Mormon spoke of the Lamanites as falling into decline and degradation, that seemed obvious enough to any contemporary observer of the Indians. Wherever the Book of Mormon promised a redemption of the Lamanites and their eventual return to high civilization and the true religion, that, too, would occur eventually if the Mormon emissaries of the restored gospel would strive with due diligence and persistence. Once converted, the Indians would take their rightful place as Israelites with the Mormons—perhaps even ahead of the Mormons—in building the New Jerusalem and establishing a new Zion on the American continent.

The Lamanites are often described in the Book of Mormon as a fallen and degenerate people, especially in comparisons with the righteous Nephites. Of course, as the putative authors of the record in question, the Nephites were free to characterize their antagonists as they wished, and demonizing of the "other" has been a recurrent process in all of human history (Pagels 1995). Some of these characterizations would understandably have been given racial connotations, not only by the early Mormons but also by nearly any nineteenth-century American readers—and probably most other white Americans even down to recent times. Mormon scholars, both Indian and non-Indian, have pointed out that the Mormon characterizations of Indians or Lamanites have always been influenced by European and Anglo-American images from at least Puritan times. One of these images was "the Noble Savage," which to Europeans originally connoted a *cultural* rather than a racial category. Of course, this image was itself a double-faceted paradox, at once "savage" (benighted and barbarous) and "noble" (dignified, and, in some ways, even civilized). These two aspects of the image were applied by white Mormons alternately and differentially, depending on the nature of their experiences with given Indian peoples (Hafen 1984; Pagán 1989b; Vickers 1998).

In the Book of Mormon narrative, for example, the Lamanites were described early on by Nephi as having "dwindled in unbelief . . . [and having become] . . . a dark and loathsome, and a filthy people, full of idleness and all manner of abominations" (1 Nephi 12:23). Accordingly, they were given by God "a sore cursing, because of their iniquity . . . [in which] the Lord God did cause a skin of blackness to come upon them," so that they would no longer be attractive to the righteous Nephites (2 Nephi 5:21)—a means of discouraging religious intermarriage. Several centuries later, "the skins of the Lamanites were [still] dark, according to the mark which was set upon their fathers . . . because of their transgression and their rebellion . . ." (Alma 3:6).

Yet the divine role in this seemingly racial transformation is not always so clear. In the very same chapter of Alma, for example, a Nephite faction (Amlicites) went over to the Lamanite side and therefore suffered a similar curse and mark (3:13–19). In this case, however, the offending faction fulfilled the divinely promised curse by *marking themselves* on the forehead as a sign of their rebellion. All the Nephites had been warned from the beginning that unless they remained faithful to their religion they would suffer the same fate as the Lamanites, "whom ye hate because of their filthiness and the cursing which hath come upon their skins, . . . [but] I fear that unless ye shall repent of your sins that their skins will be whiter than yours when ye shall be brought with them before the throne of God" (Jacob 3:5, 8). After the resurrected Christ came among them, the Nephites and Lamanites were virtually all converted and then amalgamated as one people again during a golden age of two or three centuries. Finally, near the end of the Nephite record, as the golden age was collapsing once again toward civil war, the prophet Mormon predicted that the Lamanites (now identified by *religion,* no longer by lineage) would again "become a dark, a filthy, and a loathsome people, beyond the description of that which ever hath been amongst us . . ." (Mormon 5:15).

At the same time, there are indications that the divine promise could work both ways—that is, if unrighteousness brought a curse of darkness, then repentance and a return to righteousness might remove the curse. For example, at one point in the narrative, a faction of the Lamanites is converted to the true faith and joins with the Nephites, whereupon "their curse was taken from them, and their skin became white" (3 Nephi 2:15–16). The Lamanites had received an early promise that once they came to understand their true religious heritage they would rejoice before God, and the "scales of darkness shall begin to fall from their eyes . . . and . . . they shall [become] a pure and delightsome people" (2 Nephi 30:6). Interestingly enough, prior to 1981, this last passage read "*white* and delightsome" in some earlier editions of the Book of Mormon (emphasis added). In 1839, Joseph Smith and the Nauvoo High Council approved a third edition of the Book of Mormon containing a few revisions, including changing "white" to "pure" in this passage. However, this edition was soon displaced by one published independently by the apostles in England in 1841, which did not contain the Nauvoo changes. (Other revisions that Smith apparently had also planned were not completed before his death.) Accordingly, "white" (instead of "pure") remained in the official text until the 1981 edition, when church scholars made a thorough historical investigation of all previous versions and manuscripts and turned up the Nauvoo changes among others (D. Campbell 1996). Several other references in the Book of Mormon to righteous Nephites and Lamanites as "delightsome" were never accompanied by references to color. Note, too, that earlier in this same passage the "darkness" accompanying the curse was not a darkness of skin but "scales of darkness" on the *eyes.*

Although Joseph Smith presented the Book of Mormon to the world as his translation of an ancient document, it is generally regarded by non-Mormons as a nineteenth-century product, whether or not it was divinely inspired. Accordingly, passages like those excerpted above are taken as simply reflections of nineteenth-century American racist understandings about the origins of various peoples of color. Such conventional wisdom seems justified both by the mysterious provenance of the Book of Mormon itself and by the meanings that Mormons themselves have traditionally attributed to such passages. Yet it is not entirely certain that Joseph Smith himself or even most others of his immediate family and contemporaries would have understood these passages in quite the same literal sense that modern readers have.

As one consideration, the Book of Mormon does not use the term *race* at all. In an 1842 letter (known in Mormon history as the Wentworth letter), the one recorded case in which Smith used the term in reference to the Book of Mormon, he was distinguishing *not* between Lamanites and Nephites but between them and the Jaredites, all of which parties he obviously considered to be peoples of the same Semitic origin (Joseph Smith 1989, 432). Furthermore, Smith, before his death, had begun replacing the seeming skin-color references with terms that clearly referred instead to spiritual quality. Finally, a comprehensive review of the Book of Mormon text as a whole shows that it uses *white* almost always as a figurative synonym for *pure, clean, luminous,* and similar concepts, not in reference to such "racial" traits as skin color (D. Campbell 1996, 131–35).

From Religious to Racial Identity Constructions for the "Old Lamanites"

Whatever ambiguity there might be about Joseph Smith's original understandings and intentions, however, there can be little doubt that at some point the *dominant* Mormon image of Lamanites came to be the "dark, degenerate, and savage" Indians of the American West rather than the people of destiny in the Book of Mormon. Such a shift of image would have been a fairly natural outcome of the early and continuing frustration of the Mormon aspirations for a rapid and enduring conversion of the Indians, who at first seemed to have been providentially paired with the Mormons by the shared experience of forced removal to lands west of the Mississippi. As the Mormons came to recognize how great an obstacle the traditional Indians' way of life was to their eventual conversion and return to the ideal civilization of the Book of Mormon, church leaders then adopted a missionary strategy that envisioned "civilizing" the Indians—i.e., assimilating them—prior to (or at best concomitant with) their spiritual or intellectual conversion. Only through this two-stage process of assimilation-to-conversion was the divine curse on their ancestors eventually to be removed (Coates 1978, 440–41; C. Peterson 1975, 24).

With the focus on removal of the "curse," Mormon attributions about Lamanites (and therefore about Indians) had acquired implications of a more racial kind in the physical sense, whereas previously some might have seen the Lamanite designation as more cultural or religious in nature. Certainly by the time the Mormons in Utah had been working (and skirmishing) with Indians for a decade, their "dark features" and "filthy habits" seemed especially salient to Parley P. Pratt; and George A. Smith expected any removal of the "curse of the Almighty" to require generations (both quoted in Bringhurst 1981b, 133). Yet to Brigham Young (1857), if dark skins, wickedness, and loathsomeness could be imposed on a people by a divine curse, then presumably the eventual removal of such a curse could make them once again "white and delightsome," as the Book of Mormon had promised in its original language (2 Nephi 30:6). Whatever the chronology or process, then, a shift of emphasis from an essentially religious to a more explicitly racial characterization of Lamanites as Indians seems to have occurred at least by the middle of the nineteenth century. This change of image, in turn, permitted the Mormon conscience to assume a more militant and defensive posture toward Indians, which seemed appropriate for survival in their new Utah homeland. Even during the twentieth century, long after hostile military encounters with Indians had become distant memories, racist characterizations by Mormons and others still continued in somewhat more subtle forms, including even poetry, hymnody, and other arts (Hafen 1984 and 1985; M. Hicks 1989, 209–27; Vickers 1998).

As indicated in chapter 3, some early Mormons, including the founding prophet, had entertained the possibility of intermarriage with converted Indians as one means of removing the "curse" of their darkened skins (Arrington and Bitton 1992, 195; Walker 1993, 10; Whittaker 1985, 35). However, from at least the Utah period on, Mormons were inclined to look instead for a miraculous lightening of the skin as a sign of the conversion of their Indian converts. This expectation was periodically articulated in Mormon discourse during the second half of the nineteenth century, especially when large-scale conversions of Indians seemed promising. It can be seen, for example, in the commentary on the conversion of a colony of northwestern Shoshone under Sagwitch after their resettlement in northern Utah during the 1870s (S. Christensen 1999, 21–23).[2] Also, the last major Mormon missionary campaigns among Indians toward the end of the nineteenth century were motivated largely by the belief of Wilford Woodruff (apostle and church president) that some of the Indian peoples of northern Arizona and New Mexico ("Zunis, Lagunas, and Isletas") were so civilized and light-skinned, because of the "purity of their national blood," that they were probably surviving Nephites or white Lamanites and thus especially receptive to the gospel message (Woodruff [1909] 1986, 521–27 [quote on 521]). Even in more recent times, Spencer W. Kimball, champion though he was of the Lamanite peoples, occasionally expressed publicly his expectation that conversion would be accompanied by a literal lightening of their skins—as in the case of a converted sixteen-year-old girl he had met in the Indian Student Placement Program, who "was several shades lighter than her parents" (1960a, 33–34; and 1960b, 922–23 [quote]).[3] Thus, while the Lamanites-as-dark-skinned-Indians seemed to justify the Mormon conception and treatment of them as inferiors *prior to* their conversion, the Lamanites-as-Israelites carried the expectation of a kind of racial change *after* conversion that would vindicate their membership in the family of Abraham along with Mormons and other Israelites.

Yet, as late as the mid-1960s, when the church programs for Indians at BYU and elsewhere were gaining the momentum that was to last for decades, even some of the professional educators leading these programs were anticipating skin-color changes as their Indian charges successfully embraced the gospel and the new opportunities available to them through the church. This expectation can be seen, for example, in a comprehensive series of lectures on LDS Indians and their future by Paul E. Felt, one of the founding faculty of the BYU Indian education program (Felt 1964, Lecture 1). At about the same time, another BYU academic concluded a master's thesis in religious education by declaring, among other things, that Indians who were accepting the gospel and were taking advantage of the opportunities offered them through the church were literally becoming "white and delightsome" (Dutson 1964, 105). After the new edition of the Book of Mormon was published in 1981, when this phrase was replaced by "pure and delightsome," the traditional racist connection between skin color and spiritual condition began to recede from Mormon discourse, but it still appeared even as late as 1987 in a paper presented by a senior member of the BYU religion faculty at an official campus symposium (R. Turner 1987), although (to be fair) the main burden of his remarks focused on the eventual removal of the "Lamanite mark." An even more official endorsement of this traditional belief can be seen in the introductory heading to 3 Nephi, chapter 2, of the 1981 edition of the Book of Mormon (an editorial insertion), where the reader is alerted that in the chapter to follow "converted Lamanites become white"—and this despite the change from "white" to "pure" that had already been made in 2 Nephi.

Of course, as I have argued earlier, any Mormon tendency to see differences of race or lineage in spiritual terms should be understood as part of the contemporaneous cultural and historical context of Europe and America generally, not just of the Mormon heritage in particular—a point emphasized for me by a Mormon anthropologist of Lamanite ancestry (Pagán 1989b). Throughout the nineteenth century and beyond, intellectual currents in Europe and America had begun glorifying the history and destiny of the white "race" and discovering various kinds of "inferiority," both scriptural and anthropological, in the darker skinned "races" of the world (Wood 1990). The Mormons, for their part, eventually adopted an implicit theological framework that rank-ordered various lineages from most to least favored according to the different divinely ordained destinies assigned in a premortal existence (recall chapter 2). In this rank-ordering, the position of the American Indians became somewhat ambiguous. On the one hand, they enjoyed the divine favor and glorious destiny prophesied for the various Israelite lineages. On the other hand, their ancestors the Lamanites had fallen from divine grace and had been cursed, at least temporarily, with a dark skin. This theological ambivalence was only exacerbated by the actual historical experience of the Mormons with the Lamanites-as-Indians of the West, who had proved so difficult to convert and civilize.

Mormon ambivalence toward Indians clearly persisted to the end of the twentieth century and perhaps beyond, even though it was largely unconscious. If racial condescension could be expressed with innocence and benign intentions by such prominent advocates as Kimball, a wider resolution of racial or religious ambivalence at the Mormon grassroots could hardly be expected. The Mormons' two traditional *uses* of the Lamanite identity, delineated so well by Keith Parry (1972), still remained at the end of the century—namely, the "missionary" use to characterize a people in need of conversion (perhaps despite themselves) and the "pioneer" use to characterize a benighted and hostile people standing in the way of progress. Both characterizations, of course, call for a program of assimilation and wholesale destruction of native cultures.

Mormon Conceptions about Indians in Twentieth-Century Surveys and Encounters

Such characterizations seem obvious enough, but ultimately they have to be inferred mainly from historical accounts and discourse. It is difficult to find much systematic data on white Mormon attitudes toward Indians, even during more recent years, since indicators of such attitudes rarely, if ever, appear in general surveys. However, it happens that I was involved in administering surveys of limited scope to samples of people in the mostly Mormon settlements of northern Utah (1968) and Cardston, Alberta (1980). Results of the first study compared systematic samples of 334 Mormons with 118 non-Mormons drawn from the telephone directory of Logan, Utah (Douglas and Mauss 1968). This survey focused on local white attitudes toward blacks (or "Negroes" as they were then called), but a number of questions about Indians were also included, and the distributions of responses to them were analyzed.[4]

Two main indicators of discriminatory tendencies were included in the analysis: (1) social distance, as measured by the traditional seven-step Bogardus Social Distance Scale; and (2) the respondent's intention to move away if a family of a certain other race moved into the neighborhood. Comparisons of the Mormon and the non-Mormon samples revealed a consistently greater tendency for the Mormons to give discriminatory responses, no matter what the "other" race was. However, the Mormons in the sample disproportionately had grown up in Utah, especially northern Utah, whereas the non-Mormons had come mostly from elsewhere; it therefore seemed likely that the more discriminatory Mormon responses reflected a local *cultural* parochialism at least as much as a religious one. This hypothesis was borne out when controls were imposed on the data for the degree of exposure a respondent had had to other races (specifically "Negroes"). Such exposure largely neutralized the general differences between the Mormon and the non-Mormon subsamples. Controls for other kinds of intervening variables, however, did not produce any systematic differences between Mormons and others.

In comparisons based on the main indicators of social distance, both Mormons and non-Mormons in this study tended to prefer associations with Jews or "Orientals" over other ethnic groups. Mormons and non-Mormons both ranked American Indians *second* among their preferred associates on these two measures. However, both Mormons and others tended to discriminate most of all against blacks as neighbors or close associates. The basic similarity of the Mormon and non-Mormon responses in this study precludes a finding of *unique* Mormon attitudes toward Indians; rather, the Mormons mainly seemed to *share the ambivalence* toward Indians in white society generally. Controls in the data for various "secularizing" influences in respondents' backgrounds, particularly exposure to other races, enhanced the favorable attitudes toward Indians somewhat more among Mormons than among non-Mormons. This could indicate an underlying disposition among Mormons in the study to see Indians somewhat more favorably through the prism of the Book of Mormon. With samples so small and so limited geographically, however, it is difficult to be certain about very much in this study. A study of six hundred Utah and California college students around the same time by a BYU doctoral student found no differences between Mormons and non-Mormons in willingness to extend *compensatory education* to Indians and other minorities—a less direct indicator of discrimination (M. Johnson 1973).

Of course, attitudes toward various "outgroups" are not really put to a *behavioral* test except in a context of direct and immediate conflict over political or economic interests. For example, the Mormons of nineteenth-century Utah no doubt felt freer to entertain benign aspirations about redeeming the Lamanites while reading the Book of Mormon than while resisting raids on their villages and cattle by local bands of Indians. Even in the middle of the twentieth century, when violent military encounters no longer occurred, the Mormon capacity for charitable responses to Indian claims was sometimes put to the test. In one case, during the 1960s and 1970s, a long-running political struggle ensued between the traditional white power structure, which was mostly Mormon, and the dominant Navaho population on the nearby reservation over control of the board of supervisors and other public offices in Apache County, Arizona (Pagán 1989c). The Navaho finally gained meaningful access to power only with the help of federal laws and courts. The conflict generated lingering bitterness on both sides, expressed for many of the Mormons involved by a sometime county recorder, who declared, even in a much later reflection on the incident, "I used to think of them as my Lamanite brethren, but now they're just damned Indians" (quoted in Pagán 1989c, 13).

A still later example occurred in 1980, when once again Mormon beliefs about Indians were subjected to the stress of immediate interracial conflict. In the spring of that year, a controversy arose in southern Alberta between the Canadian federal government and the Blood Indians on the reserve near Cardston.[5] The Bloods claimed title to land recently relinquished by the Canadian Pacific Railway, which they believed was supposed to revert, under the law, to the reserve upon release by the railway company. An accompanying claim was that a related strip of Indian land had been sold, without the tribe's permission, to Cardston residents. Initially, the Blood leaders looked to the Canadian federal government for redress, dramatically drawing nationwide attention to their claims with a 2,000-mile relay run to Ottawa to present their petition. After seeing little movement on the issue for a few months, the Indians decided to use their proximity to Cardston for additional leverage, apparently in the belief that if the residents of that town were sufficiently inconvenienced, they would put some additional pressure on the federal government to resolve the matter.

When the Indians began in July to boycott Cardston businesses, threatened to withdraw from Cardston schools, and eventually blockaded roads and highways in and out of the town, the hapless Cardstonites were astonished and outraged. The religious issue was always just beneath the surface, for Cardston had been established a century earlier by Mormon pioneers from Utah, who had eventually built there one of the few Mormon temples of the time. At least 80 percent of the residents of Cardston were still Mormon, who tended to see themselves as benefactors of the Indians and as sincere believers in the teachings of the Book of Mormon about the eventual divine destiny of these Lamanites (Card 1999). As Keith Parry's study (1972) makes clear, however, both the Cardstonites and the Indians brought to this confrontation a history of mutual suspicion about each others' true intentions and good faith. To be sure, many Indians were looking for good relations with Cardston, and a few had even converted to Mormonism. Similarly, many in Cardston wished the Indians well and looked upon them as potential converts and believers in the faith. Yet before the confrontation of 1980 had been brought to a close by some belated government responses, the stereotypic feelings and images on both sides were made very evident in the local press.

As it happened, the religious and church sensitivities of the Cardston residents were probably heightened by an unscheduled visit during July from George P. Lee, the only general authority of the church who was a Native American (Navaho). Lee gave an address at a multistake "fireside," in which he noted that he was there as a visitor, not "on assignment," but he made a series of comments drawing heavily on traditional LDS teachings about Lamanites, particularly about white Mormons' obligations to make them partners in building the New Jerusalem and preparing for the Lord's Second Coming. Within that theological context, Lee called on his audience to empathize with the plight of the Indians in their midst and to do everything possible to bring the current conflict to an early and peaceful resolution. This visit might have been made at the invitation of the local church leaders in hopes of neutralizing some of the acrimony that had developed among the members, or it might have been made on the initiative of Lee himself—or even some of his colleagues in the general church leadership. He said only that he had come informally as a visitor, but it seems unlikely that his visit would have been either a random event or an inconsequential one under the circumstances.[6]

When I arrived at the beginning of July to teach a couple of summer courses in the nearby University of Lethbridge, even before Lee's visit to Cardston, the situation there seemed to present an ideal context in which to study Mormon religious attitudes under stress. I was invited to join Keith Parry, then a professor in the university's Department of Anthropology, in seeking a small grant from the university to finance a survey of Cardston residents. Most of the funds were used to pay for a small number of interviewers and the printing of interview guides or questionnaires. With the help of some volunteers, during July, August, and September, we interviewed a sample of about 10 percent of the households listed in the Cardston telephone directory, soliciting opinions and beliefs about the issues involved in the crisis there. This effort yielded more than 70 interview schedules, of which 67 turned out to be usable. Electronic processing and tabulation of these data were not completed before the funds were exhausted, but I did some manual tabulations based on a small set of the interview questions.

Because of the traditional religious identity Mormons had constructed for the local Indians, the first task in this study was to establish the salience of the "Lamanite" label among the various respondents. Accordingly, I first divided the questionnaires into three groups: (1) Group A: those Mormons who definitely attributed the Lamanite identity to the Bloods *and* spoke of it in generally *favorable* terms (N = 28); (2) Group B: those Mormons for whom the Lamanite label for Bloods was either not applicable, not salient, or not favorable (N = 25); and (3) Group C: non-Mormons, who typically did not recognize the label at all (N = 14). Women outnumbered men by about two to one in this survey generally but by three to one in Group A.

Next was to determine whether there were *differential response patterns* among these three groups in the opinions they gave on issues relating to (1) the right of the Indians to the disputed land; (2) the highly publicized "run to Ottawa" by the Indians to call attention to their grievances; (3) several of the other tactics used by Indians, such as boycotts and blockades; and (4) judgments about what the residents of Cardston should have done or should do next in response to the Indians' campaign. Each of these four issues was indicated in more than one way in the interview schedule, so I had to make a summary estimate, as objective as possible, of whether the respondent's overall opinion on each issue was "sympathetic" to the Indians, "unsympathetic," or "mixed/neutral."

The tabulations in Table 5.1 indicate the nature of responses by each of the three Cardston groups to each of the four issues involving the Bloods. Because of the global and imprecise nature of my estimates of the various kinds of Cardston people and their attitudes, only the largest differences in percentages across the three columns are very meaningful.[7] It does seem clear, however, that respondents in Group A were much more likely than those in the other groups to give sympathetic responses to the questions about their views of the local Indians. Very few Cardstonites of any kind were supportive of the more militant and disruptive Indian tactics (the third issue), but, as Table 5.1 indicates, there were very large differences between those in Group A and those in the other groups in their attitudes toward the Bloods. In other words, there is evidence that looking upon the Indians through a "favorable" (if condescending) Lamanite label tended to be accompanied by a sympathetic outlook on the Indians' political exertions.

In a more qualitative examination of comments made in the interviews, I found that certain beliefs about the Indians and government policy were widely shared by the Cardston whites, regardless of differences among them

Table 5.1. Attitudes toward Cardston Indians by Beliefs about "Lamanite" Identity

Issues on Which Cardstonites Are Sympathetic[a]	Group A (n = 28)	Group B (n = 25)	Group C (n = 14)
Indian rights to disputed land	39%	24%	29%
The "Run to Ottawa"	64	36	43
Most other Indian tactics (boycotts, blockades, etc.)	7	0	7
Preferred Cardston reactions to Indians	61	20	29

a. Percentages are *only* for those giving globally "sympathetic" responses. Unsympathetic or other responses are not included.

in religious commitments. These are the kinds of views that have often been expressed by North American whites for generations, and they reflect a pervasive and fundamental disdain for Indians, quite apart from any given crisis or episode of the kind that occurred in 1980. One recurrent belief was that government policy had had the effect of cultivating a mentality of dependence among the Indians, so that they expected support and "hand-outs" without working. A related belief was that the reservation lifestyle or culture itself was to blame, for it encouraged idleness and drinking and deterred Indians from obtaining legitimate work off the reservations (or "reserves," as they are called in Canada). These characterizations were sometimes accompanied by calls for government evenhandedness, for Indians to be treated "just like everyone else," reflecting a white preference for an assimilationist government posture rather than a pluralist or multicultural one.

Beyond general stereotypes about the Indians, Cardston whites tended to share certain opinions about the crisis in question, how it had developed, and what should be done about it. First of all, some of their comments reflected a sense of regret (in some cases outrage) that they had been dragged into a controversy, not of their own making, between the Indians and the federal government. Some tended to blame government bungling, irresponsible local news coverage, and agitation by outside Indian militants and young Indian "hotheads," rather than the local tribal elders, for the deteriorating situation. They often praised both the responsiveness and the restraint of the police detachment (RCMP) and urged its continuing resoluteness to prevent damage to life or property. The respondents in Group A tended to offer, with somewhat more frequency than those in the other groups, explanations for the crisis that deflected blame from either side. These Mormons were especially likely to point to outside agitators and media distortions, while admitting that both whites and Indians bore some responsibility for mutual prejudice and misunderstanding. At the same time, they were especially likely to make self-serving and condescending declarations about how good the Cardston people had been to the Indians, how the local church leaders had urged restraint, and how much commitment the Mormons felt to Indians as their teachers, missionaries, and the like (reminiscent of the standard white characterizations criticized by Ainsworth [1986]; Mitchell-Green [1987]; and D. Sanders [1985]).

An underlying religious sentiment might thus be seen in the way in which these Mormons looked at the situation in 1980. More explicit religious sentiments about Lamanites in particular were much less frequent but still occurred in suggestive ways. Three of the respondents in Group A cited the traditional Mormon belief that Indians would someday become white. One in Group B made a similar prediction after emphasizing the importance of the original curse, but two others in that group denied that the Lamanite question was involved at all in what was essentially a matter about Indians. One respondent in this group gave especially dramatic expression to many fellow Mormons' belief that the local Indians were not even Lamanites. When asked directly if he thought that the Blood Indians were Lamanites, he declared, "Hell, no! These ain't Lamanites. Lamanites are down there in Mexico and Latin America . . . or maybe in Polynesia."

Toward a Nonracist Construction of Lamanite Identity

As indicated earlier, it is not clear to what extent Joseph Smith and other Mormons of the 1830s would have agreed with the sentiments expressed in Cardston. Even if the Book of Mormon is taken as a nineteenth-century work, the earliest Mormons might not have shared the racist disdain for Indians that later Mormons came to have, along with Americans generally. Let us recall that Joseph Smith sent his first missionary expedition to the Indians in the belief that they, not his own white converts, were supposed to take the lead in building the new Zion, after they were taught about the true gospel and the true heritage once embraced by their ancestors. Some even contemplated extensive intermarriage with these newly discovered Israelites. Furthermore, all the Indian tribes and bands the Mormons encountered in their pre-Utah years seemed fairly docile and "civilized" to them, so it is by no means obvious that they would have seen these earliest interactions primarily in racist terms. However, as chapter 3 also makes clear, the tense encounters with the Plains Indians on the way to the West and especially the Utah experience after 1847 gave the Mormon imagination a new, more immediate, and more sinister referent for what they read in the Book of Mormon about the Lamanites. It is primarily from that point on that Mormon discourse reflects an explicitly racist and demeaning understanding of the American Indians and their future.

Whatever the earlier constructions of Lamanite or Indian identity that have permeated white Mormon ways of thinking in the past, Hugh W. Nibley, a professor at BYU, has reminded modern Mormons that they need not read passages in the Book of Mormon about Lamanite "darkness" or "blackness" in racial terms (1967, 246–50). Differences between Lamanites and Nephites can be understood in terms primarily cultural and religious, rather than racial, since both peoples shared a common lineage.[8] It is thus both hazardous and unnecessary for white Mormons to read standard American racist interpretations into the Book of Mormon's characterizations of Lamanites. The universalistic call in the Book of Mormon (2 Nephi 26:33) for people of all colors and conditions to come unto Christ is itself a repudiation of racism in divine affairs, however frequently overlooked. Eugene England (1985), in a compelling essay, made clear that there are other ways of reading the relevant passages in the Book of Mormon that would be free of racial connotations and would also prove much more compatible with efforts to reach those native peoples offended by the conventional interpretations. For example, in modern colloquial English (or American), we sometimes speak of people as having "thick" or "thin" skins, without intending any literal dermatological meaning. Attributions of "white" versus "black" or "dark" skins could be read in a similarly figurative manner, as they might have been by Joseph Smith himself (or by his Nephite authors). The reader therefore need not attribute racist intentions when the Book of Mormon uses such terms as *dark* or *filthy* versus *white* or *pure,* especially when "racial traits," such as skin color, are not even explicitly mentioned—which is the case most of the time.

A modern preference for nonracial or even nonphysical definitions of the differences between Lamanites and Nephites can be seen in the quasi-official *Encyclopedia of Mormonism* (Ludlow 1992). Several articles in this encyclopedia deal in one way or another with the various peoples described in the Book of Mormon, but almost all of them manage to distinguish between the Lamanites and Nephites entirely on religious, cultural, and political grounds, without mentioning race or skin color. An exception is the entry on "Native Americans" (Chadwick and Garrow 1992), which opens with an acknowledgment of the traditional LDS conception about skin color differences but then explains that, by the end of the Book of Mormon story (4 Nephi), the reunification of Nephites and Lamanites had brought a complete mutual assimilation, obliterating whatever "racial" differences might have developed in earlier centuries.

Constructions and Uses of Lineage Identity by Mormon Indians

If the white Mormon attributions about Indians were complicated by theology and history, the perspectives of Indian Mormons were no less complex and varied. Of special interest here, however, is the potential variety in the different *uses* by Mormon Indians of their Lamanite identity. In attempting to ascertain this variety, I did not have access to a random sample of Indian Mormons, nor did I interview any such Lamanites (except Clemmer [1999], a special informant for the previous chapter). Yet I was able to get some idea of the range and variety of their feelings by studying the comments some of them made in theses or dissertations, publications, and formal oral history interviews (Embry 1992d). I also interviewed a few white informants who had had extensive experience and relationships with Mormon and non-Mormon Indians, on and off reservations. (I benefited especially from the interviews with Ainsworth [1986]; Mitchell-Green [1987]; and D. Sanders [1985].) My information about the personal beliefs and feelings of Mormon Indians is thus secondhand, but it might still be useful to the discussion at hand.

As might be expected, the Lamanite identity had different meanings and uses depending on the experiences and relationships that the Indian Mormons had had with their white coreligionists and the church more generally. In this respect, the struggle of Indian Mormons with identity was not so different from that of Indian converts to other Christian religions (Bear Chief 1992; Benedek 1995; Treat 1996; Udall 1969). It has been similar also to that confronting most immigrant peoples. Although the reservations were located within the territory of the United States (or Canada), they were culturally separate countries (or colonies). Indian Mormons—especially youths—leaving the reservations for life in white Mormon communities or for BYU campus life would have culture shock and other experiences akin to those of immigrants from overseas. Like Mormon converts from elsewhere in the world, these Indians would face the predicament of adjusting simultaneously to the Anglo-American and the Mormon cultures, which were similar but not identical. Like other immigrant peoples, the Indians carried the stigma and ambiguous status of "outsiders," far more so than had the many European converts to Mormonism. In their attitudes toward the Mormon church and people, therefore, much depended on how fully assimilated the Indian converts had become to the Anglo-Mormon way of life, or—to put the matter somewhat differently—how remote in the biographical past the reservation experience was. For those whose parents or grandparents had already "immigrated" to white America, assimilation was, of course, well underway, with or without Mormon conversion, but generational conflict often remained.

It was within this stressful context that Mormon Indians had to negotiate for themselves, individually and collectively, the meaning of the "Lamanite" identity. Naturally, the Indian converts would bring to this process all that they had learned about that identity, both ideologically and experientially, from their white Mormon teachers and associates. At the same time, during visits with friends and relatives on the reservations or in urban areas, they would be exposed to alternative identities offered by the emerging American Indian Movement and Native American religions. For some, the Mormon Lamanite identity ultimately failed to meet the existential demands life placed on them, so they left it behind for a return to the "Indian" identity, despite considerable assimilation. One sees this pattern, for example, in the life of Ella Bedonie, a Navaho from Arizona, who nevertheless had mainly pleasant recollections of her years as an active Mormon and product of the Indian Student Placement Program (Benedek 1995, 99–117). Several of the respondents in the BYU Oral History Collection also commented on how frequently fellow Mormon Indians had dropped out, even after considerable church involvement, and reverted to the ways of the reservation or to a non-Mormon lifestyle (Embry 1992d).[9]

Even for those who retained their Mormon ties, however, the salience of the Lamanite identity seems almost always to have been problematic. In reviewing the dozens of BYU oral history transcripts, one is struck by how rarely the issue of Lamanite identity is even mentioned, whether in a positive or a negative light. It is as though the Indian respondents simply recognized that "Lamanite" is the peculiarly Mormon way of referring to them, but they do not really embrace its fundamental theological implications; or, if they do, they evaluate the label with an ambivalence similar to that which white Mormons bring to it. Some Indians have found in the Lamanite identity a kind of common "rallying ground" for uniting Indians and distinguishing them and their religious styles from those of white Mormons (Harris 1985, 147–51; Pagán 1989a and 1990).[10] "Lamanite" thus serves as a kind of Mormon equivalent of "Pan-Indian," a political and cultural construct that has emerged among the North American tribal peoples (Hafen 1984; Murphy 2000, 185–86).

Even Indian church members of long standing and generally devout sentiments reported being "turned off" by their experiences in white Mormon congregations, where they perceived a flaunting of power and prosperity as part of Mormon religious life.[11] A particularly constructive reaction to this feeling, for one devout and highly assimilated Mormon Indian couple in Canada, took the form of deliberately returning to the Sarcee Reserve near Calgary as professional social workers, attracted there in part by the "Lamanite culture" and its focus on "more time for peace and reflection . . . on . . . the important and essential aspects of the gospel" (M. Cannon 1991). To the extent that such feelings are shared, they are understandably accompanied by a preference for separate Indian congregations and social activities, despite an effort by church leaders to begin phasing out "segregated" wards and branches. One young man, who had been a BYU student but had moved to Salt Lake City for work, traveled back to Provo every Sunday to attend church there in the "Indian" (144th) Ward.[12]

Of course, there were other Mormon Indians who took the "Lamanite" label seriously and personally. Some reacted to it quite negatively, partly because of the recurrent portrayal of Lamanites in the Book of Mormon as degraded or degenerate people but more often because of the Indians' perceptions about the harmful uses of that label by white Mormons. That is, the Indians were less distressed by the Book of Mormon treatment (which, after all, prophesies eventually a divine role and destiny for Lamanites) than they were by the Mormon treatment at the hands of ignorant if well-meaning fellow church members and leaders. In some cases, an indignant reaction against the "Lamanite" label was expressed by a conscious embrace of the Indian heritage (dances, celebrations, headbands, etc.), despite a high degree of assimilation into Mormon life generally (Harris 1985, 148–49).[13] Even George P. Lee, as a student at BYU, had resisted efforts there to eliminate or marginalize native music and dance as "pagan" or "devilish" (M. Hicks 1989, 217–18).

In general, those Indians most fully assimilated to the white Mormon way of life were less likely to have a negative reaction—or any reaction at all—to the use of the "Lamanite" label.[14] Arturo De Hoyos, an early and major leader in the Indian programs at BYU, expressed the kind of comfort with the Lamanite label generally felt by the most assimilated Mormon Indians: "I am a Lamanite. I have never resented, nor do I now resent, the term. Those who do resent the label seem to be so few that nobody else should give it a second thought. . . . [T]he most important meaning *Lamanite* has for me is that it identifies me as one for whom the most perfect book in the world was written [i.e., the Book of Mormon]. . . . [This] book tells me all I need to know to live a busy, productive, and abundant life. If I were not a Lamanite, I could not call this my book" (A. De Hoyos 1986, 16–17). Clem Bear Chief, an Alberta Blackfoot converted as an adult by a white Mormon missionary couple, presented a cogent and convincing account of his conversion that makes no reference at all to a Lamanite identity but instead finds that "the gospel gives us identity. It answers for us the slippery questions that still perplex so many of my people: What am I? An Indian? An Aborigine? An indigenous person? A grassroots person? First nation? The Church, through its prophets and scriptures, answers these questions" (1992, 149).[15]

Whether intended or not, such a wholehearted embrace of the church and the Book of Mormon carries with it an implication of assimilation almost by definition. A popular folk song composed for Mormon Indians during the 1960s ("Go, My Son") referred to them collectively as an "Indian nation" rather than as Lamanites and promoted assimilation in the form of educational and economic advancement.[16] Among some of the most assimilated Mormon Indians, an almost opposite use of the Lamanite identity is apparent, namely, as a basis for rejecting and resisting the demands and claims of the militant Pan-Indianism in America during the 1960s and 1970s. Whereas some of the Indians mentioned above were using their tribal or Indian identities to reject the negative Lamanite image *within* Mormonism—or at least to ignore it—others were embracing their Mormon Lamanite identities to avoid the image of the "wild and degraded" Indian. An example of this can be seen in the 1969 observations of a BYU graduate student of Taos-Pueblo origins, later a member of the faculty and an accomplished musician:

> [T]he Lamanite student is being shackled by the old identity. . . . When a so-called Indian student comes here, who knows nothing of his dances and so on, he feels that he has to learn these dances to identify as an Indian on this cam-

pus. . . . [However], the new look . . . is that we aren't Indians, because "Indian" to us is the old image of the feather, the rattle, the medicine man, the backwardness, [and] the darkness, but we're not that any more. We're Lamanites. We . . . know who we are from the Book of Mormon. . . . [T]he Lamanite is someone . . . who has had this darkness lifted, who sees himself as an honorable, dignified son and daughter of God. . . . (J. Rainer 1976)

Some Mormon Indians attempted to use—and even celebrate—their Indian and Mormon identities simultaneously in ways that might not have pleased the speaker just quoted but nevertheless represented a sincere attempt to mediate and arbitrate between the two different social worlds, as well as between their own two personal identities. One such individual receiving prominent coverage in the BYU student newspaper was Stanley Snake of Oklahoma, who in 1972 was elected president of the National Indian Youth Council (NIYC), despite his public defense of the LDS missionary work and the foster placement program among Indians. The NIYC, founded in 1961, was one of two especially militant "Red Power" groups in the country (the other being the American Indian Movement, or AIM). Snake was criticized from both worlds, as might be expected. On the one hand, he had to "convince Mormons that Indians [who] wear beads and long hair are not necessarily bad," while, on the other hand, he periodically had to defend himself against charges of "Apple Indian" or "Uncle Tomahawk" from the more militant members of the NIYC (quoted in Clemens 1972). In straddling the two identities, Snake received high praise from both the NIYC executive director and BYU's Indian Education Department. Snake himself credited his success at NIYC to his church membership, which gave him "the priesthood and a knowledge of where I came from and where I'm going" (quoted in Clemens 1972).

Another poignant example of Mormon Indians' struggle to negotiate between the two identities (Lamanite and Indian) can be seen in the case of Lacee A. Harris, a devout and active third-generation Mormon of mixed Ute, Paiute, and Anglo ancestry and a well-assimilated product of foster placement and BYU. In a 1985 publication of his story, Harris begins with his own father's rejection of the Lamanite label as referring to "wicked people" (143). Yet, as he goes on to explain, "I knew I wasn't a Lamanite because my father said we weren't. I knew I was an Indian, but I didn't know how that fit into the Mormon system of Anglos and Lamanites" (146). Yet, later on, when a white Mormon family took him in as a foster son at the age of fifteen, his "sense of being Mormon sharpened" (146). Then, at BYU, he took a mandatory class on the Book of Mormon and "really began to learn about the Lamanites. The more I learned, the more I felt that the Church really had no place for us as 'Indians.' We belonged only if we were Lamanites" (147). He accepted the account in the Book of Mormon of the Lamanites "as apostate survivors of great nations, but taking that story personally was too much for me. Were those Lamanites *my* Indian people? My people were good, deeply spiritual, in tune with the rhythms of the earth and with their own needs. . . . How could I be a descendant of wickedness and still be good without repudiating the heritage that made it possible for me to accept Mormon goodness?" (147).

Harris is apparently able to reach only an uncomfortable resolution of this predicament by embracing for himself and his children the basic Mormon teachings, but not white LDS culture, which for him "has become more alien, not more familiar, as the years have passed." In his experience, Mormon Indians who abandon their Indian heritage altogether "do not seem to be either happier or more successful" (151–52). A fictionalized but probably realistic portrayal of the anguish of trying to live in two worlds can be seen also in the story "Tracy Sequaptewa" by Michael Fillerup (1992), a Mormon author deeply steeped in experiences with Indians of the Southwest. Tracy, a Mormon Indian woman, had spent her high school years in a white Mormon home and had eventually graduated from a university, all of which had cut her off culturally and psychologically from her reservation background. Yet, though an ostensibly "successful" adult in the white world, she could not find acceptance as a teacher in a racially mixed Arizona school (where she is undermined by a politically ambitious Indian parent), or as the wife of a white husband, or even among her LDS ward members, who continued to see her mainly as a "cute little Lamanite girl" (176). This struggle to maintain and make use of two identities simultaneously is also recurrent in the BYU oral histories, discussed earlier, as well as in James Treat's edited collection (1996). The organizational counterpart of this predicament has obviously been reflected in the church's own discouraging struggle to retain its Indian converts.

Finally, one important use of this label by Mormon Indians was a conscientious embrace of the Lamanite identity to claim special status within the Mormon church. From the evidence available to me, this seems to have been a resort of rather a small minority of Mormon Indians, but for them the identity was very salient and highly motivating. At the *individual* level, this means appropriating for oneself the myth and mystique of the Lamanite as a person of divine destiny and power, in the mode of "Samuel the Lamanite," one of the great prophets in the Book of Mormon. At the *collective* level, this means attributing the "redeemed Lamanite" identity to all actual and potential Indian Mormons, with all its doctrinal and mythological implications—an identity indirectly encouraged in official church literature (but always within the normal authority structure, of course—e.g., Watrous [1985]).

This use is especially interesting when expressed in a kind of "status displacement" or role reversal, as in the case of George P. Lee (1989), discussed in the previous chapter. Lee conscientiously appropriated the Lamanite identity from early Book of Mormon scripture and discourse and then claimed that *only* the

aboriginal American peoples—*not* the white Mormons—were the true Israelites of the church and therefore the ones charged by God to lead in the building of the New Jerusalem and its temple in the Western Hemisphere. Although
the Mormon church had been divinely commissioned to bring the true gospel and the Book of Mormon to the Lamanite remnants of the hemisphere,
white Mormons remained what the Book of Mormon had always said that they
were—namely, "Gentiles," not Israelites (except by adoption).

Lee, of course, was excommunicated for his trouble, since Mormonism had
long since redefined most Euroamerican Mormons as literal Israelites, descended mainly from the tribe of Ephraim. This had become an important
myth in Mormonism's emerging racialist rank-ordering of peoples in the
nineteenth and early twentieth centuries (as explained in chapter 2). Even
with that mythology receding into the past, Lee's colleagues in the church
leadership were not prepared to relinquish their own claims to the plans for
building the New Jerusalem or to turn over these prerogatives to the Lamanites, no matter how fully and sincerely Indians might be converted to the Book
of Mormon scenario. Nevertheless, it was a form of displacement, theologically if not ecclesiastically, that Lee was trying to achieve through a collective use of the Lamanite identity for himself and his fellow Indian Mormons.[17]
His excommunication was simply the LDS leadership's assertion, perhaps an
inevitable one, of its power to control the operational significance or *uses* of
the Lamanite identity and theology set forth in the Book of Mormon—and
not for the first time or the last, as will be seen in the later discussion of
Mormonism in Mexico.

In summary, several different patterns can be inferred from the various
uses of the Lamanite identity by Mormon Indians in North America. For
some, this identity is never really internalized and therefore has no real "use"
in their lives, except perhaps for short-term access to certain material and
educational resources accompanying membership and activity in the LDS
Church. They recognize that other Mormons, both white and Indian, might
regard them as "Lamanites," but such a label neither troubles them especially
nor motivates them to change their lives or associations in the long run.

Still others try in various ways to straddle and embrace both identities,
Lamanite and tribal, to enjoy the social benefits of each. That posture proves
very difficult to maintain indefinitely, however, so they often eventually leave
behind one or the other, depending on their experiences with other Mormons
or with the church. A third pattern is a more or less complete embrace of the
Lamanite identity, or at least the positive and ennobling aspects of it, as a basis
for full assimilation into the modern Anglo-Mormon way of life, and a rejection of the Indian traditions that conflict with that way. Finally, the fourth
pattern (a relatively rare one) adds to the third a claim to special power and
status in Mormonism deriving from the ancient Israelite and Abrahamic

prerogatives of Lamanites. By the end of the twentieth century, however, all such understandings about Lamanites in North America might have become moot, at least in most practical respects.

Constructing the Identity of the New Lamanite

To make clear the contrast intended here between the "old" and the "new" Lamanites, let us recall again the original understanding of Joseph Smith and his associates. These founders applied the term *Lamanites* operationally to the North American aboriginal peoples, first and foremost those within easy reach of the Mormon missionaries. The City of Zion itself was to be built in Missouri "on the borders by the Lamanites" (Doctrine and Covenants 28:9 and 54:8), large numbers of whom had been resettled just west of the Mississippi River by Providence and by the U.S. government on its newly acquired lands. Lamanite converts, on hearing the Mormon message about their divine heritage and destiny, were expected to flock to Zion and join in its premillennial construction and expansion. For reasons already explained, this idealistic view of Lamanites was soon displaced by the more realistic and less benign definition of them as "Indians," which (with some optimistic qualifications) obtained until the middle of the twentieth century. Then, through the leadership especially of Spencer W. Kimball, a new "day of the Lamanite" was envisioned, which would finally redeem the Lamanites to their divine destiny. When, as Indians, they failed to respond adequately to the massive church investment in that destiny, it was time to look elsewhere for Lamanites of a more receptive nature. The church looked southward, where it had already seen some encouraging signs.

Of course, Mormon missionary success in certain parts of the world has often been accompanied by a reallocation of missionary effort and resources to those places, which in turn stimulates still more church growth. The same process has also encouraged doctrinal and mythological explanations for such success, both at the official and at the folk levels of discourse. Recall the example in chapter 2 of this reciprocal relation between rapid church growth and doctrinal development accompanying Mormon success in the British Isles and Scandinavia during the mid-nineteenth century. The thousands of converts from that part of the world gave strong support to beliefs about British Israelism and Anglo-Saxon triumphalism that were imported into Mormonism and remained pervasive well into the twentieth century. Similar attributions of literal Israelite ancestry were extended to the Polynesian peoples during the same general period, as they became Mormons in disproportionate numbers (see chapter 4). Early Mormon leaders and missionaries found especially receptive Israelite descendants in many parts of the world as time went on.

It is thus not surprising that the remarkable receptivity to the Mormon message in Latin America would have been accompanied by a new outpouring of missionary enthusiasm for the prospects among the "new Lamanites" there. Not that these prospects had been ignored earlier, for Mormon forays into Mexico and Latin America had occurred several times, though never with the success that came in the late twentieth century (A. Palmer and Grover 1999; Sorenson 1985, 1–5). The rapid loss of official Mormon enthusiasm for the "old Lamanites" during the same period might seem a little more surprising at first glance, but not when we remember the reciprocal lack of enthusiasm for the Mormon message and way of life among the North American aboriginal peoples themselves. Despite the high hopes of the founders of Mormonism for the fulfillment of glorious Book of Mormon prophecies about the eventual destiny of the Lamanites, white Mormons were never able to get past their own essentially racist understanding of these Indian peoples or of why they had never been eager and enduring converts.

Deconstructing the Lineage of the "Old" Lamanites

The new successes in Latin America enabled the Anglo-Mormons gradually to reconstruct their definition of *Lamanite* in such a way as to transfer the divine destiny implied in that term to the peoples of the South, while leaving increasingly dubious the divine status of the aboriginal Indians of the North who had originally been considered the true Lamanites of the Book of Mormon. It is important to emphasize that this reconstruction of the Lamanite label has so far been only an *operational* redefinition. As will be seen, there is reason to believe that concomitant changes have been underway in the traditional Mormon theological and scriptural understanding about Lamanites, but not yet officially. However, for the "new Lamanites" to replace the "old" ones in Mormon thinking, whether operationally or theologically, some redefinition would first have to occur in the special status that Mormons had attributed to the "old" for 150 years. The first public indication of this reduced status also carried considerable official weight. It took the form of the rather strident address to a 1979 assembly of BYU's Indian students by Boyd K. Packer, discussed in the previous chapter.[18]

After chiding the young Indian BYU students for failing to maintain church commitment and service, Packer briefly criticized an apparently growing tendency for interracial marriage, which would further attenuate their identification with the chosen Lamanite lineage so important in the church's sacred history: "We counsel you . . . to marry . . . within your race. Now inter-racial marriages are not prohibited but they are not encouraged, for the blood that's in your veins is the blood of the children of the covenant. . . . You have a destiny. You are chosen to serve" (1979, 13). Pure Lamanite lineage was still important. Toward the end of his speech, Packer pointed to examples of Lamanite leaders and members who had been diligent and faithful, including George P. Lee, then still a general authority in the church, but he placed far more emphasis on examples from Latin America, where there were "ten regional representatives . . . and nearly a hundred stake presidents [and other important leaders] in . . . Lamanite stakes . . . [in] more than one of which all the members of the stake are pure-blood Indians" (1979, 11).

On the one hand, Packer was pointing to some positive and constructive role models. On the other hand, he was also making a forceful and invidious contrast between the faithfulness of the Lamanite church members in the southern parts of the hemisphere and the more desultory kind of commitment he saw among the North American tribes. As construed by Packer and other church leaders, since all the aboriginal peoples of the hemisphere were of the same "race" and lineage (H. Brown 1972; LDS Indian Committee 1971 and 1972), it behooved those in the North, who had been favored to receive the gospel the earliest, to stay with and strengthen their own kind by devoting themselves to spreading the gospel southward instead of chasing after worldly success and "diluting" their divinely favored lineage through intermarriage with whites or others.[19] While it would be an exaggeration to say that church leaders in the late twentieth century were still preoccupied with maintaining lineage identities, it would be also be fair to say that lineage considerations continued to influence their thinking, if only in pointing to role models. That is, "pure-blooded Lamanites" could be held up as examples to others of high achievement despite their disadvantaged origins. This point is occasionally made in official church periodicals, as well, such as the case of the stake president in Guatemala, who was also a respected local civic leader and, as a "full-blooded Mayan, . . . a source of pride for local Church members, [for] those with ancestry such as his are held in high esteem by their fellow Guatemalans" (Searle 1985, 23–24).

If Packer's 1979 address at BYU signaled the beginning of the end for the special church programs devoted to North American Indians, it also reflected a recognition that recent missionary efforts in Latin America had yielded a bounteous harvest. Whether in North or South America, missions among presumably Lamanite peoples had been reopened only about three decades— roughly since the end of World War II—but with vastly different results in the two regions. In the Mormon heartland or "backyard," missionary work had resumed among the tribal peoples in 1943 with the opening of the Navaho-Zuni Mission, later renamed, expanded, and divided into other missions serving primarily Indians or Lamanites. By 1980, at about the time of Packer's observations, LDS membership among these peoples could be counted only in the few tens of thousands, many of whom were no longer active, despite twenty years of heavy church investments in free education and community development programs. By contrast, in Mexico and the rest of Latin America, where missionary work had also resumed after World War II, LDS membership was already being counted in the hundreds of thousands and growing rapidly.

While Packer did not explicitly remove the "Lamanite" designation from the North American tribal peoples, the effect of his remarks at least left their status somewhat ambiguous. Since they had proved increasingly difficult to convert and retain, their "Lamanite blood" or identity seemed somehow in question or at least much less salient to Mormons than their "Indian" identity; conversely, the Lamanite label came to seem more fitting and compelling when applied to the eager and numerous converts in Latin America. This change occurred not so much in popular thinking, for grassroots church members rarely take notice of whether a term in Mormon discourse means exactly the same thing at one point in time as it meant in an earlier one. Traditional usages simply change somewhat across time, in both official and popular discourse. The use of *Lamanite* in Mormon history is somewhat like the use of the terms *Israelite* or *Gentile*. That is, all these terms have expanded or contracted somewhat in scope depending on missionary experiences and expectations. Recall that Israelite descendants (or the "blood of Israel") were once found in special abundance by Mormon missionaries in the British Isles and northwestern Europe, but eventually the harvest of Israelites there diminished drastically, while missionary success and prospects revealed the blood of Israel more abundantly elsewhere, especially in Polynesia but even in Japan.

There have been no official church pronouncements in recent years on exactly which peoples are and are not included in the term *Lamanite* (H. Brown 1972). Even church leaders themselves might not have noticed the frequency with which North American Indians have been displaced in church discourse by Latin American peoples whenever the term *Lamanite* is used. Relevant articles in the quasi-official *Encyclopedia of Mormonism* (Ludlow 1992) reveal this change in discourse. *Encyclopedia* articles entitled "Native Americans" (981–85) and "The Lamanite Mission of 1830–1831" (802–4) do recognize Joseph Smith's original understanding that the Indian tribes forcibly moved west of the Mississippi River were considered Lamanites. However, in its articles on *contemporary* LDS understandings, the *Encyclopedia* is very circumspect in avoiding identification of the Book of Mormon account with any particular peoples or places in today's world, except the Western Hemisphere in general.

For example, the article entitled "Lamanites" attributes this identity to *various* peoples, "depending on contextual specifics regarding peoples, time, and place," acknowledging only that the earliest Mormon missionaries "were sent to people *thought to have* Lamanite ancestry" (805, emphasis added); and the one entitled "Book of Mormon Peoples" identifies the Lamanites simply and generally as "dissenters [from] the Nephites" (191). The *Encyclopedia* article entitled "Book of Mormon Geography" reviews the variety of theories that Mormons have had on that subject, with particular reference to the ambiguity that has existed across time in *official* thinking and discourse (178). As Kenneth W. Godfrey indicates, church leaders over the years have had various ideas on where the Book of Mormon story took place, but they have not discouraged "students and scholars in their studies [on] Book of Mormon geography" (1999, 79). The shifting referent of *Lamanite* in recent decades seems attributable far less to explicit official preference than to the initiative and commitment of influential Mormon intellectuals and scholars, both amateur and professional. While this process became especially conspicuous and effective toward the end of the twentieth century, its origins are at least a hundred years older, and thereby hangs a tale.

Early Quests for the "New" Lamanites

Despite a whole century of focusing primarily on the North American tribal peoples as the Lamanites of the LDS scriptures, church leaders had never excluded the possibility that other aboriginal peoples might also be Lamanites (e.g., "Discovery of Ancient Ruins in Central America" 1833, 71). Even Polynesians were potentially included in this identity, particularly given the eagerness with which they began embracing Mormonism from about 1860. Yet the probable identification especially of South and Central America with the Book of Mormon story had entered Mormon thinking early on because of certain geographical clues in the text of the book, such as the "narrow neck of land" (Stephens 1842, 913). However, this hypothesis also assumed that the ancient protagonists of the story had eventually migrated northward during their intermittent hostilities, ending up in a climactic civil war in or near what eventually became upstate New York. Later in the nineteenth century and especially in the twentieth, as various archaeological explorations and discoveries uncovered advanced ancient civilizations from Mexico to the Andes, Mormons increasingly and optimistically began looking to that southerly part of the hemisphere for more definitive clues about the true origins of the Book of Mormon story.

   The Mexican Mission opened again in 1901, after earlier abortive efforts and a long pause in missionary work generally among Indians (Tullis 1987, 73–86; Tullis 1997–98). This reopening gave special impetus to the rising Mormon interest in Latin America as the stage for the Book of Mormon panorama. Beginning early in the century, a few expeditions were launched by amateur Mormon archaeologists in search of ancient cities and artifacts that could be identified with civilizations described in the Book of Mormon.

None of these efforts, however, yielded the vindication of Mormon claims that had been sought. Interestingly enough, the initiatives for exploration and research that might "prove" the Book of Mormon have usually come not from the church leadership itself but from committed academics and intellectuals. Certainly church leaders individually or collectively have sometimes given moral or even financial support to such scholarly or scientific enterprises, but the faith of most leaders in the divine origin of the Book of Mormon has been so secure that empirical "proofs" have generally seemed of secondary importance to them.[20]

Whatever significance the new focus on Mexico might have had to the leaders, it was accompanied by an adventurous optimism on the part of certain academics and others, especially Benjamin C. Cluff, president of Brigham Young Academy (now Brigham Young University). From 1900 to 1902, Cluff led a band of explorers to Colombia in search of the fabled city of Zarahemla described in the Book of Mormon. A logistical and human disaster, the expedition was aborted, yielding mainly some specimens of tropical flora for exhibit at the academy (Bergera and Priddis 1985, 10–12; S. Taylor 1978, 147–72). One of the expedition's members, however, the converted German scholar Paul Henning, was later the first Mormon to undertake professional archaeological research in Latin America, under both governmental and private auspices (Fullmer 2000). A little later, B. H. Roberts, while stoutly defending the Book of Mormon in his three-volume treatise (1909), cautioned against expecting too much from archaeological and ethnographic accounts and argued that the Book of Mormon should not necessarily be taken as a general history of the ancient peoples of the whole hemisphere (Bitton 1999, 73).

This flurry of scholarly engagement with the Book of Mormon around the turn of the century did not last very long. The Cluff debacle, national economic setbacks, and world wars all seem to have dampened for awhile any official or scholarly interest in finding archaeological support for the Book of Mormon. A reduced emphasis on the Book of Mormon generally occurred during the first half of the twentieth century (N. Reynolds 1999). This apparent decline in scholarly interest coincided with at least three other developments with which it would have been compatible. One was the long hiatus in Mormon (and American) engagement with American Indians from about 1890 to 1940. A second was the general LDS neglect of missionary work in South America during the same period (except among recent European immigrants there), perhaps in favor of work among the more receptive Polynesians.[21] Third, the soft-pedaling of the Book of Mormon, even within the church, was part of the assimilationist mode the church leadership adopted during the first half of the century, when the King James Version of the Bible (shared with most other denominations) was preferred over the peculiarly Mormon scriptures in church discourse and teaching (Mauss 1994, 102–8).

By about 1950, with the Great Depression and World War II behind them, both the LDS Church in Utah and the nation as a whole had gained a new respectability and had begun to turn again to more normal concerns. In this environment, church leaders began to promote a new interest in the Book of Mormon to accompany the new missionary initiatives among the Lamanite peoples of both North and South America. In North America, as already explained, the church programs emphasized assimilation of tribal peoples through placement of Indian children with white foster families during the school year, as well as through generous BYU scholarships for Indian youths of college age. Meanwhile, throughout Mexico and Latin America, new missions were opened by the score during the next few decades. Since it was also in this southern part of the hemisphere that important archaeological remains were increasingly discovered, Mormon scholars began again to look southward for empirical authentication of the Book of Mormon (H. Peterson 1992, 172; N. Reynolds 1999, 17–18).

With the creation of the Department of Archaeology at BYU in the mid-1940s, archaeological expeditions into Central America were resumed. Promising initial results were reported from these forays, but university officials and some church leaders were reluctant to see academic integrity compromised by conspicuously tying the mission of a university department to an ecclesiastical project, such as "proving" the Book of Mormon. To keep church-sponsored archaeological research somewhat separate from the university, some church funding was therefore diverted to the New World Archaeological Foundation (NWAF), privately established in 1952 by a group of amateurs and professionals headed by the California attorney Thomas Stuart Ferguson and the BYU anthropologist Wells Jakeman (Howell, Ranae, and Copeland 1959–95).[22] The foundation's work yielded very little evidence in support of its claims about ties between ancient America and the Book of Mormon, despite several years of exploration, research, and in-house publications, to say nothing of the expenditure of hundreds of thousands of church and private dollars. NWAF enthusiasts were inclined to make excessive claims about the nature and significance of their findings, but few of their claims stood up to the scrutiny of non-Mormon scientific peers (Bergera and Priddis 1985, 84–86; S. Brewer 1999; John Clark 1999, 22–33; Larson 1990; Larson 1996, 41–84, 175–234).

Meanwhile, a totally different approach to scholarly research on the Book of Mormon was being advocated by Hugh W. Nibley, who joined the BYU faculty in 1946. Depending primarily on literary, textual, and historical criticism, Nibley argued that the strongest evidence for the authenticity of the Book of Mormon is in the pages of the book itself, not in archaeology. His approach has consisted largely of demonstrating literary and historical parallels between the text of the Book of Mormon and histories of the ancient

Near East, which could not have been known to Joseph Smith (D. Salmon 2000). Nibley's publications are voluminous, but much of his work remains controversial, especially to non-Mormons, because so few academic peers are able to give it the kind of interdisciplinary critique that is required, and because his writing style is not only verbose but digressionary and obfuscating. However, among his many valuable writings, three books have remained enduring contributions to Mormon popular literature at the "high-brow" level (Nibley 1950, 1951, and 1957). The first two of these were serialized in church magazines before their publication as books; the third is derivative of the first two and was once used throughout the church as the official priesthood study manual for adult males.[23]

FARMS, BYU, and the Construction of the "New" Lamanite Identity

The disappointments of Mormon scholars in the results of archaeological research, combined with the appeal of Nibley's alternative approach to vindicating the Book of Mormon, led eventually to the establishment of the Foundation for Ancient Research and Mormon Studies (FARMS) in 1979. Originally based in California with its principal founder, John W. Welch, FARMS soon moved to Provo, Utah, when Welch joined the faculty of the J. Reuben Clark School of Law at Brigham Young University. FARMS functioned for nearly two decades as a private foundation with the approval of both BYU and the church, but without funding from either, until it was amicably brought under BYU's administration in 1997. This development certainly enhanced the resource base of FARMS, both materially and intellectually, but only time will tell how much its intellectual independence has been compromised, if at all, by the new and closer relationship with the church through the university. To be sure, one reason that the BYU "takeover" was so amicable was that FARMS had always understood its mission as fundamentally helping to vindicate LDS truth-claims, particularly about the Book of Mormon as ancient scripture (Reynolds 1998 and 1999, 37–40).

This is not the place for a full description of the impressive work done by FARMS, which has included the production of regular research papers, videos, and books by affiliated scholars; the publication of Hugh Nibley's collected works; the semi-annual *Journal of Book of Mormon Studies* (since 1990); reprints of research articles by non-Mormons on topics directly or indirectly supportive of the historicity of the Book of Mormon and the Bible; special projects on ancient scripture not related to the Book of Mormon, such as the Dead Sea Scrolls; and many other projects.[24] However valuable all these products are, my main interest here is in the part FARMS has played in the recent process of constructing a new or revised identity for the Lamanites.

A key figure in this process has been John L. Sorenson, professor emeritus of anthropology at BYU. If it was Boyd Packer who, in 1979, first directed the gaze of BYU southward, away from the North American Indians, it was John Sorenson (1985) who offered a specific and credible theory about just *where* in the South the church might expect to find most of the "new Lamanites." In this effort, Sorenson soon acquired the backing of Welch and most of the other scholars at FARMS.

In *An Ancient American Setting for the Book of Mormon,* Sorenson is careful to make no explicit claim of "proof" that the Book of Mormon story literally took place in one or another specific location in Latin America.[25] Instead, through a meticulous study of the text itself, he details the spatial and temporal relationships among such major topographical features as seas, lakes, rivers, and mountains, as well as the estimated days of travel from place to place, all as given in the narrative. Then he creates an abstract or generic map (or series of maps) showing all those landmarks in relation to one another. It is as though he were sketching the map(s) on large transparencies and then looking for visual correspondence, as it were, between the "transparency" and the various locations on actual maps of the Southern Hemisphere. He finds the closest correspondences in Mesoamerica, a stretch of a few hundred miles of southern Mexico (including Yucatan) and Guatemala, homeland primarily of the Maya peoples. He then looks for additional and corroborating correspondences between, on the one hand, the flora, fauna, and certain other features now found in that area and, on the other hand, those described in the Book of Mormon. Sorenson's conclusion is not that the Book of Mormon necessarily took place in Mesoamerica, but that *if* it took place in the Americas, that area seems an especially likely location.

Notice that in this approach Sorenson has made use of at least two techniques that avoid the disappointments (and even ridicule) resulting from earlier Mormon efforts to find specific archaeological and artifactual "proofs" for the authenticity of the Book of Mormon. First, like Nibley, he starts with the text of the Book of Mormon itself and looks for *parallels* "on the ground," as it were. This approach carries its own hazards, of course (D. Salmon 2000), but an "argument by parallel" offers plausibility without falsifiability, making it especially appealing to believers. In this way, it can be argued that a certain element in the Book of Mormon is *consistent with* a similar or parallel occurrence elsewhere, without claiming that the two are necessarily connected. (Scientists must sometimes depend on such "reasoning from consistency" when they have a plausible theory but insufficient evidence for causal inferences.) Second, the Sorenson model, with its basis mainly in geography and topography, is not dependent on *archaeological* evidence as such, the *absence* of which could be taken as countervailing evidence by his critics. In other words, if the location he proposed "makes sense" in terms of spatial and topographical relationships, it does not matter whether any La-manite artifacts have yet been found there.

This general approach, by the way, has characterized much of the work done by FARMS generally on the Book of Mormon—namely, pointing to geographic and historical parallels rather than specific archaeological artifacts (N. Reynolds 1998). Occasional resorts to archaeological evidence, when consistent with the text, have usually been limited to discoveries already published by non-Mormons. The risks inherent in such selective reliance on science are starting to appear in recent evidence from research in genetics and DNA ("The Problematic Role of DNA Testing in Unraveling Human History" 2000). Such evidence might prove a two-edged sword. On the one hand, it has the potential of identifying which aboriginal peoples of the Western Hemisphere, if any, have genetic traits that might link them to Hebrew or Semitic origins; on the other hand, the same kind of evidence can fail to show any such connection for any of these aboriginal peoples. This two-edged sword has recently been drawn, perhaps inadvertently, in a project at BYU itself (Egan 2000). Nevertheless, the monthly newsletter *Insights* and the semi-annual *Journal of Book of Mormon Studies*, both published by FARMS, regularly feature discoveries by non-Mormon archaeologists and other scientists that seem consistent with the narrative in the Book of Mormon (and occasionally even when not consistent—e.g., Stubbs [2000] and "Asiatic Origin of Na-Dene Languages [Navajo and Relatives]" [1999]). Recently *BYU Studies* has also featured special articles in the same general vein (e.g., Houston 1999)—not surprising considering that since 1991 the editor of that publication has been John W. Welch.[26]

Of course, the continuing interest of LDS publications in ancient American civilizations *generally* is not particularly noteworthy, for that interest has been apparent throughout the twentieth century. Much more to the point here is the special focus on Mesoamerica. This region had been considered before, even by church leaders, as a promising location for the discovery of archaeological traces of the Book of Mormon story (e.g., M. Hunter 1956; and Romney 1957). Yet the frequency and intensity of the focus on Mesoamerica by FARMS and BYU have surely been unprecedented since the appearance of John Sorenson's (1985) work. It seems fair to infer that what might be called the Sorenson thesis, outlined above, has become the operative premise of FARMS and BYU. It would not even be much of a stretch to regard this thesis as the one most favored by the Mormon leadership, given the quasi-official endorsement in the *Encyclopedia of Mormonism* that Sorenson's work "has placed the study of the ancient American background of the Book of Mormon on a scholarly footing as [has] no previous work" (Ricks 1992, 208). More recently, a major film produced by the church for popular consumption, Mormon and non-Mormon, relied heavily on Sorenson's (1998) visualizations of the lands and peoples of the Book of Mormon.[27]

Some official approbation could already be reasonably inferred from the space allocated to Sorenson's work (1984) in successive issues of the official magazine *Ensign* in obvious anticipation and promotion of his major 1985 book. In such a popular medium, Sorenson's ideas would also be far more accessible than the book itself to Mormons at the grassroots. In these articles, as in the book, Sorenson is careful to leave many historical and archaeological issues open and to distinguish his "scholarly" approach from "official Church teachings." Nevertheless, after duly reviewing the evidence from historians and archaeologists, Mormon and non-Mormon, Sorenson concludes that "only one area qualifies in all respects" as the locale for the Book of Mormon account, namely, Mesoamerica (1984, 1:30). It seems significant in retrospect, though perhaps not premeditated, that this new Mesoamerican focus in official church publications was occurring just as the church was phasing out its long-standing special programs for the Lamanites of North America (during the 1980s).

Besides Sorenson's books and derivative work, evidence is not hard to find for this virtually exclusive preoccupation with Mesoamerica and the Mayan region as the setting for the Book of Mormon story. FARMS has sponsored conferences and publications that have considered a variety of possible geographies for the Book of Mormon story (e.g., John Clark 1989, a review of Hauck 1988). Yet the Mesoamerican location favored by Sorenson continues to get by far the most attention, for rarely is any other New World location suggested in FARMS publications as an alternative. For example, the 1999 FARMS catalogue lists a dozen of Sorenson's publications dealing, in one way or another, with Mesoamerica, plus a few others on Mesoamerica by FARMS-affiliated scholars. The *Journal of Book of Mormon Studies* has also published many important articles and news items on ancient Mayans and Mesoamericans, with topics ranging from serpent worship to warfare. Especially noteworthy in this focus on the Mayan heritage was the rather extraordinary effort that produced a FARMS translation of the *Popol Vuh,* a pre-Columbian Maya text, which the translator offers readers for its many "traditions and concepts that are generally found only in cultures familiar with the Hebrew Bible."[28]

Whether or not formally backed by the church leadership, this focus on a Mesoamerican identity for the Lamanites continues to receive BYU endorsement in a variety of informal (and even commercial) ways that can be expected to popularize the conception and facilitate its filtration to the grassroots for some time to come. Every year the BYU Department of Travel Study features cruises and tours to Mesoamerican sites ostensibly (but not explicitly) associated with the Book of Mormon story. These are frequently led by current or retired employees of the church or of BYU. For example, an August 1995 brochure from that BYU department, entitled *The Mayas and the Times of the Book of Mormon,* while acknowledging that the "Church has taken no official position on Book of Mormon sites," nevertheless goes on to lay out a number of similarities between the Mayas and characteristics of "the Book of Mormon peoples" and then invites its readers to send in a deposit for a tour to Mexico and Guatemala over Christmas vacation. A similar brochure from the same source in June 1997 under the title *Choice above All Other Lands* carries the usual disclaimer about any official church endorsement of Central America as the site of the Book of Mormon account. Yet it goes on to identify Guatemala and the Maya people as "likely possibilities" and then cites a 1996 visit to Guatemala by the president of the church, who is quoted as referring to his LDS audience there as "sons and daughters of Father Lehi." Even a Florida cruise company has sought a "piece of the action," appealing to presumably LDS customers by featuring John L. Sorenson as a lecturer on a week-long cruise in the same region to "Catch the Spirit of Zarahemla."[29]

Uses of Constructed Identities by the New Lamanites

If the Anglo-Mormon establishment has found renewed interest in attributing Lamanite identity to the peoples of Mesoamerica, Mormon converts from the region have found reasons of their own for appropriating and using that same identity. They appear to have done so somewhat more readily than did their cousins among the North American tribes, who have been designated above as the "old Lamanites." There are understandable reasons for this difference. In North America, the Anglo-Mormons never quite succeeded in distinguishing themselves, at least in Indian eyes, from white America more generally. While the Mormon program for Indians had benign intentions and was more comprehensive and sophisticated in the mid-twentieth century than it had been in the mid-nineteenth, its major objective remained assimilation. To the native peoples and their leaders, this had always meant the wholesale destruction of the native cultures, at best, and sheer genocide, at worst. By contrast, in Mexico and in Latin America generally, conversion to Mormonism (or to most Protestant faiths) has not required a complete abandonment of the aboriginal or mestizo cultures and languages, at least not by definition. Converts have therefore been able to make such adaptations and uses of Mormonism in their lives as they have found comfortable, without being culturally taken over and absorbed by the Mormon religion—a point made in passing by both Thomas Murphy (1997) and Eduardo Pagán (1989b).

The appropriation of the Lamanite identity in Latin America occurred first in Mexico, well before the special new FARMS emphasis on Mesoamerica. From 1901, when the first permanent Mormon mission was established in Mexico, until the mid-1930s, about three thousand Mexicans were convert-

ed by only a few missionaries. For its time, this was one of the more successful missions in the church and until 1925 the only one in Latin America. By
this time, much more had been discovered than in Joseph Smith's day about
the ancient cities of Mexico and Latin America. Mormon leaders and missionaries were routinely assuming and preaching that such archaeological
remnants had been left by the civilizations described in the Book of Mormon.[30] Accordingly, the Mormon message in Mexico emphasized the Lamanite heritage of these converts and potential converts. Such lore was thus already traditional among Mesoamerican Mormons by the time of the newly
emphasized focus on that region led by the scholars at FARMS. Yet the crucial question is whether this Lamanite identity has been internalized by the
Mormon converts there. We cannot be sure about this without a general
survey, but there have been some indications.

The first indication occurred in their widespread and enthusiastic acceptance of an unofficial book published by Margarito Bautista Valencia (1935),
a convert and amateur scholar born in 1878.[31] This work was a rather poorly
organized 500-page blending of materials from the Old Testament, the Book
of Mormon, certain pseudepigrapha, and some of Joseph Smith's writings.
Bautista not only took seriously what the missionaries had taught him about
his own Lamanite lineage but also used that concept as the central idea in a
general theory about the divine destiny of Mexico and the Mexicans as the
true Israelites—in contradistinction to the Gentiles (including white Mormons) of Europe and North America.[32] Bautista also challenged the legitimacy of control from Utah over the affairs of the Saints in Mexico, basing
his position partly on the claim that Anglo-Mormons were Israelites not by
actual lineage, as they had been assuming, but only by "adoption." The true
Israelite lineage in the hemisphere was to be found among the descendants
of the Lamanites. (Here he was anticipating by half a century the claims of
George P. Lee, mentioned earlier.) Since Bautista's book constituted a strong
argument for the conversion of all Mexicans to Mormonism, he apparently
expected to be rewarded with church publication of his book and an appointment as mission president in Mexico.

Bautista, however, had seriously overestimated the appeal of his book to
the Utah leaders and underestimated their reaction to his critique of their
ecclesiastical control. He eventually had to resort to a local publisher for his
book, and the next mission president was neither Bautista nor any other
Mexican but, again, an Anglo-Mormon. Furthermore, the Utah leadership
strenuously criticized him and his numerous sympathizers, directing them
to fall in line behind the leaders God had appointed over them. The eventual result was a 1936 schism that drew away a third of all Mexican Mormons
in a movement called the Third Convention—so called because it was the
third of three gatherings that local Mormons had held since 1932 over their

dissatisfactions with the Utah leadership (Murphy 2000, 203–6; Tullis 1987, 137–68; Tullis 1997). Bautista and other leaders of the movement were eventually excommunicated. However, the movement continued to grow, alongside mainstream Mormonism in Mexico, until 1946, when a new and more conciliatory church leadership arose in both Utah and Mexico. At that point, most of the schismatics returned to the church. Bautista, for his part, not only was never reconciled but became increasingly radical and eventually joined in the creation of an even smaller schismatic movement (Murphy 2000, 205–6; Tullis 1987, 145–59). Yet his ideas continued to influence Mexican and other Latin American Mormons, probably even to the present time.

One indication of this influence can be seen in the career of Agrícol Lozano Herrera (1926–99), two generations later (Murphy 2000, 205–6; Tullis 1987, 201–10). Lozano was a second-generation Mormon and the first Mexican Lamanite to preside over a Mormon stake (diocese). He went on to receive virtually every other high position in the church leadership, short of the general authority level. His service included presiding over one of the missions in Argentina, so his influence extended beyond Mexico proper. He also enjoyed a successful law career, negotiating, among other things, the formal registration of the LDS Church with the Mexican government in 1993. As a loyal Latter-day Saint throughout his life, Lozano was highly regarded by church leaders and in regular contact with them. His *Historia del Mormonismo en México* (1983) was much more supportive of the conventional LDS ecclesiastical structure and authority than was Bautista's tome. Furthermore, Lozano was harshly critical of the Third Convention, especially of Bautista and the role he had played as an apostate. Despite that criticism, Lozano's ideas strongly suggest the continuing influence of the major themes originally introduced into LDS Mexican lore by Bautista.

Like Bautista, Lozano embraced the Lamanite identity for himself and other Mexicans. Much more so than Bautista, however, he acknowledged and accepted the negative light in which the Lamanites are usually cast in the Book of Mormon, and he admonished his readers to reject the ancient Lamanites' tendencies toward rebellion and criticism of church leaders (Murphy 2000, 196–99, 207–8). For the faithful Mexican Saints, he promised prosperity, a divine destiny, and important roles in church leadership, as Bautista had done. However, he portrayed Euroamericans as fellow Israelites ("Brother Ephraim") rather than as Gentiles and praised the joint struggle shared by the two kinds of Israelites (Anglo and Mexican) in building the kingdom of God in his country. All of this would certainly have garnered the approval of the Anglo-Mormon leadership, for there was no counterclaim of the Bautista kind against the legitimacy of Utah control over the church in Mexico. Like Bautista before him, Lozano also asserted unequivocally (and without official objection) that the story of the Book of Mormon took place in Mexico among the ancestors of Toltecs, Mayas, and Aztecs; in fact, he explained, the name Mexico is derived from the Hebrew word for Messiah. Yet the Mexicans share a kinship with the other "Lamanite" peoples of North and South America, as well as those in the Pacific Islands.

Perhaps Lozano's more conciliatory posture toward the Utah leadership was partly a reflection of some moderation of the national and ethnic sensitivity that had been aroused among Mexican Mormons in Bautista's time and expressed in his ideas. Yet those ideas have continued to have a profound impact. As F. LaMond Tullis explained it, "Mexican Mormons did not read Bautista's book in the detached way most North Americans then and now would read it, but fully emotionally, as if they were reading their own family history. Searching for a proud national heritage, they welcomed grand stories of the noble Aztecs and Mayas, . . . of their ancestors who had formed great, civilized, chosen nations [and of] the future prophesied for Israel's American descendants" (1987, 124–25).[33] As Murphy summarized the matter, "Mexican converts to Mormonism innovatively adapted racist stereotypes for their own purposes, surprisingly employing them in a self-affirming ethnic identity" (1999, 471).[34] Jorge Iber (2000, 60, 91) and Orlando Rivera (1978) pointed to the same process among Mexican and other Hispanic converts who had immigrated to Utah.

Appropriations and uses of the Lamanite identity to foster ethnic pride have not been limited to Mexican Mormons. LDS converts throughout Latin America have been able to use the Lamanite identity to claim a special or divine distinction in contrast to both their Hispanic colonial conquerors and their Anglo-Mormon coreligionists. Already in 1972, Latin American Mormons were being encouraged to do so in the official church magazine itself. An important article recognizes the variety of legitimate ways in which Latin Americans might identify themselves but then goes on to counsel the Saints in Peru and the surrounding countries that they are "remiss" if they fail to "dignif[y] the Indian part of [their] *mestizo* . . . origins . . ."; for the "'chosen people' heritage of the Lamanites is fruitful [i.e., useful] where national leaders have been inspired to help dignify the Indian heritage, where tribal groups have retained a sense of ethnic dignity on their own . . ." (H. Brown 1972, 62, 63).

Murphy (1996 and 1997) has found convincing evidence that the Mayan and Ladino converts in Guatemala have been taking such counsel seriously. One expression of it has been the occasional use of the Book of Mormon to claim literal Israelite (Lamanite) ancestry and to validate the *Popol Vuh*, a traditional Mayan epic. Other expressions have included a local adaptation of the Mormon dietary code, or Word of Wisdom. In Bolivia, too, according to the anthropologist David Knowlton, the rural Aymara people have found the value of their ethnic heritage strengthened in the Book of Mormon, while simultaneously the urban mestizos have used the same source to validate their "ethnic and social position" in contrast to the encroaching peasantry (1988, 150; see also 1996).

Polynesian Mormons have made similar uses of their constructed Israelite heritage for more than a century. Despite a rather tenuous basis in the Mormon canon for the Polynesian claim to such an identity, the claim has been widely embraced among Mormons in both North America and Polynesia.[35] New Zealand's Maoris have received more attention in that regard than perhaps most of the other island peoples, with the possible exception of the Hawaiians. About 10 percent of the Maoris of New Zealand today are members of the LDS Church. As one might expect, more than half of all Maoris are affiliated with either the Church of England or the Roman Catholic church, which are, of course, predominantly white or Pakeha in membership. Yet the Mormon church in New Zealand has a much stronger Maori presence than these percentages would indicate, because most Maori Mormons actually attend church with some regularity and because Maoris are more fully integrated with Pakehas at the congregational level than in those larger denominations (Barber 1995; Britsch 1981; Lineham 1991; Mol 1966; Newton 1996 and 1998).

Of special interest for our purposes here is the interesting analysis by Grant Underwood (2000) of the Maori Mormons' blending of their native oral traditions with the Bible and the Book of Mormon to provide a basis for their claim to authentic Israelite identity (see also Midgley 1999). One of the important uses of this combined religious and ethnic identity by the Maoris was as a means of resisting the assimilation the British settlers were attempting to impose on them. Hans Mol has pointed to a related function, somewhat reminiscent of the one in Latin America: The LDS religion "offers a modern *non-Maori* culture [i.e., American] which [is] also *non-Pakeha* [meaning, in this instance, non-British]. This resolves to some extent the Maori ambivalence toward cultural change [and is a way to] advance economically and still remain distinct from the Pakeha majority" (1966, 59). The Mormons in Tonga provide still another Polynesian example of identity construction using Mormon materials (Gordon 1988).[36] These Mormon examples appear to be only special cases of a much more general process of identity construction and reconstruction occurring whenever a given people is required by circumstances to synthesize older and newer claims on their identity. Chinese Christians in America are another example (Yang 1999).

Conclusion

One of the underlying themes of this book, especially this chapter, has been the construction and uses of identity by one people to enhance its power relative to another people. Often an identity is claimed to modify or resist the imposition of a less desirable or a denigrating identity from the outside, especially from a source with superior power. Such was the use, for example, with the Israelite identity claims in early Utah, as was discussed in chapter 2. The Mormons became a separate people—almost a distinctive ethnic group—within a national context in which they were generally regarded as a pariah people. Drawing partly on nineteenth-century intellectual currents and theories in Europe and America and partly on their own theological innovations, early Mormons were able to identify themselves with a combination of ancient Anglo-Saxon and biblical lore, claiming descent especially from the tribe of Ephraim. This enabled them to draw invidious comparisons between themselves, as a divinely chosen people, and their more powerful American detractors and persecutors. The social and psychological benefit of this strategy, whether calculated or not, was that the more abuse the Mormons suffered, the more vindicated they felt, and the more fully they acted out that identity. Even after political capitulation, the Mormons as a people had a psychological security that enabled them to swim successfully into the cultural mainstream of American assimilation.

One can also put the "power shoe on the other foot," as it were, and see the Mormons as the more powerful side of the struggle in their relations with the tribal peoples of North America. As the previous chapters have demonstrated in some detail, the Mormons, in projecting the Lamanite identity on these Indian tribes, were able to understand them simultaneously as divinely designated objects of conversion and as backward and benighted savages to be "civilized." In the beginning, Joseph Smith and his earliest associates seem to have expected the Indians to be converted quite readily, just as soon as they were taught their true origin and divine destiny from the Book of Mormon. Their "civilizing" would naturally follow at the hands of their Mormon tutors and benefactors, with whom they would join as one people in building Zion. While some of the tribal leaders living near the early Mormons seem to have been intrigued to some extent by the Mormon vision for them, they never really embraced it, nor did the Mormons have a realistic opportunity to pursue this vision until after their own forced migration to the Utah Territory.

Once in Utah, however, the Mormons found themselves among a more powerful and more hostile group of tribes than those who had been their neighbors in Illinois. As the daily realities of this situation settled into the Mormon consciousness, the savage and fallen aspects of the Lamanite identity came to loom much larger than did the divinely destined redemption. The convert-and-civilize sequence envisioned by Joseph Smith was soon reversed by Brigham Young; for the increasingly frequent transactions between Mormons and Indians made clear to the Utah missionaries just how great a cultural chasm would have to be bridged before any enduring conversions could be achieved. Yet, as often as they were required by military and diplomatic necessity to deal with the natives as "Indians," the Mormons never forsook their own optimistic vision of these peoples as "Lamanites" with an ultimately divine destiny. Even this posture was paternalistic and condescending, to be sure, but it seems to have been more benign and less cruel than the treatment the Indians received at the hands of most other white settlers and governments.

In their identification of the Indians with the Lamanites of the Book of Mormon, the Latter-day Saints certainly made a special theological assumption not shared by the rest of the Christians. Yet this distinction must often have been lost on the Indians, who were inclined to see all Euroamericans, whether Mormons or other Christians, as encroaching on their hereditary lands and sustenance. Missionaries from all the religious factions talked a lot about religion, but they also joined with the white settlers and soldiers generally in trying to replace the Indian ways of life with those of the whites. Assimilation in some form was always on the white agenda. All Christians, including the Mormons, shared the ambivalence toward Indians that is inevitable when they are approached as both potential converts and aliens to be civilized.

The Indians had their own ambivalence. They admired much of the technology that could be learned from the whites, and even the Christian religion was palatable for many. Mormons, as well as other missionaries, eventually claimed thousands of Indian converts (depending on the tribe), few of whom, however, endured very long in the faith. In the final analysis, the whites' ways proved all too costly in Indian land, blood, and culture. Three or four waves of Mormon missionaries were sent out during the nineteenth century to various parts of Utah, Nevada, Arizona, and even northern Mexico, with only temporary success. When the massive renewal of Mormon efforts began again in the middle of the twentieth century, they started essentially from zero.

As was seen in the previous chapter, however, even that extensive and comprehensive Mormon investment in Indian missions, education, and technical training, sustained for at least three decades after 1950, once again yielded rather few enduring converts. Whatever the construction of the Lamanite identity entailed for the Mormon missionaries, teachers, and leaders, it carried different meanings for Mormon Indians. Some, such as George P. Lee, sincerely embraced the vision in the Book of Mormon of a divine and glorious destiny for the native peoples, as over against their erstwhile "fallen" condition. He thus saw in the Lamanite identity a basis on which to claim more power and resources for Indian members, even as his white colleagues in the LDS leadership had decided to reduce greatly the church's investments in Indian missions and programs. Others, such as John Rainer, the BYU Indian musician, saw in the Lamanite identity a means for maintaining an essentially assimilated relationship with the LDS Church while resisting demands for his loyalty from activists in the contemporaneous American Indian movement.

Still others, including many of the LDS Indian students who obtained BYU scholarships or who passed through the foster family placement program, seem to have remained ambivalent about their Lamanite identity. On the one hand, they were clearly put off by the traditional Anglo-Mormon portrayal of their Indian cultures as degraded and obsolete—the "Lamanite-as-fallen" image. On the other hand, they recognized the material and cultural advantages accruing to them, as various tribal peoples and as individuals, by participating in the optimistic Mormon vision of their future, despite the concomitant assimilation process. Accordingly, at least during their sojourn in that process, they seem to have embraced the Lamanite identity in varying degrees and with varying success. Yet once they left behind their church sponsorship, whether to seek urban employment or resume life on the reservation, the Lamanite identity did not long survive for many of them. Such is another way of understanding the meaning of Packer's implicit criticism of their fecklessness in the church as he pronounced, in effect, an end to the "day of the Lamanite," at least for the North American tribes.

The "new Lamanites" to the south had their own reasons for embracing and acting on their identity as explained in the Book of Mormon. Especially in the context of rising Mexican nationalism, Bautista's embrace of the Lamanite identity enabled him simultaneously to explain his country's political predicament, indict its colonial oppressors, and claim the moral and spiritual high ground for his people. The influence of Bautista and his less strident successors, such as Lozano, had already prepared the ideological climate of Mormonism in Mesoamerica for the more academic validation of the Lamanite identity promulgated by FARMS and its supporters by the end of the twentieth century. Accordingly, that identity seems to have acquired a receptivity and a usefulness there (and perhaps elsewhere in Latin America) far greater than that which it had ever acquired among the tribal peoples of North America. The needs and interests of a missionary church seem to have converged remarkably well with those of a people in search of a new identity (see also Livingston [2002] on this point).

Notes

1. Smith saw the hand of God in the federal government's removal of Indians to the West, placing them in the immediate vicinity of the prophesied city of Zion to be built in western Missouri (Doctrine and Covenants 28:9, 57:2–3). An Israelite origin for these

Lamanites has yet to find appreciable support in either archaeology or genetics, but modern Native American scholars have also been critical of conventional archaeological theories about crossings from Siberia that ignore aboriginal creation accounts (Deloria 1995; Weaver 1998b).

2. Somewhat ironically, however, such skin-lightening as did occur in this colony resulted from the intermarriage of their descendants with the surrounding whites (S. Christensen 1999, 185–206).

3. This expectation was not entirely one-sided in all cases, since the Catawba converts mentioned in chapter 3 apparently shared the belief that spiritual progress was correlated with lightening of skin color, which in their case also occurred usually through intermarriage (G. Hicks 1977, 64–67).

4. A random sample of every thirteenth name was drawn from the local telephone book, but the return rate from the mailed survey was only 45 percent, despite an elaborate follow-up system. Comments volunteered by respondents on the survey instruments indicated some degree of community hostility to the survey, in keeping with the contemporaneous context of racial tension in the nation.

5. The controversy became especially tense during July and August of 1980, when the main newspaper in nearby Lethbridge, Alberta, carried front-page stories nearly every day. See *Lethbridge Herald* issues during those months.

6. I am indebted to William G. Hartley for furnishing me with a brief secondhand account of this visit and address, which was given to him during an interview with Lee himself. The address was apparently unrehearsed and never written down (Hartley 1980).

7. Interested readers are invited to test my categorizations and tabulations against their own. The "raw" interview forms collected in the survey are deposited with my papers in the archives of the Utah State Historical Society.

8. As though having been persuaded by Nibley in this matter, the creators of a recent church film portrayed all the actors in the Book of Mormon story as having essentially the same skin color. Although the actors had various other physical characteristics indicating origins in Europe, Polynesia, or aboriginal America, they all had the same skin color in the film. The didactic point was deliberate if subtle, since it had obviously been necessary to use coloring makeup on the lighter-skinned actors, especially those of European origin. (See *The Testaments of One Fold and One Shepherd* [2000].) For earlier and perhaps less "authentic" artistic renditions of Book of Mormon characters, see Swanson (2001).

9. See, for example, DF, OH 981; JRH, OH 1181; and KS, OH 1184. Here and in future references to this oral history collection, I am using the initials and transcript numbers (OH) of the respondents.

10. Pagán, for example, pointed to the general Mormon tendency to expect Indian church members to imitate whites in dress, speech, and behavior in order to enjoy full social acceptance: "Mormons have a hard time recognizing that much of [their] experience is spiritualized Anglo-Saxon experience; that our behavior as Mormons, our methods of praying, bearing testimonies, giving talks in Church, etc., are . . . Anglo-Saxon modes of expression" (1989a; see also Pagán [1990]).

11. DF, OH 981; JRH, OH 1181; LN, OH 1167.

12. AL, OH 985; DN, OH 1187; GHC, OH 1171; LN, OH 1167. Of course, there is no monolithic "Indian" viewpoint on anything, including the preference for separate wards. Whatever their degree of assimilation to white Mormon culture, LDS Indians expressed

at least some ambivalence about "All-Lamanite" wards and branches. (See Embry 1990a and 1992b.)

13. See also AL, OH 985; DF, OH 981; and JRC, OH 1180.

14. JLD, OH 1198; JRH, OH 1181; KS, OH 1184; ON, OH 1149.

15. After years of struggling with alcoholism, Clement Bear Chief eventually found his conversion a life-transforming experience, and so did his family. When the story containing this quotation was reprinted in Treat (1996, 223–31), Bear Chief was professional director of welfare for the Siksika nation in Alberta and a leader in the Strathmore Ward of the LDS Church.

16. This song was composed by two young Mormon Indians (Smoot 1968). P. Jane Hafen credited this composition with being true to "native American values of tribal recognition and community" through its portrayal of educational and economic advancement as benefits to the Indians collectively, not just at the individual level (1985, 141).

17. The BYU oral histories from LDS Indians, many of which were collected soon after Lee's excommunication, revealed an interesting range of opinions about the significance of Lee's career and his downfall—and thus derivatively about the validity of his efforts at "displacement." See especially OH numbers 1171, 1180, 1181, 1184, 1187, 1198, and 1488; see also Pagán (1990).

18. Both V. Con Osborne (1986) and David J. Whittaker (1985, 40) also recognized this Packer address as indicating a major policy shift from North to South. The same is implicit even in the title of the apostle Mark E. Petersen's (1981) book.

19. Although considered a problem by many church leaders, intermarriages, particularly between Anglo and Indian Mormons, were occurring with some frequency (Harris 1985, 148; D. Sanders 1985).

20. The two most important examples of active involvement by general authorities of the church in scientific and scholarly research on putative geographical settings for the Book of Mormon were both members of the First Council of Seventy: Brigham H. Roberts (1857–1933) and Milton R. Hunter (1902–75). See Bitton (1999); Roberts (1909); and Hunter and Ferguson (1950).

21. Mormon missionary work in Argentina, Brazil, and other South American countries, though begun in 1925, concentrated almost entirely on European immigrants in those countries until after World War II (Ludlow 1992, 1392–1400; Williams and Williams 1987). The first enduring presence of Mormons in Polynesia dates from the 1860s in Hawaii. Since about 1890, Mormon missionary success throughout Polynesia has been truly remarkable. By the end of the twentieth century, LDS membership in Polynesia and Oceania exceeded 100,000 (Britsch 1992, 1022–26; Shumway 1992, 1110–12).

22. A flurry of enthusiasm for the resumption of archaeological research can be seen in the pages of the official LDS *Improvement Era* during the mid-1940s, just as the BYU Department of Archaeology was being established. Most of these articles were written by that department's Charles E. Dibble. The decision to move church-related archaeology from BYU to the NWAF is reflected in the sudden disappearance of *Improvement Era* articles on this topic after 1948 (Butt 1966; Harold B. Lee Library 1957).

23. The first two also appear together in volume 5 and the third in volume 6 of Nibley's *Collected Works* (1988).

24. See any recent catalogue for FARMS, PO Box 7113, Provo, UT 84604; 1–800–327–6715. The quality and quantity of FARMS publications has been impressive enough for Protestant evangelicals to wonder whether Mormon scholarship is getting the better of

them in the battle of scholarly apologetics, especially where the Book of Mormon is concerned. See Mosser and Owen (1998).

25. But see Sorenson (1990 and 1998) and Sorenson and Raish (1990) for extensions of this 1985 work that develop more explicitly his ideas about the pre-Columbian and Mesoamerican origins of the Book of Mormon.

26. Only three articles on ancient American archaeology had appeared in earlier issues of *BYU Studies,* according to the index for that journal.

27. I am again referring to the film *The Testaments of One Fold and One Shepherd,* issued in 2000 and shown more or less constantly for visiting tourists and church members in the theater of the Smith Memorial Building next to Temple Square in Salt Lake City. Although the film contains at the outset an explicit statement that the exact location of the Book of Mormon events is not known, the architecture and artifacts portrayed are strongly suggestive of Mesoamerica and obviously inspired by the Sorenson (1998) book.

28. See Christenson 2000. The quotation here comes from the FARMS newsletter *Insights* (July 2000, 2). Parallels between the Book of Mormon and the *Popol Vuh* had been claimed by leaders in LDS general conferences at least as early as the mid-1950s (M. Hunter 1956, 50–51; Romney 1957, 80–81). Gordon M. Romney had been president of the Central American Mission and recounted personal interviews with two Maya "chiefs," who, he said, claimed literal descent from Israel and Palestine on the basis of their oral traditions.

29. Copies of these brochures are in my personal files. I hasten to add that I see nothing unethical or inappropriate in these solicitations. I am interested in them here only as vehicles for the popularization of the FARMS construction of the "new Lamanite" identity.

30. One of the most prominent and regular promoters of the idea that the native peoples of Latin America were Israelites and Lamanites was Rey L. Pratt (1878–1931), a general authority of the church who was reared in the Mormon colonies of northern Mexico and devoted nearly all of his adult life to missionary service and leadership in Mexico.

31. My understanding of Bautista's career is based on my reading of Murphy (1999 and 2000, 188–206) and Tullis (1987, 109–68).

32. I am grateful to Dr. Bill L. Smith of the University of Idaho for calling my attention to the similarities between some of Bautista's ideas and those of the contemporaneous scholar José Vasconcelos (1979, e.g., xix, xx, xxvi, 8, 14–16, and 36). The two also had some fundamental differences, but both wrote within the context of the racialist theories popular in Europe and America during the late nineteenth century and early twentieth.

33. In these views, Bautista and his followers would have found support in many public statements by Rey L. Pratt and Anthony W. Ivins, both of whom were also basically sympathetic to the Mexican Revolution (see Livingston 2002, 376–98).

34. I am grateful to Murphy for calling my attention to the perpetuation, even at the dawn of the twenty-first century, of this idea among Mexican Mormon scholars. In a recent reissue of Tullis's *Mormons in Mexico* (1987) in Spanish, a special preface ("Comentario") is added by the translator that sets Tullis's account squarely in the context of the Mormon racialist heritage, even to the extent of quoting the racialist exponent Bruce R. McConkie (1966b, 616) on the premortal foreordination of certain lineages to specific races: "'La raza y nación en la cual el hombre nace en este mundo es un resultado de su vida en la preexistencia . . .'" ("Comentario" in Tullis 1997, ix; see also Murphy [2002]).

35. This is not the place for a general review of the extensive history and uses of Mor-

monism among the various Polynesian peoples, but see Britsch (1986 and 1992) and Shumway (1992). The only basis in Mormon scripture for linking Polynesians to the Book of Mormon account is Alma 63:5–8, which mentions a departure by sea of an expedition from ancient America about 100 B.C.E. Since the expedition never returned, the popular Mormon myth developed that these Lamanites eventually discovered and settled Polynesia, even though the party in the missing expedition was a Nephite one (Loveland 1976; Midgley 1999). Scripture aside, the myth survives on the highly pragmatic basis of long-standing missionary success.

36. I am grateful to Grant Underwood for calling my attention to this convergent research on identity construction.

6. Christian and Mormon Constructions of Jewish Identity

Jesus saith unto [the Jews], if ye were Abraham's children, ye would do the works of Abraham. But now ye seek to kill me. . . . Ye are of your father, the devil. . . . And because I tell you the truth, ye believe me not.

—John 8:39–40, 44–45 (King James Version)

O ye Gentiles, have ye remembered the Jews, mine ancient covenant people? Nay, but ye have cursed them, and have hated them, and have not sought to recover them. But behold, I will return all these things upon your own heads, for I the Lord have not forgotten my people.

—2 Nephi 29:5 (Book of Mormon)

EVEN IN THE genocidal history of twentieth-century Europe, the mass murders of the Jews seem to have been uniquely systematic and extensive. That Christian Europe, which has rightly taken such pride in its centuries of civilization, should have turned its wrath on a minority that had contributed so much to that civilization certainly cries out for an explanation. It is more than a little ironic that so much of the explanation has its origin in the Christian religion itself. As a variety of that religious heritage, Mormonism has shared in the Christian struggle to understand the place of the Jews in the divine scheme of things. Although sometimes called "the Jewish problem," the problem is, of course, actually a Christian one. The Mormon construction of this problem is both similar to and different from the form it has taken in the rest of Christianity, as will be seen, but first let us review the more general Christian legacy, as its development is explained in contemporary scholarship (American Interfaith Institute 1993 and 1994; R. Brown 1994; Crossan 1995; Gager 1983; Pagels 1995; E. Sanders 1985; Segal 1986).

Jewish Identity in Traditional Christian Beliefs

In the decades since the Holocaust, or *Shoah*, of World War II, scholars in many disciplines have studied the history and development of Christian-Jewish relations in an effort to understand how such a disaster could have occurred (Adorno et al. 1950; Gerber 1986; Isaac 1964; Myers [1943] 1960; Novick 1999; Parkes 1963). Psychological, sociological, and economic factors have all been cited as contributing to the particularly vicious and fatal forms of anti-Semitism in the history of Europe (and sometimes in America, as well), but all such factors seem to have their genesis in a religious ideology that defines Jews (at best) as apostate from the Abrahamic religion of the Bible or (at worst) as diabolical enemies to the true Christian religion. For centuries, this identity was imposed on Jews by Christians in the belief that it was justified by such biblical passages as the one attributed to Jesus in the epigraph that opens this chapter. More recent historical studies and biblical criticism, however, have indicated that such expressions are the retrospective attributions of much later Christian writers influenced by the political struggles in first-century Palestine (Anti-Defamation League of B'nai B'rith 1982).

The earliest surviving account of the ministry of Jesus and his contemporaneous conflicts with the Jewish establishment is found in the Gospel of Mark. Some of this account, like Matthew's, might have been influenced by an even earlier source, which no longer survives and is known to scholars only as "Q." The Gospel of Mark has been dated by scholars to the generation just after Jesus, or to about 65–70 C.E., which places it in the context of the general Jewish uprising against the Romans in that period. The apostle John wrote his gospel a generation later, near the end of the first century, and the gospels of Matthew and Luke were produced somewhere between those of Mark and John. According to Elaine Pagels, drawing largely on the work of earlier scholars, all of the gospels were influenced by two simultaneous political struggles underway during the decades after the Jewish uprising: (1) the Roman crackdown and ongoing military campaign to control and pacify Judea or Palestine, and (2) the conflict among at least three different Jewish factions over how to deal with the Romans (1995, xxii, 5–8; see also R. Brown 1994).

In this context, the Jesus movement, then emerging from its Jewish roots, had no desire to join the struggle against the Romans, given its eschatological expectations for the imminent arrival of the kingdom of God on earth. The movement's interests were best served by distinguishing itself, especially in the Roman mind, from the Jews, whose political and religious leaders had, in any case, always been enemies of Jesus and his followers. Having collaborated at times with the Romans, this Jewish establishment was seen by the Jesus movement as now getting its just desserts when Rome finally crushed the revolt. The new movement wanted a separate identity from all this. As Christianity acquired an increasingly Gentile constituency during the first century, the desire for a clear separation from the Jews became even more important.

Thus the Jews came to be identified increasingly as potential rivals and enemies of Jewish Christians, with the Gentiles as the main potential converts (Pagels 1995, 8–11, 27–34). The identification of the Jews as *the Other* occurs in the context of a great cosmic struggle between good and evil (or God and Satan), a framing that becomes increasingly emphatic across time, from the Gospel of Mark, through Matthew and Luke, to John. By about the end of the first century, the earlier distinction between the hostile Jewish leadership itself and the Jews as a people had been largely lost. In the earlier gospels, the Jews as such are rarely mentioned, but by the time we get to John, they are mentioned more than seventy times, usually in pejorative terms. By that point too, the Jews have been transformed from a specific, unbelieving people into a synonym for an unbelieving world and thus a symbol of human evil (Pagels 1995, 9–15, 85–91, 98–105).

With the end of the next Jewish uprising against Rome (the Bar Kokhba Revolt in the mid-second century, 135 C.E.), Palestine had been fully pacified and the Jews there largely scattered to the diaspora, so the main enemies and persecutors of Christians were then the Roman regime and the Gentiles of its empire (Rokeah 1989). However, by that time, the accumulating Christian canon, oral and written, had established the Jews as those who had departed from the true God of Abraham, had rejected the divine dispensation of a new gospel and kingdom, and had connived with the Romans to crucify the prophet and son of God bringing that dispensation. Thenceforth the ancient covenant between God and Abraham would find its efficacy only in the gospel of the Messiah Jesus, which gospel, having been rejected by the Jews, would now be taken to the Gentiles, and lineage of any kind would become irrelevant (Pagels 1995, 86–89).

If the Romans had had their political reasons for despising the Jews, the Christians now had their religious ones. By the middle of the fourth century, when Christianity finally became the state religion of Rome, the stage was set for centuries of hostility against the Jews of Europe, ranging from the calumny in the Passion Play of Oberammergau to the pogroms of eastern and central Europe. Not only the four gospels themselves but also the accumulated theological commentary on them created a conventional understanding, among both Catholics and eventually Protestants, that went something like this: The Jews have always rejected the prophets sent by God, even in Old Testament times. Finally they rejected the ultimate prophet—the Messiah, or Christ Jesus—and killed him (Matthew 27:25: "His blood be upon us and upon our children"). For that sin, they and their apostate religion have been rejected by God, and their just punishment is to suffer scattering, hardship, and persecution until they accept the Messiah and the true religion of Christianity, which has now superseded the religion of the Torah (themes explored in Isaac [1964, 39–147]; and Parkes [1963, 57–73]).

Recent Reconstructions of Christian-Jewish Relationships

Only in the wake of the twentieth-century Holocaust did Christian scholars and ecclesiastical leaders finally begin to recognize the considerable contribution that such historic *religious* characterizations of the Jews had made to *secular and political* anti-Semitism. This recognition, in turn, has produced a burgeoning of new scholarship and a fundamental reconsideration in Christian denominations of the traditional doctrines and scriptural interpretations relating to Jews. One of the first and perhaps the most important of the revisionist documents was *Nostra Aetate* (In our age), issued in 1965 during the Vatican Council II. As if in response to the scholarly literature just mentioned, the Roman Catholic church in this document formally repudiated the general anti-Semitic charge of deicide and acknowledged the common spiritual heritage of Catholics and Jews. At that time, few other denominations followed the Vatican II example, but by the end of the century such historical reconsiderations had become interdenominational (Anti-Defamation League of B'nai B'rith 1983; E. Fisher 1984; Glock and Stark 1966, xviii–xix; Neusner 1993; Stendahl 1995).

For the Roman Catholic church especially, the process had only begun at Vatican II (Efroymson 1994). Considering its antiquity, its universality, and its manifest political entanglements with the secular history of Europe, the church has understandably come in for special historical scrutiny and criticism in its relationships with Jews, particularly during the Holocaust era and the papacy of Pius XII. The resulting scholarly and polemical literature has revealed the anguish of numerous ironic confrontations pitting abstract ethical idealism against moral and political relativity and all these, in turn, against political imperatives for organizational survival or protection (Carroll 2001; Phayer 2001). Progress in the ongoing Catholic-Jewish dialogue has been assessed also in periodic conferences and symposia. For example, in April 1985, the Anti-Defamation League of B'nai B'rith joined a number of Catholic organizations to sponsor a special conference in Rome on developments since Vatican II (Anti-Defamation League of B'nai B'rith 1985a). Several speakers at that conference identified still more specific declarations and policy changes needed by the church. A number of declarations and documents have subsequently been issued by the Vatican to refine and in some ways strengthen the impact of *Nostra Aetate,* including a "declaration of repentance" by Pope John Paul II as late as March 2000 (Walsh 2000). Yet many critics, even within the church, have called for still more strenuous and extensive repudiations by the pope and the hierarchy of the ancient anti-Semitic traditions (Carroll 2001).

The effort to redefine the historic Christian portrayal of Jews has focused primarily on the text of the four New Testament gospels themselves, especially the Gospel of John. The chief issue here is the appropriate interpretation of scriptural references to the Jews, especially where they seem to be implicated in the crucifixion of Jesus. If these references are taken, in their traditional meaning, as condemnations of the Jews as an entire people, then the charge of deicide is engraved in holy writ and seems to have a divine origin, at least for Christians. The most effective strike at the deicide charge, therefore, because it is the most radical, is a reinterpretation of the meaning of "the Jews" in the Gospels.

Biblical scholars have used a two-pronged attack in this reinterpretation. First, they have reminded us that almost *all* the principals in the life and ministry of Jesus were Jews, including his disciples and the general Judean public to which he brought his ministry. Jewish ubiquity was, of course, the case also in the so-called Old Testament, where the Jews are frequently condemned by their own prophets for their errant ways.[1] Therefore, even the widest reasonable interpretation of "the Jews" in such a context would be simply as a synonym for "the people" or "the public" of those specific times and places, *not* for all Jews always and everywhere. Second, the intended meaning of "the Jews" in the Gospels was, in any case, usually a reference to the religious and political *elite* of Roman Judea; the broadening of this meaning to refer to *all* Jews was the product of much later editing and emendations influenced by political conflicts among differing Jewish parties, especially the emerging Christian Jews (a main theme in Pagels 1995; see also American Interfaith Institute 1996a; Efroymson 1997; Harrington 1994; and Kee 1997).

Having achieved this redefinition of exactly who "the Jews" of the four gospels were, Christian and Jewish scholars have worked together in recent decades to see that this newer understanding is reflected in popular versions of not only the Bible itself but also derivative teaching texts. Various newer translations of the Bible have rendered "the Jews" as "the leaders," "the crowd," or (at most) "the people" (Burke 1995; Kee 1996). Various catechisms, as well as the so-called Passion narrative in its popular forms—most notably the annual dramatic rendition at Oberammergau—have also undergone revisions that reflect more neutral and less pejorative references to the Jews in the life and death of Jesus (Anti-Defamation League of B'nai B'rith 1985b; R. Brown 1995; E. Fisher 1996; Kelly 1997). All of these efforts and many other initiatives by scholars and organizational activists have been attempts to neutralize or eliminate the charge of deicide that has been aimed at the Jews as a people for so many centuries.

Beyond the vexing deicide charge have been other issues that have complicated relationships between Jews and Christians. Perhaps the most troublesome of these is supersessionism, the traditional Christian claim that the ancient Abrahamic covenant has been "superseded" by Christianity as a new dispensation brought from God by the Messiah Jesus. The effect of this claim, of course, is to invalidate the entire Jewish religion as the obsolete and divinely rejected relic of an apostate people. (The supersession issue is reviewed in the essays in Kee and Borowsky [1994]). In some of the New Testament, especially the writings of Paul, supersessionism also redefines the identity of the "chosen people" such that the term no longer applies to the Jews but applies only to those who accept Christ, meaning mainly the Gentiles.[2] The supersessionism rationale, in turn, has provided the motivation for Christian proselyting among Jews, which, however benignly intentioned, is extremely offensive to them. Jews widely regard it as de facto a form of anti-Semitism to be resisted, not only by internal Jewish education but also by external political action. In recent years, most Christian denominations—except for the more evangelical Protestant bodies, such as the Southern Baptist Convention—have backed away from attempting to convert Jews (American Interfaith Institute 1996b; Perlmutter and Perlmutter 1982).

Jewish Identity in Traditional Mormonism

Since the earliest Mormons were all converts from some variety of Christian background, many of them, perhaps most, were familiar with the inherited religious lore about Jews, even if they had never personally known any Jews. Nineteenth-century Mormon religious discourse occasionally reiterated such traditional ideas as the historic suffering of the Jews in consequence of their having rejected and condemned their own prophets and the true Messiah. Mormon preaching and literature of the time also reflected an assumption of dispensational supersession: Since the Jews and their religion had forfeited divine favor, a new dispensation of the true gospel had gone to the Gentiles instead. However, the "times of the Gentiles" would eventually be "fulfilled," and God would once again offer the Jews a chance to embrace the truth as his chosen people—or so the preaching usually went in Utah, according to excerpts discussed by Hugh Nibley (1985–95, 13:169–72).

　　Yet it is important to emphasize that the historic "Jewish perfidy" (as it is sometimes called in traditional Christian literature) was never understood by Mormons as uniquely Jewish. Like the Old Testament itself, Mormon scriptures portrayed a cyclical history of human relations with the divine. If Jews and the rest of Israel had periodically been chastened for turning their backs on God, so had the pre-Israelite biblical peoples in the times of Adam, Enoch, and Noah; so had the Nephites and Lamanites of the Book of Mormon; and so had the Christian Gentiles themselves after the apostolic era. Mormons typically understood the waywardness attributed to Jews in biblical and Christian writings as simply a normal and recurrent human tendency (Norman 1999). Furthermore, Joseph Smith and many of his earliest disciples could easily sympathize with the Jewish rejection of mainstream Christianity, which Mormons themselves considered an apostate tradition responsible for centuries of merciless persecution of Jews and others (Epperson 1989). Such is the context in which Mormons have always understood the juxtaposition of the two scriptural passages that appear at the head of this chapter.

Mormon and Jewish Identities as Mutually Legitimating

A special Mormon sympathy for the Jews developed as part of the emerging understanding among Anglo-Mormons of the 1830s and 1840s that they were themselves actually descendants of the tribe of Ephraim and thus shared Israelite ancestry with the Jews (Glanz 1963, 51–55, 69–75; Widtsoe 1960, 398–400). This claim referred to literal genealogy and thus went far beyond the common Protestant evangelical claim to "spiritual" or "symbolic" Israelite descent (M. Wilson 2000). I and others have traced this Mormon doctrinal development and its consequences in some detail elsewhere (A. Green 1999; Mauss 1999). Here it will suffice to explain that by the end of Joseph Smith's life, Mormonism had embraced a variant of Anglo-Israelism that was perhaps already embryonically implicit in the Book of Mormon. As this doctrine developed, Mormons came to understand that two Israelite gatherings, not just one, were divinely destined to occur before the millennial return of the Messiah. The ancient Kingdom of Judah, the Jews, would be gathered to Jerusalem, and the "lost" tribes constituting the Kingdom of Israel, prepared and led by the tribe of Ephraim, would be gathered to Zion, located in America. This system of "dialectical holy lands," in the phrase of Gershon Greenberg (1994, 227), came as a great surprise to Jews, of course, but it carried several important implications for the ways in which Mormons identified both themselves and the Jews (Cain 1992; Glanz 1960, 41–50, 95–107).

One implication was that the restored Church of Jesus Christ, namely the Mormons, would bear responsibility in the final dispensation for the gathering to Zion, under Ephraim, but *not* for the gathering to Jerusalem, under Judah. Christ himself, of course, was behind both gatherings, but the divine charge of the Mormon elders was to find and convert the lost remnants of Israel and gather them to Zion in America. The gathering of the Jews was a different process, which might occur either before or after their conversion to the true Messiah, but however it was to occur was a matter best left in God's own hands. Individual Jews might occasionally be encountered and converted by Mormon missionaries (and a handful of Jews did convert during the earliest years of Mormonism—Glanz 1963, 145–55; A. Green 1999, 217). However, the massive gathering promised in the scriptures (e.g., Zechariah 12–14) was not to occur under the Mormon aegis. The gathering to Zion and the building of a new temple in the New Jerusalem there would be quite enough responsibility for the tribe of Ephraim. Along with the Anglo-Mormons, other descendants of Ephraim and of his brother Manasseh would also join in building Zion. These were, of course, the Lamanites of the Book of Mormon.

A second implication of this dual gathering concept was that Mormons and Jews were literally related by blood. Nineteenth-century Mormons, as literal descendants of the lost tribe of Ephraim, were being mystically gathered by the promptings of the Holy Spirit from around the earth (but especially from northwestern Europe and America). Modern Jews, of course, were literal descendants of the tribe of Judah; they might not yet understand that Jesus is the true Messiah, but eventually they would. They might not yet recognize the divine destiny they shared with Mormon Ephraimites to gather and prepare the two holy sites for the millennial reign of the Messiah, but eventually they would come to understand that, too. In the political developments already taking place by 1840 in America, Europe, and Palestine itself, there were signs of Jewish gathering to the original homeland (A. Green 1994–95; Higham 1957; Mauss 1999, 134–35). The Mormon press on either side of the Atlantic regularly reported or reprinted news events about such developments from the 1840s on (Glanz 1963, 284–93). Mormons were thus inclined to look upon Jews respectfully as partners in the divine program for the end times.

A third implication was the importance of this dual partnership and blood tie for the ongoing construction of the identity of the Mormons themselves. In the first chapter of this book, I reviewed briefly the work of E. Theodore Mullen Jr. on the Jews' reconstruction of their identity after their Babylonian captivity, and I suggested some parallels with the Mormon case in the nineteenth century. Here I am making a somewhat different but related point: By highlighting the special importance of Israelite identity for both Jews and Mormons as part of the divine plan for the last days, the Mormons enhanced their own legitimacy as a chosen people. The Mormons claimed special divine commissions under both Christian and Hebrew dispensations, or under both Testaments, as it were. In recovering Ephraim and the other lost tribes and bringing them to a new Zion, the Mormons were restoring and fulfilling the ancient Abrahamic covenant of the Old Testament. At the same time, by restoring the New Testament church, which had been lost in a general apostasy after the original apostles, the Mormons were bringing in the final dispensation of the gospel of Christ, to the Gentiles as well as to Israel. The millennial world would thus eventually be united under the true Messiah, even if there were two Zions.

As the Mormons' construction of their own Israelite identity developed, the Jews became increasingly important, in a collective sense, as a kind of "theological alter ego" to that identity. Mormons increasingly saw parallels between their own historical experience and that of the Jews (Ellern 1977; Greenberg 1994, 227–58). The Mormons' exodus to the promised land in Utah not only was led by a Moses figure but also took them to an arid homeland, where a fresh lake and a salty lake were connected by a river—which, of course, they named the Jordan. The Mormons even suffered their share of the persecution imposed on the chosen lineage—only for a couple of generations, to be sure, but still the parallel to the Jewish experience was unmistakable and called for a degree of reverence in remembering the sacrifices punctuating both of those histories. The two Zions also were similar in that each would have a political and territorial, as well as a religious, basis. Scriptural prophecies made clear that both were equally important in the divine plan for the end times.[3] In all of these respects, then, the special identity the Mormons claimed for themselves depended in part on endorsing the parallel claims of the Jews to their special divine destiny and homeland.

Variations in Mormon Doctrinal Development regarding Jews

This emphasis on a shared chosen lineage and dual Israelite gatherings, as important as that is, cannot obscure the considerable ambiguity and complexity in the Mormon doctrinal portrayal of the Jews more generally. Among the founding generation of Mormons, different spokesmen have emphasized different elements of Christian lore about the Jews, and the prophet Joseph Smith himself promulgated a somewhat novel mixture of new and old ideas. Even historians who have tried to articulate a common "Mormon" characterization of the Jews have produced somewhat different pictures and have been forced to recognize the ambiguities in all of them (starting with Glanz [1963]). Arnold H. Green, a history professor at BYU, identified seven main "strands" in the various traditional Mormon versions of the history and destiny of the Jews: divine judgment; chosen lineage; Judeophilia; Jewish-Mormon partnership; Jewish return to Palestine; eventual Jewish conversion to Christ; and the universal applicability of the Abrahamic covenant to all who accept Christ, whether Israelite or Gentile. In Mormon discourse across time, said Green, these seven themes have emerged in different combinations, then "ebbed, reemerged, and continue to entwine in various configurations" (1994–95, 141).

In a later essay, Green (1999) offered a somewhat sharper focus on two of those seven strands which have tended to dominate Mormon discourse, namely the "lineage primacy" theme and the "universalism" theme. In the thinking of the founding prophet Joseph Smith himself, Green maintained, these two themes were given about equal emphasis quantitatively, stamping early Mormon discourse and scriptures with a somewhat bifurcated portrayal of Jews. This divergence was never resolved by Smith but continued to be debated along with the other accumulated concepts about Jews. After Smith, however, some of his most prominent disciples associated themselves more or less strongly with the one or the other of the two dominant themes.

In Green's conceptual framework, the "lineage primacy" theme was apparent especially in the preaching of Brigham Young, Wilford Woodruff, and John Taylor, whereas the main exponents of universal gospel applicability (and therefore of imminent Jewish conversion) were the Pratt brothers, Parley and Orson. (See illustrative citations of official and unofficial LDS sources in A. Green [1994–95, 144–56]; and A. Green [1999, 207–28].) Each of these "camps" was able to identify scriptural passages, as well as comments from Smith himself, for authoritative support of its expectations about the Jews. Each camp expressed some degree of "Judeophilia" and some expectation of an eventual Messianic reign based in two world centers (Palestine and America). Yet such favorable portrayals of the Jewish future were accompanied in each camp by occasional resorts to the traditional Christian predictions of divine judgment and eventual conversion, sometimes in rhetoric that today would be considered anti-Semitic. During the next century, Mormon commentators continued to emphasize one or the other of the two dominant themes of lineage primacy and universalism. References to Jews, as they appeared in official and unofficial publications, were often made in the context of world events affecting Jews and seemingly pointing toward their imminent gathering and conversion. However, Green contended, by the end of the twentieth century, the theme of universalism had come to dominate official Mormon discourse at the expense of the lineage primacy theme, which was only rarely cited.

Steven Epperson (1992), writing a few years earlier than Green, had also reduced the various strands or themes in traditional Mormon thought about Jews to only two general tendencies. Like Green, his sometime BYU colleague, Epperson found these two tendencies (or "models," as he sometimes called them) in the earliest discourse of the Mormon founders. Although Epperson's descriptions of the two tendencies resemble Green's, he traces their origins to slightly different founding figures. In Joseph Smith himself, Epperson does not see the equivalence that Green finds between the two major emphases of universalism and lineage primacy but instead sees lineage as much more salient: "For Smith . . . Israel's example and integrity loomed large and led him to foster its covenantal role in the redemption of the world" (1992, 125; see also 113–37). The "restoration of all things" included not only the gathering but also the establishment of an earthly kingdom and homeland, with a priesthood and a temple for special covenantal rites connecting the Latter-day Saints to previous dispensations. It was thus to Israel's prophets and perennial aspirations that Smith and his disciples turned "for the terms, symbols, and syntax of their own gathering" (Epperson 1992, 127).

Oliver Cowdery, one of Smith's earliest disciples and once his "assistant president," was selected by Epperson to represent the contrasting Mormon emphasis on universalism. Like Sidney Rigdon, another early member of the inner circle of Mormon leadership, Cowdery was more focused than Smith on the traditional and universal Christian requirement that "every knee shall bow . . . and every tongue confess" that Jesus is the Savior and God (Philippians 2:10–11). According to Epperson, Cowdery's preoccupation was reclaiming and restoring the primitive Church of Jesus Christ, "a church of visible Saints awaiting the imminent end of the world and the demise of the ungodly. This church was an embattled, exclusive sect of the righteous set apart by its apocalypticism and its confrontation with [the world's] religious culture. . . . Thus Cowdery's vision of Mormonism was fundamentally hostile to rival covenantal traditions and communities . . . [and to] the autonomy and integrity of the Jewish people" (1992, 124–25).

While Green's accounts concentrate on the development of Mormon doctrines about Jews *after* Joseph Smith, Epperson's book focuses mainly on Smith's own understanding of the Jews and their destiny and on how that understanding developed across time. Smith's innovative effort to combine Old and New Testament themes in this process was portrayed by Epperson as standing in clear contrast to the more orthodox Christian understandings of Cowdery, Rigdon, and the Pratt brothers. Smith's ideas about the primacy of lineage seem to have been echoed instead by some of his other apostles, mainly Brigham Young, Orson Hyde, and Heber C. Kimball. Epperson recognizes that Smith's affirmations of the continuing relevance of the Jewish covenantal heritage was "neither normative nor preeminent during the first decade. The dominant sentiments of the Saints during the 1830s were apocalyptic and primitivist" (1992, 210–11).

Yet later Mormon doctrinal development showed the increased influence of Smith's special appreciation for the Jews and their divine destiny.[4] Epperson attributes this increase to developments both internal and external to Smith and his emerging church. First was a growing estrangement between Mormons and the surrounding Christian churches, which helped make Smith feel somewhat freer to look beyond the Christian heritage to Israel's scriptures, myths, symbols, and covenantal history as part of his prophetic mission to "restore all things."[5] Second was the delay of the millennium and its new kingdom, deflating Mormon apocalyptic hopes and requiring a reinterpretation of failed prophecies (Epperson 1992, 211–12; Norman 1983). To all this might be added the growing exposure of Smith and his missionaries to things Jewish, starting with their relationship with Joshua Seixas, their Hebrew instructor, in the mid-1830s, as well as the influence of recurrent news reports during the 1840s (many reprinted in the church's *Times and Seasons* and *Millennial Star*) about the strife, migrations, and gatherings to Palestine of Europe's Jews (Epperson 1989 and 1992, 73–111; Walton 1981; Zucker 1968).

One of Smith's responses to these developments was to dispatch the apostle Orson Hyde to Palestine in 1841, where, in a private prayer on the Mount of Olives, he dedicated that land for the return and gathering of the Jews.[6] About a year after Joseph Smith's assassination, the Quorum of the Twelve Apostles issued a long proclamation to the people and rulers of the world, in which, among other things, they called on the Jews to return to Palestine and on the rest of the world to facilitate that return (*Proclamation of the Twelve Apostles of the Church of Jesus Christ of Latter-day Saints* 1845).

The Legacy of Joseph Smith: Philo-Judaism and Proselyting Reticence

Epperson, in his analysis of Joseph Smith's portrayal of the Jewish identity and destiny, emphasizes the contrast between the innovative vision of Smith and the more orthodox position of some of his colleagues, such as Cowdery. In so doing, Epperson might have overdrawn the distinction between the two Mormon theological "camps" to emphasize the importance Smith ascribed to the Jews in divine history—particularly in the final days of that history in which the early Mormons were then living. Epperson seems to be arguing that Smith came to believe in a kind of "side deal" that God had made with the Jews. Such a view would have stood in clear contrast to the universalistic and exclusivist impulses in Mormonism, as in the rest of Christianity. Yet it remains true that neither Smith nor his immediate successors launched missionary campaigns to convert the Jews, as other Christian denominations and missionary societies did; and this despite a generalized Mormon proselyting ethos and several missionary campaigns directed specifically at other ostensibly Israelite peoples, such as the British, the Scandinavians, the American Indians, and the Polynesians. When Orson Hyde and later delegations traveled to the Holy Land to "dedicate" it for the fulfillment of God's purposes, these dedications were for the *gathering* of the Jews, not for their conversion. To be sure, the conversion was definitely expected to occur eventually, but its schedule and process were left mainly up to God.

Especially in the light of what we have learned from modern scholarship about the sources of traditional Christian antipathy toward Jews, many have welcomed Epperson's discovery of ideas like Smith's that seem to neutralize the anti-Jewish residue in Mormonism (Norman 1999). However, Epperson has also been criticized, sometimes quite severely, for claiming that Smith proposed a kind of exceptionalism for Jews that would exempt them from eventual conversion to Christ. Grant Underwood found in Epperson's book such a selective packaging of Smith's writings about Jews as to verge on deliberate dishonesty (1994–95, 120–23). Arnold Green explicitly used the word *dishonest* in a passing reference to Epperson's book, viewing it as partly an

effort to associate Joseph Smith's ideas with contemporary Christian scholarship (1999, 220–22). Epperson was charged with ignoring or truncating
passages from the Book of Mormon and elsewhere that seem to pronounce
severe divine judgment on the Jews in perpetuity and clearly call for their
eventual conversion to Christ as part of their redemption. Even the Jewish
scholar Seymour Cain, in a generally favorable review of Epperson's book,
found passages in the Book of Mormon, particularly in 1 Nephi and 2 Nephi,
that "raise . . . serious questions about Epperson's thesis," and he regarded
the author's "attempted explanations . . . [as] rather lame" (1993, 33).

My own assessment of Joseph Smith's portrayal of the Jews and their identity is somewhat sympathetic to Epperson's position, with the caveat that he
probably overstressed the differences between the Smith-Young-Hyde
"camp" and the Cowdery-Rigdon-Pratt "camp" in early Mormonism. Epperson no doubt was influenced by the post-Holocaust literature on Christian-Jewish relations, as Underwood and Green suggested. I suspect he was
also employing a rhetorical strategy, in other words, deliberately exaggerat-
ing Smith's Jewish exceptionalism to make more stark the distinction between the two early Mormon camps, as though to "clarify" the ambiguities
in Mormon discourse outlined in the articles by Green (1994–95 and 1999).
Yet even Green recognized the existence of essentially the same two camps
and their persistence in Mormon discourse all the way to the end of the twentieth century.[7] Moreover, Epperson's critics did not adequately take into account the *chronological* dimension in Smith's theological development, and
probably Epperson himself could have emphasized that dimension more
strongly. Here I am referring to the *evolving* nature of Smith's ideas (and of
others' through him) about the Jewish identity, role, and destiny.

Those ideas would have emerged out of their original Christian context
in the late 1820s, while Joseph Smith was working on the Book of Mormon.
It is therefore understandable that they would have reflected the kinds of
traditional Christian judgments against Jews seen early in that book, particularly in 1 Nephi and 2 Nephi. Almost all of the evidence cited against Epperson by his critics came from about the first fourth of the Book of Mormon. If we look instead at the commentaries on Jews by the mature Smith
in the 1840s, for example, in the pages of Nauvoo's *Times and Seasons,* Epperson's case seems somewhat stronger (Epperson 1989 and 1992, 73–111). By
that time, Smith had been studying Jews and the Hebrew language for more
than a decade, and his understanding about the role of Jews in divine history would certainly have evolved as part of the expanded Hebraic layer in his
thinking that Jan Shipps (1998) has identified.[8]

Epperson seems to have gone too far, however, in the degree of Jewish "exceptionalism" that he attributes to Smith when he says that the conversion of
Jews "is never mentioned nor advocated in the Book of Mormon" or in oth-

er Mormon scriptures (1992, 36), a position argued earlier by W. D. Davies (1978, 83) and criticized by Seymour Cain (1992, 61–63; and 1993, 33). Yet it is also true, as Underwood conceded, that "Joseph Smith rarely commented on the conversion of the Jews" and that "Smith and his associates rejected contemporary missions to the Jews" as disregarding both the divine timetable and the divinely appointed manner of Jewish conversion (1994–95, 113, 115). Brigham Young, too, until the end of his life, taught that the Jews "cannot now believe in Jesus Christ," for to do so "would prove that they are not Jews" (1866b, 279). Here Young, unlike Smith, was not taking a sympathetic posture toward Jewish rejection of Jesus but was reflecting his own uncharitable view that the Jews would remain under a divine curse until they gathered to Jerusalem and were there forced to accept Christ by the extremity of the apocalyptic circumstances foreseen in Zechariah 12–14 (A. Green 1999, 204–7, 227–28). Until then, claimed Young, the Jews simply would not be "ready" for conversion by Mormon missionaries or anyone else: "Jerusalem is not to be redeemed by our going there and preaching. . . . It will be redeemed by the high hand of the Almighty. . . . [I]t is impossible to convert the Jews until the Lord God Almighty does it" (quoted in Nibley 1985–95, 13:170–71).

It must be added that most of the passages in the Book of Mormon ostensibly referring to Jewish "conversion" are not really calls for active proselyting among Jews but rather *prophecies and expectations* of eventual Jewish acceptance of the true religion (e.g., 2 Nephi 6:11, 9:2, 10:7–8, 30:7–8). In practical terms, then, Epperson and his critics are not very far apart in explaining the obvious historical reticence among Mormons about "converting the Jews." As Underwood pointed out, Joseph Smith and those who thought as he did simply looked to God himself "personally [to] participate in the conversion of his ancient people [which] is probably the biggest factor in understanding why the Mormons still have rarely mounted any missionary effort among the Jews" (1994–95, 116). In the light of this operational reality, the theological "exceptionalism" for which Epperson has been criticized does not seem very important. He and his critics agree that Mormons have rarely included Jews in the proselyting enterprise extended to the rest of the world's peoples. Whether the main reason for this policy is to be found in an "exceptionalist" strain originating with Joseph Smith or in something more pragmatic depends largely on which interpretations one prefers in early Mormon discourse.[9]

The Modern Mormon Religious Posture toward Jews

Joseph Smith's own appreciation for the Jews is, at the very least, probably the main reason for the Hebraic stamp on Mormonism that Jan Shipps and other non-Mormons have observed. It was the Jewish scholar Seymour Cain himself who noted that "biblical Judaism, more exactly the religion of Israel, has been the paradigm for the Mormon historical experience. This has happened before in the history of Western religion, but never with the generative power and social and cultural effect of the Mormon movement" (1991, 26). Furthermore, throughout the nineteenth and twentieth centuries, Mormons uniformly offered moral and other support for the establishment and success of the new state of Israel, which all Mormons have traditionally considered an essential harbinger of the millennial reign or at least concomitant with it. In the 1920s, Heber J. Grant, the church's president, was among those pointing to the Balfour Declaration of 1917 as a divine portent and calling for the Saints to look forward to the establishment of a Jewish state in Palestine. After that actually occurred in 1948, President George Albert Smith, both publicly and privately, assured prominent Jews of church support for the new state. Such support was never contingent on Jewish receptivity to the Mormon religion (Goodman 1976, 217; Grant 1921; Tobler 1992, 59–68; Zucker 1981, 44).

Mormon Proselyting Episodes among Jews

Yet, as already indicated, individual Mormons, from the very beginning, have certainly attempted to convert Jewish friends and acquaintances, at least subtly, even if their efforts have rarely produced converts. Mormon leaders, including the apostles themselves, have also periodically launched brief proselyting forays among the Jews, again without any appreciable success. Yet the church generally has not had a sustained program for Jewish conversion, despite its massive and historic commitment to missionary work among most other peoples. The dedicatory visits of Mormon leaders to Palestine, beginning with Orson Hyde in 1841, did not establish missions to the Jews, even though conspicuous Jewish colonies began to appear there from about 1880 onward.

    The church did, however, establish a mission in the Middle East at the end of 1884. Called the Turkish Mission, it was directed less to Muslim Turks than to their neighboring and subject peoples, such as the Armenians and other Christians. With only limited success, this mission was closed in 1909 and reopened in late 1921 as the Armenian Mission. Since the Armenian population was decimated and scattered during conflicts with the Turks, the name and focus of the LDS mission was changed again in 1933 to the Palestine-Syrian Mission. This mission was closed with the arrival of World War II in 1939 but reopened in 1947. The name was changed yet again in 1950 to the Near East Mission, but that, too, was closed a year later (*Deseret News Church Almanac* 1975, D8–D24; and 1990, 225–42). It must be emphasized that none of the missionary work in this region was directed at the Jews, and even among the various non-Jewish populations, conversions never totaled more than a few score during the several decades. It is clear from the record that the church was so preoccupied with trying to relocate and sustain various impoverished and refugee groups throughout this region that it was never able to focus on proselyting as such. Since the middle of the twentieth century, the church has never found a cost-benefit rationale for resuming missionary work in that conflict-ridden area (Lindsay 1966; D. Peterson 1992, 325–69).

There have, however, been Mormon proselyting campaigns among Jews, few and brief though these efforts have been. These were reviewed by the historian Arnold H. Green in a master's thesis and derivative scholarly article (1968) covering the history up through 1965. Green makes the passing observation (which others have discussed more fully) that the Mormons in Utah made no attempts to proselyte among the Jews, who were arriving there in numbers large enough to have established half a dozen congregations in various towns by 1876. Yet Mormon-Jewish relationships were so warm that the Jews were invited to celebrate Rosh Hashanah on Salt Lake City's Temple Square as early as 1865, and the president of the church was invited to lay the cornerstone for a new synagogue in 1903. In 1916, Utah became the second state in the Union to elect a Jewish governor. (Heavily Mormon Idaho was first in 1914.) During the 1920s, President Heber J. Grant, well known as a strong critic of anti-Semitism, was also a booster of the Jewish National Fund, which supported the creation of a new Jewish state in Palestine. As in the nineteenth century, Mormon spokesmen such as Grant were still convinced that any appreciable Jewish gathering to Palestine was strongly portentous of the imminent return of the Messiah, and the British mandate after World War I seemed to verify that conviction (A. Green 1968, 431). Yet there was no Mormon proselyting among Jews in Palestine.

The first Mormon program for converting Jews was a later effort initiated in the Eastern States Mission in 1926 by Brigham H. Roberts, a senior church official and its leading intellectual, who had been sent to preside over that mission in 1922. New York City, of course, had the largest concentration of Jews in America, and Roberts encountered there a Christian Jew who encouraged him to contribute articles to a monthly publication entitled the *Redeemed Hebrew.* In a series of three such articles, directed at a fictional (or at least pseudonymous) rabbi named Rasha, Roberts reviewed key LDS doctrines on deity, Christology, and the Book of Mormon as a new witness for the divinity of Jesus. In 1932, the three articles were combined with supplementary material and published as *Rasha—The Jew,* which served for several years as a proselyting tract for use with Jewish prospects. This missionary effort seems to have attracted a certain amount of curious attention, rarely favorable, and it resulted in no Jewish converts to Mormonism (A. Green 1968, 432).

This New York campaign had arrived with the tide of enthusiasm for Jewish prospects in Palestine after World War I. A generation later, after World

War II, the actual establishment of the new state of Israel in 1948 inspired extravagant hopes in some Mormon quarters that the apocalyptic gathering of Jews was at last under way.[10] LeGrand Richards and a few of his colleagues in the Quorum of the Twelve Apostles were convinced that, in his words, "the 'times of the Gentiles' are now fulfilled to the point where we should carry the message to this chosen branch of the House of Israel" (1954a, 434). Richards, a dynamic and determined preacher, expected that the First Presidency of the church would soon be starting such missionary work and apparently began nudging them in that direction, for they soon authorized him to set up "experimental" missions for Jews in a few areas. In preparation, he published a book, *Israel! Do You Know?* (1954b), which came to be very well known among Mormons and provided the basis for a major new missionary campaign in southern California. The book drew heavily on the traditional Mormon claim of parallel Israelite lineage with the Jews and the derivative responsibility of the church, as the house of Joseph and Ephraim, to carry the gospel to its cousins in the house of Judah—a theme regularly reiterated by Richards in general conferences of the church (e.g., 1956, 23–26; and 1969, 31; see also A. Green 1968, 434).

The largest Mormon missionary campaign ever launched for Jewish converts arose in the Los Angeles Stake of the church in 1955 (A. Green 1968, 434–39; Reid 1973). This was, of course, right in the center of a major concentration of American Jews, second only to that in New York City. The president of that stake was willing to try Richards's "experiment" and appointed special assistants for that purpose, including a Jewish convert to Mormonism who even relocated from Ogden, Utah, to Los Angeles for this new calling. Richards was aware also of another important resource there, namely, a unique Mormon woman by the name of Rose Marie Reid, who had spent much of her life among Jews in New York City and southern California. As a professional swimsuit designer, she had made many Jewish friends in the textile industry and was convinced that she knew how to approach them with the Mormon message in unoffensive ways. With Richards's encouragement, Reid prepared a manuscript of her missionary lesson plans for Jews, which was eventually reviewed by the Missionary Committee of the church and published in 1958. Although it was never officially promulgated as a part of the general church program, the *Suggested Plan for Teaching the Gospel to the Jewish People* was published by the church press and widely used in southern California and elsewhere for several years.

The *Suggested Plan* emphasized certain features intended to appeal to Jewish contacts and to avoid offending them at the outset with a strong message about Jesus as Christ. Jesus was not to be mentioned at all until the fourth lesson. The earlier lessons focused on similarities between Jews and Mormons; their common heritage of persecution; their shared descent from

Abraham through (respectively) Judah and Joseph (not his sons Ephraim and Manasseh, perhaps less familiar to Jews); the Mormon use of temples for special worship services; and other ostensible similarities. The lessons relied on the Old Testament section of the Bible, not on the New Testament, so that all the references to deity would be to God or Lord, not to Jesus or Christ. Scriptural passages were, of course, given a Mormon interpretation in proof-text fashion. When the time came, in lesson four or later, to discuss Jesus and his divine mission, the resurrection was emphasized over the crucifixion, the blame for which was explicitly directed away from the Jews. Participants were reminded that Jesus had laid down his *own* life, as an act of divine will, and that, in any case, he had called upon Heaven to forgive his crucifiers, "for they know not what they do" (Reid 1973, 114–27).

Aside from content, the pedagogical method advocated was also interesting: the avoidance of references to Jesus or Christ in the earlier lessons; the use of visual aids to curtail questions or comments from the Jewish listeners during the presentation; the deflection of critical comments or questions without explicitly contradicting Jewish participants when they did talk; and the careful use of logic, analogy, and evidence drawn from scripture or from experience (Reid 1973, 113–14). Few of the missionaries chosen by stake leaders had the skill or commitment that Reid required, and Jewish converts themselves were not to be used to contact other Jews, for fear that they would immediately be considered "traitors" to the Jewish heritage (Reid 1973, 135–36).

Reid deplored local Mormons' resistance to proselyting among Jews and the ignorance about Jews (even occasional anti-Semitism) among those who were appointed to use her teaching plan (1973, 128–30, 148–55). She was equally candid about the enormous social and psychological costs of conversion for the few Jews who did convert, even if they had been only "cultural Jews," as it were, to begin with. The kinds of costs she discussed would be easily recognized by social scientists as typical of people trying to manage fundamental identity transformations of various kinds and should be understandable as well to any Mormons who themselves have been converted from drastically different cultural or ethnic backgrounds (Reid 1973, 154–59).

By 1960, Mormon missionary work, with or without the Reid program, had also been initiated in several centers outside southern California, most notably San Francisco; Ogden and Salt Lake City, Utah; Portland, Oregon; Washington, D.C.; and again in New York City (Jewish Mission Files 1955–58; Reid 1973, 134–35, 139–42). Most of these missions resulted from the personal visits or encouragement of Richards, and in some locations missionaries were quite systematic in their attempts to identify, locate, and canvass Jewish prospects (A. Green 1968, 436–39; Reid 1973, 133–41, 161–62). Correspondence between Richards and leaders of the Utah stakes chosen to "pilot" the new program for Jews reveals a valiant effort on the part of a very few stake missionaries (whose names and activity reports are sometimes included in the correspondence). Periodic expressions of high hopes are followed by disappointing results and "stiff upper lips," as it were. Despite an impressive investment of volunteer time and other resources for three to five years, these missionary forays produced fewer than fifty Jewish converts in all the sites combined and none at all in several locations. In 1959, the First Presidency called a halt to all special missions among Jews, with the instruction that the gospel should simply be offered to individual Jews encountered in the course of normal missionary activity throughout the world, just as would be the case with any other individuals.[11]

By that point, the southern California program had already evolved in a somewhat different direction anyway. Reid and her colleagues in the missionary effort there had discovered that a major deterrent to their success was the ignorance and naïveté about Jews among the Mormons themselves. Jewish friends and investigators occasionally visiting LDS meetings were sometimes offended by ignorant comments and questions directed at them quite innocently by their Mormon hosts (Reid 1973, 148–50, 157–58). Accordingly, the missionary program there was transformed from one of straightforward proselyting into the Understanding Israel Program, developed and recommended by the church leaders in nearby San Bernardino. This program focused on teaching Mormons about ancient and modern Judaism in the hope of enhancing their "understanding . . . and a genuine friendship for Jewish people" (A. Green 1968, 441). All this, it was hoped, would create goodwill toward Mormons and eventually open more Jewish doors and hearts to regular missionary work. Even this modified program died a natural death with the 1959 decision by the general church leadership.

Judged by the intensity and duration of the effort and the investment of material and human resources, this campaign during the 1950s would have to be considered the most sustained and important program ever undertaken by the church to convert Jews. It is the only such effort mentioned in the official one-volume history of the church (J. Allen and Leonard 1992, 568–69). It might also have to be considered the most successful, even though very few Jewish converts resulted. In Rose Marie Reid's interview, she estimated that about fifty Jews in New York City had joined the LDS Church during and after the 1950s and perhaps a few hundred throughout the United States, mainly in southern California. These estimates would probably be considered exaggerations by Arnold Green, who estimated some thirty in southern California and another two or three each in Ogden, Salt Lake City, San Francisco, Portland, and Washington, D.C. (A. Green 1968, 436–39). In most of these sites, fewer than a dozen missionaries worked with Jewish prospects, mostly on a part-time or irregular basis. In southern California, however, more than a hundred missionaries were involved, and records for 1957 and

1958 show that they delivered some twelve hundred lessons to Jewish homes during ten thousand hours of proselyting in producing only those thirty converts (Reid 1973, 137–39).

Nevertheless, before the twentieth century ended, still another missionary campaign was briefly directed at Jews in the United States, this time by President Spencer W. Kimball, with the enthusiastic support of his apostolic colleague Ezra Taft Benson. In an April 1975 seminar with regional Mormon leaders, President Kimball declared that the Jewish people "must hear the gospel; they must accept Jesus Christ as their Lord and Master, and that day . . . cannot come until we, the witnesses of Jesus Christ, get busy and present the message to them" (quoted in "Missionary Discussions for the Jewish People" 1979). Acting on that dictum, the Missionary Department of the church published in 1978 the *Missionary Training Manual for Use in the Jewish Proselyting Program* and then, in April of 1979, *Missionary Discussions for the Jewish People,* to be used in actual proselyting ("Missionary Discussions for the Jewish People" 1979). The training manual, intended for the missionaries themselves, provided orientation and information on Jewish history, terminology, and social demography, with suggestions on effective and inoffensive ways to approach Jewish contacts. The missionary discussions were in three parts: the first introduced Joseph Smith as a prophet in continuity with the ancient Hebrew prophets and discussed the Book of Mormon as a product of his prophetic ministry; the second focused on Old Testament prophecies about the Messiah and showed how Jesus fulfilled them; and the third identified additional Old Testament prophecies anticipating the wholesale apostasy of Christianity after the original apostles, thus demonstrating the need for the LDS message as a restoration of ancient Christianity. Following these three special lessons for Jewish investigators, the missionaries were to switch to standard lessons and approaches used in the general missionary program ("Missionary Discussions for the Jewish People" 1979). Various visual aids and six pamphlets were also provided for use with Jews (B. Christensen 1986), including the *Message to Judah from Joseph,* originally delivered as a speech by Ezra Taft Benson (1976).

Benson's message was a polite but direct sermon, with no punches pulled, calling for Jewish conversion. Even though his actual and intended audiences were Jewish, his rhetoric contained little of the elaborate, indirect, and more diplomatic approach attempted in the Reid program of the 1950s. To be sure, Benson emphasized his own "credentials" as a friend of Israel, with references to his several visits there and his personal relationship with such leaders as David Ben Gurion. He also hit hard and repeatedly on the general theme of a common and literal lineage connection between Mormons (Joseph) and Jews (Judah). The main burden of his message, however, was a Mormon exegesis on the proper interpretation and understanding of various Old Testament passages supporting the Messianic claims of Jesus; the predictions of the scattering and subsequent gathering of all Israelite tribes; and the divine mission of the modern lineage of Joseph (i.e., Mormons as Ephraimites) to assist the Jews in recovering the true religion and God's ancient covenant, from which they had strayed (Benson 1976).

However, by the time the *Missionary Training Manual* and the *Missionary Discussions* had been announced and described in the church magazine *Ensign* ("Missionary Discussions for the Jewish People" 1979), they represented a culmination more than an initiation of the most recent proselyting efforts among Jews. Even before the 1975 Kimball dictum, mentioned above, Mormons had already been looking again upon Jews as proselyting prospects, despite the dubious results of the 1950s campaign. Certain events, both external to the church and internal, probably contributed to this renewed Mormon optimism. One was an end to the Vietnam military draft, which had limited the size of the Mormon missionary corps until the mid-1970s. Another was the outbreak in 1967 and again in 1973 of Arab-Israeli wars, which after the earlier hostilities of 1948 and 1956, seemed especially portentous to many Latter-day Saints and their leaders as they reflected on prophecies about the Jewish gathering and struggle in the Holy Land.[12]

Internally, too, there had been an important turnover in church leadership since the proselyting program for Jews in the 1950s. Three presidents of the church since then had come and gone by the time Kimball took the office at the end of 1973. His career as an apostle had already been distinguished by a massive commitment to gathering and redeeming the Israelites of North America (i.e., American Indians), as previous chapters have explained. It is not surprising, in retrospect, that he would have considered the gathering and redemption of the Jews as an important part of the same divine program, especially in the light of portents from the Middle East. Whatever all the reasons might have been, church publications in the 1970s had an increased frequency of articles about Jews, their conversion, and the importance of the state of Israel. My review of an index of official Mormon publications, such as the *Improvement Era*, the *Ensign*, and the *Church News*, indicated that nearly twice as many articles appeared during the 1970s as during the 1960s on the topics of "Jews," "Hebrews," and "Israel" (LDS Historical Department 1961–90).

Although the final framework for a new proselyting approach to Jews apparently did not appear until 1978, a decision for it must have been made much earlier in the decade. Well before President Kimball's 1975 announcement, the official magazine seems to have anticipated the new missionary campaign. The May 1972 issue of the *Ensign* was devoted entirely to articles on Jews and Israel, historical and contemporary. The issue had a special guest editor (itself an unusual practice for the *Ensign*), Daniel H. Ludlow (1972), then director of instructional materials for the church and a major educator and curriculum specialist. Besides the distinguished guest editor, this special *Ensign* issue featured substantive and interesting articles by sixteen other specialists in the Church Education System. An implicit theme in the issue was the imminent gathering of the Jews to Israel and the nature of the land and environment they would be dealing with there. Even a year earlier, the *Ensign* had carried important articles on the Jews and the Holy Land, and others appeared periodically throughout this decade and the next (e.g., Murray 1971; E. Rasmussen 1971).

The new proselyting program, as it was launched by President Kimball, received special trials in key eastern cities containing concentrations of Jews, according to the account of Thomas B. Neff (1977), who was president of the New York City Mission of the church from July 1974 to July 1977. He reported receiving inquiries from the Church Missionary Department in early 1975 soliciting his help in inaugurating the new program. He apparently identified Irving Cohen, a Mormon convert of Brooklyn and Scotia, New York, as someone who could help prepare pamphlets and offer advice. Most of these pamphlets were eventually approved and printed by the Missionary Department, but some missionaries who had been converted from Judaism found parts of them objectionable and preferred to write their own. Missionaries in the various cities who were specifically assigned to work with Jews were organized separately into "Jewish Zones" of their missions. These zones were more in the nature of administrative than geographical designations, but missionaries focused their efforts mainly in residential areas known to contain large Jewish populations.

In December of 1975, Loren C. Dunn of the Seventy called a meeting in Harrisburg, Pennsylvania, of mission presidents based in several eastern cities to discuss proselyting experiences and strategies. All the presidents reported that the efforts of their missionaries so far had been met with friendly but firm rejections in selected Jewish neighborhoods. Many Jewish people seemed to have generally favorable feelings toward Mormons and were willing to listen politely during an initial visit but were unwilling to accept follow-up visits. "Some success" and "several baptisms" (not otherwise defined by Neff) were reported in New York and elsewhere. The missionaries' approach emphasized the beliefs and experiences that Mormons and Jews presumably held in common, including literal descent from Abraham and a heritage of persecution. However, it is not clear whether the special lessons were as elaborate or as tightly outlined as the Reid program had been twenty years earlier. In early 1977, Dunn reported to the mission presidents that a new and improved "Jewish program" was nearly ready, but it had not appeared by the time Neff left his post. Presumably Dunn was referring to the materials described in the *Ensign* article mentioned above ("Missionary Discussions for the Jewish People" 1979), which finally appeared a couple of years later.

As far as the record indicates, this proselyting campaign among Jews in eastern cities during the 1970s was the final Mormon effort of its kind. It is difficult to assess its results, but they were probably no more encouraging than those obtained from the 1950s program. There is no further mention of it in church periodicals, and the 1977 biography of Spencer W. Kimball makes no mention at all of converting Jews, despite the urgency he had given the matter in his 1975 seminar with regional leaders ("Missionary Discussions for the Jewish People" 1979). Neff, in his concluding comment about this campaign, seemed to express well the recurring Mormon experience with all such efforts to convert Jews: "We continued our proselyting of the Jewish people, but it was . . . difficult and discouraging" (1977, 11). The work was so discouraging that Neff found himself unable to keep missionaries assigned to a "Jewish Zone" for longer than six months, usually even less, without risking their spiritual morale.[13] It appears that this special program for Jews, like the one for American Indians, did not survive the presidency of Spencer W. Kimball, who died late in 1985.

The Emerging Modus Vivendi

As the twentieth century ended, a new and less assertive posture toward Jews and their conversion had already begun to emerge in the church leadership. It involved a new focus on Israel and Jerusalem rather than on American Jews, and it was initiated by study groups visiting from Brigham Young University rather than by apostles. Begun even before 1970, these visits brought delegations large enough and frequently enough eventually to form the nuclei for small Mormon branches in Jerusalem, Tel Aviv, Haifa, and Galilee by the end of the decade (D. Peterson 1992, 343–53). The Mormon presence in Israel grew at the same time as the Kimball missionary initiatives just described but was separate from them. The church branches there were products *not* of missionary activity but mainly of Mormon expatriation from various other locations for professional or occupational reasons. In deference to Israeli sensitivities, if not to Israeli law itself, the LDS Church has conscientiously abstained from proselyting in Israel proper. The modest but significant Mormon presence there is therefore best understood as an *alternative* to the proselyting programs that had proved so unproductive in the past, a reflection of a changed policy, not merely a disguised missionary presence.

Outreach without Proselyting This new policy is more in the spirit of Orson Hyde's 1841 mission, namely, a relaxed friendship with Jews and periodic visits to Jerusalem until the Jews are ready to hear the fuller gospel. Symbolically enough, Hyde's name was evoked when the church in 1972 considered a plan to construct the Orson Hyde Memorial Garden at the Mount of Olives. This new spirit was symbolized also by the initiative of the apostle Howard W. Hunter. Even well before his own brief term as president of the church, Hunter had often shown an open and universalistic posture toward all peoples and a special sensitivity about Jewish feelings concerning prose-lyting (Scott 1994–95). After appropriate negotiations with the Israeli gov-ernment and purchase of the necessary land, the garden was eventually finished and dedicated in October 1979. It has generally been accepted as intended, namely, as a goodwill offering from the Latter-day Saints to Jeru-salem visitors of all religions for their meditation and aesthetic enjoyment (D. Peterson 1992, 343–45).[14]

The nearby BYU Jerusalem Center for Near Eastern Studies on Mount Scopus was also constructed in the Hyde spirit and dedicated by Hunter in 1989 (Galbraith 1984; D. Peterson 1992, 345–52; Scott 1994–95). This center, however, received strident opposition at every stage from the chief rabbin-ate and the Orthodox religious groups in Israel and even from some of the Christian denominations there ("BYU President Defends School's Jerusalem Center" 1985; D. Fisher 1986; Friedman 1985; Indinopulos 1985). Plans were submitted to the Israeli government in early 1981 and approved three years later. By that time, a large opposition movement had formed out of fears in some Israeli circles that the LDS Church was not sincere about its pledge not to proselyte and that the Mormons were preparing various techniques for surreptitious missionary work. In response, the church bent over backward in several ways, canceling informational ads in Israeli newspapers, destroy-ing church pamphlets on hand in English and Hebrew, and stopping all sales of the Book of Mormon in Hebrew. By 1985, BYU felt it necessary even to hire a prominent Israeli public relations firm to reassure the public about the purposes and motives of the new center (D. Peterson 1992, 347–48).

The Israeli public and most of its leaders seem to have realized that, in Daniel Peterson's words, "the dispute was not really about [the Mormons] at all [but] primarily a battle about the nature of Israeli society and the Israeli state" (1992, 348). The eventual dedication of the center not only was facili-tated by the special efforts of Mayor Teddy Kollek and other Israeli moder-ates but also had the public support of several Jewish American organizations, including the Anti-Defamation League. No doubt it helped matters that Kollek's office could report that for sixteen years three hundred Mormon stu-dents had been coming to Israel annually, with no reports in all that time of any Jewish conversions or even criticisms of Mormon conduct (Indinopulos 1985, 1124). The eventual edifice of more than 100,000 square feet, sitting on four well-landscaped acres and costing $15 million, was regarded by Mayor Kollek as an architectural masterpiece with an inspiring view of the city (Scott 1994–95, 11–12). Since its dedication, the center has been put to its intended academic uses, with about a hundred BYU students normally in residence

(Galbraith 1984, 1–4). Continuing vigilance by critics has rarely produced any complaints about proselyting or any other offenses to local sensitivities. An oversight committee of Israeli officials monitors the lectures, recitals, concerts, and other public events at the center to watch "for any evidence of secret missionary agendas" (D. Peterson 1992, 350; see also A. Pratt 1986).[15]

Aside from the scrupulous nonproselyting policy at the BYU Jerusalem Center, Latter-day Saint academics and leaders have proved very responsive in other ways to Jewish sensitivities about the various kinds of costs that history has exacted from the Jews as a people. For example, the "Scholars Conference on the Holocaust and the Churches" was held at BYU in early March 1995. The conference featured as a keynote speaker Congressman Tom Lantos (Democrat from California), a non-Mormon Hungarian Jew and Holocaust survivor, as well as a number of others being honored at the conference for their work in research, museums, films, and other aspects of the Holocaust. One of the organizers of the conference was Douglas F. Tobler, a BYU German language professor and a former LDS mission president in Germany who has written on the Holocaust (1992).[16] However, perhaps no incident so well typifies the new Mormon legitimation of Jewish sensitivities as LDS leaders' rapid response in 1995 to Jewish complaints about the vicarious temple baptisms of deceased Holocaust victims. In a gesture rife with both symbolic and political significance, the church forthwith ceased all these Jewish baptisms, even though they would presumably have had no spiritual or theological efficacy except to Mormons themselves. In the light of this incident, one might be tempted to conclude that the Mormons have given up (at least for now) on efforts to convert even those Jews who have departed to the next world. (See Moulton [1995] and similar articles in the national press during April and May 1995.)

The low-key approach of the LDS Church as an institution toward Israel and the Jews has been supplemented by the efforts of the occasional Jewish convert to Mormonism. Mention has already been made of the few who have written testimonials, pamphlets, and or even books, often privately produced, to share with other Jews their discovery of the complementary nature of Judaism and Mormonism. Besides the usual claim of "Hebrew Christians" (Jewish converts to Christianity) that Jesus of Nazareth was the Messiah promised in Hebrew scriptures, LDS converts from Judaism typically emphasize the Mormon doctrine of a common Israelite ancestry with Jews. The conversion of a few Jews is seen as a harbinger of the eventual uniting of the house of Judah with the house of Joseph in the divine plan for the last days.

The most visible of the Mormon Jews' private initiatives has been the Ensign Foundation, established by the convert Daniel Rona (né Rosenthal) with a Utah headquarters and extensive activities in Israel. A brochure describes the Ensign Foundation as "a non-profit charitable organization which assists in preparing people who consider themselves of the House of Israel to become an Ensign to the nations. The Ensign Foundation facilitates the open exchange of dialogue, travel, science, culture, education, and economic trade between the peoples of Joseph and Judah."[17] Rona is a Palestine-born resident of Israel, American-reared and educated, with dual citizenship. He advertises himself with the fourfold designation of Jew, Mormon, American, and Israeli and "the first and only licensed LDS guide and tour operator in Israel." As his Web site makes clear, he is also an extraordinarily imaginative and successful entrepreneur.

A longtime leader in the small Mormon congregations of Israel, Rona has kept his church ties strong. He and his foundation clearly enjoy the unofficial backing of the church, too, since he typically uses church buildings on his lecture tours in the United States and elsewhere, and the foundation produces instructional materials in Hebrew and English to supplement the official lessons in Mormon Sunday schools. Yet the church has been quite meticulous in avoiding public endorsement of the activities of Rona and his foundation, while they, in turn, have kept those activities far enough removed from direct proselyting, at least within Israel itself, to avoid trouble with the government or to jeopardize Rona's tour guide license.

Opening to the Palestinians If the Jews in Israel and elsewhere have resisted the Mormon theological embrace, one of the effects might have been a dampening of the traditionally one-sided Mormon enthusiasm for the Israeli cause in Palestine: Given the Jewish reluctance to accept the gospel of Jesus—thereby postponing the millennium still further—then perhaps there is still time to do some proselyting among others of Abraham's literal lineage, such as the Arabs. Nor would there seem to be the same urgency that some earlier Mormon leaders saw about completing the Zionist hegemony of the Jews over their ancestral homeland as the final gathering place for the Messianic apocalypse prophesied by Zechariah. Whether or not such a rationale has been articulated explicitly by church leaders, it is certainly fair to say that as their proselyting among Jews has suffered resistance and decline, their posture toward Arabs and the Palestinian cause has become more sympathetic. This important change began to appear in both official and unofficial Mormon discourse toward the end of the twentieth century.

Indications of increased Mormon acknowledgment of Arabs, Palestinians, and their important religious heritage could be seen already in the 1970s as the church was winding down its one last missionary campaign among American Jews. Two important articles appeared in the same issue of the official magazine *Ensign,* one by Howard W. Hunter (1979), who would become church president in a few years, and other by James B. Mayfield (1979), an academic specialist in the Middle East at the University of Utah. Outreach toward Islam at the academic level could also be seen a little later in an important conference and derivative collection of essays produced under the auspices of BYU (S. Palmer 1983). The *Ensign* articles were especially noteworthy in so pointedly calling for recognition that the "sons of Ishmael are our brethren, too" and, along with the descendants of Isaac, entitled to the blessings and covenants of their common father, Abraham. As "a new threshold in the gospel's expansion throughout the world" has been reached and as "Africa and Asia become part of our great missionary program," we cannot, Mayfield insisted, "disdain or ignore" the "histories, cultures, and religions of these areas" (1979, 24–25).

Hunter was even more pointed:

> As members of the Lord's church, we need to lift our vision beyond personal prejudices. . . . Sometimes we unduly offend brothers and sisters of other nations by assigning exclusiveness to one nationality of people over another. [As an example], the present problem in the Middle East—the conflict between the Arabs and the Jews. . . . We believe [the prophecies concerning the Holy Land] . . . but this does not give us justification to dogmatically pronounce that others of our Father's children are not children of promise. . . . Both the Jews and the Arabs are . . . children of promise, and as a church we do not take sides. (1979, 74)

In a similar vein, David B. Galbraith, a longtime resident of Jerusalem and a local LDS Church leader there, even as he was about to take charge of the new BYU Jerusalem Center building, emphasized the evenhandedness that had become church policy: "We . . . need to be politically objective and neutral in considering the rights and problems of both the Israelis and Arabs" because, first, neither side is right, and neither side is wrong; and, second, scriptural promises about gathering in the Holy Land do not refer to Jews alone (quoted in A. Pratt 1986; see also Lubeck 1982). Still later, in 1993, Galbraith asked "How should we as Latter-day Saints view events in the Middle East? Should we passively wait for an inevitable Armageddon? Or is there something we can do to actively and affirmatively promote peace?" His response: "We seem to believe that there is a right and a wrong to every situation. But partiality can breed divisiveness and closed-mindedness. . . . If we take sides in a political context, we compromise our ability to reach out to both sides" (Ogden and Galbraith 1983, 53). The Mormon outreach to Palestinians has not yet involved much proselyting, but important academic research in their country has been started under BYU auspices for improving family, education, and community life there (Fronk and Huntington 1998).

If this new posture toward the Palestinians represents an appropriate "balance" in the Mormon view, it has not been universally welcomed by Israeli commentators, some of whom regard such "neutrality" as tantamount to anti-Semitism (Siporin 1991, 116). While the controversy was still underway in Israel about the BYU Jerusalem Center, the catalogue of nefarious and surreptitious activities for which the church was periodically suspected included sympathies and initiatives favoring the Palestine Liberation Organization (PLO). Admonitions like Galbraith's about not "taking sides" were actually turned against the LDS cause by one leading Israeli opponent of the center, Moshe Dann, who claimed that Mormons were not really special friends of Israel or of Jews but simply indiscriminate and opportunistic world proselyters. He went on to identify several prominent Mormons as boosters for various Palestinian causes and charged BYU's David M. Kennedy Center with clear Arab biases (1987, 10–11).[18]

Since Dann's article appeared, the Mormons have tried to be quite scrupulous in their evenhandedness *and* in honoring their pledge not to proselyte, so most Israelis seem to have relaxed about the Mormon "threat." Yet, given the historic Mormon commitment to world proselyting, the Israelis are not without grounds for assuming that the church still has aspirations for eventual missionary work in their country. Although the church was fully willing to promise not to proselyte in Israel as long as it was not approved by the government, church leaders were not willing to make such a promise for all eternity; or, in the words of James E. Faust of the First Presidency, "We will never say never" (quoted in D. Peterson 1992, 349).

Conclusion

From the historical record reviewed in this chapter, it remains difficult to say with certainty just how the Latter-day Saints today define the identity and divine destiny of the Jews. Arising out of the Christian heritage almost two centuries ago, the Mormon movement could hardly have avoided absorbing a certain amount of the general Christian lore about Jews. Much of that lore was rather hostile, but in recent decades Christian historians and theologians have undertaken a major redefinition of the status of Judaism and the Jews and the Christian relation to both. Mormons, too, might have been influenced somewhat by this redefinition, but not necessarily. The Mormon tradition itself, while mixed and ambiguous about the Jews in some respects, has always contained a strong philo-Judaic, or philo-Semitic element. Throughout most of Mormon history, that element seems to have suppressed both the proselyting programs and the anti-Semitism so common in the rest of Christianity, despite the well-known Mormon missionary zeal among other peoples. Only in the twentieth century, and then only for brief periods, did the Mormons launch any special missionary programs among Jews, and these proved rather unproductive, especially when compared with Mormon missionary success elsewhere.

One might well ask why Mormons have not made more inroads among the Jews. Considering the Hebrew lore and Old Testament usages embraced by Joseph Smith and largely perpetuated by his successors, we might have expected more. Mormons have regularly pointed to the parallels between their religion and Judaism, especially their traditional claims (emphasized at least until recently) of a common ancestry of the two peoples (that is, between the tribes of Ephraim and Judah). The mutual goodwill existing between Mormons and Jews in Utah, from the earliest days onward, has received heartwarming commentary from both sides (Glanz 1963, 184–232, 284–320; Goodman 1976; Siporin 1991; Zucker 1981). Yet even in Utah, it has been rare for a Jew to convert to Mormonism or for Mormons even to seek Jewish converts. Why? In seeking an explanation, many plausible reasons might come to mind, from both the Mormon and the Jewish sides of the relationship.

From the Mormon side, as already indicated, not much proselyting has ever been attempted, even in Utah. Such evidence as is available from Jewish converts to Mormonism (only anecdotal, not systematic) indicates that most of them were already marginal to the Jewish heritage before encountering the Mormons (see, e.g., Glanz 1963, 145–55; Goodman 1976; *Why I Joined the Mormon Church* 1972; and Rothman 1986). It might well be that the unusual Mormon reticence about proselyting among Jews arises ultimately from the theological ambiguity in the legacy of Joseph Smith about Mormon responsibility for the eventual destiny of the Jews. The manifest shortage of practical results from such proselyting as *did* occur would not have helped overcome this traditional theological reticence.

From the Jewish side, many obstacles to conversion have been remarked on by Jews themselves and even by the occasional convert who has overcome these obstacles to become Mormon (or even just Christian). First of all, a thorough Jewish upbringing, even if it is not fully Orthodox, instills an iron Jewish identity forged on the anvil of a unique history. Using a different metaphor, Steve Siporin observes that the "Holocaust has seared the consciousness of all Jewish children" (1991, 116). Even well into the most recent generations, Jewish history has been permeated with discrimination, exclusion, persecution, and genocide, of which the Nazi Holocaust was only the most disastrous. This history has understandably inculcated in the very Jewish identity a sensitivity about outside forces that could threaten overtly or subtly the existence of the Jews as a people. Even in North America, where anti-Semitism was always mild compared with that in Europe—and lately seems almost nonexistent (at least to Gentiles)—Jews still fear a "silent holocaust" through the convergence of two forces that remain serious threats to their identity and their peoplehood: *assimilation* to Gentile culture and *conversion* to an alien or outside religion, especially Christianity (Siporin 1991,

118, citing Reines 1989 and Waxman 1989). The cross, after all, was a profound-
ly threatening symbol to Jews long before the swastika appeared in Germany (Norman 1999, 171–72).

These two distinct but related forces (assimilation and conversion) are all
the more dangerous because they are not inherently violent and can thus pick
off Jews as individuals instead of taking on entire Jewish organizations or
communities.[19] From this viewpoint, it should not be difficult to understand
the survival of a "siege mentality" or a "ghetto mentality," even among many
successful Jews; nor should it be difficult to understand why so many Jews
consider Christian (and Mormon) proselyting as acts of anti-Semitism by
definition (Siporin 1991, 118–19). Mormons once reacted with similar sensitivity and withdrawal against forms of siege that were usually much less violent and of shorter duration than pogroms. That is why Utahns and others
with Mormon upbringings also usually prove difficult to convert to other
religions, even when they have become somewhat marginal to Mormonism
(S. Albrecht and Bahr 1983; Bahr and Albrecht 1989).

Social psychologists have learned that identities created under cultural and
emotional stress, that is, at high psychological "cost," are much harder to
change than those internalized more easily (Barth 1969b; Olzak 1992; Roosens 1989). For many more generations than the Mormons, Jews have been
passing along this "high cost" identity to their children, along with a rich and
powerful lore, which succeeding generations have so far been unwilling to
shelve for the sake of conversion to a different identity. Mormons ought to
be able to understand that, and perhaps they do to some extent. Meanwhile,
assimilation of Jews through intermarriage has proceeded at alarming rates
in the United States, further justifying the sensitivity of Jewish leaders and
families (Reines 1989; Singer and Grossman 2001; Waxman 1989).

Against all of that background, the official Mormon posture toward Jews
at the end of the twentieth century seemed not only sensitive and charitable
but also rational from the cost-benefit and the public relations viewpoints.
In relationships with Israelis and Jews throughout the world, Mormons seem
to have come to the realization, however reluctantly, that prospects for the
conversion of Jews in any appreciable numbers are extremely remote for the
foreseeable future. Meanwhile, Mormons continue to build on the common
ground and common interests already in place. Of course, theologically and
theoretically, Mormon leaders still expect that sooner or later "every knee
must bow and every tongue confess" that Jesus is the Christ, and that includes
the Jews. However, it is questionable that many Mormon leaders today would
expect such a spiritual consummation of the world's history to be imminent.

Continuing Jewish resistance to Mormonism, if not to Mormons generally, has encouraged church leaders to think a little more about the rest of

Abraham's children in Palestine (A. Green 2001). In the earliest years after the establishment of the new state of Israel in 1948, comments by Mormon leaders, whether in public or in private, had revealed a strong pro-Israel sentiment, based primarily on their inherited religious eschatology about the significance of the "return of the Jews" to the Holy Land. Also, like other Americans, most Mormons tended to approve of the new state as an entitlement for Jews in the wake of the Holocaust experience and to see the resistance by Palestinians and certain Arab states as illegitimate in the face of both divine and U.N. mandates. Later in the century, however, as the power and prosperity of the state of Israel made it seem much less the "underdog" in the region, Mormons seem to have separated opinions about the state of Israel from their favorable feelings toward Jews more generally. By the end of the century, Mormon leaders and members had adopted a much more balanced perspective on Israeli conflicts with the Palestinians (A. Green 2001). It remains to be seen whether and when this relatively new Mormon awareness of the Arab peoples of Palestine can be translated into effective missionary outreach into the Islamic world, especially in an age of a newly aroused religious fundamentalism there.[20]

Notes

1. This issue is reviewed by Craig Evans (1993), who cites examples of specific Old Testament verses in Isaiah 1, 30, and 57 and in Jeremiah 3, 7, 9, and 11.

2. Somewhat ironically, the question of who the "chosen people" *really* are has become controversial even in Israel and among some of the world's Jews. See Y. Cohen (1999); and Sandmel (1997).

3. This "dual Zionism," as it might be called, is reflected in the standard LDS interpretation of Isaiah 2:1–4 ("out of Zion shall go forth the law, and the word of the Lord from Jerusalem . . .") as referring to two separate holy sites during the millennial reign. Similarly, the two "sticks" described in Ezekiel 37:15–20 are understood by Mormons to refer not only to the two kingdoms of Judah and Ephraim but also to two separate books of scripture (the Bible and the Book of Mormon), both equally valid. Recall also Gershon's term *dialectical holy lands.*

4. One sees here an interesting parallel to the "Jewish racial mystique" later embraced by converts to Hebrew Christianity (Sobel 1966).

5. This contributed to the development of what Jan Shipps (1998) has called the second or "Hebraic" layer of doctrine and lore that emerged during Smith's innovative career.

6. This was the first and most important of several such Mormon visits to dedicate Palestine, but, as Arnold Green pointed out, "only for the return of the Jews, not for the preaching of the gospel of Jesus Christ" (1994–95, 144). Later visits are described in Epperson (1992, 209); Greenberg (1994, 234–50); and D. Peterson (1992).

7. A "hard" version of the Cowdery-Rigdon position, perhaps overdrawn in the opposite direction from Epperson's, can be seen in Millett and McConkie (1993). In Epperson's review of this book, he finds characterizations of the Jews that are implicitly and in places even explicitly anti-Semitic (1994–95, 128–34).

8. For a more recent example of the lasting intellectual impact on an orthodox Mormon of sustained exposure to Hebrew teaching and traditions, see D. Rasmussen (1981).

9. Rudolf Glanz also emphasized how rare Jewish conversions to Mormonism were even in nineteenth-century Utah, where the surrounding Mormon presence might have been overwhelming and where at least some Jewish conversions might have been expected simply for political or economic expediency (1963, 145–55).

10. According to the tabulations of Gordon Shepherd and Gary Shepherd, the period between 1950 and 1980 brought the first increase of the twentieth century in the frequency and saliency in official Mormon discourse of references to Israel and the Jews in God's plans (1984, 242).

11. Reid attributed this official shutdown mainly to the influence of Henry D. Moyle, who in 1959 had replaced Stephen L. Richards in the First Presidency (1973, 132–34, 143–46). Stephen L. Richards was a cousin of LeGrand Richards and shared his enthusiasm for proselyting among Jews. Moyle, however, was unenthusiastic about it, perhaps because of the influence of his father, James H. Moyle, who had much earlier succeeded B. H. Roberts as mission president in the Eastern States Mission and had closed down Roberts's program there.

12. The pro-Israeli sentiment of most Mormons during this period was reflected in folklore about supernatural interventions on Israel's behalf during one or another of the wars between 1948 and 1973. The folktale differed in details from one telling to the next, but it usually involved a miraculous appearance in Palestine by one of the "Three Nephites" to turn the tide of battle just in time to save a beleaguered and surrounded Israeli army (W. Wilson 1978). For more on the legend of the Three Nephites, see Fife (1940); and W. Wilson (1988).

13. More information about the results of this final missionary campaign might be found in the H. Ronald Zeidner files, 1975–84 (five boxes), "Jewish Mission Task Committee," 1975, also located in the LDS Church Archives, but these files were among several on proselyting among Jews that were restricted and not available to me.

14. An extensive record (with photos) of the acquisition and construction of the Hyde Memorial Gardens can be found in the LDS Church Archives, MS #6427 and #10959.

15. Since this writing, the violence of 2001–2002 in Palestine has forced the LDS Church to close its Jerusalem Center and otherwise greatly reduce its presence in Israel.

16. An advertisement and registration form (copy in my personal files) describes this 1995 event as an "Annual Scholars Conference," so it might have been neither the first nor the last of its kind.

17. Quoted from a brochure, in my personal files, obtained at a public lecture by Rona in January 2002. The brochure also refers readers to the Web site <www.israelrevealed.com>, which indicates the foundation has an extensive range of activities, including lecture tours by Rona, books, tours, newsletters, videos, musical productions, and many other activities supported wholly or partly by foundation funds.

18. Dann is identified by Dan Fisher (1986) as an expatriate American academic who converted to Orthodoxy and was a spokesman for one of the Israeli groups in opposition to the LDS Jerusalem Center. Dann's list of suspects included the Arab Mormon Omar Kader (then a BYU professor), a few other active Mormons with commercial ties to the Middle East, and David M. Kennedy himself, once the U.S. secretary of the treasury.

19. There is a large and growing literature, which I will not attempt to review here, on contemporary Jewish assimilation in America. One article, however, is especially inter-

esting in the present context because it deals with the decline in Jewish identity among Reform Jews in Salt Lake City (Gephart, Siegel, and Fletcher 1974).

20. In an effort to enhance its readers' understanding of Islam, the editors of *BYU Studies* prepared a large, special issue of that journal even before the events of September 11, 2001 (Toronto, 2001).

7. Mormons and Secular Anti-Semitism

> There should be no ill will, and I am sure there is none, in the heart of any true Latter-day Saint, toward the Jewish people. . . . And let no Latter-day Saint be guilty of taking any part in any crusade against these people. I believe in no other part of the world is there as good a feeling in the hearts of mankind toward the Jewish people as among the Latter-day Saints.
> —Heber J. Grant, 1921

> I have perceived no sign of anti-Semitism in any office, school or government, where I was known, and known to be a Jew. . . . *This* may safely be said: there is probably no Christian-Gentile culture which is less disposed to anti-Semitism than the Mormon culture here in Zion.
> —Louis C. Zucker, 1981

THESE TWO EPIGRAPHS, the first from a venerable president of the Mormon church and the other from a prominent Jewish citizen of Utah, capsulize the message of the previous chapter: Mormon teachings and policies seem to have contravened and neutralized the anti-Semitism inherited from traditional Christianity.[1] Yet the relation between ostensible religious beliefs, on the one hand, and actual behavior, on the other, can never be taken for granted, as both the clergy and the critics of religious communities can attest. The question in this chapter is whether and how the *religious* beliefs of Mormons are translated into *secular, civil* attitudes and behavior toward Jews.

The question is not, of course, whether anti-Semites or anti-Semitism are found among the Mormons. No doubt they are. Mormons living in Christian countries have, after all, been exposed to the same religious lore and myths about Jews as have other residents of those countries (illustrated by the recent experience of Keith Norman [1999, 168]). Furthermore, at any given point since the middle of the twentieth century, most Latter-day Saints have been converts to Mormonism and thus likely to have reached at least their teenage years without such neutralizing influences as might have been provided by traditional Mormon philo-Semitism. But what is the extent of anti-Semitism among Mormons, and how do Mormons compare with other Christians when similar measures are used? There is much evidence available. Some of the evidence is qualitative and anecdotal, yet there is also a great deal of systematic empiri-cal evidence from surveys of Mormons and other religious denominations.

Personal and Historical Accounts

The account by Louis Zucker (1981), from which the epigraph is taken, is especially useful because its author was a publicly committed and observant Jew who had lived with his family among the Mormons for more than half of the twentieth century as a professor of English at the University of Utah. He had had regular contact with prominent Mormon and non-Mormon leaders in religion, politics, business, and academia, as well as with friends and peers of all kinds. He certainly was not attracted to the Mormon reli-gion and was, in fact, critical of the religious naïveté of most Mormons, even prominent ones, and was particularly critical of the retrospective appropri-ation and distortion of the Hebrew scriptures in church sermons and lessons. He also referred candidly to a few instances of anti-Semitism and dishones-ty on the part of some Mormons in business dealings. Yet he concluded that the Utah environment was one in which Jews and their religion could thrive and in which his children had thrived among their Mormon school peers and teachers. Taken by itself, this account might appear too good to be true.[2]

More recently, Steve Siporin (1991), another Jewish professor of English, responded to an invitation to reflect on a much shorter but still meaningful sojourn in Logan, Utah (a more conservative town than Zucker's Salt Lake City). Siporin's account also was candid in acknowledging occasional in-stances of anti-Semitism he and his children had encountered, but he regard-ed these as the "normal" or traditional Christian kind, nothing special. He emphasized that he did not find the LDS Church or religion per se to be anti-Semitic, not even in the form of subtle proselyting efforts. Some of his Mor-mon neighbors even sent him greeting cards for Jewish holidays. He attrib-uted this fairly friendly environment to "the Mormon assumption of a special Mormon-Jewish relationship" (1991, 114). He and his family found it difficult to live so far away from a Jewish congregation and community, especially at holiday times, but he saw far more acceptance and appreciation for his her-itage than anti-Semitism among his Mormon friends. Very few other ac-counts of life among the Mormons by Jews have been left behind.[3]

Three historical accounts of Jewish life among the Mormons have been published. The first was by the New York scholar Rudolf Glanz (1963). His book covered Mormon-Jewish relations only during the nineteenth century and was a generally uncritical presentation of documents, quotations, and excerpts from other accounts about Mormons and Jews. Glanz was very re-spectful and appreciative of the Mormon and Utah treatment of Jews, re-marking particularly on the fact that this "new religion of the Mormons [was able to] contribute to the consolidation, socially and spiritually, of the oldest European religious community in the New World, [representing] one of the most astonishing phenomena in the history of ideas" (1963, 332). Diffuse though this book might be, it is a unique and useful collection of material on early Mormon-Jewish relationships and illustrates the historic philo-Judaism of the Mormon religion and people.

The well-known Mormon historian Juanita Brooks (1973) had considerable difficulty in acquiring the necessary information and understanding about Jewish life and religion, but eventually she published a history of the Jews of Utah and Idaho. Apparently under the critical guidance of Louis Zucker, who actually wrote one of the chapters himself, Brooks finally finished the six-year project. Like Glanz's book, this one is a useful collection of historical facts and details arranged chronologically; unlike Glanz's, it largely bypasses Mormon-Jewish relationships per se in favor of narrative *Jewish* history, which was the purpose for which it had been privately commissioned. In more than two hundred pages, plus appendixes, it takes the history of Jews in Idaho and Utah (primarily the latter) up to about 1970.

The third general history of Jews among the Mormons is the shortest but also probably the most accessible and the most skillfully written of the three. A Jewish journalist, scholar, and longtime resident of Utah, Jack Goodman maintained that Jews have thrived in Utah as an integral part of the political, economic, and other institutional structures because "overt anti-Semitism is largely unknown. . . . Utahns have generally accepted Jews as neighbors, as business associates, as fellow citizens, and as folks next door" (1976, 217–18). The first two Jews ever to be elected state governors in the United States were Simon Bamberger of Utah in 1916 and Moses Alexander of Idaho in 1914 (Brooks 1973, 127–34, 163–74; Goodman 1976, 208–10). Jewish children growing up in Utah, claimed Goodman, "unhappily discovered anti-Semitism for the first time" only when they went away to major universities in the Ivy League and elsewhere (1976, 214). Goodman conceded that the relatively small number of Jews in Utah (perhaps 0.1 percent) might simply make them seem less threatening and more acceptable to the citizens there, but he credited mainly the special Mormon theology about Jews.

All of these historical treatments are, like this chapter, set in the United States, where almost all interactions between Mormons and Jews have taken place. There are fragmentary accounts of such interactions elsewhere, particularly in Germany, where Nazi policies toward Jews created serious and tragic rifts in Mormon religious ranks. Of course, that is a topic for a different book or article (but see Keele and Tobler 1980; King 1979; Schnibbe 1984; and Tobler 1992, 72–90). Let us move now from personal and historical accounts to a more systematic and quantitative review of attitudes toward Jews among Mormons and others.

Anti-Semitism in General Surveys

The Christian Context in America

As was discussed in the previous chapter, Christian and Jewish scholars after the Holocaust began serious reassessments of the contributions traditional Christian teachings might have made to that tragedy and to earlier historic pogroms and persecutions of European and American Jews. As part of that effort, surveys of American public opinion and attitudes toward Jews seemed desirable, especially in the light of periodic anti-Semitic incidents still occurring long after the end of the Nazi era. The systematic data that general surveys might yield about the nature, magnitude, and distribution of anti-Semitic expressions were, of course, of special interest to the Anti-Defamation League (ADL) and other Jewish organizations. Accordingly, the ADL sponsored and financed a number of such surveys over the years.

One of the earliest of the ADL-sponsored surveys was a five-year study conducted by Charles Y. Glock and Rodney Stark at the Survey Research Center of the University of California, Berkeley, starting in the early 1960s. The first volume of the several projected over the five-year period was published in 1966 as *Christian Beliefs and Anti-Semitism*. This volume was based mainly on a large, systematic survey of Protestant and Catholic church members in the San Francisco Bay Area, augmented with a comparative national sample by members of the same Berkeley team. These two data sets, regional and national, were designed to permit analyses that would provide both breadth and depth for the findings about the origins and implications of anti-Semitism among Christians. The various publications that eventually came out of this project established early benchmarks of existing levels of anti-Semitism for comparisons with later studies, as well as for comparisons with my own data from Mormons, collected at about the same time.[4]

The theoretical process employed by Glock and Stark (1966) traces the roots of anti-Semitism to certain religious beliefs and cognitive styles, and the authors devised means for measuring each of these elements with a cluster of questions. For example, people who gave clearly affirmative answers to questions about belief in God, in the divinity of Jesus, in an actual devil, and in biblical miracles were considered "orthodox" Christians. The more such beliefs they affirmed and the stronger their affirmation, the higher were their scores on orthodoxy. The same basic method was used to measure other religious elements theoretically implicated in the genesis of secular anti-Semitism. In summary, what these scholars learned from their research was that orthodoxy and other expressions of traditional Christian belief were potentially productive of anti-Semitism but *only if* linked with a specific outlook of religious hostility toward *contemporary* Jews (1966, 132, figure 2). Such hostility was expressed in the belief that God is still punishing the Jews for the crucifixion of Jesus; the belief that Jews cannot be forgiven until they accept Jesus as Christ or Messiah; and other unfriendly notions. Only with those hostile elements do Christian beliefs lead to anti-Semitism or to any other specific kind of prejudice. Or, as summarized in a more recent Dutch replication of this work, "For those who believe that [today's] Jews are damned on religious grounds, it is only a small step also to believe that they are clannish, dishonest, unpatriotic, and subversive" (Eisenga, Konig, and Scheepers 1995, 215).

The Glock and Stark study (1966) was the first large-scale demonstration in the social science literature of how certain traditional Christian beliefs have contributed to secular anti-Semitism, and it specified which beliefs were primarily responsible. As might have been expected, the work received a great deal of attention from other scholars and the partisans of various religious communities. The assessments of the work were not entirely favorable (e.g., Dittes 1967; Furfey 1966; Hoge and Carroll 1975; Kirsch 1972; Mayer et al. 1966; Middleton 1973; and Roof 1974). Glock and Stark (1973) mounted a vigorous defense, pointing to the controls imposed on their analysis to rule out the influence of social, psychological, and other traits of a nonreligious kind. They also pointed to replications of their work that had produced very similar findings, starting with their own replications from national data (not just California) and from clergy data (Stark et al. 1971, 1–14), as well as replications by other scholars (e.g., Kersten 1970; and Mauss 1968 and 1970). Supportive replications continued into the 1990s (Eisenga, Konig, and Scheepers 1995).[5] Many of the reviews of Glock and Stark's *Christian Beliefs and Anti-Semitism,* from a variety of disciplines, were actually very favorable, even uncritical. The Berkeley project itself went on to produce additional follow-up studies on anti-Semitism with the use of various other data sets (e.g., Selznick and Steinberg 1969; Stark et al. 1971; and Quinley and Glock 1979). Some of the original work, fortunately, was available to the appropriate committees during the Second Vatican Council and thus was able to make a contribution to the deliberations that eventually produced the papal declaration *Nostra Aetate* of 1965, mentioned in the previous chapter.

Surveys on Mormons and Anti-Semitism

The occasion for surveying Mormons about anti-Semitism did not arise from any institutional interest in doctrinal reconsiderations of the kind that occurred during Vatican II. Although there have always been Mormon anti-Semites, there is little or no reason to believe that church indoctrination has been responsible for their *secular* ideas about Jews. As was discussed in the previous chapter, traditional Christian teachings about Jews seem to have been largely neutralized by a general Hebraic overlay in early Mormonism and by a unique and specific Mormon claim of literal descent from the Israelite tribe of Joseph through Ephraim. Glock and Stark (1966) had found that orthodox Christian teachings, even when potentially hostile toward Jews, could be neutralized by a countervailing commitment to religious libertarianism. From my association with these scholars in the 1960s and my knowledge of their project at Berkeley, I postulated that the unique philo-Judaism in the Mormon tradition might function to neutralize the anti-Jewish strain inherited by Mormons from conventional Christianity, somewhat as religious libertarianism does. I reasoned that the general theoretical model of Glock and Stark might be tested to see if religious indoctrination could *work both ways*—that is, if it could *undermine* or neutralize anti-Semitism, as well as generate it.

Measuring Anti-Semitism among Mormons It seems clear from the previous chapter that certain religious beliefs about Jews have been just as important for Mormons as for Protestants and Catholics. The question in this chapter is how these religious beliefs are related to *secular* anti-Semitism among Mormons, as among others. In an earlier book, I explained how I collected data from three surveys of Mormons located, respectively, in the California East Bay Area, in urban San Francisco, and in Salt Lake City, Utah (1994, 33–59, 215–26). My survey methods were deliberately modeled on those explained by Glock and Stark (1966, 215–48). The 1964 East Bay Area survey was originally intended as a kind of pilot study for the other two but yielded two publications in its own right (Mauss 1966 and 1968). The subsequent Salt Lake City and San Francisco data provided the basis for my doctoral dissertation (1970); a derivative manuscript never published (1985); a few publications in Mormon scholarly journals (1972a, 1972b, 1976); some of the chapters in my 1994 book; and this present chapter (condensed from Mauss 2001a, chapter 8).[6]

These surveys were the first ever conducted among Mormons on such a scale and with any appreciable randomness (Mauss 1994, 222–26). They remain the only large surveys, not under church auspices or control, that represent adult Mormon populations, either in general or in specified geographic areas (Bahr and Forste 1986; Mauss 2001b, 157–63). Their main drawback, of course, is their vintage, now approaching forty years. Despite their age, however, they are valuable for future comparative purposes, because they cover the beliefs and attitudes of Mormons about not only various racial questions but many other questions and social characteristics as well. The questions of ethnic or racial prejudice under discussion here give these data special value even now, precisely because of the time period during which they were collected.

This is a point worth emphasizing. When these surveys were conducted in the 1960s, the Mormon membership still consisted primarily of lifelong members reared in Utah and the West, products of three or more generations of indoctrination in traditional Mormon teachings, including the "racial" lore about Jews and blacks (or "Negroes," as they were called then). Since that time, Mormon church growth has come largely from adult converts outside of Utah (Heaton 1992, 1525–27); but my survey data from the 1960s represent a mainly Mormon-born membership still steeped in traditional racial and ethnic conceptions of themselves and other "lineages." These Mormon surveys thus parallel those of Catholics and Protestants conducted by Glock and Stark well before any change in religious indoctrination could have occurred in the wake of Vatican II.

The Mormon, Protestant, and Catholic samples are thus highly comparable in temporal terms, as well as other respects. They provided a good opportunity to test two hypotheses about Mormons implied by the historical doctrines and relationships with Jews outlined in the previous chapter: first, when compared with other Christian denominations, Mormons show relatively low rates of secular anti-Semitism; and second, among Mormons, secular anti-Semitism is less likely for those accepting the special doctrine of Mormon *affinity* with the Jews than for those not accepting that doctrine.[7] The first of these hypotheses calls for a fairly straightforward comparison of Mormons with others in measurable rates of anti-Semitism, but the second hypothesis involves a somewhat more complex analysis of the countervailing influences of various traditional Mormon doctrines.

Before considering these hypotheses, we need an operational definition of anti-Semitism—meaning here a prejudice expressed in *secular, civil* images of Jews, not just in hostile religious ideas. Glock and Stark had conceptualized and measured three different aspects of anti-Semitism: beliefs, feelings, and behavior (1966, 101–61). For the Mormon case, I focused mainly on anti-Semitic *beliefs* because feelings and behavior are derivative. Or, as explained by Glock and Stark, the anti-Semitic beliefs are foundational, because they provide the *rationale* for the hostile feelings and behavior (1966, 105–6). Among the many beliefs about Jews indicative of anti-Semitism, Glock and Stark used six intercorrelated items to construct an additive scale of Christian anti-Semitism (1966, 123–29). I used three of those same items to construct my scale of secular anti-Semitism for Mormons.[8] When my scale was reduced, like its predecessor, to four levels for greater statistical stability, the two scales became quite comparable.[9]

Table 7.1 summarizes a great deal of data and thus obscures a number of specific variations in the data. For example, the Mormon rates of anti-Semitism tended to resemble those of the liberal and moderate Protestant denominations more than those of the conservative and fundamentalist ones (see Glock and Stark 1966, 129). Even compared with Protestant and Catholic averages, as in table 7.1, Mormon secular anti-Semitism tends to be on the

Table 7.1. Mormons, Protestants, and Catholics on a Scale of Secular Anti-Semitism

Secular Anti-Semitism Score	Mormons			Total Protestants ($n = 1654$)	Catholics ($n = 409$)
	Salt Lake City ($n = 958$)	San Francisco ($n = 296$)	Combined ($n = 1254$)		
High 4	4%	3%	4%	15%	11%
3	23	23	23	18	18
1–2	58	55	57	47	45
Low 0	15	18	16	20	26

Source: Figures for Protestants and Catholics are from Glock and Stark (1966, 129) and are based on six questions.

low side. Especially noteworthy are the relatively small Mormon figures for high anti-Semitism (3–4 percent). Similar distributions were obtained among the East Bay California Mormons (Mauss 1968, 16), so altogether the hypothesis of relatively low Mormon anti-Semitism is modestly confirmed. The sheer incidence of anti-Semitism among Mormons, however, is not nearly as interesting as the cognitive process by which it is constrained. To see that process, we must turn to the second hypothesis, namely, that Mormons tend to have lower rates of anti-Semitism if they accept the church's doctrines defining their affinity with the Jews as a chosen people.

Religious Beliefs and the Mitigation of Anti-Semitism Although Glock and Stark found traditional Christian doctrines about contemporary Jews as the main cognitive conduit for anti-Semitism (1966, 60–80), they also found religious libertarianism to have the opposite function (1966, 81–98). In other words, on the one hand, the traditional belief that the Jews were responsible for the crucifixion of Christ, plus the belief that they could not be forgiven without accepting Christ, created a theological or religious *hostility* that was readily translated into secular anti-Semitism.[10] On the other hand, if Christians also believed in *libertarian* teachings—namely, that religious outsiders (even atheists) should be permitted to participate without discrimination in secular, civil life—then the religious hostility was strongly neutralized, and secular anti-Semitism was greatly reduced, even among the most orthodox Christians (Glock and Stark 1966, 86–89, 132).

This same process was readily apparent in the Mormon data (Mauss 1970 and 1985), where religious hostility toward Jews and religious libertarianism were measured by indicators similar to those used by Glock and Stark. These indicators showed that Mormons were at least as likely as other Christians to accept the hostile beliefs about modern Jews but were also much *more* likely than other Christians to embrace religious libertarianism (Mauss 1994, 53–54). This combination suggests that Mormons had simply imported the conventional definitions of Jews in Christian lore but had also learned from their own persecutions the importance of tolerance for religious outsiders. Religious libertarianism thus tended to neutralize religious hostility toward Jews in the Mormon data, as in the Catholic and Protestant data (see figures C.1 and C.2 in appendix C, herein; compare Glock and Stark 1966, 92–98).

Yet, for Mormons, there was an important additional element in the cognitive mix: the Mormons' own historic belief in their affinity with Jews as fellow Israelites and therefore also as "chosen people" in the divine scheme of things. What evidence do we have that these Mormon doctrines about Jews would have any impact on anti-Semitism among the Mormons? If Mormons tend to share the hostile beliefs of traditional Christianity about the crucifixion and perpetual Jewish guilt, can the special Mormon doctrines about their affinity with the Jews make any difference? One way to find out is to "mix" beliefs in the two kinds of doctrines and see what impact the various combinations of belief might have on anti-Semitism. Table 7.2 shows how the "high" levels of anti-Semitism in table 7.1 change with different combinations of religious beliefs about Jews.

In considering table 7.2, let us first recall that religious *hostility* toward Jews was indicated by beliefs that Jews are still being punished by God and that Jews cannot be forgiven for their continuing perfidy until they accept Jesus Christ. A posture of religious *affinity* toward Jews was based on the beliefs that the Jews still remain "chosen people" in God's eyes and that Mormons share with Jews a literal Israelite ancestry. The interaction of these four beliefs with each other and with secular anti-Semitism is what we see in table 7.2.

This table shows that the unique Mormon teachings about Jews, to the extent that they are believed by Mormons, greatly reduce the incidence of secular anti-Semitism that is otherwise encouraged by traditional Christian beliefs about Jewish perfidy and punishment. Most Mormons hold both kinds of beliefs simultaneously (hostility *and* affinity beliefs), because both are part of a generally orthodox Mormon outlook. However, to the extent

Table 7.2. Mormon Anti-Semitism with Combinations of Beliefs about Jews

Combinations of Jew-Related Beliefs	Anti-Semitism Rates for Each Combination[a]				Percent Drop[c]
	Yes + No[b]	Yes + Yes	No + No	No + Yes	
Jews punished + Jews chosen	40%	36%	30%	22%	−18
Jews punished + Mormons as Israelites	42	37	27	26	−16
Jews unforgiven + Jews chosen	40	34	28	19	−21
Jews unforgiven + Mormons as Israelites	43	35	24	24	−19

a. Data from Salt Lake City and San Francisco combined. Figures are "high" percentages in the secular anti-Semitism score (i.e., scoring either 3 or 4 on the scale in table 7.1).

b. For each of the four combinations, "yes" refers to agreement (either "definitely" or "probably") with the belief, and "no" indicates all other responses to the same belief.

c. "Percent Drop" refers to the difference between figures in the first and fourth columns for each combination of beliefs.

that Mormons are free of the hostile beliefs, their rates of anti-Semitism drop significantly. Across the various combinations of acceptance and rejection of traditional beliefs in table 7.2, rates of anti-Semitism drop by about half (from slightly over 40 percent to around 20 percent or less) between those accepting only the hostile beliefs (first column) and those accepting only the affinity beliefs (fourth column). This table confirms, with better samples and fuller analysis, the findings I reported in my earliest article on this subject (Mauss 1968, 25, table 11).

When countervailing beliefs are paired, as in table 7.2, we can see how important the affinity beliefs are in neutralizing the hostility beliefs, in one combination after another. Yet there remains the question of how much overlap there really is in the Mormon samples *collectively*. Are there basically two kinds of Mormons—those who hold mostly the affinity beliefs but reject the hostility beliefs versus those who take the opposite posture? The answer can be seen in table 7.3. For this table, two additive indexes were created by the usual method. The index of religious hostility toward Jews combines responses to the two questions about perpetual Jewish punishment for the Crucifixion and the requirement for their conversion as a condition of forgiveness. The index of religious affinity toward Jews combines responses to the questions about the "chosen" status of the Jews and their common ancestry with the Mormons. The strong tendency for the two sets of beliefs to go together is clear in table 7.3, where virtually all (96 percent) of those Mormons high in religious hostility are also medium or high in religious affinity.[11]

Table 7.3. Mormon Affinity for Jews by Religious Hostility Levels

Religious Affinity for Jews	Religious Hostility toward Jews		
	Low ($n = 576$)	Medium ($n = 388$)	High ($n = 290$)
Low ($n = 260$)	37%	9%	4%
Medium ($n = 399$)	35	37	18
High ($n = 595$)	28	54	78
Total $n = 1,254$			

So far, three major sets of religious belief have been implicated variously in the genesis of anti-Semitism among Mormons. A graphic summary of this process is presented in figure 7.1. This figure is an abbreviated path diagram depicting how these various religious factors influence each other on the way to anti-Semitism in Salt Lake City and San Francisco.[12] The full path models appear in appendix C (figures C.1 and C.2), where there is also an explanation for the technique of path analysis (see also Stark et al. 1971, 126–27). In brief, a path coefficient indicates the weight, or impact, that one factor has on the next

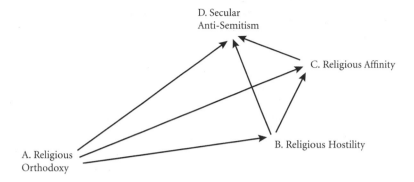

PATH COEFFICIENTS FOR THE DIAGRAM

	A→B	A→C	A→D	B→C	B→D	C→D
Salt Lake City	.422	.555	.047	.188	.100	.011
San Francisco	.359	.568	.027	.176	.162	−.116

Figure 7.1. Abbreviated Path Diagram for Religious Beliefs and Secular Anti-Semitism among Mormons in Salt Lake City and San Francisco

one when all the other factors in the full model are statistically controlled. In figure 7.1, the numbers indicate that (in Salt Lake City, for example) orthodoxy (A) has a rather strong direct influence on both religious hostility (B) toward Jews (.422) and religious affinity (C) for Jews (.555).[13] However, it has only a minimal direct impact on anti-Semitism (D) itself (.047). Religious hostility has some direct influence on anti-Semitism (.100)—double that of basic orthodoxy (.100 compared with .047)—but hostility is even more strongly related to religious affinity (.188). The most important path in the diagram, however, is that of C→D, with a coefficient of nearly zero (.011), indicating virtually no potential for anti-Semitism. A reasonable interpretation of all these figures would go something like this: Orthodoxy has little potential to generate anti-Semitism *unless* it "goes through" (or is accompanied by) religious hostility. The impact of religious hostility, in turn, is blunted to almost zero (.011) when it "goes through" religious affinity. These figures for Salt Lake City Mormons resemble the ones for San Francisco Mormons, where affinity not only blunts hostility but actually "reverses" it (−.116).

The Fuller Framework of Mormon Anti-Semitism To avoid undue repetition of research presented in earlier publications, I have deliberately truncated my analysis of Mormon anti-Semitism in this chapter. The focus here has been primarily on what is unique about the emergence of anti-Semitism in the Mormon cognitive process, particularly the influence of the belief in shared ancestry and chosen status with the Jews. If it were not for this element, the genesis and incidence of anti-Semitism among Mormons would differ little from what the Glock and Stark model amply explained about other Christians. Yet in their model, as in my adaptation of it for Mormons, the production of anti-Semitism occurs in a much larger and more complex framework of both religious and nonreligious variables. These other variables are largely ignored in this chapter, but they have been included in the theoretical models and calculations that have been published elsewhere (e.g., Glock and Stark 1966; Stark et al. 1971; and Mauss 1968, 1970, and 1994), which readers can easily consult. They are also included herein as part of appendix B and appendix C, but without the detailed explanation of conceptualization and measurement already provided in those other sources.

In addition to the religious variables of orthodoxy, hostility to Jews, and affinity with Jews, which have formed the crux of the argument in this chapter, the other religious variables in my fuller analysis consisted of particularism and libertarianism.[14] These two variables, along with orthodoxy, made up a composite religious posture that I called religious provincialism (Mauss 2001a, chapter 8). Comparable but not identical to religious dogmatism in the Glock and Stark model (1966, 94–98, 130–35), religious provincialism refers to an outlook among Mormons that not only is orthodox in basic beliefs but also claims exclusive possession of religious truth and advocates restrictions on the civil liberties of nonbelievers.[15] This outlook is roughly the opposite of cosmopolitanism, an index that was constructed and applied in an earlier book (Mauss 1994, 66–73).[16]

As Glock and Stark amply demonstrated, however, social status, education, age, and many other nonreligious factors are also related to anti-Semitism, even if not as strongly as are the religious factors (1966, 172–87). In a fuller analysis of the Mormons, I included in my general explanatory model social status (educational attainment and occupational prestige); external involvements (participation in various clubs, societies, and interest groups); and anomia (an abbreviated version of the standard Srole measure of psychological alienation or disillusionment with society). All of these variables, religious and nonreligious, are combined in the path analyses appearing in figures C.1 and C.2 in appendix C, but they are not otherwise discussed because they function in the model mainly as control variables on the relationships among the religious variables and anti-Semitism.[17]

More Recent Evidence on Anti-Semitism among Mormons

Although the surveys on which this chapter has depended are quite dated, they still retain considerable value for what they reveal about the influence of religious indoctrination among Mormons and other Christians in a period when traditional teachings about Jews were still generally held. Further-more, the cognitive *process* generating anti-Semitism and depicted in the path models retains a presumptive validity independent of the age of the survey data. The validity of this theoretical process has been confirmed by much later data, both in the Netherlands (Eisenga, Konig, and Scheepers 1995) and among American Mormons. Not a great deal of later data is available. Such evidence as there is, however, indicates that Mormon tendencies toward anti-Semitism remained low all the way to the end of the twentieth century. In particular, two surveys of more recent years can be cited here. The first of these was a nonrandom but rather extensive survey during the mid-1980s of a few hundred members of a right-wing, somewhat racist patriotism move-ment in Idaho. About a third of the respondents in this survey were Mor-mons. The second survey actually took the form of a data subset that I com-piled from the General Social Surveys of the National Opinion Research Corporation covering 1986–89 and containing two questions indicative of attitudes toward Jews (J. Davis and Smith 1996).

Mormons, Right-Wing Politics, and Anti-Semitism

During the second half of the twentieth century, Mormons in the United States came to be identified in the public mind and in political reality with the Republican party and a generally conservative political posture (Mauss 1994, 46–59). Since such a posture has traditionally carried a strain of anti-Semitism, as well as a resistance to expanded civil rights for black Americans, it seems reasonable to wonder how Mormon racial beliefs and attitudes might have been influenced in the process. Mormon relations with blacks are the subject of the next two chapters, but it is well known that the LDS Church, along with the states of Utah and Idaho, had conservative policies toward blacks until at least the 1970s. Did right-wing Mormons, like others on the Right, tend to generalize their prejudice to all racial and ethnic minorities, or were their anti-Semitic tendencies still neutralized by the traditional Mormon philo-Semitism? Such a question is all the more appropriate in the light of the success that the John Birch Society and other right-wing organi-zations once had in attracting Mormons, such as the prominent Mormon apostle (and later church president) Ezra Taft Benson and his family (Quinn 1993).[18] A study of a right-wing movement in Idaho (where the Bensons orig-inated) bears on these questions (Aho 1990).

The research by James A. Aho of Idaho State University included a valuable survey. For several years, Aho immersed himself in studying the literature, meetings, activities, and more than three hundred personal interviews with persons identified (by themselves or other key informants) as members of the so-called Christian Patriotism movement in Idaho. This movement was a loose federation of three different segments, the two largest of which were called

Identity Christians and Christian Constitutionalists. The Identity Christians tended to be members of the Church of Jesus Christ—Christian, centered in the Hayden Lake area of northern Idaho, and led by the Reverend Richard Butler. Very few people of Mormon background were members of Butler's church, partly for ideological reasons, partly because few Mormons live in northern Idaho, and partly because they were disinclined to abandon their Mormon membership for this alternative sect.[19] By contrast, 80 percent of the Mormons in Aho's study were Christian Constitutionalists, who also held memberships in such right-wing political organizations as the John Birch Society, the Freeman Institute, the Sons of Liberty, and the Posse Comitatus. Mormons constituted about a third of the Christian Patriotism movement in general (all segments), which was about the same as their proportion of the total Idaho population (Aho 1990, 22, 120–31, 177, 258–59).[20]

As already noted, racism of various kinds, including anti-Semitism, is pervasive in such movements. In particular, they promulgate theories that implicate Jews in various conspiracies to take over the world or at least the world's economic and political institutions. Aho found Jewish conspiracy theories much less prominent, however, among the Christian Constitutionalists (comprising most of the Mormons) than among the Identity Christians. Aho went to some lengths to analyze the countervailing religious heritage in Mormonism that helped neutralize this kind of anti-Semitism (1990, 114–32, 175–80). As I explained in chapter 2, Mormonism traditionally carried a strong strain of British Israelism, just as the Christian Identity and other groups have. However, in those other groups, this strain has generally been expressed in a hostile counterclaim *against* Jews and their worldwide "conspiracies," whereas the Anglo-Israel claims in Mormonism have usually been accompanied by a natural affinity *for* Jews and a resistance to anti-Semitism. That is why, according to Aho, Mormons who have joined right-wing "Patriot" causes have preferred the Constitutionalist branch of the movement to the Christian Identity branch (1990, 127–30). All in all, he tells us, "[E]xplicit anti-Semitism is rare among Mormon patriots" (1990, 22).

Yet, even the Constitutionalists are not entirely free of anti-Semitism, at least as far as financial issues are concerned. Aho encountered a certain amount of ambivalence among them about Jews and money. One who had done business with "Jewish brokers" observed that they somehow always got others rather than themselves to "take the risks." The verdict of another, however, was that the problem was not with Jews as such but with "international bankers" and that just "because a few Jewish bankers are involved, doesn't mean all Jews are bad." For Mormon Constitutionalists, in particular, Aho found even this kind of ambivalence was usually resolved by exonerating Jews altogether for banking conspiracies or one-world conspiracies, often on religious grounds: "The Lord knew what He was doing when He came through the Jews. Any nation that has gone against them has brought trouble on itself" (quoted in Aho 1990, 258–59).[21]

Aho's analysis of even recent LDS discourse leads him to conclude that for Mormons, "[w]hatever their transgressions in the past, the Jews retain God's unconditional love . . . [and] shall be regathered to possess the land of their inheritance" (assuming their eventual repentance and acceptance of Christ, of course). Despite their having strayed from the Abrahamic covenant, "the Jews have remained God's favorites, the chosen people." However presumptuous this portrayal might seem to Jews, "the Latter-day Saint sees [it] in a benign, even heroic light. The Latter-day Saint is not just a metaphorical or symbolic brother of the Jew but his own flesh and blood, [and has] an intensely jealous familial interest in harboring him from gentile persecution" (Aho 1990, 130).

It seems possible that Aho has seen his Mormon informants from the Patriot movement in an unduly optimistic light, for we are not able to determine how "representative" they might have been of Idaho Mormons or even of movement members. However, the ideas about Jews expressed by Aho's Latter-day Saints in the 1980s certainly seem consistent with what emerged from my surveys in the 1960s. Anomalous as it might seem to others, right-wing Mormons in Idaho have apparently separated anti-Semitism from whatever other conventional forms of bigotry might have been expressed in the right-wing organizations they have joined.

National Surveys

As I have explained elsewhere (Mauss 1994, 33–34, 226), social scientists have benefited for three decades from an annual spring social survey conducted under the auspices of Chicago's National Opinion Research Corporation with funding from the National Science Foundation (J. Davis and Smith 1996). Usually called the General Social Survey (GSS), it has been conducted almost every year since 1972. During most of these years, the survey has been based on face-to-face interviews by specialists using national samples of approximately sixteen hundred adults. Many of the questions are repeated every year, but many others are asked only on alternate years, or even less often, or of only half of the sample, or with other limitations. In any one annual sample, there might be fewer than fifty Mormons. Until a deliberate decision in the 1980s to weight the sample more heavily with respondents from the western states, Mormons were rarely included. However, by choosing the annual samples containing questions of special interest and then aggregating these samples across several years, it is possible to collect enough Mormons to make feasible comparisons possible with a general non-Mormon random subsample. That is what I have done here.

While the GSS often includes an extensive battery of questions about civil rights, blacks, or African Americans, only rarely has the survey had questions dealing with attitudes toward Jews, and very few such questions at that. Two questions indicative of viewpoints on Jews occurred often enough in the annual surveys to yield some useful comparisons between a minimal cumulative subsample of Mormons and a large, random subsample of non-Mormons. In the surveys of 1986, 1988, and 1989, interviewees were asked (1) to indicate on a scale from −5 to +5 how much they liked the state of Israel, and (2) to express the warmth of their feelings about Jews on a "thermometer" ranging up to 100° in 10-degree categories.[22] In the usual manner, I added these two scaled questions together to produce an index of feeling about Jews. From the three annual data sets containing *both* these questions, I was able to aggregate a sample of 75 Mormons to compare with 3,050 non-Mormons. As table 7.4 indicates, a higher proportion of Mormons express favorable feelings about Jews or Israel.

Table 7.4. Mormons and Non-Mormons on a Scale of Feelings toward Jews

Favorability of Feelings toward Jews	Mormons ($n = 75$)	Non-Mormons ($n = 3050$)
High	24%	19%
Medium	59	45
Low	17	36

Source: Data from GSS 1986, 1988, and 1989, based on responses to two questions of feelings about Israel or Jews, added and scaled (ISRAEL and JEWTEMP).

Note: Distribution was statistically significant (X^2 p = .030) for the original (uncollapsed) version of the table.

Considering the limitations inherent in the questions on which this table is based, to say nothing of the small number of Mormon cases, one cannot make any strong claims about the comparison between Mormons and others.[23] However, the table does indicate a continuing Mormon tendency to look favorably upon Jews and their Zion (Israel) and to reject anti-Semitism (note that the "low" favorability figure for Mormons is less than half that for the others). The consistency of this table with all the rest of the data in this chapter should enhance our confidence in it, but in any case it is the best we can do with data readily available from national sources.

Conclusion

For centuries, the conversion of the Jews has been regarded as "unfinished business" by most of Christianity. As followers of Abraham and as the original custodians of the scriptures received from Abraham's God, the Jews above all others were expected to embrace the new dispensation of truth brought to Abraham's descendants by the new prophet Jesus of Nazareth. Jewish reluctance was at first regarded by the disciples of Jesus as worldly obstinacy, then as willful perfidy, and eventually as outright evil. After a few centuries, when these Christian disciples had gained political control over most of Europe, they were in a position to force their religious commitments, prejudices, and requirements upon Jews through violence. Thus an essentially religious controversy was translated (as so often in history) into a vicious worldly struggle, and usually a very uneven one.

The new gospel dispensation introduced by the Mormon prophet Joseph Smith was a late arrival to this troubled historic relationship between Christians and Jews. The disciples of Mormonism thus had the benefit, such as it was, of the variety of Christian conceptions about Jews historically pervasive in Europe and America. Not only were the hostile conceptions of medieval times still alive and well, but also later theological ideas being advanced by Calvinism and other Protestant movements had become available for Joseph Smith and his followers to consider. Some of these newer ideas, especially in England, combined the traditional supersessionist doctrine with claims of Christian ties to the lineage of Abraham, at least in a figurative or symbolic sense, and added a new sense of urgency about the gathering of Israel in preparation for the millennial reign of the true Messiah.

In the inspired prophetic imagination of Joseph Smith, this entire Christian heritage was reworked and given a stronger Hebraic overlay. Mormons were understood to be the new Israelites in not only a figurative but also a literal sense. As such, they were writing the latest chapter in the long history of the Hebrew peoples and their special relationship with Jehovah. This history included Christianity, of course, but extended on either side of it, as well. The Mormon reworking also included a recognition of a literal blood tie between Jews and Mormons (as actual descendants of Ephraim), as well as a divinely destined partnership between the two, in establishing separate but parallel Zions in preparation for the coming of the Messiah. It is this unusual Mormon understanding of Jewish identity, especially in relation to the Mormons themselves, that has been behind both a reluctance to proselyte Jews and the relatively low incidence of secular anti-Semitism discussed in this chapter.

Of course, there is nothing new about the observation that Mormons seem relatively free of anti-Semitism. We have seen that claim expressed by both Mormons and Jews in anecdotes and in historical treatments of their long relationship. Evidence of this kind was reviewed at the beginning of this chapter, as well as in the previous one. The kind of evidence that has generally been lacking, however, is that which emerges from large, systematic surveys, such as those carried out by Charles Glock and Rodney Stark in the 1960s and 1970s on Protestants and Catholics. This chapter has been preoccupied with presenting and discussing that same kind of data on Mormons from about the same period.

Most of the tables and discussion presented in this chapter were descriptive and comparative in nature. Their purpose was to make clear how social scientists attempt to measure such cognitive traits as anti-Semitism and certain religious beliefs. In the first table, it was confirmed that Mormons do seem to have somewhat lower rates of anti-Semitism than others. However, the most revealing tables were the later ones that showed how the various uniquely Mormon doctrines about Jews were related to one another and to anti-Semitism. These tables revealed that Mormons who accept the doctrines claiming affinity with the Jews are far less likely than others to hold anti-Semitic beliefs, even when they simultaneously accept the religiously hostile doctrines about Jewish perfidy and punishment.

Two path diagrams, one for Salt Lake City Mormons and one for San Francisco Mormons, were presented so that the importance of those doctrines about Jews could be seen in a fuller context. The diagrams showed that such nonreligious factors as social status also play a part in restraining anti-Semitism, as does the quasi-religious factor of libertarianism toward others (especially atheists). However, the most important messages in those diagrams seemed to be that (1) general religious orthodoxy is not directly related to anti-Semitism, though it is strongly related to the various doctrines about Jews; (2) religious hostility toward Jews, by itself, contributes to anti-Semitism; but (3) when that hostility is combined with (or "goes through") religious affinity, it loses its relationship to anti-Semitism—indeed, in San Francisco, affinity reversed the connection of these doctrines about Jews to secular anti-Semitism.

All in all, when compared with other Christians studied by Glock and Stark, the Mormon case was less remarkable for its somewhat lower rates of anti-Semitism than it was for revealing *just which religious factors* are most influential in generating or suppressing anti-Semitism. What made the Mormon case different were the special importance of the doctrine of affinity with Jews and a somewhat higher level of religious libertarianism. Both of these worked to suppress Mormon tendencies toward anti-Semitism. All of these data, whether for Mormons or for others, emphasize the importance that religious indoctrination can have in influencing relationships between peoples, depending on how efficient and pervasive the indoctrination is. For Mormons, at least, there are encouraging suggestions from the later surveys in Idaho and in the GSS that religious indoctrination continued to be important in suppressing anti-Semitism at least to 1990.

Notes

1. Zucker's importance in the Utah Jewish community is made clear in Brooks (1973) and Goodman (1976).

2. An interesting side-story about an ill-fated Jewish immigrant colony in Utah a century ago is in Goldberg (1986) and is summarized in Brooks (1973, 151–61). The story is not included here because the colony had little interaction with its Mormon neighbors.

3. Not all have been as favorable as those of Zucker and Siporin. Less favorable comments have been made in recent years by certain Israelis with political concerns about Mormon influence in their country but without actual personal experience among Mormons (Bandes 1981; Dann 1987).

4. A complete reproduction of the questionnaire Glock and Stark used, along with a detailed description of their methods, appears in the appendixes at the very end of their 1966 book. Altogether their project produced nine interrelated studies of anti-Semitism. See descriptions of these in Quinley and Glock (1979, 211–23). Mormon samples were not included in any of these studies.

5. Eisenga, Konig, and Scheepers (1995) contains among its references an especially valuable updating of the critical literature published in response to the original work of Glock and Stark.

6. The dissertation and unpublished manuscripts mentioned here are deposited with my papers in the archives of the Utah State Historical Society, Salt Lake City. The survey data from my Salt Lake City and San Francisco studies (1967–69), along with complete documentation for these, can be found in electronic form in the same depository, as well as in the American Religion Data Archives (ARDA) housed at the Pennsylvania State University (University Park, PA 16802), Web site <www.thearda.com> (e-mail address for inquiries, <arda@pop.psu.edu>).

7. In Mauss (1968) this "affinity" was called "Semitic identification," but the same hypothesis was under consideration with essentially the same measures.

8. The three indicators in the scale of secular anti-Semitism for the Mormon samples were beliefs that Jews think they are better than other people; Jews are more likely than Christians to cheat in business; and Jews are inclined to be more loyal to Israel than to the United States. The scores on the scale were obtained by adding together points for two levels of agreement ("yes" and "somewhat"), and then the scale was reduced to four categories, as indicated in table 7.1. See table B.1 in appendix B for a comparison of Mormon, Catholic, and Protestant responses on all six of the beliefs about Jews. For summaries of the indexing method used for these scales, see Glock and Stark (1966, 123–29, 249–50); and Mauss (1994, 217–21).

9. The three beliefs in the Mormon secular anti-Semitism scale were chosen primarily because they proved the most coherent and discriminating in factor analysis and the most valid against "criterion variables." Cronbach alpha reliability coefficients for this index were .54 in Salt Lake City and .59 in San Francisco, identical to the six-item intercorrelations for the Glock and Stark index (1966, 124). "Unfriendly" feelings attached to the various beliefs were also important considerations (Glock and Stark 1966, 139–46). However, the "unfriendly" feelings expressed by the Mormons toward Jews for their presumed loyalty to Israel were relatively rare—16 percent of Mormons compared with at least 50 percent of the other Christians, judging from Glock and Stark (1966, 143, end of table 53). The low figures for Mormons reflect the *eschatological* meaning they attach to Jewish loy-

alty for Israel. That is, the presumption of a special Jewish loyalty to Israel comes with the "dual Zionism" in traditional Mormon teachings.

10. The Glock and Stark model actually distinguishes between religious hostility toward *historic* Jews (i.e., in the Bible) and religious hostility toward *contemporary* Jews, finding the latter far more predictive of anti-Semitism (1966, 65–74, 130–38). See also Stark et al. (1971, 73–78, 126n8). For the exact wording of their questions about contemporary Jews, see Glock and Stark (1966, 70–72). My model skips the historic element altogether.

11. The distributions of Mormon respondents on each of these separate scales can be seen in tables B.2 and B.3 in appendix B.

12. In the replication of their model with data from the clergy, Stark et al. also introduced an abbreviated path analysis containing only the religious variables (1971, 79–85).

13. For details on my construction of the Mormon index of orthodoxy, see Mauss (1994, 37–40, 220–21). (Alpha reliability coefficients were .88 in Salt Lake City and .89 in San Francisco.) The other indexes in figure 7.1 have already been explained above.

14. An index of religious particularism for Mormons was created by adding together a belief that Mormons are God's chosen people today and a belief that the LDS president is "God's only prophet" on the earth today (somewhat equivalent to the traditional Catholic idea of papal infallibility). See the partial explanation in Mauss (1968, 18, table 3; and 1994, 39). For my index of religious libertarianism, I used the same indicators as those in Glock and Stark (1966, 88, table 36). See Mauss (1994, 53–54, table 4.7). The libertarianism index has alpha reliability coefficients of .76 for Salt Lake City and .84 for San Francisco.

15. On a 5-point scale of the index of religious provincialism, 40 percent of the Salt Lake City sample and 20 percent of the San Francisco sample ranked at 4 or 5 (combined average of 35 percent). Yet the alpha reliability for this index was only around .200 in the two samples, because the orthodoxy element was not exceptionally well correlated with the other two (< .280).

16. The cosmopolitanism index is made up of two clusters, one representing social status and the other representing external involvements—that is, the extent to which a respondent was involved in meaningful social participation outside of the LDS Church. When alpha reliability coefficients were calculated for these two clusters separately, the figures for social status were .64 in Salt Lake City and .72 in San Francisco; those for external involvement were .49 in Salt Lake City and .59 in San Francisco. These two clusters were, however, employed separately as variables in the path diagrams (see figures C.1 and C.2 in appendix C). The combined index of cosmopolitanism was negatively correlated with provincialism in these Mormon samples (−.192 in Salt Lake City and −.327 in San Francisco). The negative correlation of cosmopolitanism and simple orthodoxy was not nearly as strong (−.063 and −.238). There are some interesting reasons for these differences in correlation between the Salt Lake City and San Francisco samples, but space does not permit further discussion of this point here. One relevant observation would be that the "cosmopolitan" outlook, as measured here, would imply many more non-Mormon influences and social ties in San Francisco than in Utah (see also the discussion of location in appendix C).

17. In the construction of these path models, religious particularism did not survive the test of statistical significance as an independent factor, so it is not included with the other indicators of religious provincialism (orthodoxy and libertarianism).

18. See Mauss (1994, 49–54 and 108–20); Quinn (1997, chapters 66–115, 314–406); and Quinn (1993). Benson's personal promotion of the John Birch Society during the 1960s

was a continuing source of conflict even with his politically conservative colleagues in the church leadership, and he tended to see the danger of a communist conspiracy everywhere, including in the national civil rights movement.

19. Larry R. Gerlach (1982) found the Mormon proportion of membership even in Utah's chapter of the Ku Klux Klan to be relatively small during the heyday of the KKK in the first half of the twentieth century.

20. Of course, most Idaho Mormons live in the southeastern part of the state, where they constitute more than a third of the population. Altogether Aho's sample included 124 Mormons, most of whom were Christian Constitutionalists, not Identity Christians.

21. Glock and Stark had also found that a belief that Jews dominate international banking did not necessarily imply hostility toward Jews (1966, 127).

22. In the GSS Codebook (J. Davis and Smith 1996), the labels for these two variables are ISRAEL and JEWTEMP. The first of these variables appeared in thirteen of the annual surveys, but the second was employed only in 1986, 1988, and 1989.

23. Despite the small Mormon sample and the different referents in these two questions (Israel in the one and Jews in the other), the responses to the questions were correlated ($r = .243$, gamma $= .225$), and the correlation was statistically significant ($p < .001$). The distribution of the data in table 7.4 is also statistically significant ($p < .030$).

8. The Curse of African Lineage in Mormon History

Any man having one drop of the seed of [Cain] . . . in him cannot hold the priesthood, and if no other prophet ever spake it before I will say it now.
—Brigham Young, 1852

When all the other children of Adam have had the privilege of receiving the priesthood . . . it will be time enough to remove the curse from Cain and his posterity.
—Brigham Young, 1854

BOTH THE LATTER-DAY SAINTS and the nation passed through tumultuous and fundamental social changes during the century or more after these declarations.[1] In some of these changes, the Mormons were simply in tandem with the nation; other changes caused great tension between the two. The main outline of the national race relations story is well known. It is the Latter-day Saint strand of the story that is the main subject of this chapter. In this scenario, a church and people struggle to come to terms with a glaring but inherited contradiction in an otherwise racially egalitarian and universalistic religious framework. The contradiction was toxic enough for the church itself, but perhaps the most adverse consequence was to delay for generations the extension of the powerful Mormon missionary program to a segment of humanity that it might have benefited greatly.

Africans and African Americans presented an anomaly to the usual LDS eagerness for missionary outreach to the varied peoples of the earth, for the church itself resisted proselyting among black populations for more than a century. The anomaly has been difficult to explain, especially for recent church leaders and spokesmen. As a result, even though the troublesome church policy has finally changed, a contradictory and confusing legacy of racist religious folklore hangs like a cloud over LDS relationships with American blacks, even those who have joined the church. How did this predicament arise for the Mormons, and what has developed since?

The Mormon Posture toward Blacks before the Age of Civil Rights

As a result of the meticulous research primarily of two scholars (both of Mormon background),[2] we now have quite a full account of the changing definitions of the place of blacks within the Mormon church.[3] With so much already in print on that topic, I need provide only a brief overview from such sources. The most important historical point is that the LDS Church, which in principle has always had a universal lay priesthood for its male members, denied access to that priesthood until 1978 for anyone known to have any black African ancestry. A derivative policy, for obvious practical reasons, called for avoiding the formal proselyting among blacks in any country (Bringhurst 1981b, 132–34, 151).

The origins of these policies are obscure. They almost certainly did not originate with the founding prophet, Joseph Smith, and there is no contemporaneous documentation indicating that they did. Smith doubtless shared with other Americans of the time the belief that blacks were descendants of biblical lineages under divine curse, but he does not seem to have connected such remote lineages to ineligibility for the priesthood, as did Brigham Young and others. Smith himself, after all, had written the second LDS Article of Faith rejecting inherited punishment, at least for "Adam's transgression," and he had certainly dictated the text of 2 Nephi 26:33 in the Book of Mormon asserting that "all are alike unto God," including "black and white, bond and free."

Origins of the Church Policy and Doctrine about Blacks

At least until after Smith's death in 1844, then, there seems to have been no church policy of priesthood denial on racial grounds, and a small number of Mormon blacks were actually given the priesthood. The best known of these, Elijah Abel, received the priesthood offices of both elder and seventy, apparently in the presence of Smith himself (Bringhurst 1979).[4] Thus the egalitarian motif generally found in early Mormonism originally applied to priesthood access as well. The late 1840s, however, brought an especially chaotic period in Mormon history, one that threatened a total fragmentation and disappearance of this new religious movement. The main surviving body of Mormons moved in phases across the Great Plains, eventually to a new gathering place in Utah under Brigham Young, starting in mid-1847. After the Mexican War, Utah became part of a large federal territory, with Young as governor, and in 1852 the first territorial legislature met. The collective trauma of their expulsion, as well as the constant struggle for organizational and physical survival, fundamentally changed the Mormons' relationship with the rest of the United States. No longer would they feel any commitment to the future of the nation; instead, they would focus on building their own New Jerusalem with its unique institutions.

Of course, those institutions themselves were very much in flux at this stage, with something less than unanimity among the leaders about the organizational forms, policies, and even doctrines that would eventually obtain in the new Zion. Meanwhile, their political and emotional detachment from the rest of the country freed the Mormons from either the need or the desire to be involved in the rising crescendo of sectional strife that was soon to culminate in the Civil War. Brigham Young and many others saw that war in apocalyptic terms as another sign of the impending millennium. Since the Mormons had been abused by politicians and citizens from both the North and the South, they tended to pronounce a pox on both sections as the war approached.

On the one hand, as converts mainly from the northern states and Great Britain, most Mormons had little appreciation for slavery. On the other hand, like most Americans even in the North, Mormons were wary of "abolitionism," a radical movement demanding an immediate end to slavery, with the social and economic "chips" falling wherever they might. At the same time, many Mormons also sympathized with the southern desire for greater sectional autonomy, if not outright secession. In these respects, the Mormons, as long as they lived in the states, fell well within the range of American popular opinion generally, at least in the North. The same could be said for their views of relations between the races more generally, quite aside from slavery itself. That is, hardly any whites, Mormon or non-Mormon, believed in racial equality or intermarriage (L. Bush 1973, 11–15, 51n22).

It was against this background of political, organizational, and ideological ferment that the policy of the LDS Church toward blacks eventually emerged after Joseph Smith. We might never know all the reasons, but they seem to have been both external and internal in nature.[5] The external influences came from Mormon relations with the rest of the country before and after the exodus to Utah. The internal factors were partly organizational and partly ideological or doctrinal. The personalities of key leaders might also have had some influence, starting with Brigham Young himself. Both Smith and Young, like their contemporary Abraham Lincoln, would be considered "racists" by today's norms because they all believed in the natural and inherent inferiority of Africans and their descendants and because they favored public policies that would ratify such a belief in more or less benign and protective ways. Smith seems to have attributed black social and intellectual deficits largely to environmental influences, whereas Young found such deficits mainly in the divine curse placed on the entire "lineage of Cain."[6] Like Lincoln, Smith advocated an eventual end to slavery with a federal "buy-out" of slave owners and a wholesale return, or "recolonization," of the freed slaves to Africa. Young—perhaps like Thomas Jefferson—opposed slavery in principle but was willing to tolerate it (in Utah) temporarily for certain practical reasons (Dutson 1964).[7]

Formalization of the Church Racial Policy and Supporting Doctrine

Slavery was a different issue, of course, from the church policy on priesthood access, but because Mormon leaders had had to make pragmatic concessions over slavery in Missouri and then later in Utah, a few scholars have suggested that in some derivative way the leaders found a restrictive church policy on priesthood to be more appropriate than it had seemed earlier.[8] Also, during the confusing transition in church leadership in the late 1840s, a few unhappy incidents involving black members and leaders had raised questions about their right to the priesthood (Bringhurst 1981b, 85–92). In any case, what can be established with certainty is that from 1852 on, Brigham Young, whatever his reasons, made the kinds of declarations with which this chapter opened, and he did so on his own authority, without reference to any known precedent from Joseph Smith or anyone else. This was the first formal and official statement in Mormon history denying the priesthood to blacks as a matter of church policy. It was made during the opening session of the first Utah territorial legislature by Young in his capacity as territorial governor. This might seem a peculiar setting unless we keep in mind that the Mormons in those days did not often make the conventional American separation between church and state. It might well be significant also that it was during this same session of the legislature that slavery was legalized for blacks and Indians. The place of blacks in the civic and ecclesiastical life of the Mormons was thereby established by 1852.

Slavery itself was to come to an end in another decade. Whether in law or as a practical matter, it had never been a significant part of Utah social or economic life (Bringhurst 1981b, 68–70). The restrictive policy on priesthood, however, lingered on. It was periodically reconsidered after Brigham Young's death in 1877, usually in response to a petition from a black member or sympathizer. The first of these reconsiderations occurred as early as 1879, when Young's successor, John Taylor, responded to a petition from Elijah Abel (the sole surviving black member to have received the priesthood) that he be admitted to the sacred temple rites of the church. Taylor's consultations turned up a claim by two prominent local church leaders that in the mid-1830s they had heard Joseph Smith declare that Negroes could not be given the priesthood and that Abel was supposed to have been stripped of it before Smith died (Bringhurst 1981b, 144–48).

Taylor himself, though a contemporary of these witnesses and a close associate of Smith, could recall no such instruction. The two witnesses in question were elderly men recalling an ostensible incident more than four decades earlier. The young apostle Joseph F. Smith, nephew of the prophet, disagreed with their recollections on the basis of an 1841 certificate he had seen verifying Abel's ordination as a seventy, and Abel himself had similar documentation also dated long after the supposed cancellation of his priesthood ordination. The discussion among the apostles, however, seemed to turn more on what the original prophet's policy *had* been than on what the church policy *ought* to be in 1879. To Abel's chagrin, church policy was "resolved" not by granting his petition but by sending him on a mission. He died not long afterward (Bringhurst 1979; L. Bush 1973, 31–36).

After that, each hearing and reconsideration by the church leadership simply brought another confirmation of the policy, so that by about 1920 there was an accumulation of precedents from previous leaders, as well as a rapidly receding institutional memory about the historical origins of the policy. Even the later memory of Joseph F. Smith himself eventually proved as unreliable as the memories of the older colleagues whom he had contradicted in 1879; for by 1908, as president of the church, Smith was now claiming that Abel's ordination (and presumably that of any other black) had been "declared null and void by the Prophet himself" (quoted in L. Bush 1973, 34). Also, during the generation after Brigham Young, three other important internal developments occurred that seemed to point to a divinely condoned racial restriction.

The first development was the formal canonization of the Pearl of Great Price, a collection of historical and scriptural documents revealed to Joseph Smith, mostly in the 1830s, and periodically published in various segments thereafter. It was not accepted by church leaders and members as binding scripture, however, until canonized in 1880 (Bringhurst 1981b, 41–46, 150–51; L. Bush 1973, 37–38). The Pearl of Great Price contained the only passages in Mormon scripture that referred to a cursed lineage. The second development, partly related to the first, was a fuller unfolding of the doctrine relating to premortal existence, or "preexistence," as it is usually called in Mormon parlance (Harrell 1988; Ostler 1982). The third development was the gradual adaptation, from popular and scholarly publications in Europe, of historical theories glorifying the Anglo-Saxon heritage above others and claiming literal Israelite origins for the peoples of Great Britain and northwestern Europe (Mauss 1999; and chapter 2 herein).

By the early twentieth century, these new doctrinal developments were available to provide confirmation, retroactive though it might have been, for the accumulated precedents that had denied black church members access to priesthood and temple rites after 1852. With the installment of Heber J. Grant as church president in 1918, no Mormon leader was still living who could remember when teachings and policies toward blacks had been otherwise (Bringhurst 1981b, 158–59). Finally, in an important 1931 book, *The Way to Perfection,* the scholarly young apostle Joseph Fielding Smith (son of Joseph F. Smith) synthesized and codified the entire framework of Mormon racialist teaching that had accumulated (1931, 42–48, 97–111). Integrating uniquely Mormon ideas of premortal decisions about lineage with imported British Israelism and Anglo-Saxon triumphalism, Smith in effect postulated a divine rank-ordering of lineages with the descendants of ancient Ephraim (son of Joseph) at the top (including the Mormons); the "seed of Cain" (Africans) at the bottom; and various other lineages in between. (For various perspectives on this racialist framework, see Bringhurst 1981b, 95–97, 128–35; Cooper 1990, 116–20; Hansen 1981, 190–98; Madison 1992; and Mauss 1999.)

This framework then became the template for interpreting all extant Mormon scripture and discourse that had any implications for racial differences or racial policy. Now embedded in such an elaborate and authoritative doctrinal web, the church policy toward blacks took on a special inertia and durability—even charisma.[9] To be sure, the surrounding culture of America provided a very hospitable environment for such racial thinking after Reconstruction was overturned and Jim Crow laws settled firmly upon the land (Myers [1943] 1960; Woodward 1955). At least two other external factors helped sustain the church's racial policy into the middle of the twentieth century: the tiny size of a powerless black population in a Mormon heartland settled mainly by northern Europeans (Bringhurst 1981b, 228) and the isolation of that heartland from national centers of social ferment and change. It should not be difficult to understand why the church and its people could not see any "race problem" on the horizon even in the mid-twentieth century and why they were taken so completely by surprise when the church began to come under attack in the 1950s from advocates of the new civil rights movement. Even Thomas F. O'Dea, an astute "outside" observer of Mormons, did not mention the race problem among the "sources of strain and conflict" that he foresaw for the LDS Church in his well-known book (1957), though that problem was fully recognized in his later essay (1972).

Winds of Change

Perhaps some Latter-day Saints expected that the growing national ferment over civil rights for black Americans would bypass Utah indefinitely, since the church had done no proselyting among blacks for a century and since very few had ever sought membership. Yet Utah had experienced an influx of black citizens during and after World War II; from 1940 to 1950, their population had doubled, even though it remained under 3,000 (Bringhurst 1981b,

228). In Utah, as everywhere else in the country, the new black arrivals faced various Jim Crow restrictions on their access to certain public accommodations and prohibitions against intermarriage or "miscegenation" (Bringhurst 1981b, 166–70). Nevertheless, church restrictions on priesthood and other privileges were criticized as early as 1947 in a private letter from Lowry Nelson, a prominent LDS sociologist, who had been asked by church leaders to investigate the feasibility of opening missionary work in Cuba. In response, he rebuked the leaders for the priesthood restriction, not only in racially mixed Cuba but elsewhere as well. Five years later, he went public with his rebuke in a national magazine (Nelson 1952).[10] This was only the beginning.

The Church, Civil Rights, and the Stormy Sixties

The 1950s and 1960s saw a rising wave of criticism against the LDS Church, not only for its racial restrictions on priesthood but also for its seeming reluctance (so the charges went) to back the entire civil rights agenda that was gradually becoming the national orthodoxy. In Utah particularly, the campaign against racial restrictions in the public arena was led by the state chapter of the National Association for the Advancement of Colored People (NAACP). As those restrictions began to fall in Utah and the rest of the country, the critics of the church turned to internal, ecclesiastical matters. The church leadership, as well as most of the members, took the position that internal matters, such as priesthood restrictions, were entirely church prerogatives, not subject to national policy or criticism. Since the church is a private, voluntary organization, this claim was perhaps technically valid, but this LDS definition of the situation was not widely shared outside the church.

During the 1960s and 1970s, the church therefore faced an increasingly hostile public relations environment, which was not helpful to its missionary work.[11] Even more serious, some of the most celebrated "showpiece" institutions of the church, such as BYU athletics and the venerable Tabernacle Choir, began to experience boycotts around the nation. Even the long-standing and intimate association with the Boy Scouts of America was temporarily jeopardized when it became apparent that boy leadership roles in local Mormon troops were tied to the lay priesthood, thereby effectively barring from leadership any black boys belonging to church-sponsored Boy Scout troops. Through all of this, the Mormons and their leaders did their best to counter public criticism by insisting that the internal policy on priesthood access had nothing to do with access to the civil rights of citizenship. During the October 1963 general conference of the church, Hugh B. Brown, speaking for the First Presidency, expressed church support for the emerging national civil rights efforts and addressed critics with the declaration that "there is in this church no doctrine, belief, or practice that is intended to deny the enjoyment of full civil rights by any person, regardless of race, color, or creed."[12]

There is little doubt that this was a sincere and accurate expression of the intentions of the church leadership, or at least the First Presidency, by 1963. It is also likely that the declaration was intended not only for the American public but also for the political leadership of Nigeria, with which the church had recently been negotiating for the opening of a new Mormon mission there (Bringhurst 1981b, 189–90; Mauss 1981, 16). Nevertheless, intentions, however benign, are not the same as practical consequences; so the NAACP, among other critics, continued to charge that the LDS racial policy and doctrines were not simply internal issues but were harmful outside the church because they reinforced the widespread assumptions in American culture generally about the inferiority of black people. Such a charge, plausible though it may seem, calls for empirical evidence, which was definitely lacking. In a desire to acquire such evidence, I sought the permission (but not the auspices) of local church leaders in the California East Bay area (where I was then residing) to survey the members of three wards (congregations) about their racial attitudes and many other matters (Mauss 1994, 34–45, 222–26).

This East Bay survey, mentioned in the previous chapter, eventually served as a pilot study for a much larger survey of Mormons launched a couple of years later. Even this relatively small survey, however, pointed to the hazards of facile assumptions about the connection between church policies and racial attitudes more generally. We might have expected such a survey to show Mormons, at least devout Mormons, much more likely than others to hold unfavorable views about blacks and to have less sympathy for blacks' civil rights aspirations. What the data indicated, however, was that the Mormons in this sample were remarkably similar to other Americans in their beliefs and attitudes about blacks and civil rights. Mormon responses on measures of these attitudes closely resembled national and California Protestant averages, as well as statistical portraits of specific denominations in northern California, such as the Episcopal, Presbyterian, Lutheran, and Baptist (Mauss 1972a and 1994, 51–54). Furthermore, there was little difference in racial attitudes *among* Mormons by orthodoxy or church attendance. Mormons did differ among themselves, however, by education level, occupation, and rural versus urban origin, just as most other religious denominations did (Mauss 1966).[13]

Mormon Racism in the American Context

In focusing so much on the Mormon case, however, we run the risk of forgetting the larger historical context in which the church struggled with its predicament. From the perspective of the twenty-first century, of course, all Americans of the 1950s and 1960s (and even later) were simply living in a racist society. On a comparative basis, however, these were less racist times than the earlier decades had been, and the United States was almost certainly a less racist society than most other societies in the world. Nonetheless, the civil rights movement of the immediate post–World War II years dramatized convincingly the enormous gap between the conventional treatment, in law and custom, of its nonwhite citizens and the egalitarian declarations in the nation's founding documents. Yet most white Americans had also grown up in a society still permeated with racial myths, based largely on outdated biblical interpretations, about how black people became black and why they were inferior, even in God's eyes.

Numerous national surveys from midcentury make clear just how conservative most Americans were on racial issues, even outside the South. One compilation of these survey results from the 1960s, based on a series of carefully drawn samples, shows that only 38 percent of Americans favored the racial integration of schools in 1964, long after the historic 1954 Supreme Court decision in *Brown v. Board of Education* and the 1957 confrontation at the high school in Little Rock, Arkansas. This percentage increased very little in subsequent years. In the same survey, only 41 percent of white Americans nationwide were willing to grant blacks equal access to hotels and businesses; a bare majority (53 percent) favored open housing; and a mere 27 percent approved of a general desegregation of the races socially. During the same period, 68 percent were convinced that civil rights advocates were "moving too fast," and 63 percent believed that blacks had damaged their cause by pressing for equal rights so aggressively (A. Campbell 1971, 127–54). Even in the relatively liberal San Francisco area, half of the respondents agreed that blacks did not adequately care for their property, which was why their neighborhoods were "run down." A fourth of the same respondents preferred racially segregated schools and churches and believed that blacks tended to be "immoral" (Glock and Stark 1966, 168).

In this cultural context, to find racial prejudice or discrimination in Mormon beliefs and practices was simply to find conventional American thinking in Mormon garb.[14] Even restrictions on access to the priesthood were not unique to the Mormon church. Most theological seminaries of the period, like most of the schools of law or medicine, were admitting very few black students. Since the theological schools were gatekeepers to the priesthood, very few blacks got through the gate to ordination, except in the so-called black churches (Wood 1990, 288–338, 365–84).[15] Few parishes or congregations of other denominations, therefore, were any more likely to find black priests or ministers in charge than were Mormon wards.

To be sure, the exclusion of black clergy and other sacerdotal functionaries was more *conspicuous* among the Mormons, who prided themselves on fielding a large, volunteer ministry. Lacking professional seminaries to do its gatekeeping, the Mormon church resorted directly to race-based restrictions on access to the lay priesthood. This meant that the few black men and boys who joined the church would always be conspicuously and painfully excluded from this otherwise universal (male) priesthood. It is reasonable to see this restriction as a uniquely Mormon expression of American racism, but it does not follow that the practice meant Mormons were "more racist" than others, either in church matters or in secular, civic relations outside the church. This generalization was eventually confirmed in several other studies during the period in question, which revealed the similarities between Mormons and others in race attitudes (D. Brewer 1970; Bunker and Johnson 1975; Bunker, Coffey, and Johnson 1977; Montanye, Mulberry, and Hardy 1971).

Neither is this to claim, however, that the traditional racial doctrines and folklore of Mormonism were free of consequences (Shipp 1968). They no more lacked consequences than did the racist traditions permeating American culture more generally. The historical and narrative literature of America abounds with evidence of discriminatory treatment ranging from the social humiliation of blacks to brutality and murder, all derived ultimately from traditional racist beliefs, customs, and laws. What is less often considered in this historical record is the brutalizing impact of racism on the lives and relationships of whites themselves, Mormon or otherwise, and one need not point only to such dramatic cruelty as lynchings. Many a white Mormon family can recount instances in which an interracial marriage or friendship has elicited such bigoted condemnation as to cause a permanent rupture of family relationships. Beyond qualitative and anecdotal examples of the potential consequences of indoctrination in racist ideas, what can we learn from more systematic and extensive data about Mormons in particular?

Sources of Racial Prejudice among Mormons

Historical studies of white American racial prejudice toward blacks have established beyond much doubt that religious ideas are implicated in such prejudice. Biblical interpretations and commentary have been used for centuries to "explain" the cultural and intellectual inferiority that Europeans and Americans have attributed to Africans and their descendants in the United States (Gossett, 1963; H. Smith 1972; Wood 1990). Until about 1960, perhaps even later, almost all Mormons descended from the Europeans and Euroamericans who had promulgated those hostile and condescending religious teachings. It should therefore not be surprising to find that Mormons have also partaken of the accompanying social and civic prejudice and acted on it, at rates similar to those for other white Americans.

Such is one message of this chapter so far, and such was the main purport of the sociological research that has been cited: In straight and simple comparisons between Mormons and others, differences in levels of racial prejudice were few or nil in the mid-twentieth century. But how much and how far were *religious* ideas implicated in helping generate this prejudice? Answering this question for American society as a whole is clearly beyond the scope of this chapter, and numerous studies by other scholars (including some cited above) have already addressed the matter. How about Mormons in particular? How did their specific religious indoctrination affect their rates of anti-black prejudice and discrimination during the age of civil rights? There is some specific evidence, once again from my surveys in Utah and San Francisco during 1967–69.

Measuring Prejudice and Discriminatory Tendencies

Following the same general procedure as in the previous chapter on anti-Semitism, I first devised measures for the variables that supposedly derive from the religious ideas in question. In this chapter, I focus on two: prejudice and discrimination. Since my data came from questionnaires, I am not, strictly speaking, measuring discrimination, which would require us to observe *behavior*. The questionnaire did, however, include respondents' *verbal estimates* of their own probable behavior, so that is the operational meaning here of discrimination. In the distinction between *prejudice* and *discrimination,* I am following an old but useful conceptualization by Peter I. Rose, who argued persuasively that although the two tend to go together, a person can exhibit the one without the other (1974, 97–106).[16] Charles Glock and Rodney Stark also had distinguished between anti-Semitic *beliefs* and anti-Semitic *actions* (1966, 101–61).

In my questionnaires, prejudice and discrimination were each measured by responses to three questions. *Prejudice* was indicated by affirming that "Negroes" (as they were then called) were immoral; that they had inferior intelligence; and that they did not adequately care for their homes and neighborhoods. *Discrimination* was indicated by a preference for racially separate schools, a preference for separate churches, and an intention to move away if black families moved into the neighborhood. When the Mormon responses were compared with those of Catholics and various Protestant denominations on each of the six basic questions, the Mormon distributions differed little from the others (see tables in Mauss 1994, 52; and in Glock and Stark 1966, 168). Indexes were then constructed in the usual manner by adding together the responses to the three questions for each variable. These indexes each proved highly reliable, and the two resulting scales were clearly intercorrelated, especially among the San Francisco Mormons.[17]

Intercorrelation, however, does not mean perfect correspondence. If Rose and others were correct in their conceptualization, prejudice and discrimination ought *not* be perfectly correlated, since some persons can possess and express the one without the other. Thus the Salt Lake City and the San Francisco Mormons were distributed somewhat differently on the prejudice and discrimination scales.[18] However, the distinction between prejudice and discrimination is most clearly illustrated when the two indexes were run "against" each other (see table 8.1). In this table, even the highest levels of prejudice are accompanied by strong discriminatory tendencies for only 60 percent of the total sample (34 percent plus 26 percent). Conversely, the *absence* of prejudice (the "Low" column) is only somewhat predictive of the absence of discrimination: 60 percent of those low in the one are also low in the other.

Table 8.1. Racial Discrimination by Racial Prejudice

	Index of Anti-Black Prejudice		
Index of Anti-Black Discrimination	Low ($n = 636$)	Medium ($n = 356$)	High ($n = 218$)
Low	60%	21%	13%
2	27	36	27
3	9	29	34
High	4	15	26

Note: Figures are percentages of respondents in each category of prejudice who are *also* in the respective categories of discrimination. Some cases are missing because they could not be salvaged in creating the indexes by the usual process.

Religious Ideas as Sources of Prejudice and Discrimination

The discussion of Mormon survey data so far has been limited to considering how to conceptualize and measure prejudice and discrimination in *secular, civil* affairs. We next consider some *religious* variables implicated in the genesis of prejudice and discrimination during the 1960s. The approach here in many ways parallels the examination, in the previous chapter, of the religious factors involved in anti-Semitism. Yet there are also differences, because the process by which the two kinds of prejudice were produced is somewhat different. Religious hostility toward blacks was indicated in the Mormon questionnaire by two statements in particular: (1) "Because of the wickedness of Cain and other forefathers of the Negroes, these people carry the mark of a black skin and the curse of perpetual inferiority"; and (2) "It is the will of God at present that the priesthood be withheld from Negroes."[19] With the usual system of additive scoring, these two statements were combined into a composite index of religious hostility toward blacks, which was then collapsed into three categories of hostility. (The distributions of the Mormon samples on this index are shown in the table B.6 in appendix B.)[20]

Whatever the degree of *religious* hostility toward blacks among Mormons, how does that hostility contribute to *secular* prejudice and discrimination (which are strongly correlated in table 8.1)? The answer can be seen to a considerable extent in table 8.2, which shows how secular prejudice (part A) and discrimination (part B) are distributed according to religious hostility.[21]

It is clear from table 8.2 that as religious hostility increases, so do prejudice (part A) and discrimination (part B) in all rows except the top one in each case. In that row ("Low"), the *absence* (or near absence) of prejudice and discrimination becomes *less* likely with increased religious hostility. Clearly a hostile religious belief about blacks is implicated in secular and civil attitudes toward them. Yet another question remains about religious influences: Is it specifically the hostile religious doctrines about blacks that generate prejudice and discrimination, or are all such attitudes more or less "natural" derivatives of an underlying religious provincialism?

Although the present discussion concerns attitudes toward blacks, it is worth recalling how the previous chapter demonstrated, as had Glock and Stark (1966) earlier, that secular anti-Semitism derives not from any underlying Christian (or Mormon) orthodoxy, however narrow, unless it is accompanied by religious doctrines that are hostile toward the specific "outgroup" (Jews in that case). The previous chapter also discussed briefly the concept of religious provincialism in this connection but was concerned more about the complex functions of Mormon teachings on Jews than about the importance of that general religious posture. In this chapter concerning blacks, however, it is appropriate to raise again the question of the potential contribution of an underlying religious provincialism to secular prejudice. An index of religious provincialism was created to examine this question. Although this index is based partly on beliefs in particularism (exclusivism) and intolerance toward civil liberties for religious outsiders, its most important element is basic Mormon *orthodoxy*. Table 8.3 shows how religious provincialism is related to religious hostility toward blacks as well as to secular prejudice and discrimination.

Table 8.2. Prejudice and Discrimination by Religious Hostility toward Blacks

Secular Attitudes toward Blacks	Religious Hostility toward Blacks		
	Low ($n = 286$)	Medium ($n = 424$)	High ($n = 507$)
A. Prejudice			
Low	70%	58%	38%
Medium	19	29	36
High	12	13	26
B. Discrimination			
Low	60	42	27
2	22	34	30
3	11	14	28
High	7	10	14

Table 8.3. Religious Provincialism and Attitudes about Blacks

	Religious Provincialism Index[a]				
	Low (*n* = 290)	2 (*n* = 151)	3 (*n* = 371)	4 (*n* = 239)	High (*n* = 143)
Religious hostility[b]	6%	31%	46%	63%	71%
Anti-black prejudice[c]	12	14	15	23	31
Anti-black discrimination[d]	8	11	10	14	16

Note: Figures on prejudice and discrimination (the two bottom rows) are based on slightly smaller numbers than indicated because of minor attrition from nonresponses.

a. Composite index combining earlier indexes of orthodoxy, particularism, and lack of religious libertarianism.

b. Figures are only from the "high" category of the index of religious hostility toward blacks (the other two categories of "low" and "medium" are not included here).

c. Figures are only from the "high" category of the index of anti-black prejudice.

d. Figures are only from the "high" category of the index of anti-black discrimination.

Looking across table 8.3 from left to right, we can see increases in the figures across all three rows. This pattern suggests that all three of these attitudes (hostility, prejudice, and discrimination) are related to religious provincialism, as they are to each other.[22] When we compare the distributions in the three rows, however, we see that provincialism has a much stronger impact on religious hostility than on either of the more secular attitudes. The figures rise steeply from 6 percent to 71 percent across the row for religious hostility. In general, this pattern would be expected, since both provincialism and hostility were reflections of the same basic religious indoctrination and socialization. A fully "orthodox" and observant Mormon in the 1960s would more or less "automatically" have accepted these traditional Mormon *religious* teachings about blacks as part of a general understanding of church doctrine.

The impact of provincialism on prejudice and discrimination is actually very similar to the impact of religious hostility on those same two variables (see table 8.2). Do the two religious variables (provincialism and religious hostility) have a *parallel and separate* impact on prejudice and discrimination? Or are they redundant (overlapping)? The relative and independent importance of the two religious variables can be seen in figure 8.1, where provincialism is replaced by orthodoxy, its main element, for simplicity.[23]

Figure 8.1 also starts with orthodoxy. The theory behind these diagrams is that religious orthodoxy (or alternatively provincialism) leads to religious hostility toward blacks, which, in turn, leads to secular prejudice and that, in turn, to discrimination. The coefficients for figure 8.1 (and for the fuller diagrams in the appendix C) clearly confirm this theoretical expectation: The path from orthodoxy to religious hostility (A→B) carries the greatest weight of all (.556 in Salt Lake City and .612 in San Francisco). Orthodoxy has little or no direct impact, however, on racial discrimination (A→D), with coefficients near zero (.043 and .055). Religious hostility generates prejudice

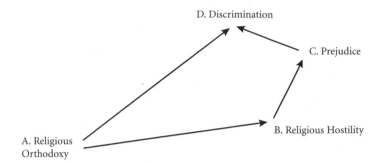

Figure 8.1. Abbreviated Path Diagram for Religious Beliefs, Anti-Black Prejudice, and Discrimination among Mormons in Salt Lake City and San Francisco

	A→B	A→D	B→C	C→D
Salt Lake City	.556	.043	.194	.402
San Francisco	.612	.055	.163	.555

(B→C), and discrimination then arises directly from prejudice (C→D), in accordance with our theoretical expectations.

It is important to remember that B→C is the key path, not A→D. In other words, the tendency to discriminate against blacks in secular, civil matters arises *not* from the basic beliefs of Mormonism but directly from beliefs in the hostile doctrines that define blacks as ineligible for the priesthood because of a divinely cursed ancestry. This point is also made, though less directly, in table 8.3. As will be seen, even though these doctrines have been officially abandoned by the church since these surveys were conducted, folklore about the "lineage of Cain" continues to circulate among white Mormons to the continuing detriment of their relationships with black Americans.

A California Bay Area study by Glock and his colleagues in the 1970s found that supernatural explanations for racial differences continued to inform the perceptions about black people for at least 20 percent of white interviewees. The general purpose of that study was to identify several different "explanatory modes" used by whites in characterizing blacks and their circumstances, so neither its objectives nor its measures of racial attitudes were comparable to those employed in the earlier surveys reviewed in this chapter. Nevertheless, that later work by Glock and others highlights the durability of traditional attributions of divine judgment on black people (and potentially on Jews and other groups as well), even in a relatively secular and liberal social environment (Apostle et al. 1983, 15–19, 23–35, 148–66, 204–9).

Conclusion

What this chapter has described and analyzed is the situation in the LDS Church and population about a decade *before* the momentous change of policy announced in June 1978.[24] At the organizational level of analysis, the church was struggling to find a modus vivendi with an American society increasingly determined to remove traditional racial and ethnic barriers to full citizenship for all. In that context, the traditional church restriction on access to the priesthood was a public relations nightmare, and it was getting worse by the year. The Mormon adherence to this policy seemed, at best, obstinately retrograde and, at worst, deliberately bigoted. Even among the church leaders themselves, there was not a clear consensus on what to do. It appears from the historical record now available that the views among the general authorities ranged from those of the conservative elder Ezra Taft Benson to those of the more liberal elder Hugh B. Brown, with the rest of the leadership distributed in degrees across that range. Benson not only opposed any change in the policy but also believed the national civil rights movement was inspired by the Communists. Brown, in a minority at the other end of the range, supported full civil rights for all and advocated dropping the church's ban on priesthood for blacks, gradually if necessary (L. Bush 1999, 241; Mauss 1981, 16; Quinn 1997, 13–17, 81, 113; F. Peterson 1999, 277). Meanwhile, "brush fires" in public relations were coming along with increasing frequency.

At the Mormon grassroots, too, opinions differed somewhat according to location, religious commitment, social status, and other variables. On the whole, Mormons were not very different from other Americans in holding rather conservative views on civil rights for blacks. On internal church questions, not all of the Saints were happy about the priesthood restriction, and many had serious doubts about other traditional teachings relating to black people. However, when pressure mounted from the outside, Mormons tended to defend their church out of loyalty, whatever their doubts (Bringhurst 1981b, 172). Such a confrontation between loyalty and personal feelings was reflected in their answers to one of the items in my questionnaire, which asked for agreement or disagreement with the statement, "I wish that Negroes could be given the priesthood in the LDS Church."

Among Salt Lake City Mormons, 39 percent demurred on this question ("No opinion" or no response), and in San Francisco, 33 percent. Thus a third or more of the Saints, at least in these locations, were as uncertain as their leaders about what should be done. In cosmopolitan San Francisco, however, the issue was salient enough for 44 percent of the Mormons to agree with the wish for change in the priesthood policy, compared with only half that figure (22 percent) among Salt Lake City Mormons. Proportions *disagreeing* with the statement were approximately the reverse: 39 percent in Salt Lake City and 22 percent in San Francisco. These percentages in disagreement might be considered the outside limits of any opposition at the grassroots to a priesthood policy change in the late 1960s. Had the change come in 1968 instead of 1978, most Mormons would almost certainly have been relieved. So why didn't the change come sooner, and why did it eventually come *at the time* that it came? What differences has the 1978 policy change made in Mormon relations with black people in the United States and elsewhere? Such questions are considered in the next chapter.

Notes

1. The statements from Brigham Young in the opening epigraphs of this chapter were made on different occasions before the Utah Territorial Legislature. They are from L. Bush (1973, 26, 57*nn* 87, 88), quoting from, respectively, a Wilford Woodruff biography by Matthias Cowley and the *Journal of Discourses* for December 1854. Brigham Young made many cognate statements about blacks during this period and later.

2. I refer especially to Newell G. Bringhurst and Lester E. Bush Jr. See Bringhurst (1981b) for the only truly book-length treatment of this history, as well as the long articles by Bush (1969, 1973, 1984, and 1999). Some of this work by these two scholars, along with my articles, appears in an edited collection (L. Bush and Mauss 1984). Also worthwhile, but of limited value by now, is the very short book by Stephen G. Taggart (1970). A long and very helpful bibliography has been published by Chester Lee Hawkins (1992).

3. I realize the term *African American* has succeeded many predecessors as the most politically correct. However, I usually use the term *black* simply as a colloquial and neutral counterpart of *white,* with no disrespect intended.

4. The office of elder is normally given to all adult males who have been members of the church in good standing for at least a year. It is the first and most basic office in the greater, or Melchizedek, priesthood of the church (the lesser priesthood is called Aaronic). The office of seventy, also a Melchizedek office, was historically bestowed on elders specializing in missionary work or training. In recent times, the Seventy (usually capitalized) are high-ranking church leaders organized in quorums of seventy just below the twelve apostles.

5. Both Newell Bringhurst and Lester Bush recognize the importance of external as well as internal factors. In general, Bringhurst tends to give more attention to external factors than does Bush. Yet Bringhurst is somewhat ambiguous about whether there was anything special about the racism among Mormons, at times citing racist passages in Mormon scriptures, while at other times conceding that Mormon ideas and behavior were not unique (Bringhurst 1981b, 10, 26, 43, 90).

6. In such religious beliefs, as well as political and social ones, Young was in the American mainstream, if we judge from the historical treatments of, for example, Gossett (1963); H. Shelton Smith (1972); and Wood (1990).

7. By 1860, such minimal slavery as there was in Utah had virtually disappeared, and no one, inside or outside Utah, envisioned Utah's admission to the Union as a slave state (Bringhurst 1981b, 68–70, 81, 111–12).

8. The so-called Missouri Thesis—that Mormons' conflicts in Missouri sensitized them to the need for tolerating slavery and, derivatively, to a need for restricting the priesthood—was the main theme of the Stephen Taggart book (1970). Though heavily criticized by Lester Bush (1969), this thesis has retained some currency among other scholars (e.g., Hansen 1981, 190–98; and Bringhurst 2001).

9. The Reorganized Church of Jesus Christ of Latter Day Saints (now called the Community of Christ), despite sharing much of the racialist heritage of early Mormonism and America generally, did not adopt formal racial restrictions in its ecclesiastical life (Embry 1992c; Madison 1992; Russell 1979).

10. The First Presidency of the church responded to Nelson's 1947 letter with a formal letter of its own in 1949, circulated churchwide, which effectively placed that top-ranking ecclesiastical body officially behind all the accumulated racial folklore (Bringhurst 1981b, 183–84, 191; L. Bush 1973, 43–44, 67nn198, 199).

11. The conflicts between the church and the larger society during the civil rights era are covered in some detail in Bringhurst (1981b, 168–89); L. Bush (1973, 44–46); and Mauss (1981).

12. This statement of the First Presidency was widely reported in the national press, starting with the *Deseret News* (Salt Lake City) on October 6, 1963, and reproduced in the *Improvement Era* in December 1963. Subsequent reiterations occurred in 1965 and 1966. See the final page of *Dialogue* 1 (2) for a 1966 statement. The events leading up to the 1963 statement are described in McMurrin (1979).

13. A complementary but more polemical analysis attempted to convince Mormons to drop their racist beliefs about curses and marks, even if the church maintained its restriction on priesthood, and to convince critics that Mormons were no more racist than others and thus should be left alone to work out their own organizational dilemma (Mauss 1967). Alas, my arguments seemed unconvincing to either audience (Bringhurst 1981b, 173, 251).

14. This is the poignant theme of a trilogy of historical novels currently in progress by Margaret B. Young and Darius A. Gray (2000–2003) about the history of black Mormons.

15. As late as 1985, black bishops in the Roman Catholic church, constituting only 3 percent of total American bishops, complained about racial bias in the church (*Los Angeles Times,* November 14, I-5).

16. For example, a prejudiced person might not discriminate if the person fears legal or social sanctions. However, someone lacking prejudice might still discriminate if local customs and sanctions require the individual to do so. (An example of such "institutionalized racism" would be the case of a typical Jewish merchant in the Jim Crow South, who—though lacking prejudice—might lose his white clientele by serving black customers [Rose 1974, 120–23].)

17. Alpha reliability coefficients for prejudice were .70 in Salt Lake City and .76 in San Francisco; for discrimination, .62 in Salt Lake City and .77 in San Francisco. Intercorrelations between prejudice and discrimination were .574 in Salt Lake City and .752 in San Francisco.

18. See tables B.4 and B.5 in appendix B. The two Mormon samples were statistically quite similar in their tendencies toward prejudice (see table B.4 in appendix B), but the San Francisco Mormons revealed somewhat less inclination to discriminate, for they tended to cluster toward the lowest end of the scale much more than did Salt Lake City Mormons (see table B.5 in appendix B). This regional difference suggests that even in the 1960s

the cultural environment in San Francisco was less hospitable than in Utah to outright discrimination (as distinguished from simple prejudice). That same "contamination" from the surrounding culture probably also accounts largely for the reduced reliability and intercorrelation of these indexes in the Salt Lake City data, as indicated in note 17. (See also discussion of location in appendix C.)

19. Respondents were asked to choose one of five responses to each question ("definite-ly" or "probably" true; "definitely" or "probably" not true; and "don't know"). Nonre-sponse to these questions was negligible.

20. Table B.6 reveals quite a difference between the two regional samples in the inci-dence of religious hostility toward blacks, with San Francisco Mormons clearly much less likely to accept the traditional religious teachings about the place of blacks in the eyes of God. The Saints in San Francisco were twice as likely as those in Utah to be "low" on this religious hostility index and only about half as likely to be "high." This difference in *re-ligious* posture between the two samples is in contrast to their general similarity in the incidence of *secular* prejudice and discrimination (see tables B.4 and B.5 in appendix B). Taken together, these tables suggest that prejudice and discrimination depended on the acceptance of traditional *religious* teachings about blacks far *less* among San Francisco Mormons than among Salt Lake City Mormons. (See also discussion of location in ap-pendix C.)

21. Gamma measures of association for hostility and prejudice were .33 in Salt Lake City and .38 in San Francisco; for hostility and discrimination .31 in both locations.

22. The gamma measures of association for provincialism and hostility were .645 in Salt Lake City and .764 in San Francisco. In both cities, gammas ranged from .300 to .390 for the associations between provincialism and either prejudice or discrimination.

23. The fuller path diagrams in figures C.3 and C.4 in appendix C reveal the impact of a variety of religious and social variables on prejudice and discrimination, and in those fuller diagrams religious provincialism has been disaggregated into its components, the most important of which is orthodoxy.

24. For a replication of this work with survey data from Mormons in the southern states, where the regional factor sometimes compounded and sometimes displaced the impact of religious indoctrination, see Ainsworth (1982).

9. The Campaign to Cast Off the Curse of Cain

[The Lord] . . . by revelation has confirmed that all worthy male members of the Church may be ordained to the priesthood without regard for race or color.
—LDS First Presidency, 1978

[The 1978 revelation] continues to speak for itself. . . . I don't see anything further that we need to do.
—President Gordon B. Hinckley, 1998

THE 1978 DECLARATION of the church leaders in the opening epigraph was widely expected to bring an end to the most important controversy in Mormondom during the second half of the twentieth century. That the church president, two decades later, was still facing questions about it suggested that the issue was not entirely dead.[1] Like most large organizations and governments, the LDS Church usually struggles with some lag between its official pronouncements and their full implementation at the grassroots. Resistance is likely to be the more protracted the more fundamental the change. Among some individuals and interest groups in any community, old ways die hard and frequently require strenuous follow-up efforts by the leadership to eliminate them entirely. Even the struggle to divest Mormonism of its polygamous heritage is still underway, at least on the margins, more than a century after the official abandonment of the practice. The more contemporary struggle to cast off "the curse of Cain" from Mormons, black and white, has persisted for a full generation, largely because the "die-hards" among white Mormons have been as reluctant as white Americans more generally to relinquish traditional prejudices and stereotypes based on race or lineage. This struggle provides an interesting case study of successes and setbacks in organizational change, sometimes behind the ecclesiastical doors but often in the public arena as well.

The Decline and Fall of the Priesthood Ban against Blacks

The process by which the LDS Church finally divested itself of the traditional restriction on priesthood for its black members is a complex story, which has been told from a variety of viewpoints and assumptions. Different authors have emphasized different elements in the process—internal, external, political, ecclesiastical, and even personal.[2] Lester Bush found reason to believe that Joseph Smith himself inadvertently set in motion certain elements in Mormonism that would later undermine the restrictive racial policy, once it was eventually established (1984, 209–10). A careful scrutiny of the Mormon historical record would likely turn up a number of acts and events with unintended consequences for racial policy. After all, the church was always looking for ways to promote its growth among various peoples of the earth, so it was always unlikely that some peoples could be indefinitely ignored, set aside, or unequally treated without creating practical and theological problems.

Outside Pressures and Tactical Adaptations

Such consequences did indeed derive from certain practical and marginal policy changes that David O. McKay, president of the church, made during his world tour in 1953 and 1954. As a result of his observations in South Africa and Latin America, especially, he became aware of how much the work and growth of the church were hampered by the traditional requirement that priesthood candidates must demonstrate "pure" lineage back to Europe before they could be ordained, even if they had no visible characteristics of African lineage. More or less summarily, President McKay simply switched the "burden of proof," so that anyone in those countries could be ordained *unless* the local church leaders provided evidence of a candidate's African ancestry.[3] In this way, the president opened the ranks of the priesthood to a great many who had been held back by "lineage questions." At the same time, of course, he opened the door for a host of later predicaments when some of the men ordained under this looser policy subsequently discovered black ancestors in the process of doing the genealogical research that faithful Mormons are all expected to do. There is evidence also that in the 1950s some of the general authorities were already discussing the racial quandary behind closed doors or even with trusted friends and relatives. In general, however, the entire issue remained remarkably quiet in the church until the next decade (L. Bush 1999, 236–38, 245; Mauss 1981, 11–14).

Especially after the arrival in 1961 of a federal administration more committed to promoting civil rights for ethnic minorities, restrictive racial policies of all kinds came under increased pressure. Various manifestations of such public pressure have been discussed at some length elsewhere (Bringhurst 1981b, 178–203; Mauss 1981, 14–19; O. White and White 1980). Internal critics also became more public during the 1960s, including the politically prominent Sterling M. McMurrin, who picked up the cudgel first waved by Lowry Nelson back in 1952. George Romney, governor of Michigan and a presidential candidate during the 1960s, was regularly embarrassed by public questioning about his church's racial policies, but he confined his own misgivings and criticisms to internal councils and leaders. The pages of *Dialogue: A Journal of Mormon Thought* during 1967 and 1968 featured regular articles and letters to the editor on church racial teachings and policies, many of them very critical, which did not endear the journal or its authors to many of the church leaders. There were even a few cases in which church policies were deliberately and publicly violated by members and local leaders hoping to dramatize the need for change. Their efforts usually resulted in their own excommunication. It would be too much to claim that all this criticism, internal and external, finally forced the church to change its racial policy, for the change came much later. Yet many leaders as well as members were stung and embarrassed at least as much by internal as by external critics (Bringhurst 1981b, 184–88; L. Bush and Mauss 1984, 4–6; F. Peterson 1999).

The next decade brought some relief from the public pummeling of the 1960s. Not that the church had changed its racial restriction on the priesthood; it was simply as though the external critics had given up on the obstinate Mormons and moved on to other causes. Now and then, of course, some prominent incident or commentator would put the church in a bad public light, but the sustained public pressure of the 1960s eased noticeably. There were some external reasons for this. Congress had passed a variety of new civil rights legislation, and most state and local racial restrictions in public life had fallen as that legislation was increasingly enforced by the courts. That was as true in Utah as elsewhere. Internal Mormon racial policies and teachings, outdated and ridiculous though they still seemed to many, were no longer seen in a context of national crisis over civil rights. That context had largely been broken down by the successes of the civil rights movement and had been replaced by new crises over the war in Vietnam and an increasingly rebellious youth culture. All such external developments helped deflect national attention away from the Mormon racial policies during the 1970s (Stathis and Lythgoe 1977; Shipps 2001).

Meanwhile, the LDS leaders were not ignoring the matter, for they were well aware of the church's tattered public image. Recall that in 1963 the First Presidency had made a public declaration (cited in the previous chapter) that the church policy on priesthood was not intended to have any implications for secular, civil relationships with blacks. Late in 1969, just at the end of President McKay's life, a second public statement on race policy was issued by two members of the First Presidency. This major statement had apparently originated as an effort by certain leaders around McKay to get his signature on a change of policy before his demise. Instead, the result was a political compromise among different factions of the general authorities, who could not quite agree on whether, when, or how to drop the priesthood restriction altogether (L. Bush 1999, 241; Mauss 1981, 17–18; Quinn 1997, 14). As the statement finally emerged, therefore, it simply reaffirmed the traditional restriction on priesthood but otherwise effectively jettisoned almost all the accumulated scriptural folklore that had been used to justify the policy. In place of all such scriptural claims, the statement simply alluded vaguely to the premortal existence as a possible explanation but otherwise offered only the simple statement that blacks had been barred from the priesthood "for reasons which we believe are known to God, but which He has not made fully known to man."[4] President McKay would probably have been willing to sign this statement had he been physically able and perhaps would have even joined in a collective decision to drop the priesthood ban altogether. However, we will never be sure, since he died within days of the 1969 statement, and his entire First Presidency was thereby dissolved. The two presidents succeeding McKay had both opposed changes in the priesthood policy all along, so there the matter rested for several years.

With the 1970s, however, a new public relations campaign was launched. The church had always had some sort of public relations program, of course, but in 1972 the new and professionalized Public Communications Department was created (since renamed Public Affairs Department). Charged with improving the public image of the church, this new bureaucracy was to be proactive, not merely reactive, and to create opportunities for enhancing public acceptance of the church and its missionaries (Shipps 2001, 59, 70n6). Spokesmen and leaders began to appear on programs in the public media (including then church president Spencer W. Kimball in 1974), where they were, of course, regularly invited to explain LDS racial and other issues as best they could. At the same time, a variety of outreach efforts were extended to the black community. At BYU, black athletes, both Mormon and non-Mormon, were recruited, many on scholarships. In 1976, the first black student body vice-president was elected at BYU. Prominent black speakers were invited to the campus, including Alex Haley in 1977 and Senator Edward Brooke in 1978. Off campus, outreach efforts included LDS fund-raising activities for black churches. Within the church, the few black members, virtually ignored before 1970, were given increasingly frequent coverage in the church media. Several black members wrote faith-promoting books about their experiences as Mormons, despite their displeasure over the priesthood policy, and these books were given wide circulation, especially in Utah. Clearly there was a new effort to make black members feel at home in the church, despite their lack of access to the priesthood. (Many more details on LDS outreach efforts to blacks, LDS and otherwise, are in Bringhurst [1981b, 194–97]; and Mauss [1981, 21–24].)

In this more accommodating environment, Mormon blacks responded in kind. In 1971, three active black Mormons approached the Quorum of the Twelve Apostles with a proposal for organizing an independent black unit of the church—in effect, a segregated branch. What eventually emerged was instead a black LDS support group with the name Genesis Group, suggesting a new beginning for black Mormons. Organized originally under the apostles, the group was eventually placed in a regular stake, not as a separate branch of the church but as a unique supplement to regular congregational activities. Genesis Group members were to attend and participate in the wards and stakes where they happened to live but then could come together on the first Sunday evening of each month and at other special times for a variety of supplemental spiritual and social activities (Bringhurst 1981b, 167, 194; Embry 1990b and 1992b; Mauss 1981, 23–24). Led by a "group presidency" of three black men, the Genesis Group has had its ups and downs but was thriving in Salt Lake City at the time of its thirtieth anniversary celebration in 2001 (Lloyd 1996; Stack 1998c).

Incremental Steps toward Ending the Restriction: A Retrospective Summary

From the vantage point of a later generation, it might seem that the momentous policy change of 1978 should have been easy to see on the horizon. After all, for the previous decade and a half the church had been taking a beating in the mass media, and to some extent in the political arena, over its racial ideas and policies. Seemingly in response, the church had issued important public statements in 1963 and 1969 attempting to sever its ecclesiastical policies from any justification for racial discrimination in the larger society. The restriction itself had been reduced in scope, so that it did not apply to island peoples of the South Seas or to cases where African lineage was not obvious and not proved. A new sensitivity and outreach to black people was apparent, both within the church and in its contacts outside. In the light of all that, surely the Mormons and the rest of the world, one might think, were impatiently standing by for the inevitable next and final step: the total removal of the ban against priesthood for people of African descent.

Yet when the announcement finally came in June of 1978 that the priesthood, by divine decree, would thereafter be extended "without regard for race or color," nearly everyone was caught by surprise (Haroldsen and Harvey 1979).[5] Why? In general, there were two main reasons for the surprise: (1) outside criticism and agitation over the priesthood restriction had tapered off in recent years, as the attention of Americans, black and white, was increasingly drawn to more crucial and pressing national issues; and (2) the marginal preliminary measures summarized in the previous paragraph had been neither very fundamental nor very widely recognized, even among Mormons themselves. Certainly LDS members had noticed controversial issues affecting their church, particularly instances of public criticism, but they understood such general conference announcements as those of 1963 and 1969 as defenses of the faith rather than as harbingers of change. Meanwhile, administrative changes in the scope of the race policy or even the creation of the unique Genesis Group would have attracted little attention outside the small networks directly involved in such developments. The delayed timing of the change also helped reassure the faithful about its ultimately divine origin; if the policy had been changed under the public pressure prevailing a decade earlier, it would have been much more difficult to avoid the implication of sheer political expediency as the main motivation for change (Mauss 1981, 26–31, 43nn111–12).

Internal Developments Requiring Change

Even as the world responded to the welcome change, much of the commentary carried a cynical tone implying just such expediency. Given the entire anguished history of Mormon conflict with the outside over this and earlier issues, a certain amount of cynicism was inevitable and understandable, especially among the traditional critics. Yet the fuller historical record makes clear that the church leaders' decision to drop the priesthood restriction was neither sudden nor attributable mainly to outside pressures. The change was driven far more directly by two kinds of *internal* pressure: (1) the missionary imperative—the deeply felt obligation to spread the gospel and build an enduring presence for the church throughout the world; and (2) the eventual recognition of the inadequate scriptural and canonical basis for connecting modern black Africans to an obscure ancient lineage once denied the priesthood. Each of these factors created a kind of "cognitive dissonance," and the two of them together greatly intensified that dissonance, making church leaders far more susceptible than they had been earlier to whatever a divine will might have prompted. Critics who ignore these factors and try to reduce the revelatory process among Mormon leaders simply to internal or external political machinations are overlooking too much—a point discussed at greater length elsewhere (Mauss 1981, 29–34).

The Missionary Imperative

The missionary motive is always present in Mormonism and could be seen already in President McKay's decisions during the 1950s to broaden access to the priesthood by giving the "benefit of the doubt" to peoples and individuals of "questionable lineage." Much more important, however, in drawing official attention to the hazards of racially restrictive policies was the unfulfilled prospect of massive missionary success in black Africa itself. This prospect was aborted in 1963, with considerable embarrassment for the church, when the government of Nigeria was apprised of Mormon racial ideas and policies and therefore refused to admit LDS missionaries, despite a considerable local Nigerian demand for them (J. Allen 1991; Bringhurst 1981a and 1981b, 188–90). As it turned out, missionary work at that time would soon have been disrupted anyway by a major civil war in Nigeria, but the potential was obviously there. When that potential eventually began to be realized with large-scale conversions after the 1978 policy change, it became painfully apparent just how many new members would have been available all along, especially in Nigeria and Ghana but also in South Africa and elsewhere.[6] By the end of the twentieth century, there were more than 100,000 Latter-day Saints in Africa, mostly in urban centers and with relatively high levels of church attendance, activity, and observance. Half of the thousand missionaries serving in Africa had been called from the African countries themselves ("News of the Church: Report of Africa Area Presidency" 1997).

In Brazil, too, probably the most racially mixed nation in the Western Hemisphere, the church had made great strides among people of all colors. Opened in 1925, originally for proselyting among Germans and other immigrants from Europe, the Brazil Mission began much more general proselyting during and after World War II. By 1974, there were four missions, nine stakes, and 41,000 Latter-day Saints in Brazil, which made it seem an especially appropriate location for the first temple in South America. The issue of priesthood eligibility there had also become thorny. The "ineligible" lineage was so intertwined with all the other lineages, often in the same family, that it became simply impossible to disentangle the thicket (Grover 1984 and 1990). Led by President Spencer W. Kimball, the church leaders nevertheless decided in 1974 to build the São Paulo Temple (announced 1 March 1975).

The church leaders must have known that this decision would put them in an untenable position if they were to maintain the priesthood restriction, since access to the priesthood is one of the qualifications for access to the temple rites. The church therefore faced the prospect that thousands of its Brazilian members would be asked for voluntary contributions of money and labor to build the temple with no expectation of being able to enjoy its privileges.[7] It seems fair to conclude that after 1975 there could have been no turning back, for an end to the priesthood restriction would have become imperative as a practical matter. When the end was finally announced in 1978, just weeks before the dedication of the new temple, it provided dramatic vindication for the faith of all who had worked and sacrificed to build it, especially those patient Brazilian Saints of the disfavored lineage (Martins 1996; Mauss 1981, 24–25).

The Dubious Canonical Basis for Racial Restrictions

Beyond these genuine considerations and concerns for extending a permanent church presence among eager new peoples of color, many of the church
leaders were increasingly uneasy with the doctrinal and scriptural basis for
denying the priesthood to those of African descent, even if they were descendants of Cain (or Ham). President McKay and others had begun to ponder
this matter at least as early as the 1950s. Few Mormons have actually questioned the connection of Africans or African Americans to the lineage of Cain,
not only prior to 1978 but all the way to the twenty-first century. Once imported into Mormonism from the time of Joseph Smith himself, this old
biblical folklore proved extraordinarily durable (L. Bush 1999, 258–59; Mc-
Conkie 1981). What came under increasing scrutiny during the 1970s, therefore, was not so much the lineage itself attributed to black people but only
the *priesthood restriction* traditionally accompanying that lineage. Two important developments of the 1960s and early 1970s presented the general
authorities with challenges to that restriction that could not be ignored.

The Book of Abraham The first came in 1967 with the discovery of some fragments of the original papyrus text from which Joseph Smith had translated
the Book of Abraham in the 1830s (Baer 1968; "Facsimile Found" 1967; "The
Joseph Smith Egyptian Papyri" 1968; Sandberg 1989; Urrutia 1969). This
unique Mormon scripture contains the only passage in the entire church
canon that declares any particular lineage ineligible for the priesthood. In an
account of the origin of ancient Egypt, Abraham refers to the pharaohs as
having descended from Ham, a lineage "cursed as pertaining to the priesthood," despite their ancient but invalid claim (Abraham 1:26–27). No reason or explanation is provided in the scripture for this proscription, and
nothing in any of the scriptures connects the lineage of the pharaohs to black
Africans in general. Not only was the passage in question rather obscure in
its meaning, but also the Book of Abraham was not published until 1842 and
then only in a series of installments in the church organ *Times and Seasons,*
which Joseph Smith did not claim, at the time, to be divinely inspired writ
(for examples of apologetic works on this subject, see Millet and Jackson 1985;
Nibley 1975; Skinner 1997; and Todd 1968). Official canonization of the Book
of Abraham, however, occurred only in 1880, as part of the Pearl of Great Price
(Todd 1969). Before then, there is little evidence that church leaders ever used
anything in the Book of Abraham as a rationale for withholding the priesthood from blacks, though some scholars have believed that the Abraham
pseudepigrapha influenced the thinking of Joseph Smith and others on racial matters from the beginning (Cooper 1990, 119–29; Esplin 1981, as cited
by Bringhurst 2001).

Once the provenance of the 1967 papyrus fragments was definitely traced to Joseph Smith and they were established as the basis for some of the Book of Abraham, it was possible for modern Egyptologists to scrutinize Smith's translation—something not feasible in the 1830s, so soon after the discovery of the Rosetta stone in Egypt. All the experts who studied the papyrus, Mormon and non-Mormon alike, agreed that it seemed to be a common funerary text from an Egyptian period much later than that of Abraham. Translated into English by the usual academic methods, the text bore no resemblance to the writings that Joseph Smith had attributed to Abraham. This discovery did not, of course, receive much publicity in the church, but it set Mormon scholars and apologists to work searching for an alternative explanation for the Book of Abraham.

While that explanation remains elusive, the authenticity of the book as revealed scripture has been upheld by simply explaining that Joseph Smith's "translations," whether of the Book of Abraham or of the Book of Mormon, are properly understood not in the usual academic sense but as products of Smith's own direct communication with the divine. The general authorities of the church did not offer their own explanations for the Book of Abraham beyond reaffirming its divine origin, but they could never again assume that this unique scripture was a "translation," in the usual sense, of any ancient document. Some question would thereafter inevitably accompany the significance of the curse "as pertaining to the priesthood" (Abraham 1:27).[8]

Historical Research Even more important in undermining the historical basis for the priesthood restriction was the exhaustive and meticulous research of Lester E. Bush Jr., a talented and persistent young Mormon scholar motivated by a personal quest for the full truth in the matter. With professional training and experience in both medical and historical research, Bush was well qualified to determine what the historical record revealed about the origins and the scriptural warrant for traditional LDS racial ideas and policies. Furthermore, during the 1960s and early 1970s, when Bush did most of this research, he had the field largely to himself. The new Arrington era in the Church Historical Department did not begin until 1972. Prior to that time, the church archives were in the custody of a few nonprofessional clerical staff headed by the apostle Joseph Fielding Smith as church historian and chief gatekeeper. Bush's (1999) retrospective account of his research journey, as well as his encounters with church leaders along the way, is itself a fascinating story. With the help and cooperation of the staff at the church archives, Bush gained access to many important primary and secondary sources. He found other relevant collections also at BYU and elsewhere, some of them in private hands.

His first published product was an extensive review essay of a short book by Stephen G. Taggart (1970). As the first serious historical analysis of the traditional LDS racial ideas, Taggart's book was an important contribution, but it depended too heavily on secondary sources and an a priori thesis that the priesthood restriction had its origins in Missouri during the 1830s (L. Bush 1969). In critiquing this work, Bush introduced a great deal of new historical data and evidence, but his fuller contribution (1973) took the form of a sixty-page article in *Dialogue,* based on a large, unpublished documentary sourcebook that Bush (1972) had collected over the entire decade of his project. For our present purposes, the most important and unavoidable conclusions from Bush's work were that (1) all or most early Mormons and their leaders accepted with little question the traditional American and European biblical lore about the origins of Africans from the lineage of Cain and Ham; (2) the founding prophet, Joseph Smith, did not connect that lineage to any restriction on the priesthood and did not withhold the priesthood from black church members during his lifetime; (3) the restriction emerged gradually during the late 1840s and was formally introduced only in 1852 by Brigham Young, who then connected it to the lineage of Cain; and (4) the resort to the Book of Abraham to justify denial of the priesthood occurred only after that work was formally canonized late in the nineteenth century.

Bush's other discoveries of what was contained (and not contained) in the historical record also proved important, but these four conclusions effectively destroyed the historical basis for denying the priesthood to male church members of black African ancestry. All that remained was the deadweight of accumulated administrative precedents, which no one in authority had questioned during the entire twentieth century. The claim that church racial policy had its basis in divine revelation actually rested only on these precedents, not on any recorded instance of divine direction. From Bush's account (1999) of his contacts and conversations with general authorities of the church while preparing his work for publication, it is obvious that by 1973, when his major article was published, the results of his work were already well known in official circles and among the newly appointed professionals in the church historian's office. Clearly, some of the church leaders were uncomfortable with his findings and particularly with the prospect of their being published. However, no one was prepared to gainsay or criticize Bush's work, and later communications expressed informally by a few church leaders made it clear that this work had a major impact on official thinking (L. Bush 1999, 252–70).

Just how that impact might have played into the eventual decision to drop the priesthood restriction in 1978 we can only surmise. We do know that a new church president, Spencer W. Kimball, was installed on the eve of 1974 and that one of the first decisions by the apostles under his leadership that year was to build a temple in Brazil. As I contended earlier, this decision made almost inevitable the one in 1978 to end all racial restrictions in the church. Surprising as that decision might have seemed outside the leadership councils of the church, it was certainly not spontaneous. It was the product of a revelatory process that began with a long, human struggle of conscience and collective anguish among church leaders and culminated in a susceptibility to spiritual promptings that most of them considered unprecedented. Their unanimity in the matter seemed palpable. Their joint experience fits well with the model of revelation in key Mormon scriptures (Doctrine and Covenants 9 and Official Declaration No. 2), even down to the language used by the First Presidency in its June 1978 announcement that God had "confirmed" by revelation that the priesthood should be extended to all people "without regard for race or color" (Mauss 1981, 29–31).

Developments in the Church after the Revelation of 1978

The revelation and policy change of 1978, in a single administrative act, removed all formal restrictions on full participation in LDS church life by people of black ancestry. What has been much slower to change, however, has been almost two centuries of accumulated racial and religious folklore among white American Mormons. This folklore had been constructed over many years to defend and "explain" to Mormons and others the erstwhile policy of withholding the priesthood from a divinely disfavored lineage. Even though the policy itself had been overturned, the folklore for rationalizing it lingered on at the grassroots, despite its manifest irrelevance to contemporary church life. In particular, the notion that blacks were descendants of Cain now seemed ironically to take on a life of its own as a post hoc "explanation" for the historical origin of the priesthood restriction (W. Wilson and Poulsen 1980). Such "explanations" were no longer offered by the general authorities of the church, but they continued to be circulated in print through authoritative books written by recently departed colleagues in the leadership. Since such ideas were never officially repudiated, they could still be promulgated by local leaders and teachers, including some in the Church Education System and even on the BYU faculty (Ostling and Ostling 1999, 106). In the apparent hope that with time all such vestiges of racism would simply die a natural death, most church leaders simply looked for ways of constructively engaging black people in the future. In this endeavor, the success of the church among blacks in North America did not keep pace with its success elsewhere.

Mormon Missionary Outreach to Black Americans

It is difficult to ascertain just how successful the Mormon missionary program has been among American blacks since 1978. Because ordinary church records do not keep track of race or ethnicity, we are dependent on unsystematic samples and anecdotal evidence. Certainly the church publications have given more exposure than ever before to stories of black conversion, the spiritual and social growth of new black members, and their inspiring encounters with divine influences. A sheer count of such stories would be misleading, however, since a disproportionate number deal with cases outside the United States. Newell Bringhurst studied how the *Church News* presented "the image of blacks as prime instruments of [church] growth and expansion" during the first decade after 1978 (1992, 113). He concluded that in strictly geographic terms the church had made great strides into large sections and populations of the world traditionally neglected by LDS missionaries. In numerical terms, however, Bringhurst found *Church News* claims of rapid black growth to be a little exaggerated in some of the countries. In the United States itself, growth was actually quite slow.

Despite the strained history of Mormon relationships with blacks and the church's studied avoidance of proselyting among them before 1978, American blacks have occasionally joined the church from the very beginning, but especially since World War II. One informed Utah journalist estimated that the church had two thousand black members even before the priesthood policy was changed (Swinton 1988). Most of these seem to have been attracted to the church through friendships with individual white Mormons encountered in the workplace or during military service. As noted earlier, such estimates can only be informed guesses, but whatever their actual number, these converts have been remarkable for their ability to look beyond all the trappings of racism to the Mormon spiritual core. A few of them have left accounts of their conversions (e.g., Bowles 1968; Cherry 1970; W. Clark 1970; Freeman 1979; Hemming 1979; Lamb 1966; Lythgoe 1972; Martin 1972; Oliver 1963; Olsen 1980; Sturlaugson 1980 and 1982; and S. Wright 1970). These accounts reveal a variety of more or less successful efforts to deal with the cognitive dissonance and external black criticism involved in joining the Mormons. I have more to say about this predicament later in the chapter.

Conversions of American blacks to the LDS Church seem to have waxed and waned with local conditions and initiatives, and by no means have missionary efforts been limited to blacks in Utah. A major drive during the early 1980s by the Mormon mission in North Carolina brought in some nine hundred black converts, but a few years later only a hundred remained active in the church (Swinton 1988, 22). O. Ken Earl, who headed the LDS mission in northern California (based in Oakland) from 1983 to 1985, gave special attention to proselyting among the large black population in the Oakland area, and his missionaries succeeded in baptizing 93 new black members, constituting 5 percent of all the converts in the mission during that period (Earl 1985). Most of these lived in two Oakland wards (congregations), and they provided the nucleus for the organization of a northern California chapter of the Utah-based Genesis Group mentioned earlier. This level of growth and enthusiasm did not long survive Earl's departure, but several black families went on to gain prominence in local Mormon congregations (Newhall 1994). The Watts area of southwest Los Angeles produced enough converts for a branch of some one hundred people in a little more than a year, almost all of whom were black (Lang 1985; a fuller discussion of black-white relations among Mormons in Los Angeles is in Orton [1987]). Missionary successes with blacks have attracted attention in other important urban centers of the nation, as well, including the South Bronx and East St. Louis (Gonzales 1994; Hart 1994). Temporary surges in missionary success with American blacks elsewhere have often been reported anecdotally.

One important source of such reports is the collection of African American oral histories compiled by the Oral History Program of the Charles Redd Center for Western Studies at BYU (see appendix A). This program is devoted to collecting oral histories from various special ethnic and other groups in the Mormon orbit. For the Afro-American Oral History Project, 225 black Mormons (mostly recent converts) were interviewed during 1985–89 by Alan Cherry, a prominent black convert of many years. Although these interviews were conducted in various parts of the United States, they constituted essentially an "opportunity sample" of black Mormons, not a representative one. Particularly overlooked in the sample were members who had dropped out of church activity. Nevertheless, the oral history interviews were numerous enough to reveal a great range of social characteristics and life circumstances among the converts, as well as a variety of experiences with conversion, disillusionment, and acceptance in the Mormon community. The quality of these experiences has been captured in an important book based on the interviews (Embry 1994), and a number of articles have been published from the quantitative data these interviews yielded (Jacobson 1991 and 1992; Jacobson et al. 1994; D. White and White 1992; O. White and White 1995).

Taken altogether, this published work is qualitatively very rich. It indicates that those American blacks who joined the Mormon church and remained active in the decade after the change in priesthood policy were disproportionately young, well educated, upwardly mobile socially, and largely of southern origin and upbringing (Jacobson 1991; D. White and White 1992). The converts claimed to have been attracted to Mormonism especially by its "Plan of Salvation," linking this life to the next, and by its emphasis on family life and values. In general, however, they seemed more attached to the general Christian teachings in the LDS Church than to the uniquely Mormon teachings. Especially southern members credited the lay priesthood with keeping them involved in the activities of the organization. Yet many who were still active offered accounts of others who had dropped by the wayside because of the insensitivity of white members, lapses in the church's retention efforts, or simply their own difficulties in trying to maintain the LDS way of life.

Through such reports from those still involved, it is possible to infer some of the reasons for an apparently large drop-out rate among black Mormons in the United States. These reasons included (in no particular order) discomfort over class and cultural differences with white Mormons in most congregations; feelings of being treated categorically as blacks instead of as individuals; exaggerated attention as "novelties" of some kind in their treatment by whites; continuing undercurrents of racism in such LDS popular beliefs as the curse of Cain; white resistance to intermarriage or even interracial dating; and in general a level of white acceptance that was considered civil but not warm. At the same time, the black interviewees recognized that these difficulties were the kinds that tended to occur between blacks and whites in the United States generally, not just in LDS congregations.

In my own interviews, black LDS leaders acknowledged that they devoted much of their time to counseling black church members who had been offended by the traditional racial teachings in Mormonism (Bridgeforth 1981 and 1985; Gray 1999; Lang 1981 and 1985). In general, these black leaders were quite restrained and philosophical about their own disappointments with racial slights by white Mormons, but they clearly shared the indignation that had so often been "unloaded" on them by the black members who came to them for spiritual counseling, as well as by many others throughout the country who had reached them by mail or telephone for the same kind of help. A recurring source of irritation was the continuing circulation among ill-informed and credulous white Mormons of the old racial myths about Cain and Ham and other dubious doctrines, especially in Utah. One black convert couple in Riverside, California, reported that their children had dropped out of the church because of the teasing by their white peers about their supposed descent from Cain (John Smith and Smith 1985).

Some irritants came out of sheer insensitivity, such as the occasion reported by Marva Collins (1985) when her ward Relief Society sisters decided to raise funds through a "slave auction," whereby members would agree to be "slaves," promising to do household tasks for the highest bidder. They totally overlooked the impact of such an idea on their only black member. In short, my own few interviews with black Mormons in southern California and Salt Lake City produced reports very much like those in the Cherry and Embry oral history interviews. While these accounts of life in the church for new black converts contained much that was reassuring and inspirational, the recurring problems with white ignorance and insensitivity were also readily apparent, even among those still active in the church. Indeed, Darius Gray, president of the Genesis Group, reported in an interview in the *Salt Lake Tribune* that the most important reason for the attrition of black church members was the attitude of some white members (Stack 1998c). Whatever the number who had been offended enough to drop out, their departure would be understandable and presumably a source of great concern to church leaders from the top down. So far, however, this official concern has focused less on challenging the racist residue among white Mormons than on preserving public relations outside the church.

Public Relations Outreach by the LDS Church

Besides the usual missionary and congregational programs, the LDS Church has tried to cultivate warmer public relationships with its black members and black America more generally. One method has been to join the national celebration of Black History Month each February or at least to encourage black Mormons to do so. Perhaps the earliest of these initiatives was taken by the black LDS community in Salt Lake City itself, with the encouragement of the church. The first annual "Ebony Rose Black History Conference" was held in the Twenty-first North Ward there on February 21–22, 1987, with a promise that the second annual one would be held in Washington, D.C. The 1987 conference included workshops on a variety of practical topics and black history, especially black LDS history, plus a worship service. One featured speaker was Mary L. Bankhead, perhaps the oldest surviving black Mormon at that time and a descendant of one of the pioneer Utah black families. The keynote speaker was Yoshihiko Kikuchi of the Seventy, a Japanese national. Incongruous as that might seem in a black LDS American gathering, Kikuchi's remarks were very well received as sensitive and supportive (Collins 1987, numbers 25 and 26).

In June 1988, at the ten-year anniversary of the priesthood policy change, the church held a special all-day conference at BYU, "LDS Afro-American Symposium," after several weeks of advance publicity (the printed program and publicity flyers are in BYU Archives). Black Mormons who had gained prominence in religious or professional roles were brought in as featured speakers from as far away as Washington, D.C., Atlanta, and Chicago. Dallin Oaks, of the Quorum of the Twelve Apostles, gave a very upbeat keynote address, in which he emphasized the spiritual and scriptural basis for the church's outreach to black people, the faithfulness of black members, and the enormous growth of the church in Africa. The concluding speaker was James D. Walker, founding president of the Afro-American Historical and Genealogical Society in Washington, D.C. This conference and various other commemorative expressions by the church were duly covered by the national press in some fairly extensive newspaper and magazine articles. Most of this coverage was very favorable and forward-looking in tone, but continuing vestiges of racism in the church were acknowledged (Chandler 1988; Cherry 1988; Chetnick 1988; "Church News" 1988; Swinton 1988; entire summer 1988 issue of *This People*).

As time went on, church-sponsored commemorations of important events in black history were no longer focused exclusively on black Mormons but looked more outward to the nation as a whole. In acknowledging the important contributions of black Americans, Mormon and non-Mormon, the church served three important public relations purposes simultaneously: (1) focusing attention particularly on the achievements of black Mormons, past and present; (2) legitimizing the celebration of black history; and (3) validating the Mormon participation in that history. The commemorations have not been limited to sites and events in Utah. An example with great visibility was a large ecumenical religious service on Sunday, January 20, 1991, sponsored by the Interreligious Council of Oakland (California) but hosted by the LDS Church at its spacious Interstake Center on the grounds of the Oakland Temple. The theme of the service was "Martin's Dream and the Drug Crisis." It featured prayers, music, and a dozen speakers from different denominations, black and white, Protestant, Catholic, Jewish, and Mormon. Most of the several hundred in attendance were black, and afterward all were served refreshments in an adjacent hall by women of the LDS Relief Society.[9]

Other large LDS buildings have also been sought by various religious organizations for commemorating Martin Luther King Day. For example, in January 1992, the San Fernando Valley Interfaith Council was offered use of the LDS Van Nuys Stake Center for a turnout of almost two thousand black, white, and other appreciative celebrants. LDS Church representatives have continued to participate in commemorating Martin Luther King Day under the auspices of the Southern Christian Leadership Conference, the Interreligious Council of Southern California, and the National Conference for Community and Justice (NCCJ—formerly National Conference of Christians and Jews).[10]

Perhaps the single most remarkable illustration of the constructive public relations impact of Mormon outreach to the black population occurred in the wake of the Los Angeles riots in May of 1992.[11] The riots had left much of South Central Los Angeles in shambles, and many of the inhabitants, black, white, and Asian, were unable to get food, shelter, utilities, transportation, or work. Some churches in the neighborhood were doing what they could, with limited resources, to provide food and shelter. Two of these were particularly important in this effort: the Mt. Zion's Baptist church and the First African Methodist Episcopal (AME) church, both of which served mainly black congregations. A few leading Mormons in the immediate vicinity and nearby launched a local campaign to bring relief. The effort went forward under the auspices and initiative especially of the stake presidents in the Palos Verdes and the Los Angeles stakes. While much of the city was still smoldering, a series of Mormon car and truck caravans began delivering food and other supplies to the First AME and Mt. Zion's churches from Mormon congregations in neighboring stakes. The campaign went on for several days, including a Sunday when some of the LDS congregations even canceled their usual meetings to collect and distribute the supplies (see also Florence 1992a and 1992b; and "News of the Church: Calming the Storm" 1992).

The AME pastor, the Reverend Cecil Murray, who had heard little about Mormons except their traditional racial doctrines, was apparently so gratified that he actually gave a public pronouncement encouraging people in the vicinity to talk with the local Mormon missionaries, who had theretofore been largely ignored or even threatened. This episode established an ongoing religious and social relationship between the AME Church and the local LDS stakes that was still active at least a decade later, when a Latter-day Saint apostle was invited in December 2001 to attend a special AME service and to receive, on behalf of the LDS Church president, this congregation's Lovejoy Award, in recognition of the outreach efforts by local Mormons in recent years.

Murray and other local black leaders apparently also intervened with Tom Bradley, who was the black mayor of Los Angeles at the time, to get his help in ending a six-year delay in the issuance of a building permit for a Mormon stake center in the area. The construction of the new stake center, in turn, pumped twelve million dollars worth of jobs and goods into the economy of South Central. Local Mormon leaders believe that the goodwill of black religious leaders such as Murray has also been responsible for protecting the new stake center against vandalism and for opening doors to Mormon missionaries. That stake center served as the site of a large conference, as part of Black History Month in February 2002, devoted to genealogical research for black Americans and sponsored jointly by the LDS Church, the African American Heritage Society, and the California African American Genealogical Society. Under the title "Discover Your Roots," the conference featured the archivist Chris Haley, nephew of Alex Haley, as keynote speaker, and was attended by some four hundred black people of various religious persuasions. The new relationship between the LDS Church and the black community in southern California was obviously still thriving as the new century opened.[12]

Black History Month each year during the 1990s and thereafter has provided opportunities for focusing the attention of the LDS Church on black Americans, Mormon or otherwise. During February of 1993, the church's *Deseret News* featured an article on the work of BYU student teachers who were working with black inner-city high school students in Washington, D.C., and in the same month the *New York Times* covered the growth of the church in Scarsdale, New York, where photos indicated clearly that the congregations were racially integrated (Goldman 1995; Schmidl 1995). On February 5 and 12, 1994, the weekly *Church News* carried special articles on black LDS families and their activities in Roswell, Georgia; East St. Louis, Illinois; and Los Angeles, California. The BYU *Daily Universe* of February 13, 1995, was devoted in large part to the need for greater ethnic "diversity" on campus. As part of the commemoration of Black History Month in particular, the *Daily Universe* featured an article on black Mormon athletes and their needs at the university and another on the first three blacks in the twentieth century to serve full-time missions for the church (Mano 1995; Nuttall 1995). Of course, these represent only a small sampling of the kinds of news coverage sought and received by the church during each Black History Month, especially in the 1990s. Nor was such coverage limited to February of each year; impressive news stories of a "human interest" kind about black Mormon converts appeared at any time of the year.

The twentieth anniversary of the priesthood policy change in 1998 was another occasion for commemorations. However, these were more limited than in 1988 and largely overshadowed, both in Utah and on the national stage, by a widely circulated news story that an official repudiation of the traditional racial doctrines was being considered by the Mormon leadership. At issue were the legends connecting Africans and their descendants with Cain and Ham, as well as some uniquely Mormon ideas about a divinely sanctioned hierarchy of lineages originating in premortal life. The news report about the impending repudiation first appeared in a *Los Angeles Times* article on May 18, 1998, and was carried around the world in various media (Stack 1998a and 1998c; Stammer 1998b and 1998c). However, when confronted by the press at a news conference, President Gordon B. Hinckley denied the report, saying that "the matter . . . has not been discussed by the First Presidency and the Quorum of the Twelve." True though that denial apparently was, the repudiation in question definitely was under discussion at lower organizational levels; and thereby hangs a tale (Ostling and Ostling 1999, 103–5; Stack 1998b; Stammer 1998a).

As recounted by the Ostlings (1999), the need for such a public repudiation had become apparent to Marlin K. Jensen, a president of the Seventy, and to some of the staff working under him in the church's Public Affairs Department. The discussions at Jensen's level, however, had apparently not yet produced any specific proposal for consideration by the Quorum of the Twelve Apostles at the time of Hinckley's comments to the press. The main issue in question was the racist residue remaining in authoritative books written by prominent Mormon leaders of the past. These books, some of them considered doctrinal "classics" among grassroots Mormons, had continued in print under church auspices long after the end of the priesthood restriction that they had ostensibly "explained" (e.g., Dyer 1966; H. Lee 1955 and 1973; McConkie 1966a, 1966b, 1981, and 1985; and Joseph Fielding Smith [1931] 1951). Yet to most white Mormons the "race problem" had been "solved" in 1978, simply by the change in priesthood policy.

Many black Mormons, if they joined the church much after that time, did so without being aware that the issue had ever existed—until they read some of the books with the offending passages. Particularly in North America, where these books were readily available in church libraries and bookstores, black Mormons could learn about these old racial doctrines, sometimes from one another and sometimes even from non-Mormon black friends. When they would raise questions about these doctrines in church settings, they would be met, as often as not, with matter-of-fact affirmations of the doctrines by local Mormon leaders, who themselves tended to accept whatever they read in "Church books." The late Eugene England, who taught English literature at Brigham Young University to the end of the twentieth century, reported that in surveys periodically administered to his classes "a majority of bright, well-educated Mormon students" continued to express belief in the old racial folklore, claiming they had learned it from parents and teachers in the church and never questioned it (quoted in Ostling and Ostling 1999, 106; see also Stack 1998b).

Some black converts, especially those who had gained a deep appreciation for their new religion, were willing simply to swallow hard and dismiss all such ideas as carryovers from the past that eventually would disappear along with the rest of American racism. Others, however, took such offense that they soon dropped out altogether. Still others were willing to give the matter some time but were not prepared to remain quiet in the interim. It was one of these less docile black converts who, with the moral support of his local home teacher, began to remonstrate with church leaders by mail. In particular, however, it was through his home teacher's personal relationship with Jensen that an ad hoc committee was created by Jensen in mid-1997 to help draft a proposal to the other general authorities. The proposal compiled examples of demeaning references to blacks in LDS literature, outlined the potential harm of such passages, and recommended an official and public disavowal of these as modern church doctrine.[13]

The twentieth anniversary of the end of the priesthood restriction seemed an especially propitious time for an announcement of such a disavowal. However, when June 1998 approached with no indication that such a statement would be forthcoming, the black member of the ad hoc committee, who had initiated the process in the first place, became impatient. In the apparent belief that the process could be accelerated with a little encouragement from the press, he got an interview with a reporter from the *Los Angeles Times* and explained what had transpired. The resulting press exposure had just the opposite of the desired effect, as church leaders refused to be prodded in their deliberations. The whole process was thereby aborted, and the "disavowal" that Hinckley finally issued turned out to be nothing more than a denial that he was considering any disavowal (Ostling and Ostling 1999, 105; Stammer 1998c). The rest of the ad hoc committee was chagrined that one of its members had leaked the story to the press, and Jensen presumably suffered some embarrassment at the raised eyebrows of some of his superiors.

Even if the proposal from Jensen had worked its way up to President Hinckley, it is by no means certain that the president would have supported the kind of public repudiation recommended. In his May 1998 demurral, he reiterated the theme that the twenty-year-old policy change "continues to speak for itself." In a later interview with the *Los Angeles Times* reporter who had broken the 1998 story, President Hinckley (having recently returned from visiting LDS congregations in Africa) added, "I don't hear any complaint from our black brethren and sisters. I hear only appreciation and gratitude wherever I go. . . . I don't see anything further that we need to do" (Stammer 1998a; see also Stack 1998b). The apparent assumption behind such comments by the president and his colleagues is that the abandonment of the restrictive racial *policy* in 1978 was meant implicitly to include an abandonment of the various traditional *doctrinal folklore* that had once been used to justify that policy. Such an assumption, of course, does little to neutralize the dubious and offending doctrinal myths that remain in older church literature, especially when it continues to appear in reprintings of that literature.[14]

The manifest confidence of President Hinckley and perhaps most other Mormons that there was no necessity for further disavowals of discarded doctrines could only have been strengthened by the remarkable invitation he received to address the Western Region One Leadership Conference of the NAACP. In the first address ever given by a Mormon president to the NAACP, on April 24, 1998, Hinckley was given a standing ovation and presented with an NAACP Distinguished Service Award by Julian Bond, chairman of the board of directors. Although the main theme of his address was the importance of strong fathers in maintaining stable families, the president also offered well-received comments about the need to improve relationships between the races. Conceding that he was "deeply concerned" about the prejudice remaining in the United States, he nevertheless expressed his typical optimism about the future, for, as he put it, he was already meeting "men and women of great distinction, tremendous capacity, [and even] brilliance in many professions [coming from] diverse ethnic and racial backgrounds." He concluded with the ringing declaration that "each of us is a child of God. It matters not the race. It matters not the slant of our eyes or the color of our skin. We are sons and daughters of the Almighty. . . . When a child comes to realize that there is something of divinity within him, then something great begins to happen" (Hart 1998; see also "News of the Church—NAACP Leadership Meeting" 1998).

Another span in the lengthening Mormon bridge to the American black community was constructed during Black History Month in February 2001. A church genealogy researcher working in the National Archives had happened on the records of the Freedman's Bank, a Reconstruction-era institution that went defunct in 1874 but left behind the banking records of thousands of freed slaves. With the backing of the church and the labor of 550 family history "buffs" who were inmates at the Utah State Prison, these banking records were electronically compiled from microfilms and collated into family groups. The project took eleven years, but with the data in that form, it was possible to identify vital statistics and family connections for nearly half a million freed slaves and their ancestors going back into the previous century. As many as ten million contemporary American blacks have ancestors identified in those records, which the church offered gratis on the Internet or at cost on electronic disks. The project was hailed by prominent scholars and black spokespersons (Falsani 2001; LDS Public Affairs Department 2001; Mims 2001).

The release of the new discs was announced during a highly publicized and well-attended press conference called by the church on February 26, 2001. Predictably, one of the reporters in attendance asked whether this project and the attendant publicity were part of a church gesture of conciliation to the nation's black people in the light of traditional racist doctrines. The church public relations official in charge bridled slightly at the question and offered a rather abrupt response. Fortunately for the Public Affairs Department, a skilled church authority was present from the Seventy and intervened with a much less defensive and more appreciative response to the reporter.[15] The point highlighted by this exchange is that even as the church was getting some credit for its generous dealings with blacks, its unrenounced racist teachings about a "divinely cursed" genealogy were still available to be cited and to cloud an otherwise successful public encounter.

The special commitment of the LDS Church to genealogical research, however, will likely prove a convenient and convivial meeting ground with black Americans in the future. As if in response to the LDS offering of the Freedman's Bank records in 2001, the National Museum of African-American History and Culture in Washington, D.C., opened Black History Month in 2002 by bringing much of its core collection to the LDS temple in Washington, D.C., for a two-month exhibit at the visitors' center there. The featured speaker on the opening day was Frederick Douglass IV, and the next night was devoted to an inspirational "fireside" meeting under the auspices of the Genesis Group from Utah. Early in the month, the church also sponsored an all-day conference there on African American family history and then offered to microfilm copies of all the materials brought for exhibit by the National Museum (*Genesis* [newsletter], January/February 2002). Another LDS-sponsored conference entitled "Discover Your Roots," held in Los Angeles during the same February, was already described earlier.

Of course, all these forms of LDS outreach to blacks are intended to convey the message that real changes have taken place in the ways in which the church regards black people and their aspirations. It is a sincere message, even if it is not always delivered skillfully and sensitively. Having dropped the ban against the priesthood for blacks a quarter of a century ago, most church leaders do not seem to see the necessity for adding a formal, official repudiation of offensive racial doctrines, for these can be expected to disappear naturally from the collective memory with the passage of time. Certainly these old doctrines have not appeared in official church discourse for at least two decades. They are mentioned in the *Encyclopedia of Mormonism* only in passing as relics of the past no longer relevant in the modern church (Embry 1992a; Flores and Flores 1992). However, as long as these doctrines continue to appear in successive reprintings of authoritative books and are freely circulated at the Mormon grassroots, they will continue to rankle many of the black Saints.

Changed Mormon Posture on Civil Rights

Meanwhile, is there any evidence that the church's recent outreach to blacks has been accompanied by corresponding changes in Mormon public opinion about civil rights for black citizens? That is, since my surveys of the late 1960s, have the political and social beliefs and attitudes of white Mormons become more favorable toward black people and their civil rights? Answers to these questions can be found in national survey data collected across three decades by the National Opinion Research Corporation as part of the annual General Social Survey, or GSS (J. Davis and Smith 1996; Mauss 1994, 226).

The tables that follow present comparisons between Mormon and non-Mormon subsamples drawn from the GSS. Together the tables cover a period starting in 1972 and ending in 1996. The LDS subsample accumulated during those years amounts potentially to as many as 452. The national subsample used for comparison is a random selection of about every tenth case during the same time span, which potentially totals about 30,000 cases. However, the actual numbers involved rarely reach those limits and actually vary a great deal because not all the questions in the surveys were used every year. The numbers for the Mormon subsample, in particular, are sometimes quite small, partly from attrition caused by skipping some questions in certain years and partly from subdividing the data by decade. Insofar as the data permit, the tables have been divided into four sections: one for each of the three decades of the 1970s, 1980s, and 1990s and one for the total time period (1972–96). In each section, the surviving Mormon subsample is compared with a corresponding (but much larger) general or national subsample (without Mormons). In table 9.1, we can see these comparisons in response to a question about whether whites have a right to live in racially segregated neighborhoods if they wish to do so.

Table 9.1. Whites Have a Right to Segregated Neighborhoods

	1972–80		1981–88	
	LDS (*n* = 53)	Other (*n* = 5,491)	LDS (*n* = 121)	Other (*n* = 7,542)
Agree strongly	13%	20%	5%	10%
Agree slightly	17	17	15	13
	30%	37%	20%	23%

	1989–96		Average, 1972–96	
	LDS (*n* = 96)	Other (*n* = 6,869)	LDS (*n* = 270)	Other (*n* = 19,902)
Agree strongly	3%	6%	6%	11%
Agree slightly	7	11	13	13
	10%	17%	19%	24%

Note: The title of the table is an abbreviated version of the statement put to respondents (GSS Variable Label = RACSEG). The remaining response categories were "disagree slightly," "disagree strongly," and "don't know" or no response. Distribution was statistically significant (X^2 p = .008).

The first three columns of this table reveal that American approval of segregated communities declined slowly but steadily during the three decades. Mormon rates of approval for segregation were smaller than the national average across all three periods and declined as fast or faster than in the national data. (There were enough Mormon cases to produce statistical significance.) On this measure, at least, the Mormons joined the rest of the nation in giving up segregationist preferences and might even have moved a little faster in that direction after the church policy on priesthood was changed in 1978.

Another indicator in the GSS of segregationist thinking was a question asking whether it was better for black and white students to go to the same schools or to separate schools. By the 1990s, so few Americans were willing to agree to separate schools that the question was dropped from the annual survey. However, we can still compare Mormons with others during the 1970s and 1980s. In table 9.2, we can see that even during the 1970s the LDS respondents were less inclined than the others to favor segregated schools, so in the 1980s the Mormons did not have as far to go as the rest of the country to reach virtual unanimity on unsegregated schools.

The GSS data also permit us to consider differences between Mormons and others in the nation (on average) on three other racial issues: (1) open housing policy; (2) willingness to have a person of the other race home for dinner; and (3) whether blacks should "push" so hard to achieve civil rights goals. In none of these three measures did the distributions prove statistically significant, probably because the Mormon numbers were too small. However, some of the differences between Mormons and others might still be

Table 9.2. Is It Better for White and Black Students to Go to the Same Schools or to Separate Schools?

	1972–80		1981–88		Average	
	LDS ($n = 53$)	Other ($n = 6,057$)	LDS ($n = 56$)	Other ($n = 4,028$)	LDS ($n = 109$)	Other ($n = 10,085$)
Same schools	93%	85%	95%	90%	94%	87%
Separate schools	6	12	5	7	6	11
Don't know or no response	2	2	0	2	1	3

Note: The title of the table is an abbreviated version of the question put to respondents (GSS Variable Label = RACSCHOL). Distribution was statistically significant (X^2 p = .007).

considered indicative. For example, in the first of these indicators (GSS Variable Label = RACOPEN), the question was whether the respondent would vote to let an owner decide who occupies his/her property or would vote to prevent the owner from discriminating on racial grounds. In the 1970s, the Mormons (68 percent) were more likely than the others (60 percent) to favor owner discretion, but by the 1990s both figures had dropped by half and no longer differed (34 percent for both Mormons and others).

On the second of these issues, having a person of the other race come for dinner (RACDIN), Mormons were less likely than others to express any objection even in the 1970s, but by the 1980s the gap (never large) had widened somewhat (88 percent of Mormons had no objection compared with 81 percent of the others). Corresponding data were not collected by the GSS for the 1990s. Finally, on the question of whether blacks should "push" so hard for their rights (RACPUSH), Mormons were a little less likely than the national average all the way along to object to black "pushing." In the 1970s, 66 percent of the Mormons and 70 percent of the others agreed (strongly or slightly) that blacks should not "push." By the 1990s, the corresponding figures were only 29 percent for Mormons and 40 percent for others.

All three of these comparisons, as well as those shown in tables 9.1 and 9.2, are consistent with the general finding that by the 1990s, if not sooner, Mormons had equaled or exceeded the national averages in their support of various civil rights for black citizens (see Mauss [1966 and 1994, 52] for 1960s comparisons). These figures are also consistent with those presented by Wade Clark Roof and William McKinney, who also analyzed GSS data but in an earlier decade (1987, 200). Their graphic presentation even then showed Mormons among the more "liberal" of the various denominations in attitudes toward racial justice (Mauss 1994, 153). With this obvious convergence between Mormons and others in secular, civil racial attitudes, we are back again to the question that was vexing Mormons in the 1960s: Why should anyone care about the Mormons' *religious* beliefs on racial matters (Mauss 1967)? The answer suggested in this chapter is twofold. First, even if Mormons are no longer as racist as most other Americans in secular or civil attitudes, their racism, *whatever* its magnitude, is partly rooted in traditional religious beliefs (such is the message of table 8.2, figure 8.1, and figures C.3 and C.4 in appendix C). Second, those religious beliefs continue to circulate among white American Mormons to the detriment of relationships with black church members, even if there are no consequences for interracial relationships outside the church.

White Mormons, Black Mormons, and the Negotiation of Mormon Identity

Mormonism, of course, has its roots and its trunk firmly planted in its Anglo-American origins. While the many new branches and grafts of the past two centuries have made the religion somewhat less generically American in its culture, its converts from other ethnic backgrounds will probably always find some strains as they try to negotiate their new identities as both Mormon and ethnic. Few, if any, have had to struggle as much with this process as the black American converts. Most peoples find in Mormonism an affirmation of their identities as cherished children of God. The clashes they experience between their new religion and some of their cultural traditions require certain modifications in their ethnic identities, but mostly around the edges. In such cases, the negotiation process has no necessary implications for their essential identities in the divine cosmic plan. If they cannot claim literal descent from the divinely favored lineage of Israel, then they are at least assured of adoption or "grafting" into that lineage after baptism. Even the "curse" on the aboriginal or native peoples of America was but a temporary cloud hanging over a divine destiny.

The traditional Mormon definition of black African lineage was something more fundamental and essential. This lineage, so the explanation went, actually originated before mortality, when a certain segment of God's spirit children was identified and set aside for its premortal sins or failings, which presumably were very serious offenses but not very clearly delineated. These "justly" stigmatized spirits were the ones sent into mortality through the lineage of Cain, the most monstrous counterfigure in scriptural lore, second only to the devil himself (and, indeed, a collaborator with the devil). The Mormon version of this lineage myth was an elaboration on a general European legend that had been increasingly applied to Africans, especially as a useful justification for black slavery. The degradation of life under that institution seemed to confirm and reinforce the myth. By the time Mormonism came along, many generations of both black and white Americans had been inculcated with this definition of black identity.

It was, of course, never a meaningful myth to Africans themselves, virtually all of whom were black, and it was less salient even in other parts of the
Western Hemisphere, where in some countries the descendants of black slaves
came to be the dominant populations. In those situations, black peoples had
some control over the kinds of images and identities about themselves that
were passed down the generations. Furthermore, white control over national myths and daily life gradually waned, so that the black populations, especially in Africa, were not constantly reminded of their inferior and oppressed
status (South Africa would be an exception, of course, until recently). In the
United States, by contrast, the legacy of slavery remained for at least a century after the Civil War and in some respects even into the twenty-first century. During all this time, the unequal opportunities and unequal treatment
of the black minority by white neighbors and institutions, even outside the
South, have continued to reinforce traditional religious and cultural myths
about the black identity. It is no wonder that a mutual wariness and suspicion can still be found between blacks and whites in the United States, even
more so than in all-black nations.

How do American blacks—and black Mormons in particular—deal with
this predicament at the level of the individual?[16] How does a black member
of the LDS Church negotiate an identity that somehow manages the cognitive dissonance between an ethnic or racial definition that she or he cannot
escape and a demeaning religious tradition that the individual was once
encouraged to accept in the process of conversion? As might be expected, this
negotiation yields different resolutions for different black Mormons, just as
the negotiation of the Lamanite identity does for American Indians, as was
seen in chapter 5. In my own interviews and informal conversations with
black Mormons in Utah and California, I have encountered several different resolutions, but the richest source of data on this question is the Afro-
American Oral History Project of Jessie Embry and Alan Cherry at Brigham
Young University, mentioned earlier (see appendix A). Those semi-structured
interviews encouraged the black Mormon respondents to talk at some length
about their experiences with the church and with other Mormons in various parts of the country. In particular, the respondents were asked to reflect
upon the meaning of the traditional Mormon teachings and policies regarding black people.

With more than two hundred such interviews, it would be an enormous
task to review, organize, and categorize all of these responses so that a general typology might be constructed. Fortunately, this task was undertaken by
two scholars (O. White and White 1995). They studied the Embry-Cherry
interview transcripts and abstracted five different modes of identity negotiation that emerged in those interviews, as the black Mormon respondents
articulated the relationship between their racial and religious identities. The

scholars enriched their analysis with illustrative quotations from the actual interviews. The five different modes seemed to arrange themselves along a conceptual continuum. At one end of the continuum were respondents who gave precedence to their newly found Mormon identity over their racial one, and at the other end were those who did the opposite. In between were different combinations of racial and religious explanations for the identities that black Mormons embraced in their relationship with God and the church.

The *first* type of identity resolution embraced the truth-claims of Mormonism while recognizing the traditional racial ideology that seemed to go with it. The erstwhile denial of the priesthood for blacks was explained as a lack of historic or even moral readiness on the parts of blacks themselves or their supposed ancestors going back to Cain or Ham rather than as any error in the church. This mode was especially common among black Mormons who had joined the church in earlier years, while the priesthood restriction was still in force. The *second* type of identity resolution also gave precedence to the Mormon religious identity, while explaining the traditional racial ideas and policies as simply a great quandary, one that all would understand sometime in the hereafter but that should not be allowed in the meanwhile to keep anyone from the true faith. The *third* mode called for relegating all racial issues in the church to the past. Whether the traditional teachings had a divine or a human origin was no longer relevant, and nothing was to be gained by rehashing it. The main thing these black Mormons wanted to do was to assert their own new identities as members of the true church and look to the future rather than to the past. Black Mormons assuming this posture were, in effect, validating the public comments of church leaders, especially President Hinckley, about the need to forget the past.[17]

The fourth and fifth modes, while still embracing a Mormon identity, put the responsibility for the traditional racist teachings entirely on the whites. In the *fourth* mode, the explanation was that the church had simply allowed human error to influence church policy, because of political compromises (in Missouri or Utah) or because of the need to mollify a few slave-owning converts. Black Mormons taking this position, even if they had joined the church before the priesthood policy change, always looked upon the racist elements in Mormonism as imported from the outside, never part of the true gospel, and certain to be changed eventually. This was the posture taken, in general, by some of the most prominent black Mormons from the pre-1978 period, including Ruffin Bridgeforth, founding leader of the Salt Lake City Genesis Group; Catherine Stokes of Chicago; and Cleeretta Smiley, of Washington, D.C., who candidly characterized the traditional Mormon racial teachings as "damnable heresies" (quoted in Broadway 1998). Finally, the *fifth* mode reversed the moral positions of whites and blacks with the argument that blacks had been denied the priesthood all those years because God knew that *whites* were not morally and spiritually ready to accept black members in full fellowship. This position implied that blacks had been tested and had demonstrated superior moral strength through their patience and forgiveness.[18] In transferring the burden of responsibility for racist teachings and policies to the whites, the fourth and fifth modes maintained a positive identity for blacks while still completely embracing the Mormon religion and identity.[19]

The reader will perhaps recall some similarities here to the discussion in chapter 5 about negotiations of clashing identities on the parts of American Indians who had become Mormons. In particular, recall the similarities to the first mode for those Indians who had embraced their Mormon identity as a means of *escaping* the stigmatized Lamanite identity in favor of full assimilation into the Mormon culture. The fifth mode here, too, is reminiscent of certain Indians in the United States and Mexico who aspired not only to reverse the positions of themselves and "white Gentiles" in the divine scheme but also in some cases even to *displace* the whites as the true Israelites (e.g., George P. Lee and Margarito Bautista).

Additional evidence of black Mormons' struggle with identity can be found in a few publications they have produced. Earlier in this chapter, I listed books that individual black Mormons had published, in some cases well before the 1978 policy change, to tell the stories of their conversions and their struggles with identity in a "white church." Besides these books, at least three periodical newsletters have emerged from the small black Mormon community in Utah. Two of these survived only a few years, despite church grants to help them get started, probably because they depended on only one or two key individuals to keep them going. *Ebony Rose* was edited and published from 1985 through 1988 by Marva Collins, assisted mainly by family members. *Let's Talk* (later changed to *UpLift*) was edited and published in Utah from 1989 through 1994 by the Latter-day Saints for Cultural Awareness (LDSCA), led by Joseph C. Smith and a few associates (Lloyd 1993). *Genesis,* published by the Genesis Group, is still being published irregularly (as of 2002), but the original publication date is uncertain. It advertises itself as "a non-correlated publication of the Church," but its parent organization, the Genesis Group, is "officially sponsored" by the church, so both enjoy a certain amount of funding (see appendix A).

All three of these newsletters have explicitly promoted the mission and teachings of the Church of Jesus Christ of Latter-day Saints. Accordingly, they all cultivate a strong Mormon component in the black convert's identity. All of them have received the public support and endorsement of the church's leaders. They have all promoted to some extent a black identity, as well, but they differ somewhat in tone and emphasis on the black heritage. *Ebony Rose* was perhaps the least "assimilationist" of the three. Taking a cue from the advice of church president Kimball against racial intermarriage, an *Ebony Rose* editorial called for the construction of a vast network through which black Mormons could meet one another and, in some cases, marry (issue 20, 1986). An earlier editorial had observed that assimilation is not entirely a good thing if it means that black Mormons must forfeit their black culture entirely. This publication also cultivated a connection with African Latter-day Saints to the point that its "Letters" section was dominated by African "pen pals."

Without taking a position on assimilation, *UpLift* (and its predecessor *Let's Talk*) devoted a large portion of each issue to black history in general (not just black LDS history) and to various expressions of "cultural awareness," meaning mainly a celebration of various aspects of the black cultural heritage. Perhaps in an effort to distinguish itself from the other publications, *UpLift* explicitly declared that its parent organization, LDSCA, "is a non-profit educational corporation . . . not a support group. Our goal is to educate in the area of cultural awareness . . ." (Editorial, vol. 3, no. 3 [1993]: 6). In denying a "support group" function, LDSCA seems to have been dropping an objective identified by earlier editorials in *Let's Talk,* namely, assisting "African-Americans with the transition into the gospel so that they do not feel separated and lonely after joining the Church, nor that they have to leave their culture behind to assimilate into the LDS culture" (Editorial, vol. 1, nos. 3–6 [1989–90]: 2). To emphasize its focus on cultural awareness, LDSCA bestowed its Ammon Award each year on persons judged to have been especially instrumental in promoting that goal (awareness) among Latter-day Saints (Lloyd 1993).[20] *UpLift* also carried articles from time to time on Africa or Africans, and LDSCA leaders were periodically enlisted by the church's Public Affairs Department to participate in receptions at church headquarters for visiting African dignitaries (vol. 1, no. 1 [1991]: 1).

The Genesis Group, organized in late 1971, has not always had a special publication of its own or a mission of outreach to Africans, American blacks, or anyone else except the struggling band of black LDS members in Utah. After the 1978 revelation extended the priesthood to black members, the raison d'être of the Genesis Group seemed increasingly in doubt. A decade later its active membership, only around fifty to start with, had diminished to half that number, and there were fears for its survival (Bridgeforth 1985; Gray 1999). Since then, the group has benefited from increased acceptance and support in Utah and at church headquarters; a productive collaboration with the "younger generation" of black Mormons in the LDSCA (while that organization lasted); and an infusion of new and younger members.[21] Its functions have expanded to fill a real and growing need for helping black Latter-day Saints throughout the country negotiate the conflicting claims on their identities from the church, on the one hand, and the black American community, on the other (Lloyd 1996).

Formally and informally, the Genesis Group has also acquired many important functions (Lloyd 1996). One of these is missionary outreach. Especially in recent years, with the priesthood restriction a thing of the past, black Mormons' efforts to proselyte among blacks have sometimes been effective. Able speakers, musicians, and other performers from the Genesis Group also periodically are invited to appear at social and religious events in various wards and stakes. Lately an important outreach function for the Genesis Group has been counseling and educating new black members and investigators of the church, as they become aware of the Mormon racial history. Especially before 1978, when the priesthood restriction was still in force, it was a shock for some blacks during and after conversion to discover that they would not be able to hold the priesthood along with everyone else in the church. Obviously a few of them joined anyway, but often only after lengthy consultations by phone and mail with Genesis Group leaders able to reassure them of the prospects for change. Even since 1978, with no formal racial distinctions any longer part of the church program, the history is still there, and so are remnants of the old folklore about divine marks and curses. When black converts discover this racist history and residue, often only after joining the church, their disillusionment requires the kind of social and spiritual nurturing that Genesis Group members are uniquely capable of offering.

Finally, the Genesis Group attempts to meet the special needs of not only black members but also racially mixed couples and families, including those families in which parents of one race have adopted children of another. In their normal LDS wards (congregations), active black members and mixed families tend to stand out as anomalies.[22] By contrast, at the periodic Genesis Group meetings and social events, they are able to feel much more comfortable, for most of the members there share the same predicament. The celebration of the unifying rather than divisive potential of "racial mixing" is apparent to anyone attending recent meetings of the Genesis Group or reading its newsletter, *Genesis.*

The functions of the Genesis Group have thus changed somewhat since its origin, but a main function still consists of helping black members cultivate strong and favorable identities as Mormons, despite the racist heritage that some of them remember all too vividly (Bridgeforth 1985; Gray 1999). The mission of the group has expanded to meet the needs of multiracial families that have been formed or recombined through divorce (or widowhood) and remarriage. In all these situations, children, especially, must learn to integrate into their identities not only their Mormonness but also their associations with parents, siblings, and church peers from a variety of racial or ethnic settings.

Meanwhile, in recognition of the potential for church growth among the large black population of southern California, the LDS public affairs office there appointed a talented young black LDS man as director of African

American affairs, and in 2002 initiated a series of bimonthly regional "fireside" gatherings for black church members and families in the region. The retention and activity of black Latter-day Saints depends on the success of these organizational efforts, and there can be no room for invidious comparisons among lineages. In this sense, the Genesis Group and related groups in other cities might represent harbingers of future Mormon efforts to reach outside regular congregational boundaries to serve the needs of black, mixed, and special populations (Embry 1990b).

Conclusion

This chapter has presented a variety of data from secondary historical sources, large-scale surveys, in-depth interviews with black Mormons, and many other documents bearing on the relationships between black and white Mormons in the United States. The evidence indicates that white Mormons as individuals and the LDS Church as an institution have sincerely tried to relegate to the past the earlier teachings and practices that for so long complicated their relationships with black Americans. This effort seems to have been more successful in secular relationships outside the church than in congregational life. There are a few racially mixed wards and branches and even some that are predominantly black in Los Angeles and other urban areas. However, the overwhelming majority of white Mormons rarely encounter blacks at church, so that a certain discomfort and wariness tend to remain whenever they do. Moreover, Mormon missionary work among American blacks does not seem to be thriving, even after the 1978 change in priesthood policy.

It is not clear how much the lingering racial myths in the Mormon religious heritage affect missionary work or the congregational relationships between blacks and whites. The tables and figures in this and the previous chapter and in appendix C have demonstrated that the religious hostility implied in those old myths has played an important part in generating anti-black prejudice and discrimination. Some three decades later, both the religious hostility and its secular implications have apparently diminished, but there is no reason to believe that any change has occurred in the *relation* between hostile religious myths and secular prejudice. In other words, the theoretical framework I advanced in the 1960s (following Glock and Stark) remains valid in its basic causal argument. Therefore, even if religious myths about premortal failings, descent from Cain, and the like, have diminished in the lore and collective memory of Mormons, any residue can be expected still to generate prejudicial and discriminatory outcomes in the thinking and behavior of white Mormons. Authoritative writings by earlier church leaders, as well as recurring anecdotes at the grassroots level, suggest that some of this residue remains and continues to rankle relationships *within* the church, even if its impact is minimal on the outside. It is for that reason that President Hinckley's call for the issue simply to be relegated to the past, without some sort of explicit and official disavowal, seems unduly optimistic to many black members.

Perhaps all religious traditions based on claims of divine revelation find it difficult to deal with major discrepancies between the received doctrines and later scientific understandings. As a relatively new religious tradition, Mormonism at least has not yet had to grapple with anything so fundamental as the legacy of medieval religious opposition to modern science. Yet, even if relatively free of the heavy baggage of ancient theological disputes and scientifically untenable dogmas, Mormonism carries more recent baggage with a special weight of its own. Many Mormons of my generation grew up with grandparents who could remember hearing the teachings of the religion from the lips of some of the founders themselves. These teachings were often a mix of canon doctrine, conjecture, and sheer folklore, but they were undeniably venerable precisely because they were so close in time to the founding era of miracles.

To repudiate any of the cherished religious lore of their immediate ancestors seems to some Mormons, especially the older ones, to be almost a repudiation of the grandparents themselves, to say nothing of *their* teachers, who might have walked with God. Thus is the accumulation of ecclesiastical precedent sanctified in a way by family bonds; and thus is the divestment of relatively recent tradition sometimes more difficult than overturning one that is centuries old. One need point only to the struggle in Utah even now over plural marriage: Despite the long arm of the law and the church's strenuous repudiation of polygamous *practices,* the traditional *doctrines* underlying plural marriage still survive even in mainstream Mormonism. Why should traditional racial doctrines be any easier to set aside?

Besides the kinds of specific racial myths at issue here, every community, indeed every family, has its own cherished *organizational* myths. A couple of these general myths seem to have grown with time in the ecclesiastical governance of the LDS Church. These are not found explicitly in scripture, policy handbooks, or even church discourse. Yet it is reasonable to infer that these myths operate under the surface in the organizational life of the church. The first is what I call the *myth of continuity,* which sees the history of Mormonism in linear, progressive terms (perhaps a little like the classical American myth of progress). There are no zigs or zags, no turning back, no repudiation of the past in Mormon church life or lore. There are changes, to be sure, but these are the products of continuous revelation. Such a linear definition of revelation is implied in a passage from the Book of Mormon: "For behold thus saith the Lord God: I will give unto the children of men line upon line, precept upon precept, here a little and there a little . . . [and] unto him that receiveth I will give more . . ." (2 Nephi 28:30; see also Doctrine and Covenants 98:12; and Isaiah 28:9–10). Even though new revelations might make the church quite different from the way it was earlier, these changes are simply the logical fulfillment of policies and teachings already anticipated by earlier prophets.

Thus, when the priesthood restriction policy was dropped in 1978, this was not portrayed as an actual reversal, because several earlier church leaders had predicted that it would happen (of course, several others, including Brigham Young, had predicted that it would never happen). Even with the abolition of polygamy, the practice was only "suspended" and could be restored at any time, since the theological basis was left intact. This myth of continuity has the important function of validating the traditional claim of continuous revelation (which *is* canonical) and protecting the church against the charge of purely pragmatic and expedient changes.

The second cherished organizational myth is related to the first: the *myth of history as time-filtered*—the organizational equivalent of the old adage that "time heals all wounds" and similarly dubious notions. This myth is typically accompanied by an organizational posture of "benign and selective forgetfulness." If the church progresses in a continuous, linear path by divine guidance, then *contemporary* realities and understandings replace those from the past, which will eventually be forgotten or filtered out by time. Obsolete ideas and practices simply do not count any more, even if they originated as divine revelations. Where discrepancies appear between the present and the past, there is no point in reminding ourselves about the past. Especially if something about the past is embarrassing, then recalling it and dwelling on it, even if only to repudiate it, merely confuses the matter. Such negative thinking has no place in the Lord's kingdom. If harm has resulted from earlier ways of thinking, then everyone involved should forgive everyone else and get on with constructing a better future. Apologies or ringing declarations of disavowal should not be necessary, since few peoples or individuals have histories free of offenses against others, and thus few are in a position to demand apologies. With time, memories of these offenses will fade automatically, and we will all be better for it. Meanwhile, if we have made the requisite changes, let's not stir up useless and uncomfortable old memories.

This myth of time-filtered history promotes organizational morale by accelerating the erosion of painful collective memories. The myth is particularly useful in an organization with a constant influx of new members or converts, who are unaware of very much in the organization's past. Almost all discrepant ideas and practices from the past can be expected to disappear from the institutional memory within a couple of generations. Along with the myth of continuity, time-filtered history means that at any given moment in Mormon organizational life, the main motif in the church will be positive, confident, and optimistic, a posture personified especially well by the current president, Gordon B. Hinckley.

Such myths promote success at the organizational level but are less effective in the retention of disillusioned individuals. As President Hinckley ap-
peals to everyone to leave the racist legacy of the church in the past and look
to the future, most Mormons will be able to do that at no cost to their own
identities or self-esteem. Many black members, however, reading recurring
passages from that very legacy in recently reprinted church books, will find
it difficult to see themselves or their identities in those passages and to remain identified with the church. In that sense, the old "curse of Cain" remains
a burden upon them and upon the mission of the church itself.

Notes

1. The 1978 passage quoted in the opening epigraph comes from Official Declaration
No. 2, dated June 8, in Doctrine and Covenants. The second one, from President Hinckley, is in Stack (1998c); Stammer (1998a); and Ostling and Ostling (1999, 104–5).

2. The most complete account of the process by which the policy was changed remains
Mauss (1981), but important aspects of the process are considered in Bringhurst (1981b,
171–203); L. Bush (1984 and 1999); Grover (1984 and 1990); and O. White and White (1980).

3. During this same general period, Fijians, New Guineans, and Philippine Negritos
were also reclassified from questionable to eligible lineages.

4. Letter to all priesthood leaders in the church, December 15, 1969, signed by Hugh B.
Brown and Nathan Eldon Tanner for the First Presidency. Reproduced (among other
places) in L. Bush and Mauss (1984, 222–24).

5. The complete text of the policy change can be found as Official Declaration No. 2,
in Doctrine and Covenants.

6. Although beyond the scope of this chapter, the eventual opening of full LDS missionary work and church activity in Africa is recounted in LeBaron (1996); Mabey and
Allred (1984); and Morrison (1990). On the legacy of apartheid in South Africa for Mormons, see A. Clark (1994).

7. The apostle LeGrand Richards was among the LDS leaders who explicitly cited this
Brazil dilemma as a strong incentive for change in the church racial policy (Mauss 1981,
30–31, 44n 118).

8. The dialogue on the Book of Abraham between believers and nonbelievers has continued into the twenty-first century. See, for example, Ashment (2000); Cook (2000); and
Ritner (2000), where some of the arguments from the 1960s are revisited and updated.

9. I am grateful to the LDS poet Carol Lynn Pearson for providing me a copy of the
printed program for this event, together with a very moving account from her own journal of her feelings while participating in the religious service (Mauss personal files).

10. These and similar accounts about LDS outreach to the black community in southern California are in LDS Public Affairs Department (1999).

11. The account that follows is a highly condensed summary of a much more extensive narrative provided in a memorandum to Robert D. Hales of the Quorum of the Twelve
Apostles from the Los Angeles office of the LDS Public Affairs Department, dated December 6, 2001, a copy of which is in my personal files. The same account appeared in
LDS Public Affairs Department (1999).

12. I received a firsthand account of this conference on February 16, 2002, from the local missionary couple who had organized and coordinated it under the auspices of the Los Angeles office of the LDS Public Affairs Department. The conference was held all morning on Saturday, February 9, at the new stake center. It featured workshops on several different family history and genealogy topics. A copy of the brochure announcing the conference is in my personal files.

13. For an accurate account of this committee's efforts and personnel (which included myself) and the eventual outcome of the effort launched by Jensen, see Ostling and Ostling (1999, 103–5). Copies of most of the committee's correspondence (1996–98) are in my personal files.

14. In response to my specific inquiry about the circulation of books with these offending passages, the owner and the buyer at a major Salt Lake City bookstore offered the following estimates, based on their joint experiences. Two of the books—McConkie (1996b and an earlier edition) and Joseph Fielding Smith ([1931] 1951)—are still "big sellers," defined as forty to fifty copies each per year at their store alone, plus perhaps four times that many at other Salt Lake City bookstores with which they are familiar. Other "big sellers" included Joseph Fielding Smith (1957–66) and Joseph Fielding Smith and McConkie (1954–56)—and this despite the fact that all these books periodically go out of print (Bench and Wotherspoon 1997).

15. The story was covered at some length in two programs on National Public Radio: Shirley Jahad on *All Things Considered,* February 26, 2001; and Howard Berkes on *Morning Edition,* February 27, 2001. The LDS black community had known about the project for several years (*UpLift* 3, no. 1 [1993]: 1–3).

16. The pathos in this predicament is dealt with sensitively and authentically in a trilogy of historical novels published at the beginning of the new century (Young and Gray 2000–2003).

17. A panel of active black Mormons in the Washington, D.C., area also took this position in a public presentation during the annual conference of the Mormon History Association in May 1998. The conference program committee (including myself) had reason to believe, however, that the black panel members had been well coached by local church leaders (Broadway 1998).

18. This attitude also appears implicit in the public comments and demeanor attributed by one journalist to two black celebrity converts to Mormonism: Thurl Bailey, a Utah Jazz basketball player and musician; and Gladys Knight, a Hall of Fame pop singer (Swenson 2001). Their comments might also partly reflect the fourth mode described here. The "divine test" idea is fully articulated in a recent issue of the *Genesis* newsletter (Hamilton 2002, 8).

19. To these five modes of identity construction, one might add the use of religious conceptions in the process of *identity quest,* illustrated by the remarkable case of the former black militant Eldridge Cleaver, who temporarily embraced Mormonism during the early 1980s as a stage in his "passage" from expatriate fugitive to loyal and law-abiding American—a passage apparently never quite completed before his death. See the story in Bringhurst (2002).

20. Ammon is a figure in the Book of Mormon who courageously took the gospel to the despised Lamanites (Alma 17).

21. *Let's Talk* (1, no. 3 [1989]) featured a front-page article on its "merger" with the Genesis Group, and then, as if to renew that relationship, Ruffin Bridgeforth, president

of the Genesis Group, was made chairman of the board of directors for LDSCA five years later (*UpLift* 4, no. 1 [1994]).

22. The religious motivations for black Mormons to seek interracial marriages, despite the social pressures against doing so, are poignantly detailed in the oral history interviews analyzed by O. Kendall White Jr. and Daryl White (2000).

10. Reprise

[The missionary] had gone out to change [the world] and was
returning, himself a changed man. . . . The conversion of the
missionary . . . results in his being not only a missionary but an
internationalist, an intermediary between . . . civilizations. Abroad
he represents a universal religion . . . ; at home he is constantly
changing the attitude of the millions of his constituency, . . .
bringing to them something of his new breadth of vision. . . .

—Earl H. Cressy, 1919

THE EPIGRAPH COMES from a book whose general theme is the enormous
impact that Protestant missionary work in China had on the missionaries
themselves during the late nineteenth century and early twentieth (Xi 1997).[1]
As the history of imported religions might lead us to expect, their Christian
message gradually underwent certain syncretic modifications under the influence of the ancient religions of the Far East. As Lian Xi observed, this
changed outlook of the missionaries carried a cost for their proselyting enterprise: "because syncretism appealed to humanistic principles and often to
scholarly refinement; rather than seeking to evoke religious enthusiasm, it
tended to become the victim of its own persuasion, arguing its way out of
the missionary cause . . ." (1997, 228). Furthermore, and probably more serious, this missionary experience, the author argued, transformed the general
theology of many of the missionaries from the traditional (especially Calvinist) particularism with which they began to the liberal and universalist
expressions of Christianity that came eventually to dominate the mainline
denominations and seminaries of America.

The consequences of this change thus extended well beyond the mission
field to the home denominations themselves, as the syncretism and relativ-
ism brought back by these missionaries contributed greatly to the conflict
and eventual schism throughout America between the "modernists" and the
"fundamentalists." No such dire consequences have occurred in the wake of
a century and a half of Mormon missionary work—at least not yet—even
though much of the Mormon proselyting has been carried on far outside of
the American homeland. The susceptibility of Mormon missionaries to syncretic and unorthodox thinking has been greatly constrained by the short

length of the standard mission (rarely more than two years, three for mission presidents), as well as by the tight controls imposed by church headquarters over the missionaries' activities and teachings.

Yet Mormonism has not remained untouched by the changes in missionaries, mission presidents, and traveling church leaders as they have returned from overseas assignments. Such is the main "story line" of this book, as indicated in the very first chapter. While missionary work did not have the divisive and schismatic impact on institutional Mormonism that it apparently had on mainstream Protestantism, it certainly did bring about changes in the ideological framework governing Mormon missionary activity. The change of greatest concern in this book, of course, has been the steady decline in Mormon thinking about the importance of some lineages over others in the divine plan, as well as an erosion of other racialist understandings and explanations for the world's many ethnic differences. Such old notions from early Mormonism (and early America) simply could not be sustained in the face of the manifest eagerness of various peoples to embrace the Mormon message. This purging of the preoccupation with lineage has been the gift of the world's peoples to Mormonism.

Religious Ideas and Constructions of Identity

A subplot in this story about the impact of Mormon missionary engagement on the religion itself can be seen in the ongoing negotiation and renegotiation of lineage or ethnic identities. The general nature of this process was described in chapter 1 with a theoretical explanation and a historical illustration from post-exilic Judaism. The Mormons' construction of their own identity was forged in the fires of calumny and persecution. This might seem at first unexpected for such a thoroughly American innovation. Earliest Mormonism and its followers, in the very beginning, would have been difficult to distinguish from other Calvinist-inspired restorationist movements emerging out of the nineteenth-century American frontier.[2] The theology in the Book of Mormon or early Mormon discourse was not very different from that familiar to the Campbellites, the Methodists, and other Protestant strains of the time. Also like their neighbors, the Mormons were all of Anglo-Saxon stock, not German Anabaptists or French Huguenots. Moreover, Joseph Smith was very much in the mold of a Jacksonian folk-hero, an American everyman who rose from among the people to become a new prophet, not just another reformer. So why the almost immediate antagonism to the new religion? Answering this question adequately would take us rather far out of focus, but in passing I would point particularly to three characteristics that produced hostility to the early Mormons: (1) the claim to exclusive divine authority; (2) the claim to new and direct divine revelations, of which the Book of Mormon was the most public; and (3) the Mormon tendency almost from the very beginning to cluster or gather, thereby raising the specter of concentrated political and economic power.

While there is obviously much more to the story of Mormon interactions with the surrounding citizenry, those interactions produced a widening rift beginning at least with the gathering of the Saints to Kirtland, Ohio, in 1831. The Mormon resistance to outside criticism and persecution took many forms, but one of these was the internal cultivation of a special identity for the Saints as a divinely chosen people, an identity regularly reinforced by the persecution itself. Had not such always been the fate of the chosen? This process of identity construction began, as explained in chapter 2, with the recognition of an allusion in the Book of Mormon itself to Joseph Smith as a literal Israelite, a descendant of the ancient Joseph (2 Nephi 3:6–18). The process continued with a growing awareness, expressed in formal patriarchal blessings, that others were also of the same chosen lineage, especially those with familial ties to the Smiths. Eventually, the earliest self-understanding of the Saints as Gentiles, charged with bringing the gospel again to the aboriginal Israelites or Lamanites of the Book of Mormon, was supplanted by the understanding that the Saints were themselves actually Israelite remnants of the tribe of Joseph, called out from a Gentile *nation* to gather all of scattered Israel. Remnants of Israel might be found anywhere in the world, however, so the missionary impulse was still ultimately universal in its orientation.

By the time the church was relocated to Utah, these early LDS constructions of lineage identity began to find powerful reinforcement and elaboration from the influences of British Israelism and Anglo-Saxon triumphalism. These two philosophies, the first a religious one and the second a more secular one, developed in Europe quite independently of Mormonism, of course. Yet they were popularly embraced, in both England and the United States, by the middle of the nineteenth century, and they were readily imported into Mormon popular thinking. They fit especially well with the Ephraimite identity that the Saints had brought to Utah. Official church literature and pulpit discourse gradually blended and articulated all of these aspects of the emerging Mormon identity with an understanding of premortal existence as the phase of divine history during which God had assigned his spirit children to the more favored lineages, the less favored, or even the disfavored ("cursed"), depending on their merits during premortal life. The outcome of this doctrinal development was a comprehensive racialist explanation for the preeminence of the Saints as a people in God's eyes, which provided a durable defense against the common outside definition of the Mormons as a despicable, pariah people. Such was the identity that underlay the collective Mormon psyche until the middle of the twentieth century: exclusivist, racial, tribal, and divinely chosen from before the earth's creation.

By that point in Mormon history, the Ephraimite identity had been given preeminence even over the fraternal identity of Manasseh accorded to the Lamanites, or American Indians. Chapter 3 opened with two apostolic declarations a century apart: The first, by Orson Pratt, envisioned a Lamanite initiative in building the New Jerusalem for the gathering of Israel on the North American continent (1855b, 178); the second, by Bruce R. McConkie a century later, pronounced such an idea a "whiff of nonsense," making it clear that Anglo-Mormon Ephraim was to take that role (1985, 519). Historical developments between these two points in time would have vindicated McConkie's understanding, since the native peoples of North America had shown little of the enthusiasm that Pratt had expected in a mass conversion to the gospel of Christ and the Book of Mormon. For understandable reasons, the Indians had responded rather casually and opportunistically to the Mormon proselyting efforts, while the Mormons—also understandably—had largely abandoned those efforts by the end of the nineteenth century.

It was the middle of the twentieth century before the Lamanite identity regained its operational salience in the church, and the Saints were willing and able to take seriously once again the divine mandate to convert the Lamanites. As chapter 4 explained, this "rediscovery" of the Lamanites was followed by a sustained effort of several decades to bring about the long-promised "day of the Lamanite," which had proved so elusive in the nineteenth century. After two or three generations on reservations, essentially cut off from the general American economic and technological progress, some of the Indians seemed more willing than their ancestors had been to consider what the Mormons had to offer. From the Mormon side, that offer was extended primarily through the initiative of strong proponents of literal Israelite identity for the Indians, or Lamanites. Some of these Mormon proponents were longtime neighbors and associates of Indian tribes in the Southwest, and a few were also found among the general authorities of the church. Of these, none was as important as Spencer W. Kimball. From the mid-1940s to the mid-1980s, the strength of the LDS commitment to the Indians rose and fell with Kimball's career. Before that commitment was exhausted, many thousands of Native Americans, especially from the southwestern tribes, had been baptized Mormons, educated through high school and college, and otherwise trained in modern occupations and professions, as chapter 4 recounts. Strictly on a cost-benefit basis, the spiritual depth and durability of these conversions ultimately did not satisfy the church leaders, but there can be little doubt about the material and economic benefit of their Mormon experience for the Indian members, regardless of whether they retained their church activity.

The cost-benefit assessment of the missionary effort among the North American tribes might not have looked so unfavorable except by comparison with the burgeoning ranks of new converts in Latin America after the mid-twentieth century. The aboriginal peoples of those countries had also long been assumed by most Mormons to be Lamanites and therefore of a favored Israelite lineage. However, since the earliest Mormons knew little about those peoples, the Lamanite identity had always had a more immediate and cogent significance when applied to the tribal peoples of the western United States. Yet the differential responsiveness to the Mormon message in the two parts of the hemisphere could not be ignored, so the "true" Lamanites, at least in an *operational* sense, came increasingly to be understood as those who "heard their Shepherd's voice" in Mexico and in the lands farther south. This operational redefinition of the Lamanite location, described in chapter 5, was clearly vindicated by the end of the twentieth century, when the LDS membership in Latin America reached nearly four million, one million in Mexico alone (Bennion and Young 1996; Knowlton 1996).

By this time, the Mormons had experienced 170 years of missionary encounters in many other parts of the world. In the process, they had been learning much about the historical and geographical variability in the usefulness of the Israelite identity. That identity had originally seemed such a promising premise for the long-standing missionary commitment to the Indian tribes of North America, but the Lamanite identity eventually came to make more sense in Latin America. In the Sandwich Islands (Hawaii), a rather tentative missionary venture in the 1850s opened the way to a startling conversion rate throughout Polynesia all the way down to New Zealand by the end of the century. This success provided a convincing vindication for the traditional Mormon interpretation of an obscure passage in the Book of Mormon seeming to extend the Nephite (and thus Israelite) identity to the Polynesian peoples (Alma 63:5–8). Yet who would have expected, at the outset, to find "the blood of Israel" among so "remote" a people?

Perhaps some of the same "blood" had traveled from Polynesia all the way to Japan, for a mission was opened there in 1901 partly on that premise—a belief that remained in the mind of the mission president even after the church had decided to close the mission in 1924 for lack of results. By the time missionary work was reopened in Japan two decades later, there was no longer much discussion of the blood of Israel, but by the end of the century there were several missions and a hundred thousand converts there, Israelites or not. A similar responsiveness to the Mormon message was found in Korea, Taiwan, Hong Kong, and the Philippines, though no one had ever anticipated a special Israelite strain in those places. To be sure, the prophet Joseph Smith had left open from the beginning the possibility of scattered Israelite seed as far away as Tibet, but the decisions to open missions in Asia during the second half of the twentieth century had far less to do with assumptions about blood lines than with cost-benefit assessments of the social and political readiness of the Asian societies for Mormon missionaries.[3]

Of course, the earliest and most abundant harvest of the lineage of Israel had been from among those descendants of Ephraim who, it was widely believed, had settled in the Nordic and Anglo-Saxon countries. Arriving in Utah by the tens of thousands from the 1840s onward, these converts seemed a living vindication of the emerging mythology that identified Ephraim's seed with those countries. Descendants from the same countries seemed to account in large part even for the success of the missionary work in other places to which they had migrated, such as Brazil and Argentina early in the twentieth century. Yet by at least 1880, the conversion rate in Europe and the British Isles had dropped to such a degree that one apostle wondered if all of Ephraim's descendants in those countries had already been converted and gathered to Zion in Utah (F. Richards 1898, 33).

All in all, as chapter 2 revealed, it became increasingly difficult to find a coherent pattern by which the favored Israelite lineage could be inferred on a priori grounds, whether theological or geographic, and then verified by sustained rates of conversion and church growth. Those LDS leaders and members still looking for salience in blood lines were left with little beyond the tautology that those who joined the church must have had the blood of Israel. Such a tautology was reinforced by a literal understanding of the "lineage assignment" in official patriarchal blessings but not necessarily by the more figurative understandings that emerged by end of the century. As the missionary enterprise discovered the blood of Israel in some very unlikely locations, it became increasingly difficult to take lineage into account at all in opening new missions or accounting for their differential success. A universal outlook made more sense after all: As the apostle Paul had taught, if the gospel is taken to the whole world, then all those who embrace it will by definition become the children of Abraham.

Lineage Identity and Racial Prejudice: The Case of the Jews

Nor was an a priori expectation of missionary success on genealogical grounds vindicated by Mormon experience with the Jews, who surely had maintained the strongest claim of all to Israelite ancestry from the beginning. For theological and political reasons going back to patristic times, Christianity in general had taken a posture toward the Jews that was not only competitive but supersessionist and hostile. It was as though the authenticity of Christianity still depended, as in the second century, on displacing the lineage-based claims of the Jews with the new divine mandate or dispensation of the church as "spiritual Israel." The Mormon solution was different. As explained in chapter 6, Mormonism has always contained a strain of traditional Christian supersessionism but usually in the *ultimate* sense that all the peoples of the earth, including the Jews, will eventually have to accept the kingship of Jesus the Christ. Meanwhile, instead of trying to displace the lineage-based religious heritage of the Jews through conversion, the Mormons simply claimed a share in that heritage. The Mormons came to see their relationship with the Jews as one of two brothers, Judah and Joseph (or Ephraim), kneeling before the same Father. Ephraim might claim a superior understanding of the Father's ultimate will and might even reach out to the more recalcitrant brother, but it is left up to the Father himself finally to bring Judah back into the tent with the rest of Abraham's children.

As condescending—even bizarre—as that Mormon outlook might seem to the Jews, it has proved historically to be a strong neutralizer of the hostile anti-Semitism characteristic of mainstream Protestantism and Catholicism. This is the case I tried to make in chapter 7. There are not many cases in history in which a form of religious "prejudice" (or at least religious particularism) helps undermine secular prejudice, but that is one way of describing the Mormon case. Relatively low rates of secular anti-Semitism among Mormons seem to have been an unintended if welcome consequence of a theological construction by which Mormons share an identity with the Jews instead of erecting a boundary against them as totally "Other." To be sure, there have always been Mormon anti-Semites, for historically all Mormons were recruited from anti-Semitic cultures. Yet there is little, if any, anti-Semitism in Mormon*ism*. Furthermore, as indicated by the tables and figures in chapter 7, the secular anti-Semitism that does exist among Mormons comes not from orthodox Mormonism itself but primarily from accepting the hostile religious teachings of traditional Christianity *without* accepting the neutralizing Mormon belief in a shared and chosen lineage.

There is an interesting irony here, in which the Mormon acceptance of the Jews' own lineage identity has had the effect, as it were, of "protecting" the Jews from sustained Mormon proselyting. This is in stark contrast to the general history of Mormon missionary initiatives, in which lineage constructions have been implicated in the early selection of certain peoples for proselyting. To be sure, some of those initiatives were continued long after they no longer yielded a steady church growth (e.g., the northwestern Europeans and the American Indians). In other cases, potentially promising lineages were abandoned by the missionaries out of cost-benefit considerations (e.g., early Japan). In still other cases, a lineage identity once applied primarily to some peoples (American Indians) came to seem much more applicable to other peoples (Latin American aborigines and Polynesians). None of these variations in the Mormon uses of lineage applied to the Jews. Instead, the Mormon construction of Jewish lineage made for a deferential reluctance about proselyting, with only a few brief and seemingly half-hearted missionary initiatives.

Lineage Identity and Racial Prejudice:
The Case of the Black Africans

The black Africans and their descendants present still a different case—one in which Mormon theological constructions of lineage virtually prevented proselyting altogether until 1978. The effect, of course, was to constrain Mormon missionary penetration throughout Africa (except for the relatively small white populations in southern Africa)—and not only in Africa itself but also among millions of African descendants in North America, the Caribbean Islands, and Latin America. When those areas were finally opened to Mormon proselyting, the change came, ironically, not from church outreach efforts to gain access to reluctant prospective converts but from the long-suffering prospective converts themselves, who reached out to the church and patiently waited for the LDS leaders to abandon their anachronistic understanding of Africans and their lineage, so that they might finally gain access to the gospel and the priesthood. We can only imagine the predicament mentioned in chapter 9, in which literally thousands of eager potential proselytes, having first learned about the new religion accidentally on their own in 1963, had been, as it were, lined up in West Africa for fifteen years awaiting the arrival of the first Mormon missionaries (J. Allen 1991). Similarly, we can imagine thousands of new black church members in Brazil, watching, praying, and contributing to the rise of a new temple there, hoping desperately to see the day when they would be free to enter it (Grover 1990).

As chapter 9 indicated, this one construction of lineage—the African, or "Cainite"—remains an obstacle to church growth among black people in North America, if not elsewhere. This is no longer an issue of politics, no longer an argument, as it was in the 1960s, over whether Mormons are "racist" in their public policy votes and preferences. Considered simply as one religious denomination among others, Mormons probably never were uniquely racist compared with most other Christians. That seems clear from the research reviewed in chapter 8. Equally clear, however, is that once the church dropped its internal racial restriction on the priesthood, Mormons in national surveys came to be among the *least* racist Americans in public policy toward blacks. After 1978, in other words, Mormon levels of secular prejudice in national surveys came steadily down until they crossed to the other side of the national average. That transition across time invites the inference that prejudice and discrimination had been kept artificially high for the otherwise egalitarian Mormons by the church's own internal racial policies and teachings about blacks. This cognitive structure was illustrated by the tables and figures in chapter 8, where an orthodox Mormon outlook strongly predicted acceptance of hostile *religious* ideas, which, in turn, predicted *secular* prejudice and discrimination. Some of that religious hostility was presumably diminished by ending the racial restrictions on priesthood and proselyting, and that is reflected in the more recent survey data.

The identification of blacks with Cain, however, has never been officially dropped or even mildly disavowed by church leaders. At least the traditional notions about the origin and significance of that lineage are no longer repeated in official discourse or literature. Yet they remain scattered throughout authoritative church books from the past that continue to be reprinted under the auspices of the church. It is ironic that these ideas were advanced originally to explain and rationalize the erstwhile Mormon denial of the priesthood to its black members. Yet a quarter of a century after that priesthood policy was overturned, the theological folklore used to support it remains in common circulation. Just how common today we cannot be sure, but only a generation ago, half of the Salt Lake City Mormons and a third of their San Francisco coreligionists still believed that blacks were under a divine curse as descendants of Cain. Such notions could be expected to linger to some extent.

Much more telling, however, are the interviews with black Mormons, reviewed in chapter 9, and regular anecdotal reports from the Mormon grassroots, all of which suggest that the "lineage of Cain" idea continues to be widely believed, even among today's younger Mormons. When criticized or questioned, they need only refer to authoritative books as the basis for their beliefs. This situation therefore remains a matter of unfinished business in the LDS Church's relationship with its black members and potential members. As long as the folklore about Cain continues to circulate among white Mormons, many of them will continue to impose an identity on blacks that will greatly complicate racial relationships and church growth; black Mormons, for their part, can never be quite sure how white Mormons look upon them.

Epilogue

As we reflect on the entire Mormon missionary experience to the end of the twentieth century, it seems fair to say that the some uses of lineage identity have been benign and even constructive. Sometimes the identities constructed in Mormon teachings for certain peoples have even been embraced by those peoples for their own purposes, as in the cases of some of the Lamanites and Polynesians, as well as the Anglo-Ephraimites themselves. In other cases, of course, the Mormon identity constructions have been met with puzzled bemusement, resistance, or hostility. The consequences of traditional Mormon ideas about lineage and its significance have often been unintended and unpredictable. Most ironic of all, the proselyting uses of lineage identity itself eventually undermined the narrow and provincial understanding of lineage among early Mormons. Thus purged of its preoccupation with chosen lineages, Mormonism could at last become a truly universal religion. That is the principal development in the historical process reviewed here.

Of course Mormonism, like many other newly revealed religions, always was universalistic in its aspirations and its ultimate theological claims. It never actually lost sight of the Pauline promise that all believers could eventually become the children of Abraham. It was only that the special experiences and teachings of the early Latter-day Saints combined to produce a racialist understanding of the priority and sequence by which the lineages of the earth would be gathered under Abraham: Ephraim and Manasseh first; Judah whenever it was ready; the other or "lost" tribes of Israel whenever they were brought out of obscurity by the divine schedule; then the Gentiles; and finally the descendants of Cain. While never spelled out in precisely this manner and largely derived from popular folklore and discourse, this process can easily be inferred from authoritative literature and discourse well into the twentieth century, which was cited extensively in chapter 2.

The point here, however, is not whether this racialist framework was true or false, divinely revealed or not. Rather, the point is to understand the *uses and functions* of that framework, beginning with the part it played in creating a powerfully supportive identity for the nineteenth-century Mormons themselves. After that, the same framework helped the Mormons to understand why they were proselyting in some parts of the world but not others and why their message was received with such eagerness by some peoples but not others. When the racialist framework ceased to be useful and began to encumber rather than facilitate the worldwide growth of Mormonism, it was gradually abandoned. While never explicitly repudiated, the traditional racialist teachings simply fell into disuse. In the final decades of the twentieth century, early Mormon universalism once again dominated official discourse, with no more references to different lineages and their special blessings or curses. Another way of summarizing the historical process is to say that any racialist understanding of access to gospel blessings became untenable in the face of the conversion and faithfulness of people from so many lineages having *no* obvious "racial" identification. All believers of all lineages thus finally became the children of Abraham, as the apostle Paul had promised.

Notes

1. Cressy's observation is quoted by Lian Xi (1997, 227–28). I am grateful to Philip L. Barlow for calling Xi's book to my attention.

2. A brief but good review of the similarities and differences between early Mormonism and certain cognate religious movements of the time is in J. Allen and Leonard (1992, 14–19).

3. The so-called cold war and various hot wars in Asia made the opening of new Mormon missions there impractical until the 1960s, except in Japan (from 1948). A review of any edition of the *Deseret News Church Almanac* indicates new missions finally opening in Korea (1962), the Philippines (1967), Taiwan (1969), and Hong Kong (1969). See also Bennion and Young (1996); and Shepherd and Shepherd (1996).

Appendix A:
Notes on Library and
Personal Sources

Published Sources

THE GREAT VARIETY of primary source materials about Mormon history and culture is apparent in Walker, Whittaker, and Allen (2001), particularly the two appendixes of that bibliographic work. See also J. Allen and Leonard (1992, 673–762). Especially useful for my purposes in this book, at least in the earlier chapters, have been official and quasi-official periodicals and other collections published under the auspices of the church. Examples of historical primary sources to which I am referring here would include *The Evening and the Morning Star* (1832–34); the *Latter Day Saints' Messenger and Advocate* (1834–37); the *Times and Seasons* (1839–46); the *Latter-day Saints' Millennial Star* (1840–1970); the *Journal of Discourses* in 26 volumes (1854–86); the seven-volume *History of the Church of Jesus Christ of Latter-day Saints* (1902–32); and *Conference Report* (1880 and 1898–present).

All of these published primary materials are available at the library of the church's Historical Department in Salt Lake City and in many other libraries, as well. Recently such works have become accessible on compact disks issued by two or three different companies in Utah. In particular, I made use of the *LDS Collectors Library '97* (1996), especially in chapter 2. Searching compact disks via key words saves an enormous amount of library time, of course, but it does not eliminate library work altogether. Original pagination and certain other details are often lost in electronic compilation, necessitating a check of the originals just to make sure that the citations are complete and accurate. For all of the electronic searching, I relied on my assistant Manfred Heim, to whom I am deeply grateful for his many hours of meticulous research. However, I did the checking of electronic printouts myself against the library originals.

A SPECIAL NOTE ON PUBLISHED SOURCES FOR
MORMON-INDIAN RELATIONSHIPS

No general history of Mormon relationships with Native Americans has ever been published. For my general overview of the early history of these relationships, I am relying on the secondary sources listed in my references, especially Arrington (1970 and 1985); Arrington and Bitton (1992, 145–60); J. Allen and Leonard (1992, 62–63, 263–81); R. Bennett (1987 and 1997); Parry (1972 and 1985); and Walker (1989 and 1993). The dissertation by Lawrence G. Coates (1969), though unpublished, is a standard and frequently cited source for such history, but it deals mainly with Mormon-Indian relationships during Brigham Young's lifetime. Many published articles by Coates, some of them derived from the dissertation, are also very valuable and are cited in my references. A more recent study of a particular historic episode that contains much useful general information is John Alton Peterson's (1998) study of Utah's Black Hawk War. While the geographical focus of Peterson's book is mainly on the Ute and other tribes from central Utah southward, Scott Christensen's (1999) biography of Sagwitch focuses northward. These are the main sources of my historical information on Mormon-Indian relations, but the *interpretations* I have imposed on that information are my own and do not necessarily coincide with those of the authors on whom I depended.

For more recent history on Mormons and Indians, I used primary and secondary sources cited in my chapters and endnotes. I also consulted certain publications from the Native American press in general and from the Native American community at Brigham Young University (BYU) in particular to get details and background information on many of the developments reviewed in twentieth-century Mormon-Indian relationships. Little of this general background information has been cited because it would have proliferated the endnotes, with considerable redundancy, and the generalizations and general arguments presented are rarely very controversial. In acquainting myself with the contents of the various Native American newspapers, I benefited greatly from the able assistance of my niece Susan C. Eliason, who reviewed back-issues of these papers well into the 1980s. We found in the *Navajo Times* regular articles featuring BYU, Mormon Indians, and other Mormon matters of potential interest to its readers, including both positive and negative reports, but usually quite evenhanded and well balanced. Mormon-related articles rarely appeared in any other publications of the Native American press around the United States (e.g., *Akwesasne Notes, Wassaja,* and *Yakima Nation Review*). The *Eagle's Eye* was the main BYU publication covering Indian affairs from 1970 on (a couple of predecessor publications had been issued irregularly in the 1950s and 1960s). We reviewed back-issues of the *Eagle's Eye* up through the spring of 1999, by which time its contents had begun to change noticeably from an exclusively Native American focus to a more general "multicultural" one featuring various ethnic groups on campus. My own files contain dozens of back-issues of this periodical covering the late 1970s and early 1980s, when the BYU programs were reaching their apex and starting to decline.

A SPECIAL NOTE ON PUBLISHED SOURCES FOR
MORMON-BLACK RELATIONSHIPS

The small LDS African American or black community has produced three kinds of newsletters, which can be considered "published" in that they were periodically reproduced privately and mailed out to subscribers. I have considered these primary sources because they reveal the interests and concerns of at least some segments of the black LDS population in the United States. The first of these is *Genesis,* published by the Genesis Group, described in chapter 9, the only enduring organization so far among Mormon blacks. The *Genesis* newsletter, however, has not been published consistently during the group's history, and I was unable to locate any archive of back-issues, even with the help of the current group leadership. I have retained only a few recent issues in my own personal files. I have more complete sets of back-issues from the other two newsletters, *Ebony Rose* and *UpLift*.

Ebony Rose was published between 1985 and 1988 by Marva Collins, a black LDS convert living in the California Bay Area during the early 1980s. Apparently intended at first for the black Mormons in that area, the newsletter was the product mainly of the labor of the Collins family. Later the family moved to Salt Lake City, where the newsletter was produced through mid-1988, when Marva Collins was transferred by her employer to Atlanta, Georgia, at which point publication ceased with what was described as the "farewell" issue in August 1988 (no. 41). In my references, Collins is considered the author of anything cited from this source. At its peak, this publication claimed more than a thousand subscribers in twenty states, England, and the West Indies.

In the case of *UpLift*, I was a charter subscriber with volume 1, issue 1 (April/May 1989), when it was called *Let's Talk*. I maintained my subscription until I received the last issue in late 1994, when it stopped coming without explanation. I learned later that the founder and editor of this publication, Joseph C. Smith, had suddenly moved away. Originally published by the LDS African American Cultural Awareness Group (AACAG), *Let's Talk* was renamed *UpLift* in 1991, after a year's hiatus, and its sponsoring organization was renamed the Latter-day Saints for Cultural Awareness (LDSCA), apparently the same people in the main. Some or all of those connected with this newsletter, including Smith, were also members of the Genesis Group (see Lloyd 1993). In its first issue of 1992, *UpLift* claimed two hundred subscribers in twenty-two states, but mostly in Utah.

Unpublished Sources

Beyond the published sources normally available in libraries, I occasionally used unpublished materials deposited in the Archives and Special Collections at LDS Church headquarters in Salt Lake City and the Harold B. Lee Library of Brigham Young University in Provo, Utah. In both these locations, I also perused various reports and documents produced by the Church Education System from 1955 to 1995 for daily religious instruction; the LDS Indian Committee (also known as the Lamanite Committee and Minority Affairs Committee, among other names), the chief coordinating agency for programs serving LDS Native Americans, from 1943 to 1983; and Social Services (also called Unified Social Services), the social and humanitarian service arm of the church, from 1969 to the present. I collected personally some of the unpublished materials cited in this book across a number of years. These are listed in the references as personal files and are deposited with the archive collection under my name at the Utah State Historical Society in Salt Lake City.

ORAL HISTORY INTERVIEWS

Two repositories of oral history transcripts were especially important in providing material for this book. One of these is the James M. Moyle Oral History Collection located in the LDS Church Archives. This project, begun in 1972, contains some 1,300 interviews by experienced scholars or historians with key leaders or figures in the LDS hierarchy, wards, stakes, missions, agencies, or programs, particularly if they had special knowledge by virtue of their positions or locations. Access to many of these interview transcripts is restricted at the request of the respondents or because they contain sensitive information, especially on persons still living. Some of these interviews provided helpful background information for this book; I have cited in the references several that were especially useful.

The second repository of interviews important to my work was the LDS Ethnic American Oral History Project, Charles Redd Center for Western Studies, Harold B. Lee Library, at Brigham Young University. The historian Jessie L. Embry is the project director and assistant center director. This project was initiated in 1985 with a focus primarily on black converts to the LDS Church, but with additional time and funding it was expanded to cover oral history interviews with other LDS ethnic groups in the United States whose voices and experiences tend to be overlooked in the usual Mormon historical narratives (Embry 1992d). I used only the oral history transcripts compiled during the 1980s and 1990s from black and American Indian respondents, but the project has collections from Hispanic American and Asian American samples, as well. I benefited also from several published analyses that had been derived from these interviews by other scholars (e.g., Embry 1990a, 1990b, 1992b, and 1994; Jacobson 1991; and O. White and White 1995 and 2000).

These interviews, whether under the Moyle program or the Redd program, were generally conducted on a "convenience" or "opportunity" basis, so they are not systematic representations of any particular populations. This is especially the case for the Redd Center collection, which is deliberately based on a "snowball" sample. All these interviews are, however, very valuable for illustrating recurrent experiences, ideas, and feelings of various individuals and certain types of interviewees. Further information on these oral history collections can be found in Embry (1992b); Walker, Whittaker, and Allen (2001, 247); and Whittaker, ed. (1995, 111–19, 167–68).

PERSONAL INTERVIEWS

Apart from the formal collections of oral histories, I conducted interviews of my own, mainly during the 1980s, with persons having special knowledge about relationships between Mormons (including the church) and either Native Americans or African Americans. These interviews, too, were conducted as opportunities could be found and by no means comprise all the key informants who might have been helpful to me. I occasionally cite these interviewees explicitly and by name, but I used their interviews mainly for background information and only rarely as sole sources for my assertions or impressions. For my research on Mormon-Indian relationships, these key informants included Charles H. Ainsworth, Janice Clemmer, Stewart A. Durrant, Bonnie L. Mitchell-Green, V. Con Osborne, and David L. Sanders.

Charles H. Ainsworth, a Ph.D. and a former student of mine, was an instructor and administrator at the Navaho Community College, Tsaile, Arizona, during the early 1980s and was also active in the local leadership of the LDS Church during the same period. In those roles, he became well acquainted with local church leaders and members, both Navaho and white, who were serving on or near the large Navaho reservation in that area and with students at the main campus and various extension campuses of the community college. During 1983 and 1984, he responded extensively to requests from LDS leaders for his observations and recommendations on how to improve church activity and retention among Navaho members. He furnished me copies of his correspondence with these leaders and granted me an extensive interview on May 15, 1986.

Janice Clemmer, who has a Ed.D. and J.D., is an educator of Wasco-Shawnee-Delaware extraction and was a member of the Indian Education—later Multicultural Education—Program at BYU until 1985. At the time of my hour-long telephone interview with her on May 26, 1999, she was still teaching in the fields of educational law and multicultural education at BYU, having also served two terms on the BYU faculty advisory council.

Stewart A. Durrant was a professional staff administrator from 1966 through 1983 for the so-called Lamanite Committee (in its various iterations and names), serving under the general authorities of the church. Though Durrant officially retired in 1983, he continued to serve on a volunteer basis for another year or so. I interviewed him in his office on August 15, 1975. More accessible to the reader than the notes from my own interview is the formal oral history interview with Durrant in 1983, which can be found in the James M. Moyle Oral History Collection in the LDS Church Archives.

Fred Gowans was a professor in the Department of History at BYU, as well as coordinator of what survives there as the Native American Studies Program, mainly a baccalaureate minor in that field. He granted me a very brief telephone interview on May 27, 1999, in response to two or three specific questions on the status of his program at that time.

Bonnie L. Mitchell-Green was the supervisor of adult and community education for the Utah Navaho Development Council, 1980–83, and the director of the Multi-Cultural Center at Southern Utah State College (now Southern Utah University), 1983–87, when she left to resume work for her doctoral degree. In those roles, she often saw the LDS Church and its programs through the eyes of the Indians who had encountered them. She favored me with a lengthy interview on September 2, 1987, and I have maintained periodic contact with her since then. After completing her Ph.D. and a series of temporary professional positions, she returned to Southern Utah University as a member of the anthropology faculty in 2001. Aside from specific details she provided, I relied on her primarily to help me understand the Mormon-Indian relationships from the Indian perspective, with which she had become very familiar.

V. Con Osborne was closely associated with teaching and administration for Indian students at BYU during at least two decades and was head of the Department of Indian Education, 1978–85. He completed a doctoral dissertation and other documents on Indian education at BYU (all cited in my references), and he kindly granted me three different interviews on June 2, 1981, August 20, 1986, and July 12, 1999, respectively, which enabled me to understand especially the "winding down" period of Indian education as it occurred at BYU.

David L. Sanders, whom I interviewed in the summer of 1985, was at that time an attorney in Tustin, California, and the bishop of the La Sierra Second Ward, Riverside West Stake. He had been a student at BYU during the early 1970s, with a minor in American Indian Studies (but eventually a law school graduate). Throughout his BYU days, he was active in the Lamanite Generation and the Tribe of Many Feathers, as well as other social and recreational activities for campus Indians, though he was clearly Anglo-Mormon. He married an Indian woman from North Dakota, who had been Miss Indian BYU in 1971–72. The couple maintained extensive contact with various LDS Indians from their BYU days and from her tribal origins. Besides their own nine children, they took three Indian foster daughters for two years each in the Indian Student Placement Program.

I relied on several black Mormon friends and colleagues as key informants on Mormon-black relationships. These included Ruffin Bridgeforth, O. Ken Earl, Darius A. Gray, Robert L. Lang, John M. Smith, and Elnora V. Smith.

Ruffin Bridgeforth, president of the Genesis Group from its origin in 1971 until his death in 1997, had been a member of the church since the 1950s and had reconciled his own LDS religious commitments and his belief that the church policy on racial restrictions had always been fundamentally wrong. Over the years he had frequently been called on for counseling and encouragement by other black Mormons feeling less successful in that reconciliation effort. He granted me two long interviews, one by telephone on June 2, 1981, and one in his home on May 23, 1985.

O. Ken Earl was not a black LDS member but was president of the California Oakland Mission of the church from 1982 through 1985. I made his acquaintance when he sought me out as a speaker at a mission conference in September 1983 to explain to his missionaries and many members the history of the struggle in the church over its traditional racial policies and conceptions. Besides my visit with him on that occasion, I had an extensive telephone conversation with him in 1985, during the fall, as I recall (I failed to record the date). During his tenure as mission president, he gave special attention to proselyting among the black citizens of the Oakland area, and he was very helpful to Marva Collins as she organized Genesis II there (a "chapter" of the Genesis Group in Salt Lake City).

Darius A. Gray was a founding member of the Genesis Group and the successor to Ruffin Bridgeforth as president of that group. He played a major role in the transition of this group from a small, all-black support group to a large, supplemental program of monthly spiritual and social activities for Mormon families of mixed races, not just black members. He had also succeeded in garnering increased financial and other forms of support from LDS Church headquarters for this rather unique institution and was devoting a great deal of personal time to pastoral counseling of both black and other members of the group. As the twenty-first century opened, Gray was coauthoring a trilogy of historical novels about the black Mormon experience (Young and Gray 2000–2003). He granted me a long telephone interview on May 25, 1999, and three or four informal conversations thereafter.

Robert L. Lang was president of the Southwest Los Angeles Branch during the early 1980s and later was a high councilor in the Los Angeles Stake. Lang's branch (about a hundred members) had a mixed-race membership but was mostly black by virtue of its geographic location. He faced many challenges in maintaining church activity in the branch and in getting the rest of his stake to see it as something *other* than a de facto "black branch," which all black members in Los Angeles should be urged to attend. He granted me two long interviews by telephone, one on June 10, 1981, and the other on May 21, 1985.

John M. Smith and Elnora V. Smith of Riverside, California, were a black couple with teenaged children. The family had been converted to the LDS Church a year or so before my interview with them in their home on November 23, 1985. I actually interviewed three or four black LDS families in the same general vicinity of southern California, but this couple in particular had experienced, as new Mormons, some demoralizing disappointments that they were willing to share with me at some length. They attributed these difficulties to the insistence of well-meaning white members of their ward that they (the Smiths) were descendants of Cain, for which their children were being hazed by their white Mormon peers.

In addition to the Smiths, I interviewed three other black LDS families in the Riverside area during 1985. I have not made much explicit use of these interviews in this book except (again) as background, since the information I obtained from them duplicated much that was obtained in other interviews or in the Redd Center oral histories at BYU. Beyond these interviews (face-to-face or by telephone), I also enjoyed correspondence with several knowledgeable colleagues, whose letters remain in my personal files. They are occasionally cited in this book among the other references or in the endnotes to some of the chapters.

Appendix B:
Supplementary Tables
for Measuring Mormon Beliefs about
Jews and Blacks

THE ORIGIN AND NATURE of the survey data in chapters 7 and 8 are explained at some length in my earlier book (1994, especially 33–60, 215–28). Note that the data in these tables were collected during 1967–69. In generating and analyzing these data, I followed closely the survey methodology in Glock and Stark (1966, especially their appendix). Where necessary, I have occasionally added further explanations but generally have avoided repeating those provided in earlier publications. To minimize interruptions in my narrative, I have included in the chapters themselves only a few tables and figures from the survey data. A few additional tables and figures, with more extensive analyses of the same data, have been provided in this appendix for their potential interest to certain readers. Appendix C presents a few figures, as well.

Table B.1. Indicators of Secular Anti-Semitism

	Salt Lake City Mormons ($n = 958$)	San Francisco Mormons ($n = 296$)	Total Protestants ($n = 2326$)	Catholics ($n = 545$)
"Avaricious Jew" Image				
1. Jews more likely than others to use shady business dealings	30%	29%	33%	29%
2. Movie and TV industries run by Jews	64	67	72	74
3. International banking run by Jews	55	55	48	45
"Egocentric Jew" Image				
4. Jews tend to believe they are better than others	49	47	40	36
"Unpatriotic/Subversive Jew" Image				
5. Jews are less likely than others to oppose Communism	16	18	15	21
6. Jews are inclined to be more loyal to Israel than to America	47	47	31	26

Note: Percentages responding "yes" or "somewhat" to the question of whether "you think Jews tend to be like this." Percentages not responding or responding no are not included. The actual questions appear here in abbreviated form. Items 1, 4, and 6 were used to construct a composite index of secular anti-Semitism. The corresponding index in Glock and Stark (1966) was based on six items, some of them different from any of these three, but the indexes in the two studies are quite comparable.

Table B.2. Mormons and Religious Hostility toward Jews

	Religious Hostility Levels		
	Low	Medium	High
Salt Lake City sample ($n = 958$)	42%	33%	25%
San Francisco sample ($n = 296$)	58	25	17
Combined sample ($n = 1254$)	46	31	23

Note: The figures in this table result from combining responses to two questions, one about the ongoing punishment of Jews for the Crucifixion and the other about the requirement for their conversion as the condition for their forgiveness.

Table B.3. Mormons and Religious Affinity for Jews

	Religious Affinity Levels		
	Low	Medium	High
Salt Lake City sample ($n = 958$)	17%	33%	50%
San Francisco sample ($n = 296$)	31	29	40
Combined sample ($n = 1254$)	21	32	47

Note: The figures in this table result from combining the responses to two questions, one about the shared ancestry of Mormons and Jews and the other about the continuing "chosen" status of the Jews.

Table B.4. Mormons and Anti-Black Prejudice

	Index of Anti-Black Prejudice		
	Low	Medium	High
Salt Lake City sample ($n = 925$)	50%	31%	19%
San Francisco sample ($n = 290$)	60	25	15
Combined sample ($n = 1215$)	52	30	18

Note: The table was collapsed to three categories from a more extended original version. Percentages are totals for each category of the index based on responses to three indicators of prejudice. The total for the data set was 1254 (958 + 296); however, 39 cases, mostly nonrespondents from Salt Lake City, proved unsalvageable by the usual method of surrogate coding.

Table B.5. Mormons and Anti-Black Discrimination

	Index of Anti-Black Discrimination			
	Low	2	3	High
Salt Lake City sample ($n = 926$)	35%	32%	22%	11%
San Francisco sample ($n = 291$)	54	22	12	12
Combined sample ($n = 1217$)	40	30	19	11

Note: The table was collapsed to four categories from a more extended original version. The validation process against criterion variables indicated the need for four rather than three categories to maintain statistical homogeneity within each category. A few cases are missing, mostly from Salt Lake City, because they were not salvageable by the usual method.

Table B.6. Mormons and Religious Hostility toward Blacks

	Index of Religious Hostility toward Blacks		
	Low	Medium	High
Salt Lake City sample ($n = 958$)	19%	35%	46%
San Francisco sample ($n = 296$)	39	33	28
Combined sample ($n = 1254$)	24	34	42

Note: The figures in this table result from combining the responses to two questions, one asking whether blacks are cursed as "descendants of Cain" and the other asking whether God's will requires withholding the priesthood from them (questions and data from the 1960s).

Appendix C:
Path Diagrams as Summaries
of the Formation of Mormon Attitudes
toward Jews and Blacks

A Brief Explanation of Path Diagrams for the Nonspecialist

A PATH DIAGRAM is a graphic portrayal of the relationships among the several factors ("variables") that theoretically lead to a certain outcome. For example, in the diagrams that follow, the "outcome" in each case is a discriminatory attitude or disposition toward an ethnic group. The labels indicate which factors are theoretically implicated in producing this outcome, and the arrows connecting the labels indicate how these factors are theoretically related to each other "on the way" to the outcome. The decimal numbers with the arrows are called standardized partial regression coefficients (or "beta weights") and indicate the *relative weight* or impact of each factor on the next one in the process. If a number is negative, that means the factors on either end of the arrow are *inversely* related; that is, if one factor increases, the other decreases.

In the construction of a path model, an analyst's selections of the factors to be included or excluded are typically made on three main criteria: (1) is a reliable measure of a given factor available from the data? (2) judging from previous research or analysis, is there a *theoretically* significant reason to include or exclude the factor? (3) in the statistical analyses that lie behind each path model (i.e., regression equations), does the factor prove *statistically* significant?[1]

Since no path model can encompass more than a small number of all the factors that might contribute to a given outcome, there is no expectation that all the coefficients in a given model will explain all the variation in the outcome in question. The "residual," or unexplained, portion is often in excess of .90, as indicated by the external figure at the upper right end of each diagram. What a path model *is* expected to do is to provide confirmation for a given *theoretical process* consistent with the analyst's hypotheses about which factors lead to which others and with what differential weights or impacts. (For a succinct textbook treatment of the nature and use of path analysis in social science research, see M. Allen [1997, 156–65].)

Path Models for Secular Anti-Semitism among Mormons

Figures C.1 and C.2 are diagrams of the process through which secular anti-Semitism (SAS) has traditionally been generated among Mormons in (respectively) Salt Lake City and San Francisco.[2] With the explanation given above, one can easily interpret most of the paths and coefficients. The factors of greatest importance for my theoretical argument—namely, the religious beliefs about Jews—have already been pointed out in chapter 7, with the abbreviated figure 7.1 and the surrounding discussion.[3] These factors are presented again here only as part of the larger matrix that includes *nonreligious* factors, as well: social status, external social involvements, libertarianism, and anomie. In summary, this path diagram shows that orthodoxy has strong positive effects on both religious hostility and religious affinity toward Jews, but none of these three has much direct impact on secular anti-Semitism.[4] The effect that religious hostility does have on anti-Semitism is strongly blunted by the religious affinity that almost always accompanies it. Although the data on which these diagrams are based were collected in the 1960s, the *cognitive process* illustrated in the data is presumably valid across time and place.

What about social influences apart from religious teachings? Social status (SOCSTAT), measured mainly by formal educational attainment and occupational prestige, is somewhat influential in these diagrams, producing at least modest relationships directly with secular anti-Semitism (−.131 in Utah) and with religious hostility toward Jews (−.145) but scarcely any with orthodoxy (−.051). Notice, however, that these relationships are all *negative*, which means that the higher the social status of the Mormons, the *less* they possess secular anti-Semitism *or* religious hostility. The other main kind of social influence, external involvements outside the church (EXTINV), is clearly derivative of social status but essentially unrelated to anything else in the diagram. ANOMIA is as much a psychological as a social variable, but it is scarcely related to secular anti-Semitism anyway and only negatively to orthodoxy and libertarianism, meaning that Mormons with those qualities are *less* likely to be anomic. (The concept of anomia or anomie, as measured by the Srole method, might be defined most simply as a general or global disillusionment with society.)

Another, more implicit, social variable, however, is suggested by the contrasts between our two main samples. This variable is *location*, defined here operationally as the difference between Salt Lake City Mormons (see C.1) and those living in downtown San Francisco (see C.2). We might anticipate that secularizing influences would have a greater impact in San Francisco (even in the mid-1960s) than in the more socially and intellectually homogeneous Salt Lake City. Figures C.1 and C.2 bear out this expectation. Social status among San Francisco Mormons is more strongly related to *both* orthodoxy (−.192) and religious libertarianism (.318) than among those in Salt Lake City (but not to religious hostility). Social status is essentially unrelated to secular anti-Semitism (.050) in San Francisco. What seems especially interesting, though, are the *similarities* between San Francisco and Salt Lake City in the relationships among the key *religious* variables.

In general, then, the "tale of two cities" seems to be that social status has a bigger impact in San Francisco than in Salt Lake City on religious orthodoxy (negatively) *and* on libertarianism (positively). However, *if* the Mormons in *either* location are orthodox or lacking in libertarianism, they are about *equally* likely to have religious hostility *and* religious affinity for Jews. Furthermore, those Mormons lacking a belief in religious affinity are even more likely to translate their hostility into anti-Semitism in San Francisco (.162)

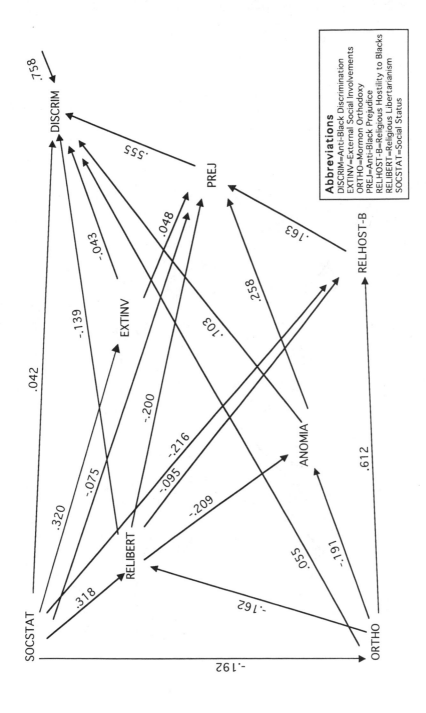

Figure C.1. Path Diagram for Determinants of Anti-Semitism: Salt Lake City Mormons

Abbreviations
DISCRIM=Anti-Black Discrimination
EXTINV=External Social Involvements
ORTHO=Mormon Orthodoxy
PREJ=Anti-Black Prejudice
RELHOST-B=Religious Hostility to Blacks
RELIBERT=Religious Libertarianism
SOCSTAT=Social Status

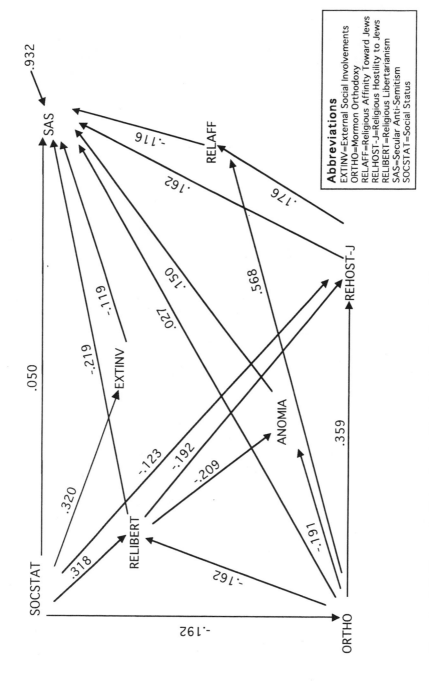

Figure C.2. Path Diagram for Determinants of Anti-Semitism: San Francisco Mormons

Abbreviations
EXTINV=External Social Involvements
ORTHO=Mormon Orthodoxy
RELAFF=Religious Affinity Toward Jews
RELHOST-J=Religious Hostility to Jews
RELIBERT=Religious Libertarianism
SAS=Secular Anti-Semitism
SOCSTAT=Social Status

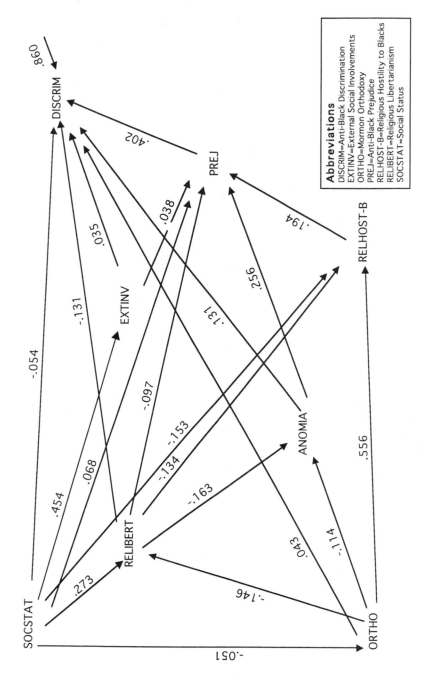

Figure C.3. Path Diagram for Determinants of Discrimination against Blacks: Salt Lake City Mormons

Abbreviations
DISCRIM=Anti-Black Discrimination
EXTINV=External Social Involvements
ORTHO=Mormon Orthodoxy
PREJ=Anti-Black Prejudice
RELHOST-B=Religious Hostility to Blacks
RELIBERT=Religious Libertarianism
SOCSTAT=Social Status

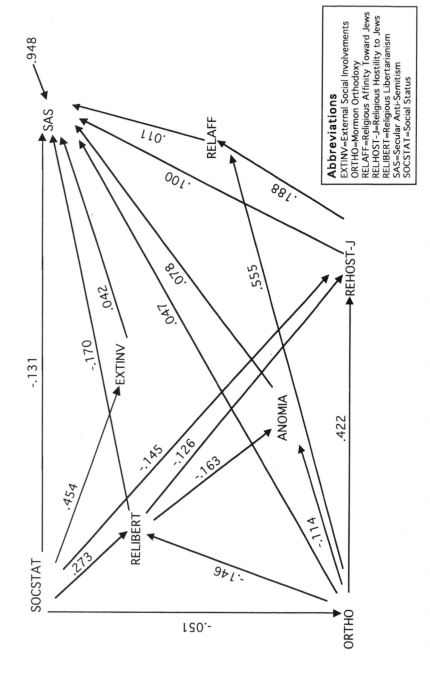

Abbreviations
EXTINV=External Social Involvements
ORTHO=Mormon Orthodoxy
RELAFF=Religious Affinity Toward Jews
RELHOST-J=Religious Hostility to Jews
RELIBERT=Religious Libertarianism
SAS=Secular Anti-Semitism
SOCSTAT=Social Status

Figure C.4. Path Diagram for Determinants of Discrimination against Blacks: San Francisco Mormons

than in Salt Lake City (.100). Finally, where *both* kinds of beliefs about Jews are present, affinity *reverses* the impact of hostility on anti-Semitism in San Francisco (−.116) and blunts it to nearly zero in Salt Lake City (.011).

Path Models for Anti-Black Prejudice and Discrimination among Mormons

In the path models for the traditional Mormon belief system about Africans and African Americans, we can apply the same basic logic, but now there is a slightly different theoretical process. Traditional Mormon beliefs about blacks included no counterpart of a special affinity such as the Mormons felt for the Jews. Unlike most (if not all) other Christian religions, Mormonism elevated discrimination against blacks to an article of faith, not merely a racist custom inherited from American history. The cognitive process involved was discussed in chapter 8 and illustrated, in abbreviated form, in figure 8.1, which focused only on the religious variables implicated in producing anti-black prejudice and discrimination. Figures C.3 and C.4 provide the larger matrix of religious and social variables leading to these outcomes. As in figure 8.1, Mormon orthodoxy itself does not have an appreciable direct impact on discriminatory tendencies (.043 and .055). However, orthodoxy does lead to hostile *religious* beliefs about blacks (i.e., the curse of Cain and divinely mandated restriction of the priesthood). Then that religious hostility leads to secular prejudice, which, in turn, powerfully predicts discrimination (.402 and .555).

The combination of coefficients on this right side of the diagram also suggests an interesting difference between the two Mormon samples: Religious beliefs about blacks are less likely to lead to secular prejudice among San Francisco Mormons than among Salt Lake City Mormons, but *if* religious beliefs lead to prejudice, then discrimination is more likely to follow in San Francisco than in Salt Lake City. This difference suggests that the cultural and political environment in San Francisco is less accommodating of discrimination (even among the prejudiced) than is the environment in Salt Lake City.

As with anti-Semitism, certain other factors in the diagram also have impacts, either positive or negative, on prejudice, discrimination, or religious hostility (e.g., social status, religious libertarianism, and anomia). The several factors also interact in various ways among themselves. However, our main interest here is in that portion of the path model that sets in context the process by which religious beliefs might or might not contribute to discriminatory tendencies toward black people. Of course, a decade after these data were collected, the LDS Church dropped its own ecclesiastical discrimination against its black members. However, the *process* described in the diagrams is still relevant, for to the extent that Mormons today retain any of the old hostile religious beliefs about blacks, they might also retain the potential for continued *secular* prejudice and discrimination.

Notes

1. *Statistical significance* refers not to how "important" a relationship is but to the likelihood that it could have occurred by chance. In the social sciences, the maximum acceptable likelihood is, by convention, 5 percent ($p = .05$), typically calculated by the chi-square test for tables. Since significance tests are heavily dependent on the sheer size of the sample, the great majority of the statistical relationships in this book remained at or below

the .05 probability level. In calculating the coefficients for the path diagrams, I automatically eliminated those that exceeded the .05 level.

2. I am grateful to my son Edmund A. Mauss for the final camera-ready versions of the four path diagrams in appendix C, which he rendered electronically from rough drafts that Julie C. Nelson had prepared much earlier.

3. Religious particularism, a variable that played a part in generating anti-Semitism in the Christian samples in Glock and Stark (1966, 19–40), proved statistically weak on an independent basis when included in these path diagrams for Mormons, so it was dropped.

4. This accords with the original finding by Charles Glock and Rodney Stark (noted earlier) that Christian orthodoxy *in itself* is not directly related to anti-Semitism but is related only to the extent that it is carried over into hostile beliefs *about the Jews specifically.* Subsequent (and somewhat critical) studies also found orthodoxy to be unrelated or even negatively related to secular anti-Semitism. See, for example, Middleton (1973); and Hoge and Carroll (1975). Thus in the research literature generally, orthodoxy seems to have been largely exonerated as a direct "cause" of anti-Semitism. These later authors, however, differ from Glock and Stark in finding considerably smaller relationships between orthodoxy and hostile doctrines about Jews. The weights (coefficients) for the paths from religious hostility to anti-Semitism are, however, quite similar across all our studies (Hoge and Carroll 1975, .15; Stark et al. 1971, .20; and Mauss, .100 for Salt Lake City and .162 for San Francisco).

References

Adams, David W. 1995. *Education for Extinction: The American Indians and the Boarding School Experience, 1875–1928.* Lawrence, Kans.: University Press of Kansas.

Adams, Stirling. 1987. "'Y' Turns Back on Indian Education Program." *Student Review* (Provo, Utah) 2 (8): 1, 16.

Adorno, T. W., E. Frenkel-Brunswik, D. J. Levinson, and R. N. Sanford. 1950. *The Authoritarian Personality.* New York: Harper and Row.

Aho, James A. 1990. *The Politics of Righteousness: Idaho Christian Patriotism.* Seattle: University of Washington Press.

Ainsworth, Charles H. 1982. "Religious and Regional Sources of Attitudes toward Blacks among Southern Mormons." Ph.D. diss., Washington State University.

———. 1986. Interview by author, Olympia, Wash., May 15.

Alba, Richard D. 1990. *Ethnic Identity: The Transformation of White America.* New Haven, Conn.: Yale University Press.

Albrecht, David A. 1985. "A Conversation about Changes in the Indian Student Placement Service." *Ensign,* February, 76, 80.

Albrecht, Stan L., and Howard M. Bahr. 1983. "Patterns of Religious Disaffiliation: A Study of Lifelong Mormons, Mormon Converts, and Former Mormons." *Journal for the Scientific Study of Religion* 22 (4): 366–79.

Allen, James B. 1991. "Would-Be Saints: West Africa before the 1978 Priesthood Revelation." *Journal of Mormon History* 17: 207–47.

———. 1998. "The Rise and Decline of the LDS Indian Student Placement Program, 1947–1996." In *Mormons, Scripture, and the Ancient World,* edited by Davis Bitton, 85–119. Provo, Utah: Foundation for Ancient Research and Mormon Studies.

Allen, James B., and Glen M. Leonard. 1992. *The Story of the Latter-day Saints.* 2d ed. Salt Lake City: Deseret Book.

Allen, Michael P. 1997. *Understanding Regression Analysis.* New York: Plenum.

Allred, Richard D. 1997. "The Lord Blesses His Children through Patriarchal Blessings." *Ensign,* November, 27–28.

American Interfaith Institute, Philadelphia. 1993. Seminar. *Explorations* 7 (2): entire issue.

———. 1994. Seminar. *Explorations* 8 (2): entire issue.

————. 1996a. "Debate: John Dominic Crossan vs. Raymond E. Brown." *Explorations* 10 (1): 1–3; 10 (2): 2–3.

————. 1996b. Interdenominational Commentary on SBC Decision to Proselyte among Jews. *Explorations* 10 (3): 4–5.

Anderson, Benedict. 1991. *Imagined Communities: Reflections on the Origin and Spread of Nationalism*. London: Verso.

Anderson, C. Leroy. 1981. *For Christ Will Come Tomorrow: The Saga of the Morrisites*. Logan: Utah State University Press.

Anderson, James H. 1933. *The Present Time and Prophecy*. Salt Lake City: Deseret News.

————. 1937. *God's Covenant Race from Patriarchal Times to the Present*. Salt Lake City: Deseret News.

Anderson, Talmadge, ed. 1990. *Black Studies: Theory, Method, and Cultural Perspectives*. Pullman: Washington State University Press.

Anti-Defamation League of B'nai B'rith, New York City. 1982. "The Parting of the Ways: Rabbinic Judaism and Early Christianity." *Face-to-Face: An Interreligious Bulletin* 9 (Winter/Spring): entire issue.

————. 1983. "Martin Luther and the Jews." *Face-to-Face: An Interreligious Bulletin* 10 (Spring): entire issue.

————. 1985a. "Nostra Aetate: Twenty Years Later." *Face-to-Face: An Interreligious Bulletin* 12 (Fall): entire issue.

————. 1985b. "Oberammergau: Christian Folk Religion and Anti-Judaism." *Face-to-Face: An Interreligious Bulletin* 12 (Winter): entire issue.

Apostle, Richard A., Charles Y. Glock, Thomas Piazza, and Marijean Suelzle. 1983. *The Anatomy of Racial Attitudes*. Berkeley: University of California Press.

Arrington, Leonard J. 1970. "The Mormons and the Indians: A Review and Evaluation." *Record* (Pullman, Wash.) 31: 4–29.

————. 1985. *Brigham Young: An American Moses*. New York: Alfred A. Knopf.

————. 1987. "A Mormon Apostle Visits the Umatilla and Nez Perce in 1885." *Idaho Yesterdays* 31 (1–2): 47–54.

Arrington, Leonard J., and Davis Bitton. 1992. *The Mormon Experience*. 2d ed. Urbana: University of Illinois Press.

Asante, Molefi K. 1987. *The Afrocentric Idea*. Philadelphia: Temple University Press.

————. *Afrocentricity*. 1988. Trenton, N.J.: Africa World Press.

Ashment, Edward W. 2000. "Joseph Smith's Identification of 'Abraham' in Papyrus JS1: The 'Breathing Permit of Hôr.'" *Dialogue* 33 (4): 121–26.

"Asiatic Origin of Na-Dene Languages (Navajo and Relatives)." *Journal of Book of Mormon Studies* 8 (1): 75–76.

Backman, Milton V., Jr. 1983. *The Heavens Resound: A History of the Latter-day Saints in Ohio, 1830–1838*. Salt Lake City: Deseret Book.

Baer, Klaus. 1968. "The Breathing Permit of Hor: A Translation of the Apparent Source of the Book of Abraham." *Dialogue* 3 (3): 109–34.

Bahr, Howard M., and Stan L. Albrecht. 1989. "Strangers Once More: Patterns of Disaffiliation from Mormonism." *Journal for the Scientific Study of Religion* 28 (2): 180–200.

Bahr, Howard M., and Renata T. Forste. 1986. "Toward a Social Science of Contemporary Mormondom." *BYU Studies* 26 (1): 73–121.

Baird, J. Edwin. 1968. *A Program for the Urban Lamanite*. Instruction Manual, Department of Seminaries and Institutes, Church Education System. Archives and Special Collections, Harold B. Lee Library, Brigham Young University, Provo, Utah.

Ballard, Melvin J. 1924. Address. In *Conference Report,* October, 27–32. Salt Lake City: Deseret News.

———. 1926. Address. In *Conference Report,* October, 33–41. Salt Lake City: Deseret News.

———. 1930. Address. In *Conference Report,* April, 153–58. Salt Lake City: Deseret News.

———. 1938. Address. In *Conference Report,* April, 42–46. Salt Lake City: Deseret News.

Ballif, Ariel S. 1992. "Stake Patriarch." In *Encyclopedia of Mormonism,* edited by Daniel H. Ludlow, 1064–65. New York: Macmillan.

Ballif, Serge F. 1909. Address. In *Conference Report,* April, 77–81. Salt Lake City: Deseret News.

———. 1917. Address. In *Conference Report,* April, 116–20. Salt Lake City: Deseret News.

———. 1920. Address. In *Conference Report,* October, 89–91. Salt Lake City: Deseret News.

———. 1923. Address. In *Conference Report,* October, 93–97. Salt Lake City: Deseret News.

Bandes, Hanna. 1981. "Gentile and Gentile: Mormon and Jew." *Midstream* 27 (February): 7–12.

Barber, Ian. 1995. "Between Biculturalism and Assimilation: The Changing Place of Maori Culture in the Twentieth-Century New Zealand Mormon Church." *New Zealand Journal of History* 29 (October): 142–69.

Barklay, LeRoi G., Jr., Harold C. Brown, Royal V. Ellis, Kent E. Morgan, Gary L. Wade, and Arland L. Welker. 1972. "A Study of the Graduates of the Indian Placement Program of the Church of Jesus Christ of Latter-day Saints." M.S.W. project, Marriott Library, University of Utah.

Barkun, Michael. 1994. *Religion and the Racist Right: The Origins of the Christian Identity Movement.* Chapel Hill: University of North Carolina Press.

Barnhill, J. Herschel. 1986. "Civil Rights in Utah: The Mormon Way." *Journal of the West* 25 (4): 21–27.

Barth, Fredrik. 1969a. Introduction to *Ethnic Groups and Boundaries: The Social Organization of Culture Difference,* edited by Fredrik Barth, 9–38. Boston: Little, Brown.

———, ed. 1969b. *Ethnic Groups and Boundaries: The Social Organization of Culture Difference.* Boston: Little, Brown.

Bates, Irene M. 1991. "The Transformation of Charisma in the Mormon Church: A History of the Office of Presiding Patriarch, 1833–1979." Ph.D. diss., University of California at Los Angeles.

———. 1993. "Patriarchal Blessings and the Routinization of Charisma." *Dialogue* 26 (3): 1–29.

Bates, Irene M., and E. Gary Smith. 1996. *Lost Legacy: The Mormon Office of Presiding Patriarch.* Urbana: University of Illinois Press.

Bautista Valencia, Margarito. 1920. "A Faith Promoting Experience." *Improvement Era,* September, 983–84.

———. 1935. *La evolucion de México: Sus verdaderos progenitores y su origen, el destino de America y Europa.* Mexico City: Apolonio B. Arzate.

Bear Chief, Clem. 1992. "Plucked from the Ashes." *Dialogue* 25 (4): 140–49. (Reprinted in *Native and Christian: Indigenous Voices on Religious Identity in the United States and Canada,* edited by James Treat, 223–31 [New York: Routledge, 1996].)

Bench, Curt, and Dan Wotherspoon. 1997. Letter to author, November 8.

Benedek, Emily. 1995. *Beyond the Four Corners of the World: A Navajo Woman's Journey.* New York: Alfred A. Knopf.

Benedict, Jeff. 2000. *Without Reservation: The Making of America's Most Powerful Indian Tribe, and Foxwoods, the World's Largest Casino.* New York: HarperCollins.

Bennett, Archibald F. 1930. "The Children of Ephraim." *Utah Genealogical and Historical Magazine* 21 (April): 67–85.

———. 1950. *Saviors on Mount Zion.* Salt Lake City: Deseret Sunday School Union Board.

Bennett, Richard E. 1987. *Mormons at the Missouri, 1846–1852: "And Should We Die."* Norman: University of Oklahoma Press.

———. 1997. *"We'll Find the Place": The Mormon Exodus, 1846–1848.* Salt Lake City: Deseret Book.

Bennion, Lowell L. 1933. *Max Weber's Methodology.* Paris: Les Presses Modernes.

Bennion, Lowell C., and Lawrence A. Young. 1996. "The Uncertain Dynamics of LDS Expansion, 1950–2020." *Dialogue* 29 (1): 8–32.

Benson, Ezra T. 1976. "A Message to Judah from Joseph." *Ensign,* December, 67–72.

Berger, Peter, and Thomas Luckmann. 1967. *The Social Construction of Reality: A Treatise on the Sociology of Knowledge.* Garden City, N.J.: Anchor Books.

Bergera, Gary J., and Ronald Priddis. 1985. *Brigham Young University: House of Faith.* Salt Lake City: Signature Books.

Birch, J. Neil. 1985. "Helen John: The Beginnings of Indian Placement." *Dialogue* 18 (4): 119–29.

Bishop, Clarence R. 1960. "An Evaluation of the Scholastic Achievement of Selected Indian Students Attending Elementary Public Schools of Utah." M.A. thesis, Brigham Young University.

———. 1967. "A History of the Indian Student Placement Program of the Church of Jesus Christ of Latter-day Saints." M.S.W. thesis, University of Utah.

Bitton, Davis. 1999. "B. H. Roberts and Book of Mormon Scholarship: Early Twentieth Century—Age of Transition." *Journal of Book of Mormon Studies* 8 (2): 60–75.

Blodgett, Terry M. 1994. "Tracing the Dispersion: New Linguistic Studies Help Tell Us about the Scattering of Israel." *Ensign,* February, 64–70.

Böhmann, Fred. 2000. Telephone interview by author, December 7.

Book of Mormon. [1830] 1981. Salt Lake City: Church of Jesus Christ of Latter-day Saints.

Bourdieu, Pierre, and J. C. Passeron. 1977. *Reproduction in Education, Society, and Culture.* Beverly Hills, Calif.: Sage.

Bowles, Carey C. 1968. *A Negro Mormon Views the Church.* Maplewood, N.J.: Privately published.

Bradley, Donald. 1997. "People of the Book: The Biblical Roots of the British and Mormon Identities." Paper. Archive of Restoration Culture, Brigham Young University, Provo, Utah.

Brewer, David L. 1970. "Religious Resistance to Changing Beliefs about Race." *Pacific Sociological Review* 13 (2): 163–70.

Brewer, Stewart W. 1999. "The History of an Idea." *Journal of Book of Mormon Studies* 8 (1): 12–21.

Brewster, Hoyt W., Jr. 1998. *The Promise: The Prophesied Growth of the Church of Jesus Christ of Latter-day Saints in the Netherlands and Belgium and All of Western Europe.* November edition. Amsterdam: LDS Church.

Bridgeforth, Ruffin. 1981. Telephone interview by author, June 2.

————. 1985. Interview by author, Salt Lake City, May 23.

Bringhurst, Newell G. 1979. "Elijah Abel and the Changing Status of Blacks within Mormonism." *Dialogue* 12 (2): 22–36.

————. 1981a. "Mormonism in Black Africa: Changing Attitudes and Practices." *Sunstone,* May–June, 15–21.

————. 1981b. *Saints, Slaves, and Blacks: The Changing Place of Black People within Mormonism.* Westport, Conn.: Greenwood.

————. 1992. "The Image of Blacks within Mormonism as Presented in the *Church News,* 1978–1988." *American Periodicals* 2 (Fall): 113–23.

————. 2001. "The 'Missouri Thesis' Revisited: Early Mormonism, Slavery, and the Status of Black People." Paper presented at the annual Sunstone Symposium, Salt Lake City, August.

————. 2002. "Eldridge Cleaver's Passage through Mormonism." *Journal of Mormon History* 28 (1): 80–110.

Britsch, R. Lanier. 1981. "Maori Traditions and the Mormon Church." *New Era,* June, 37–46.

————. 1986. *Unto the Isles of the Sea: A History of the Latter-day Saints in the Pacific.* Salt Lake City: Deseret Book.

————. 1992. "Oceania, the Church in." In *Encyclopedia of Mormonism,* edited by Daniel H. Ludlow, 1022–26. New York: Macmillan.

Broadway, Bill. 1998. "Black Mormons Resist Apology Talk." *Washington Post,* May 30, B-9.

Brodie, Fawn M. 1972. *No Man Knows My History: The Life of Joseph Smith the Mormon Prophet.* 2d ed. New York: Alfred A. Knopf.

Brooke, John L. 1996. *The Refiner's Fire: The Making of Mormon Cosmology, 1644–1844.* Cambridge: Cambridge University Press.

Brooks, Juanita. 1944. "Indian Relations on the Mormon Frontier." *Utah Historical Quarterly* 12 (1): 1–48.

————. 1962. *The Mountain Meadows Massacre.* 2d ed. Norman: University of Oklahoma Press.

————. 1973. *The History of the Jews in Utah and Idaho.* Salt Lake City: Western Epics.

Brown, Douglas S. 1966. *The Catawba Indians: The People of the River.* Columbia: University of South Carolina Press.

Brown, Gayle O. 1992. "Premortal Life." In *Encyclopedia of Mormonism,* edited by Daniel H. Ludlow, 1123–25. New York: Macmillan.

Brown, Harold. 1972. "What Is a Lamanite?" *Ensign,* September, 62–64.

Brown, Raymond E. 1994. *The Death of the Messiah.* 2 vols. New York: Doubleday.

————. 1995. "The Narratives of Jesus: Passion and Anti-Judaism." *Explorations* 10 (3): 6–8.

Brown, S. Kent. 1992. "Israel." In *Encyclopedia of Mormonism,* edited by Daniel H. Ludlow, 706. New York: Macmillan.

Buchanan, Frederick S. 1987. "The Ebb and Flow of Mormonism in Scotland, 1840–1900." *BYU Studies* 27 (2): 27–52.

Bunker, Gary L., Harry Coffey, and Martin A. Johnson. 1977. "Mormons and Social Distance Multi-Dimensional Analysis." *Ethnicity* 4 (December): 352–69.

Bunker, Gary L., and Martin A. Johnson. 1975. "Ethnicity and Resistance to Compensatory Education: A Comparison of Mormon and Non-Mormon Ethnic Attitudes." *Review of Religious Research* 16 (December): 74–82.

Burke, David G. 1995. "Translating *Hoi Ioudaioi* in the New Testament." *Explorations* 9 (2): 1–7.

Bush, Lester E. 1969. "A Commentary on Stephen G. Taggart's *Mormonism's Negro Policy.*" *Dialogue* 4 (4): 86–103.

———. 1972. "Compilation on the Negro in Mormonism." Collection of notes and facsimiles. Archives and Special Collections, Harold B. Lee Library, Brigham Young University, Provo, Utah, and LDS Church Archives, Salt Lake City.

———. 1973. "Mormonism's Negro Doctrine: An Historical Overview." *Dialogue* 8 (1): 11–68.

———. 1984. "Whence the Negro Doctrine? A Review of Ten Years of Answers." In *Neither White nor Black: Mormon Scholars Confront the Race Issue in a Universal Church,* edited by Lester E. Bush and Armand L. Mauss, 193–220. Salt Lake City: Signature Books.

———. 1999. "Writing 'Mormonism's Negro Doctrine: An Historical Overview' (1973): Context and Reflections, 1998." *Journal of Mormon History* 25 (1): 229–71.

Bush, Lester E., and Armand L. Mauss, eds. 1984. *Neither White nor Black: Mormon Scholars Confront the Race Issue in a Universal Church.* Salt Lake City: Signature Books.

Bush, William S. 1970. Telephone interview by author, July 4.

Bushman, Richard L. 1976. "The Book of Mormon and the American Revolution." *BYU Studies* 17 (1): 3–20.

———. 1984. *Joseph Smith and the Beginnings of Mormonism.* Urbana: University of Illinois Press.

———. 1997–98. "The Visionary World of Joseph Smith." *BYU Studies* 37 (1): 183–204.

Butt, Newbern I. 1960. "Index to Conference Reports of the Church of Jesus Christ of Latter-day Saints—50th and 68th–129th." Typescript. Harold B. Lee Library, Brigham Young University, Provo, Utah.

———. 1966. "*Improvement Era* Index, Volumes 59–68 (1956–65)." Typescript. Harold B. Lee Library, Brigham Young University, Provo, Utah.

"BYU President Defends School's Jerusalem Center." 1985. *Ensign,* October, 73–74.

Cain, Seymour. 1991. "The Mormon Quest for the Kingdom of God." *Midstream* 37 (November): 24–27.

———. 1992. "Judaism and Mormonism: Paradigm and Supersession." *Dialogue* 25 (3): 57–65.

———. 1993. "Mormons and Jews." *Midstream* 39 (October): 31–34.

Callister, Raymond J. 1970. "An Adult Indian Religious Education Program of Personal Involvement." Ed.D. diss., Brigham Young University.

Campbell, Angus. 1971. *White Attitudes toward Black People.* Ann Arbor, Mich.: Institute for Social Research.

Campbell, Douglas. 1996. "'White' or 'Pure': Five Vignettes." *Dialogue* 29 (4): 119–35.

Cannon, Brian Q. 1999. "Adopted or Indentured, 1850–1870: Native Children in Mormon Households." In *Nearly Everything Imaginable,* edited by Ronald W. Walker and Doris R. Dant, 341–57. Provo, Utah: Brigham Young University Press.

Cannon, George Q. 1880. Discourse, October 31, 1880. In *Journal of Discourses,* 22:128–30. London: Latter-day Saints Book Depot, 1854–86.

———. [1890] 1988. "The Church in Polynesia." In *Collected Discourses Delivered by Wilford Woodruff, His Two Counselors, the Twelve, and Others,* edited by Brian H. Stuy, 2:1–9. Burbank, Calif.: Brian H. Stuy.

Cannon, Mike. 1991. "'Brava' Characterizes Work on Reserve." *Church News,* August 24, 4.

Card, Brigham Y. 1999. "Mormons." In *Encyclopedia of Canada's Peoples,* edited by Paul R. Magocsi, 979–97. Toronto: University of Toronto Press.

Carroll, James. 2001. *Constantine's Sword, the Church, and the Jews: A History.* Boston: Houghton Mifflin.

Carter, Edward L. 1997. "Mailman Gets Yet Another Name: 'Bear Who Leads with Dignity.'" *Deseret News* (Salt Lake City), July 26, B-10.

Carter, Kate B., comp. 1964. "The Indian and the Pioneer." In *Daughters of the Utah Pioneers Lessons,* October, 61–124. Salt Lake City: Daughters of the Utah Pioneers.

Carver, James A. 1971. "A Comparative Study of the Teaching Methods of the LDS and Non-LDS Religious Educational Movements among the Indians in Southeastern Utah since 1943." M.Ed. thesis, Brigham Young University.

Chadwick, Bruce A., and Stan L. Albrecht. 1994. "Mormons and Indians: Beliefs, Policies, Programs, and Practices." In *Contemporary Mormonism: Social Science Perspectives,* edited by Marie Cornwall, Tim B. Heaton, and Lawrence A. Young, 287–309. Urbana: University of Illinois Press.

Chadwick, Bruce A., Stan L. Albrecht, and Howard M. Bahr. 1986. "Evaluation of an Indian Student Placement Program." *Social Casework* 67 (November): 515–24.

Chadwick, Bruce A., and Thomas Garrow. 1992. "Native Americans." In the *Encyclopedia of Mormonism,* edited by Daniel H. Ludlow, 981–85. New York: Macmillan.

Chandler, Russell. 1988. "Mormonism: A Challenge for Blacks." *Los Angeles Times,* August 12, I-1, 28–30.

Cherry, Alan G. 1970. *It's You and Me, Lord!* Provo, Utah: Trilogy Arts Publications.

———. 1988. "Silent Songs We've Never Heard." *This People* 9 (2): 24–27.

Chetnick, Neil. 1988. "Embracing the Black Mormon." *San Jose Mercury News,* August 13, C-1, 14.

Christensen, Bryce J. 1986. "Mormons and Jews." *Midstream* 32 (January): 8–11.

Christensen, Scott. 1999. *Sagwitch: Shoshone Chieftain, Mormon Elder, 1822–1887.* Logan: Utah State University Press.

Christenson, Allen J., trans. and ed. 2000. *Popol Vuh: The Mythic Sections—Tales of First Beginnings from the Ancient K'iche'-Maya.* Provo, Utah: Foundation for Ancient Research and Mormon Studies.

"Church News." 1988. *Standard-Examiner* (Ogden, Utah), June 4.

Clark, Andrew. 1994. "The Fading Curse of Cain: Mormonism in South Africa." *Dialogue* 27 (4): 41–56.

———. 1995. Telephone interview by author, August 1

Clark, E. Douglas. 1992. "Abraham." In *Encyclopedia of Mormonism,* edited by Daniel H. Ludlow, 7–9. New York: Macmillan.

Clark, James R., ed. 1965–75. *Messages of the First Presidency of the Church of Jesus Christ of Latter-day Saints,* 6 vols. Salt Lake City: Bookcraft.

Clark, Janice. 1975. "Combating the Life-Shorteners." *Ensign,* December, 24.

Clark, John E. 1989. "A Key for Evaluating Nephite Geographies." *FARMS Review of Books* 1: 20–21.

———. 1999. "A New Artistic Rendering of Izapa Stela 5." *Journal of Book of Mormon Studies* 8 (1): 22–33.

Clark, Richard O. 1967."A Manual of Instructions for Area Coordinators of the Indian Seminary Program." M.S. thesis, Brigham Young University.

Clark, Wynetta Martin. 1970. *I Am a Negro Mormon.* Ogden, Utah: Privately published.

Clemens, Dave. 1972. "Mormon Tells of NIYC Views." *Daily Universe* (Brigham Young University), May 1, 1.

Clemmer, Janice. 1999. Telephone interview by author, May 26.

Clinton, Lawrence, Bruce A. Chadwick, and Howard M. Bahr. 1973. "Vocational Training for Indian Migrants: Correlates of Success in a Federal Program." *Human Organization* 32 (1): 17–27.

Coates, Lawrence G. 1969. "A History of Indian Education by the Mormons, 1830–1900." Ed.D. diss., Ball State University.

———. 1972. "Mormons and Social Change among the Shoshone, 1853–1900." *Idaho Yesterdays* 15 (4): 3–11.

———. 1976. "George Catlin, Brigham Young, and the Plains Indians." *BYU Studies* 17 (1): 114–18.

———. 1978. "Brigham Young and Mormon Indian Policies: The Formative Period, 1836–1851." *BYU Studies* 18 (3): 428–52.

———. 1985. "The Mormons and the Ghost Dance." *Dialogue* 18 (4): 89–111

———. 1987. "The Spalding-Whitman and Lemhi Missions: A Comparison." *Idaho Yesterdays* 31 (1–2): 38–46.

———. 2000. Letter to author, December 29.

Cohen, Anthony P. 1985. *The Symbolic Construction of Community.* New York: Tavistock.

Cohen, Yoel. 1999. "Covering Israel's Religious Wars." *Religion in the News* 2 (3): 16–17.

Collins, Marva. 1985. Oral history interview. Afro-American Oral History Project, Charles Redd Center for Western History, Brigham Young University, Provo, Utah.

———. 1985–88. *Ebony Rose* (newsletter).

Cook, Bradley J. 2000. "The *Book of Abraham* and the Islamic *Qisas Al-Anbiya* (Tales of the Prophets) Extant Literature." *Dialogue* 33 (4): 127–46.

Cooper, Rex E. 1990. *Promises Made to the Fathers: Mormon Covenant Organization.* Salt Lake City: University of Utah Press.

Conference Report. Salt Lake City: Deseret News, 1880, 1889–present.

Cornell, Stephen. 1988. *The Return of the Native.* New York: Oxford University Press.

Cowdery, Oliver. 1835. "Letter No. VIII." *Messenger and Advocate* 2 (1): 195–202.

Cristy, Howard A. 1978. "Open Hand and Mailed Fist: Mormon-Indian Relations in Utah, 1847–52." *Utah Historical Quarterly* 46 (3): 216–35.

Crossan, John Dominic. 1995. *Who Killed Jesus? Exposing the Roots of Anti-Semitism in the Gospel Story of the Death of Jesus.* San Francisco: HarperCollins.

Cuch, Forrest S. ed. 2000. *A History of Utah's American Indians.* Logan: Utah State University Press.

Cummings, David W. 1961. *Mighty Missionary of the Pacific.* Salt Lake City: Bookcraft.

Dann, Moshe. 1987. "The Mormon Church, Israel, and the Arabs." *Midstream* 33 (May): 10–11.

Davis, Garold N. 1998. "Book of Mormon Commentary on Isaiah." *Ensign,* September, 54–60.

Davis, James A., and Tom W. Smith. 1996. *General Social Surveys, 1972–1996.* Chicago: National Opinion Research Corp.

Davies, W. D. 1978. "Israel, Mormons, and the Land." In *Reflections on Mormonism,* edited by Truman G. Madsen, 79–97. Provo, Utah: Religious Studies Center, Brigham Young University.

Deem, Woodruff J., and Glenn V. Bird. 1982. *Ernest L. Wilkinson, Indian Advocate and University President.* Provo, Utah: Privately published.

De Hoyos, Arturo. 1986. "Letter to the Editor." *Dialogue* 19 (3): 15–17.

De Hoyos, Genevieve. 1992. "Indian Student Placement Services." In *Encyclopedia of Mormonism,* edited by Daniel H. Ludlow, 679–80. New York: Macmillan.

De Hoyos, Genevieve, and Arthur De Hoyos. 1973. "The Indian Placement Program of the Church of Jesus Christ of Latter-day Saints." Draft for private circulation. Harold B. Lee Library, Brigham Young University, Provo, Utah.

Deloria, Vine. 1969. *Custer Died for Your Sins: An Indian Manifesto.* New York: Macmillan.

———. 1973. *God Is Red.* New York: Grosset and Dunlap.

———. 1992 *God Is Red: A Native View of Religion.* 2d ed. Golden, Colo.: North American Press.

———. 1995. *Red Earth, White Lies: Native Americans and the Myth of Scientific Fact.* New York: Scribner's.

Deseret News Church Almanac. 1974–present. Salt Lake City: Deseret News.

DiPadova, Laurie N., and Ralph S. Brower. 1992. "A Piece of Lost History: Max Weber and Lowell L. Bennion." *American Sociologist* 23 (Fall): 37–51.

"Discovery of Ancient Ruins in Central America." 1833. *Evening and Morning Star* 1 (9): 71–72.

Dittes, James E. 1967. "Review of Glock and Stark." *Review of Religious Research* 8 (Spring): 183–87.

The Doctrine and Covenants of the Church of Jesus Christ of Latter-day Saints. 1981. Salt Lake City: Church of Jesus Christ of Latter-day Saints.

Douglas, Ella D. Lewis, and Armand L. Mauss. 1968. "Religious and Secular Factors in the Race Attitudes of Logan, Utah, Residents." *Proceedings of the Utah Academy of Sciences, Arts, and Letters* 45 (2): 467–88.

Durrant, Stewart A. 1975. Interview by author, Salt Lake City, August 15.

———. 1983. Oral history interview by Richard L. Jensen, June 8. James M. Moyle Oral History Collection, LDS Church Archives, Salt Lake City.

Dutson, Roldo V. 1964. "A Study of the Attitude of the Latter-day Saint Church in the Territory of Utah toward Slavery as it Pertained to the Indian as well as the Negro from 1847 to 1865." M.Ed. thesis, Brigham Young University.

Dyer, Alvin R. 1966. *Who Am I?* Salt Lake City: Deseret Book.

Earl, O. Ken. 1985. Telephone interview by author, Fall.

"Economic Restoration of Lamanite Israel." 1970. Summary of a seminar for mission presidents, October 14. Personal files.

Efroymson, David P. 1994. "Assessing Changing Winds within Catholicism regarding Jews and Judaism." *Explorations* 8 (2): 6–8.

———. 1997. "Let *Ioudaioi* be *Ioudaioi*: When Less Is Better." *Explorations* 11 (2): 5.

Egan, Dan. 2000. "BYU Gene Data May Shed Light on Origin of Book of Mormon Lamanites." *Salt Lake Tribune,* November 30, B-1 and B-3.

Eisenga, Rob, Ruben Konig, and Peer Scheepers. 1995. "Orthodox Religious Beliefs and Anti-Semitism: A Replication of Glock and Stark in the Netherlands." *Journal for the Scientific Study of Religion* 34 (2): 214–23.

Ellern, Ahoran. 1977. "Zion in the Far West: A Modern Israeli View of the Mormons." *BYU Studies* 18 (1): 119–21.

Embry, Jessie L. 1990a. "Lamanite/Indian Branches." Paper. Personal files.

———. 1990b. "Separate but Equal? Black Branches, Genesis Groups, or Integrated Wards." *Dialogue* 23 (1): 11–37.

———. 1992a. "Blacks." In *Encyclopedia of Mormonism,* edited by Daniel H. Ludlow, 125–27. New York: Macmillan.

———. 1992b. "Ethnic Groups and the LDS Church." *Dialogue* 25 (4): 81–97.

———. 1992c. "Separate and Equal? American Ethnic Groups in the RLDS and LDS Churches—A Comparison." *John Whitmer Historical Association Journal* 12: 83–100.

———. 1992d. "Speaking for Themselves: LDS Ethnic Groups Oral History Project." *Dialogue* 25 (4): 99–110.

———. 1994. *Black Saints in a White Church: Contemporary African American Mormons.* Salt Lake City: Signature Books.

England, Eugene. 1985. "'Lamanites' and the Spirit of the Lord." *Dialogue* 18 (4): 25–32.

Enterprise Mentors. 1994. *News and Views* 4 (2): entire issue. Personal files.

Epperson, Steven. 1989. "Jews in the Columns of Joseph's *Times and Seasons.*" *Dialogue* 22 (4): 135–42.

———. 1992. *Mormons and Jews: Early Mormon Theologies of Israel.* Salt Lake City: Signature Books.

———. 1994–95. "Some Problems with Supersessionism in Mormon Thought." *BYU Studies* 34 (1): 125–36.

Evans, Craig A. 1993. "Polemics or Anti-Semitism?" *Explorations* 7 (2): 3.

"Facsimile Found: The Recovery of Joseph Smith's Papyrus Manuscripts." 1967. *Dialogue* 2 (4): 50–64.

Falsani, Cathleen. 2001. "CD-Rom to Aid Black Genealogists." *Chicago Sun-Times,* February 19, 10.

Faust, James E. 1995. "Heirs to the Kingdom of God." *Ensign,* May, 61–63.

Felt, Paul E. 1964. *The Book of Mormon, the Lamanite, and His Prophetic Destiny.* Provo, Utah: Brigham Young University Press.

Fife, Austin E. 1940. "The Legend of the Three Nephites among the Mormons." *Journal of American Folklore* 53 (1): 1–49.

Fillerup, Michael. 1985. "Hozhoogoo Nanina Doo." *Dialogue* 18 (4): 153–82.

———. 1992. "Apple Indian." *Dialogue* 25 (4): 173–91.

Fisher, Dan. 1986. "Mormon Issue Splits Israelis into Two Camps." *Los Angeles Times,* February 25, A-1.

Fisher, Eugene J. 1984. "A New Maturity in Christian-Jewish Dialogue: An Annotated Bibliography, 1973–83." *Face-to-Face: An Interreligious Bulletin* 9 (Spring): 29–43.

———. 1996. "The Catechism and 'Our Elder Brothers in the Faith.'" *Explorations* 10 (2): 5.

Flake, David K. 1965. "A History of Mormon Missionary Work with the Hopi, Navaho, and Zuni Indians." M.A. thesis, Brigham Young University.

Florence, Giles H., Jr. 1992a. "City of Angels." *Ensign,* September, 35–39.

———. 1992b. "City of the Saints." *Ensign,* September, 39–45.

Flores, Cassia C., and Enoc Q. Flores. 1992. "Race, Racism." In *Encyclopedia of Mormonism,* edited by Daniel H. Ludlow, 1191–92. New York: Macmillan.

Foundation for Indian Development. 1993. *Voice* (newsletter), Spring.

Freeman, Joseph. 1979. *In the Lord's Due Time.* Salt Lake City: Bookcraft.

Friedman, Thomas L. 1985. "Mormons in Israel Alarm the Orthodox." *New York Times,* August 13, 3.

Fronk, Camille, and Ray L. Huntington. 1998. "The Palestine Refugee Family Study." *Newsletter* (BYU Religious Studies Center) 12 (3): 1–4.

Fullmer, Robert W. 2000. "Paul Henning: The First Mormon Archaeologist." *Journal of Book of Mormon Studies* 9 (1): 64–65.

Furfey, Paul H. 1966. "Sociology and Anti-Semitism." *Commonweal* 84: 558–59.

Furniss, Norman F. 1960. *The Mormon Conflict, 1850–1859.* New Haven, Conn.: Yale University Press.

Gager, John G. 1983. *The Origins of Anti-Semitism: Attitudes toward Judaism in Pagan and Christian Antiquity.* New York: Oxford University Press.

Galbraith, David B. 1984. Oral history interview by Ava F. Kahn. James M. Moyle Oral History Collection, LDS Church Archives, Salt Lake City.

General Bishop's Minutes: Presiding Bishopric. 1876. January 8 and 13. LDS Church Archives, Salt Lake City.

Genesis Group. *Genesis* (irregular newsletter).

Gephart, Jerry C., Michael A. Siegel, and James F. Fletcher. 1974. "A Note on Liberalism and Alienation in Jewish Life." *Jewish Social Studies* 36 (3): 327–29.

Gerber, David A., ed. 1986. *Anti-Semitism in American History.* Urbana: University of Illinois Press.

Gerlach, Larry R. 1982. *Blazing Crosses in Zion.* Logan: Utah State University Press.

Getches, David H., Charles F. Wilkinson, and Robert A. Williams Jr. 1993. *Cases and Materials on Federal Indian Law.* 3d ed. St. Paul, Minn.: West Publishing.

Gibbons, Francis M. 1979. *Heber J. Grant: Man of Steel, Prophet of God.* Salt Lake City: Deseret Book.

Gibson, Arrell M. 1980. *The American Indian: Prehistory to the Present.* Lexington, Ky.: D. C. Heath.

Gileadi, Avraham. 1991. *The Last Days: Types and Shadows from the Bible and the Book of Mormon.* Salt Lake City: Deseret Book.

Givens, Terryl. 1997. *A Viper on the Hearth: Mormons, Myths, and the Construction of Heresy.* New York: Oxford University Press.

Glanz, Rudolf. 1963. *Jew and Mormon: Historic Group Relations and Religious Outlook.* New York: Waldon.

Glock, Charles Y. 1989. "The Ways the World Works." *Sociological Analysis* 49 (2): 93–102.

Glock, Charles Y., and Rodney Stark. 1966. *Christian Beliefs and Anti-Semitism.* New York: Harper and Row.

———. 1973. "Do Christian Beliefs Cause Anti-Semitism? A Comment." *American Sociological Review* 38 (1): 53–59.

Godfrey, Kenneth W. 1999. "What Is the Significance of Zelph in the Study of Book of Mormon Geography?" *Journal of Book of Mormon Studies* 8 (2): 76–80.

Goldberg, Robert A. 1986. *Back to the Soil: The Jewish Farmers of Clarion, Utah, and Their World.* Salt Lake City: University of Utah Press.

Goldman, Ari. 1995. "Mormon Tradition and Zeal Inspire Growth in the Northeast." *New York Times,* February 7, 35, 41.

Gonzales, David. 1994. "Spreading the Word in the South Bronx." *New York Times,* November 16, B-1, B-2.

Goodman, Jack. 1976. "Jews in Zion." In *The Peoples of Utah,* edited by Helen Z. Papani-kolas, 187–220. Salt Lake City: Utah State Historical Society.

Gordon, Tamar G. 1988. "Inventing Mormon Identity in Tonga." Ph.D. diss., University of California, Berkeley.

Gossett, Thomas F. 1963. *Race: The History of an Idea in America.* Dallas, Tex.: Southern Methodist University Press.

Gottlieb, Robert, and Peter Wiley. 1984. *America's Saints: The Rise of Mormon Power.* New York: G. P. Putnam's Sons.

Gowans, Fred R. 1999. Telephone interview by author, May 27.

Grant, Heber J. 1902. Address. In *Conference Report,* April, 45–49, 60–61, 79–81. Salt Lake City: Deseret News.

————. 1921. "Attitude of the Latter-day Saints towards the Jews." *Improvement Era,* June, 747.

Gray, Darius A. 1999. Telephone interview by author, May 25.

Green, Arnold H. 1968. "A Survey of LDS Proselyting Efforts to the Jewish People." *BYU Studies* 8 (4): 427–43.

————. 1994–95. "Jews in LDS Thought." *BYU Studies* 34 (4): 137–63.

————. 1999. "Gathering and Election: Israelite Descent and Universalism in Mormon Discourse." *Journal of Mormon History* 25 (1): 195–228

————. 2001. "Mormonism and Islam: From Polemics to Mutual Respect and Coopera-tion." *BYU Studies* 40 (4): 199–220.

Green, Doyle L. 1955. "Southwest Indian Mission." *Improvement Era,* April, 233–35, 262–65.

Greenberg, Gershon. 1994. *The Holy Land in American Religious Thought, 1620–1948: The Symbiosis of American Religious Approaches to Scripture's Sacred Territory.* Lanham, Md.: University Press of America.

Grover, Mark L. 1984. "Religious Accommodation in the Land of Racial Democracy: Mormon Priesthood and Black Brazilians." *Dialogue* 17 (3): 23–34.

————. 1990. "The Mormon Priesthood Revelation and the São Paulo, Brazil Temple." *Dialogue* 23 (1): 39–53.

Hafen, P. Jane. 1984. "A Pale Reflection: American Indian Images in Mormon Arts." M.A. thesis, Brigham Young University

————. 1985. "'Great Spirit Listen': The American Indian in Mormon Music." *Dialogue* 18 (4): 133–42.

Hales, Robert L. 1963. "A Book of Mormon Course of Study for Indian Students in Re-leased Time Seminaries." M.Ed. thesis, Brigham Young University.

Hall, Gerald R. 1970. "A Weekend Foster Parent Program Designed to Aid in the Devel-opment, Education, and Instruction of the Latter-day Saint Indian Youth Attending Federal Boarding Schools." Master's thesis, Brigham Young University.

Hamilton, Keith N. 2002. "The Test." *Genesis.* April.

Hangen, Tona J. 1997. "A Place to Call Home: Studying the Indian Placement Program." *Dialogue* 30 (1): 53–69.

Hansen, Klaus J. 1972. "The Millennium, the West, and Race in the Antebellum Ameri-can Mind." *Western Historical Quarterly* 3 (4): 373–90.

————. 1981. *Mormonism and the American Experience.* Chicago: University of Chicago Press.

Harmer, Earl W. 1940. *Joseph Smith and Our Destiny: A Brief Historical Outline of God's Covenant Race from Patriarchal Times to the Present.* Salt Lake City: Deseret News.

Harold B. Lee Library, Brigham Young University. 1957. "*Improvement Era* Index, Volumes 39–58" (1936–1955). Typescript.

———. 1961. "Index to the Church Section of the *Deseret News*." Typescript.

———. 1967. "Subject Guide to Manuals, 1891–1962: Priesthood, Sunday School, and M.I.A." Typescript.

Haroldsen, Edwin O., and Kenneth Harvey. 1979. "The Diffusion of 'Shocking' Good News." *Journalism Quarterly* 56 (Winter): 771–75.

Harrell, Charles R. 1988. "The Development of the Doctrine of Pre-Existence, 1830–1844." *BYU Studies* 28 (2): 75–96.

Harrington, Daniel J. 1994. "The Problem of 'the Jews' in John's Gospel." *Explorations* 8 (1): 3–4.

Harris, Lacee A. 1985. "To Be Native American—and Mormon." *Dialogue* 18 (4): 143–52.

Harrison, J. F. C. 1979. *The Second Coming: Popular Millenarianism, 1780–1850*. New Brunswick, N.J.: Rutgers University Press.

Hart, John L. 1994. "East St. Louis Branch Blossoms Again." *Church News*, February 5, 8–10.

———. 1998. "Fathers Needed as 'Pillars of Strength.'" *Church News*, May 2, 3.

Hartley, William G. 1980. Letter to author, August 25.

———. 1981. Letter to author, May 8.

———. 1983. "The Seventies in the 1880s: Revelations and Reorganizing." *Dialogue* 16 (1): 62–88.

———. 1985. Interview by author, Provo, Utah, August 29.

Hauck, Richard F. 1988. *Deciphering the Geography of the Book of Mormon*. Salt Lake City: Deseret Book.

Hawkins, Chester Lee. 1992. "Selective Bibliography on African-Americans and Mormons, 1830–1990." *Dialogue* 25 (4): 113–31.

Heaton, Tim B. 1992. "Vital Statistics." In *Encyclopedia of Mormonism*, edited by Daniel H. Ludlow, 1518–37. New York: Macmillan.

Hechter, Michael. 1987. *Principles of Group Solidarity*. Berkeley: University of California Press.

Hefner, Robert W. 1993. "Introduction: World Building and the Rationality of Conversion." In *Conversion to Christianity: Historical and Anthropological Perspectives on a Great Transformation*, edited by Robert W. Hefner, 3–44. Berkeley: University of California Press.

Hemming, Jan. 1979. "Black Author Discovers the 'Mormon Way.'" *Church News*, May 19, 10.

Heperi, Vernon. 1998. "Fair but Not Equal." *Eagle's Eye*, May, 1–3.

Hertzberg, Hazel W. 1971. *The Search for an American Indian Identity: Modern Pan Indian Movements*. Syracuse, N.Y.: Syracuse University Press.

Hicks, George L. 1977. "Separate but Similar: Adaptation by Two American Indian Groups." In *Ethnic Encounters: Identities and Contexts*, edited by George L. Hicks and Philip E. Leis, 63–83. Scituate, Mass.: Duxbury.

Hicks, Michael. 1989. *Mormonism and Music*. Urbana: University of Illinois Press.

Higham, John. 1957. "Social Discrimination against the Jews in America, 1830–1930." *Publication of the American Jewish Historical Society* 47 (1): 1–33.

Hill, Jonathan D. 1996. "Introduction: Ethnogenesis in the Americas, 1492–1992." In *History, Power and Identity: Ethnogenesis in the Americas, 1492–1992*, edited by Jonathan D. Hill, 1–19. Iowa City: University of Iowa Press.

Hinckley, Gordon B. 2001. *Stand a Little Taller: Counsel and Inspiration for Each Day of the Year.* Salt Lake City: Deseret Book.

Hoge, Dean R., and Jackson W. Carroll. 1975. "Christian Beliefs, Non-Religious Factors, and Anti-Semitism." *Social Forces* 53: 581–94.

Horsman, Reginald. 1981. *Race and Manifest Destiny: The Origins of American Racial Anglo-Saxonism.* Cambridge, Mass.: Harvard University Press.

Houston, Stephen D. 1999. "Classic Maya Religion: Beliefs and Practices of an Ancient American People." *BYU Studies* 38 (4): 43–72.

Howell, W. K., D. Ranae, and E. Copeland. 1959–95. *Papers of the New World Archaeological Foundation.* Provo, Utah: Brigham Young University.

Hudson, Charles M. 1970. *The Catawba Nation.* Athens: University of Georgia Press.

Hunter, Howard W. 1979. "All Are Alike unto God." *Ensign,* June, 72–74.

———. 1991. "The Gospel—A Global Faith." *Ensign,* November, 18–19.

Hunter, Milton R. 1956. Address. In *Conference Report,* April, 48–53. Salt Lake City: Deseret News.

Hunter, Milton R., and Thomas Stuart Ferguson. 1950. *Ancient America and the Book of Mormon.* Salt Lake City: Bookcraft.

Iber, Jorge. 2000. *Hispanics in the Mormon Zion, 1912–1999.* College Station: Texas A & M University Press.

"Indian Alcoholism Board Claims Cooperation Lack." 1972. *Lewiston [Idaho] Morning Tribune,* September 12, 2.

Indian Education Department, Brigham Young University. 1976. "Fact Sheet." May. Archives and Special Collections, Harold B. Lee Library, Brigham Young University, Provo, Utah.

———. 1977a. *Financial Aids for Indian Students.* Brochure. Archives and Special Collections, Harold B. Lee Library, Brigham Young University, Provo, Utah.

———. 1977b. *Native American Studies Minor.* Brochure. Archives and Special Collections, Harold B. Lee Library, Brigham Young University, Provo, Utah.

———. 1978a. *Indian Week, 1978.* February. Archives and Special Collections, Harold B. Lee Library, Brigham Young University, Provo, Utah.

———. 1978b. *You Can Succeed.* Brochure. Archives and Special Collections, Harold B. Lee Library, Brigham Young University, Provo, Utah.

———. 1981. *American Indian Education at Brigham Young University.* Brochure. Archives and Special Collections, Harold B. Lee Library, Brigham Young University, Provo, Utah.

Indinopulos, Thomas A. 1985. "Mormon-Jewish Turmoil in Zion." *Christian Century* 102 (December 4): 1123–26.

Institute of American Indian Services and Research, Brigham Young University. 1966. "Research Policies, Services, Personnel, and Publications." Typescript. Archives and Special Collections, Harold B. Lee Library, Brigham Young University, Provo, Utah.

———. 1972. *Paths to Progress for American Indians.* Pamphlet. Archives and Special Collections, Harold B. Lee Library, Brigham Young University, Provo, Utah.

———. 1978–85. *Buffalo Hide.* Institute newsletter, published five times annually. Archives and Special Collections, Harold B. Lee Library, Brigham Young University, Provo, Utah.

Irving, Gordon. 1973. "The Mormons and the Bible in the 1830s." *BYU Studies* 13 (4): 473–88.

Isaac, Jules. 1964. *The Teaching of Contempt: Christian Roots of Anti-Semitism.* New York: Holt, Rinehart and Winston.

Ivie, Lloyd O. 1926. Address. In *Conference Report,* April, 94–96. Salt Lake City: Deseret News.

Ivins, Anthony W. 1901. Address. In *Conference Report,* April, 57–58. Salt Lake City: Deseret News.

———. 1926. Address. In *Conference Report,* October, 13–21. Salt Lake City: Deseret News.

———. 1929. Address. In *Conference Report,* October, 92–101. Salt Lake City: Deseret News.

Jackson, Helen Hunt. 1881. *A Century of Dishonor: A Sketch of the United States Government's Dealings with Some of the Indian Tribes.* New York: Harper.

Jackson, Lynne M., and Bruce Hunsberger. 1999. "An Intergroup Perspective on Religion and Prejudice." *Journal for the Scientific Study of Religion* 38 (4): 509–23.

Jacobson, Cardell K. 1991. "Black Mormons in the 1980s: Pioneers in a White Church." *Review of Religious Research* 33 (December): 146–52.

———. 1992. "Religiosity in a Black Community: An Examination of Secularization and Political Variables." *Review of Religious Research* 33 (March): 215–28.

Jacobson, Cardell, Tim B. Heaton, E. Dale LeBaron, and Trina Louise Hope. 1994. "Black Mormon Converts in the United States and Africa: Social Characteristics and Perceived Acceptance." In *Contemporary Mormonism: Social Science Perspectives,* edited by Marie Cornwall, Tim B. Heaton, and Lawrence A. Young, 326–47. Urbana: University of Illinois Press.

Jenson, Andrew. 1901–36. *Latter-day Saint Biographical Encyclopedia.* 4 vols. Salt Lake City: Andrew Jensen History Company and Memorial Association.

———. 1913. Address. In *Conference Report,* April, 77–81. Salt Lake City: Deseret News.

———. 1925. Address. In *Conference Report,* April, 104–12. Salt Lake City: Deseret News.

———. 1930. Address. In *Conference Report,* April, 149–52. Salt Lake City: Deseret News.

Jewish Mission Files, 1955–58. LDS Church Archives, Salt Lake City.

Johnson, Lane. 1975. "When Schools Are Few." *Ensign,* December, 20–21.

Johnson, Martin A. 1973."A Comparison of Mormon and Non-Mormon Ethnic Attitudes." Ph.D. diss., Brigham Young University.

Jones, Chris L. 1975. "Seminary for Six-Year Olds." *Ensign,* December, 21–22.

Jones, Sondra. 2000. *The Trial of Don Pedro León Lujan: The Attack against Indian Slavery and Mexican Traders in Utah.* Salt Lake City: University of Utah Press.

"The Joseph Smith Egyptian Papyri: Translations and Interpretations." 1968. *Dialogue* 3 (2): 67–105.

Journal of Discourses. 26 vols. London: Latter-day Saints Book Depot, 1854–86.

Keane, Colleen. 1982. "Where Have All the Children Gone? Controversy over Native Child Placement by the Mormon Church." *Wassaja/The Indian Historian* 15 (3): 12–13.

Kee, Howard C. 1996. "Children's Bible Publishers Are Modifying References to Jews." *Explorations* 10 (2): 4.

———. 1997. "What Is the Meaning of 'the Jews' in the New Testament?" *Explorations* 11 (1): 2

Kee, Howard C., and Irwin J. Borowsky, eds. 1994. *Removing Anti-Judaism from the Pulpit.* Philadelphia: American Interfaith Institute.

Keele, Alan F., and Douglas F. Tobler. 1980. "The Fuehrer's New Clothes: Helmut Huebener and the Mormons in the Third Reich." *Sunstone,* November–December, 20–29.

Kelly, Jack. 1997. "A Hundred Years" Effort at Reform of Passion Plays." *Explorations* 11 (1): 5.

Kersten, Lawrence. 1970. *The Lutheran Ethic: The Impact of Religion on Laymen and Clergy.* Detroit: Wayne State University Press.

King, Christine E. 1979. "Strategies for Survival: An Examination of the History of Five Christian Sects in Germany, 1933–45." *Journal of Contemporary History* 14: 211–34.

Kimball, Edward L., and Andrew E. Kimball Jr. 1977. *Spencer W. Kimball: Twelfth President of the Church of Jesus Christ of Latter-day Saints.* Salt Lake City: Bookcraft.

Kimball, Heber C. 1840. Letter to the Editor, December 15, 1840. *Times and Seasons* 2 (4): 250–51.

———. 1845. "Excerpts from H. C. Kimball's Journal." *Times and Seasons* 6 (2): 787–90.

Kimball, Spencer W. 1960a. Address. In *Conference Report,* October, 32–37. Salt Lake City: Deseret News.

———. 1960b. "The Day of the Lamanite." *Improvement Era,* December, 922–23.

Kimball, Stanley B. 1985. "The Captivity Narrative on Mormon Trails, 1846–65." *Dialogue* 18 (4): 81–88.

Kirsch, Paul J. 1972. "Another Look at Anti-Semitism." *Lutheran Quarterly* 24 (3): 227–39.

Knowlton, David C. 1988. "Searching Minds and Questing Hearts: Protestantism and Social Context in Bolivia." Ph.D. diss., University of Texas.

———. 1996. "Mormonism in Latin America: Toward the Twenty-First Century." *Dialogue* 29 (1): 159–76.

Lamb, John. 1966. "My Responsibility." *Improvement Era,* January, 36–37.

Lang, Robert. 1981. Telephone interview by author, June 10.

———. 1985. Telephone interview by author, May 21.

Larsen, Dean L. 1965. "Church Programs for the Indian People Today." Paper. Archives and Special Collections, Harold B. Lee Library, Brigham Young University, Provo, Utah.

Larson, Stan. 1990. "The Odyssey of Thomas Stuart Ferguson." *Dialogue* 23 (1): 55–93.

———. 1996. *Quest for the Gold Plates: Thomas Stuart Ferguson's Archaeological Search for the Book of Mormon.* Salt Lake City: Freethinker Press and Smith Research Associates.

"The Latest in the 'Social Genocide' Field: Adoption of Indian Children by White Families." 1971. *Akwesasne Notes* 4 (4): 10–11.

LDSCA (Latter-day Saints for Cultural Awareness). 1989–94. *UpLift* (formerly *Let's Talk,* newsletter).

LDS Church Education System. 1960. "The Program of the Church of Jesus Christ of Latter-day Saints for the Benefit of the Indian." Manuscript. Archives and Special Collections, Harold B. Lee Library, Brigham Young University, Provo, Utah.

———. 1971. "Lamanite Seminary Program of the Church of Jesus Christ of Latter-day Saints." Mimeographed draft. Archives and Special Collections, Harold B. Lee Library, Brigham Young University, Provo, Utah.

LDS Collectors Library '97. 1996. 3d ed. Provo, Utah: Infobases.

LDS Historical Department. 1961–90. "Index to Periodicals of the Church of Jesus Christ of Latter-day Saints." Typescript. Library of LDS Church Historical Department; copy in personal files.

———. 1980. *Index to Mormonism in Periodical Literature,* vol. 5, *1976–1980.* Salt Lake City: Church of Jesus Christ of Latter-day Saints.

LDS Indian Committee. 1965a. "Directory of Indian Units." July. Typescript. Archives and Special Collections, Harold B. Lee Library, Brigham Young University, Provo, Utah.

———. 1965b. *Foster Parent Guide.* April. Brochure. Archives and Special Collections, Harold B. Lee Library, Brigham Young University, Provo, Utah.

————. 1966. "Enrollment Report for the School Year 1965–66 and Drop-out Report for the School Year 1964–65." Report. Archives and Special Collections, Harold B. Lee Library, Brigham Young University, Provo, Utah.

————. 1967. *The Indian Student Placement Program of the Church of Jesus Christ of Latter-day Saints: School Year 1967–68.* Brochure. Archives and Special Collections, Harold B. Lee Library, Brigham Young University, Provo, Utah.

————. 1968. *Lamanite Handbook of the Church of Jesus Christ of Latter-day Saints.* June. Archives and Special Collections, Harold B. Lee Library, Brigham Young University, Provo, Utah.

————. 1971. *Who Are You?* Pamphlet. Archives and Special Collections, Harold B. Lee Library, Brigham Young University, Provo, Utah.

————. 1972. *And the Lamanites Shall Blossom.* Pamphlet. Archives and Special Collections, Harold B. Lee Library, Brigham Young University, Provo, Utah.

————. 1973. *And the Lamanites Shall Blossom.* Pamphlet. Archives and Special Collections, Harold B. Lee Library, Brigham Young University, Provo, Utah.

LDS Public Affairs Department, Los Angeles Office. 1999. "Interfaith Relations in California." Special Report to the Area President, December. Office files; copy in personal files.

————. 2001. "Freedman's Bank Records." News Release and Fact Sheet, February 26. Office files; copy in personal files.

LDS Research Information Division. 1982. "Indian Student Placement Evaluation Study." May. Draft. Personal files.

LDS Social Services. 1970. *Natural Parent Guide.* November. Pamphlet. Archives and Special Collections, Harold B. Lee Library, Brigham Young University, Provo, Utah.

————. 1973. *Indian Student Guide.* May. Pamphlet. Archives and Special Collections, Harold B. Lee Library, Brigham Young University, Provo, Utah.

LeBaron, E. Dale. 1996. "Mormonism in Black Africa." In *Mormon Identities in Transition,* edited by Douglas J. Davies. 80–86. New York: Cassell.

Lee, George P. 1975. "A Comparative Study of Activities and Opinions of Navajo High School Graduates among Four Selected School Models." Ed.D. diss. Brigham Young University.

————. 1980. "The Mormon Student Placement Program." *Wassaja/The Indian Historian* 13 (1): 53

————. 1987. *Silent Courage: An Indian Story.* Salt Lake City: Deseret Book.

————. 1989. "The Lee Letters" (and introductory article, no author). *Sunstone,* August, 47–55.

Lee, Harold B. 1955. *Youth and the Church.* Salt Lake City: Deseret Book.

————. 1973. *Decisions for Successful Living.* Salt Lake City: Deseret Book.

Lee, Jerry. 1976. "A Study of the Influence of the Mormon Church on the Catawba Indians of South Carolina, 1882–1975." Master's thesis, Brigham Young University.

Lewis, Bernard. 1975. *History—Remembered, Recovered, Invented.* Princeton, N.J.: Princeton University Press.

Lindquist, Geraldine T. 1974. "The Indian Student Placement Program as a Means of Increasing the Education of Children of Selected Indian Families." M.S. thesis, Utah State University.

Lindsay, Rao H. 1966. "The Dream of a Mormon Colony in the Near East." *Dialogue* 1 (4): 49–67.

Lineham, Peter. 1991. "The Mormon Message in the Context of Maori Culture." *Journal of Mormon History* 17 (1): 62–93.

Litt, Mike. 1980. "The Only Alternative." *Intermountain Health Review* 1 (1): 28–31, 43.

Livingston, Craig. 2002. "From Above and Below: The Mormon Embrace of Revolution, 1840–1940." Ph.D. diss., Temple University.

Livingstone, John P. 2000. "Establishing the Church Simply." *BYU Studies* 39 (4): 127–60.

Lloyd, R. Scott. 1993. "Group Seeks to Expand LDS Cultural Awareness." *Church News,* September 4, 11.

———. 1996. "Genesis Group Notes Silver Anniversary." *Church News,* October 26, 6.

"Locked Gates Meet March on Temple." 1973. *Salt Lake Tribune,* April 9, A-3.

Loveland, Jerry K. 1976. "Hagoth and the Polynesian Tradition." *BYU Studies* 17 (1): 59–73.

Lozano Herrera, Agricol. 1983. *Historia del Mormonismo en México.* Mexico City: Editorial Zarahemla.

Lubeck, Kathleen. 1982. "David B. Galbraith—Teacher on the Mount." *This People* 3 (October–November): 31–34.

Ludlow, Daniel H., ed. 1972. *Ensign,* special issue on Jews, May.

——— 1992. *Encyclopedia of Mormonism.* New York: Macmillan.

Lyman, Melvin A. 1982. *As a Rose.* Delta, Utah: Kenninghouse.

———. 1985. *Out of Obscurity into Light.* Salt Lake City: Albany Books.

Lythgoe, Dennis L. 1972. "Interview with Lucille Bankhead." Transcript. Personal files.

Mabey, Rendell N., and Gordon T. Allred. 1984. *Brother to Brother: The Story of the Latter-day Saint Missionaries Who Took the Gospel to Black Africa.* Salt Lake City: Bookcraft.

Madison, Robert B. 1992. "Heirs according to the Promise: Observations on Ethnicity, Race, and Identity in the Two Factions of Nineteenth-Century Mormonism." *John Whitmer Historical Association Journal* 12: 66–82.

Madsen, Brigham D. 1985. *The Shoshoni Frontier and the Bear River Massacre.* Salt Lake City: University of Utah Press.

Mano, Jon. 1995. "Black Athletes Must Adjust to Lack of Diversity." *Daily Universe* (Brigham Young University), February 13, 2.

Martin, Wynetta W. 1972. *Black Mormon Tells Her Story.* Salt Lake City: Hawkes Publications.

Martins, Marcus H. 1996."The Oak Tree Revisited: Brazilian LDS Leaders' Insights on the Growth of the LDS Church in Brazil." Ph.D. diss., Brigham Young University.

Mathews, James D. 1968. "A Study in the Cultural and Religious Behavior of the Navaho Indians Which Caused Animosity, Resistance, or Indifference to the Religious Teachings of the Latter-day Saints." M.Ed. thesis, Brigham Young University.

Mauss, Armand L. 1966. "Mormons and Secular Attitudes toward Negroes." *Pacific Sociological Review* 9 (2): 91–99.

———. 1967. "Mormonism and the Negro: Faith, Folklore, and Civil Rights." *Dialogue* 2 (4): 19–39.

———. 1967–69. "Mauss Surveys of Mormons, Salt Lake City and San Francisco, 1967–69." Electronic data files and documentation, American Religion Data Archives, Pennsylvania State University, University Park.

———. 1968. "Mormon Semitism and Anti-Semitism." *Sociological Analysis* 29 (Spring): 11–27.

———. 1970. "Mormonism and Minorities." Ph.D. diss., University of California, Berkeley.

———. 1972a. "Moderation in All Things: Political and Social Outlooks of Modern Urban Mormons." *Dialogue* 7 (1): 57–69.

———. 1972b. "Saints, Cities, and Secularism: Religious Attitudes and Behavior of Modern Urban Mormons." *Dialogue* 7 (2): 8–27.

———. 1976. "Shall the Youth of Zion Falter? Mormon Youth and Sex, a Two-City Comparison." *Dialogue* 10 (2): 82–84.

———. 1981. "The Fading of the Pharaohs" Curse: The Decline and Fall of the Priesthood Ban against Blacks in the Mormon Church." *Dialogue* 14 (3): 10–45.

———. 1985. "Mormons and Minorities: A Study in the Implications of Religious Ideas." Manuscript. Armand L. Mauss Papers, Utah State Historical Society Archives, Salt Lake City.

———. 1990a. "Mormons as Ethnics: Variable Historical and International Implications of an Appealing Concept. In *The Mormon Presence in Canada,* edited by B. Y. Card, H. C. Northcott, J. E. Foster, Howard Palmer, and G. K. Jarvis, 332–52. Edmonton: University of Alberta Press.

———. 1990b. "Rodney Stark: The Berkeley Years." *Journal for the Scientific Study of Religion* 29 (3): 362–66.

———. 1994. *The Angel and the Beehive: The Mormon Struggle with Assimilation.* Urbana: University of Illinois Press.

———. 1999. "In Search of Ephraim: Traditional Mormon Conceptions of Lineage and Race." *Journal of Mormon History* 25 (1): 131–73.

———. 2001a. "All Abraham's Children: Changing Mormon Conceptions of Race and Lineage." Fuller manuscript of the present book. Armand L. Mauss Papers, Utah State Historical Society Archives, Salt Lake City.

———. 2001b. "Flowers, Weeds, and Thistles: The State of Social Science Literature on the Mormons." In *Mormon History,* by Ronald Walker, David J. Whittaker, and James B. Allen, 153–97. Urbana: University of Illinois Press.

May, Dean L. 1980. "Mormons." In *Harvard Encyclopedia of American Ethnic Groups,* edited by Stephen Thernstrom 720–31. Cambridge: Harvard University Press.

Mayer, H. T., C. Y. Glock, R. Stark, M. E. Marty, and R. Johnstone. 1966. "A Round Table Review." *Concordia Theological Monthly* 37 (9): 597–605.

Mayfield, James B. 1979. "Ishmael, Our Brother." *Ensign,* June, 24–32.

———. 1992. "Covenant Israel, Latter-Day." In *Encyclopedia of Mormonism,* edited by Daniel H. Ludlow, 330–31. New York: Macmillan.

McConkie, Bruce R. 1966a. *Doctrinal New Testament Commentary.* 3 vols. Salt Lake City: Bookcraft.

———. 1966b. *Mormon Doctrine.* 2d ed. Salt Lake City: Bookcraft.

———. 1979–81. *The Mortal Messiah.* 4 vols. Salt Lake City: Deseret Book.

———. 1981. "New Revelation on Priesthood." In *Priesthood,* edited by Bruce R. McConkie, 126–37. Salt Lake City: Deseret Book.

———. 1982. *The Millennial Messiah.* Salt Lake City: Deseret Book.

———. 1985. *A New Witness for the Articles of Faith.* Salt Lake City: Deseret Book.

McMurrin, Sterling M. 1979. "A Note on the 1963 Civil Rights Statement." *Dialogue* 12 (2): 60–63.

McPherson, Robert S. 1985. "Paiute Posey and the Last White Uprising." *Utah Historical Quarterly* 53 (3): 248–67.

———. 1992. *Sacred Land, Sacred View: Navajo Perceptions of the Four Corners Region.* Salt Lake City: Signature Books.

Merrell, James H. 1984. "The Indians' New World: The Catawba Experience." *William and Mary Quarterly* 41 (3): 537–65.

Middleton, Russell. 1973. "Do Christian Beliefs Cause Anti-Semitism?" *American Sociological Review* 38 (1): 33–52, 59–61.

Midgley, Louis. 1999. "A Maori View of the Book of Mormon." *Journal of Book of Mormon Studies* 8 (1): 4–11.

Millet, Robert L., and Kent P. Jackson. 1985. *The Pearl of Great Price.* Salt Lake City: Randall Book.

Millet, Robert L., and Joseph F. McConkie. 1993. *Our Destiny: The Call and Election of the House of Israel.* Salt Lake City: Bookcraft.

Mims, Bob. 2001. "Ex-Slave Files a Prize for History Buffs." *Salt Lake Tribune,* February 21, A-1.

"Miss Indian America Warns Youth against Militants." 1971. *Brigham Young University Today,* August.

"Missionary Discussions for the Jewish People." 1979. *Ensign,* April, 72–73.

Mitchell-Green, Bonnie L. 1987. Interview by author, Salt Lake City, September 2.

Moench, Melodie. 1979. "Nineteenth-Century Mormons: The New Israel." *Dialogue* 12 (1): 42–56.

Mol, Hans. 1966. *Religion and Race in New Zealand.* Christchurch, New Zealand: National Council of Churches.

Montanye, Theodore, Ronald F. Mulberry, and Kenneth R. Hardy. 1971. "Assessing Prejudice toward Negroes at Three Universities Using the Lost-Letter Technique." *Psychological Reports* 29 (October): 531–37.

Morrison, Alexander B. 1990. *The Dawning of a Brighter Day: The Church in Black Africa.* Salt Lake City: Deseret Book.

Mortimer, William J. 1992. "Patriarchal Blessings." In *Encyclopedia of Mormonism,* edited by Daniel H. Ludlow, 1066–67. New York: Macmillan.

Mosser, Carl, and Paul Owen. 1998. "Mormon Scholarship, Apologetics, and Evangelical Neglect: Losing the Battle and Not Knowing It?" *Trinity Journal of Theology* 19: 179–205.

Moulton, Kristen. 1995. "Mormons to Stop Baptizing Holocaust Victims." *Standard-Examiner* (Ogden, Utah), April 29, B1–2.

Mulder, William. [1957] 2000. *Homeward to Zion: The Mormon Migration from Scandinavia.* Minneapolis: University of Minnesota Press.

Mullen, E. Theodore, Jr. 1993. *Narrative History and Ethnic Boundaries: The Deuteronomistic Historian and the Creation of Israelite National Identity.* Atlanta: Scholars Press and the Society for Biblical Literature.

———. 1997. *Ethnic Myths and Pentateuchal Foundations: A New Approach to the Formation of the Pentateuch.* Atlanta: Scholars Press and the Society for Biblical Literature.

Murphy, Thomas W. 1996. "Reinventing Mormonism: Guatemala as Harbinger of the Future?" *Dialogue* 29 (1): 177–92.

———. 1997. "Guatemala Hot/Cold Medicine and Mormon Words of Wisdom: Intercultural Negotiation of Meaning." *Journal for the Scientific Study of Religion* 36 (2): 297–308.

———. 1999. "From Racist Stereotype to Ethnic Identity: Instrumental Uses of Mormon Racial Doctrine." *Ethnohistory* 46 (3): 451–80.

———. 2000. "Other Mormon Histories: Lamanite Subjectivity in Mexico." *Journal of Mormon History* 26 (2): 179–214.

———. 2002. "Review Essay." *Journal of Mormon History* 28 (1): 280–89.

Murray, Herbert F. 1971. "Arab-Israeli Conflict." *Ensign,* January, 21–23.

Myers, Gustavus. [1943] 1960. *History of Bigotry in the United States.* Reprint, New York: Capricorn Books.

Nagel, Joane. 1986. "The Political Construction of Ethnicity." In *Competitive Ethnic Relations,* edited by Susan Olzak and Joane Nagel, 93–112. New York: Academic Press.

———. 1994. "Constructing Ethnicity: Creating and Recreating Ethnic Identity and Culture." *Social Problems* 41 (1): 152–76.

Neff, Andrew L. 1940. *History of Utah, 1847 to 1869.* Salt Lake City: Deseret News.

Neff, Thomas B. 1977. "Proselyting the Jewish People." Report. Microfilm #6968, 10–11. LDS Church Archives, Salt Lake City.

Neil, William. 1975. *Harper's Bible Commentary.* New York: Harper and Row.

Nelson, Lowry. 1952. "Mormons and the Negro." *Nation* 174 (May 24): 488.

Neusner, Jacob. 1993. *Judaism and Christianity: The New Relationship.* Hamden, Conn.: Garland.

Newhall, B. Falconer. 1994. "Black Family Comfortable with the Mormon Faith." *Contra Costa Times* (Contra Costa, Calif.), November 26, 4B.

"News of the Church: Calming the Storm." 1992. *Ensign,* September, 46–47.

"News of the Church: George Patrick Lee of the First Quorum of the Seventy." 1975. *Ensign,* November, 136–37.

"News of the Church—NAACP Leadership Meeting." 1998. *Ensign,* July, 74.

"News of the Church: Native American Conference." 1997. *Ensign,* October, 75–76.

"News of the Church: Report of Africa Area Presidency." 1997. *Ensign,* September, 79–80.

Newton, Marjorie. 1996. "From Tolerance to 'House Cleaning': LDS Leadership Response to Maori Marriage Customs." *Journal of Mormon History* 17 (1): 72–91.

———. 1998. "Mormonism in New Zealand: A Historical Appraisal." Ph.D. diss., University of Sydney.

Ng, Sik Hung. 1996. "Power: An Essay in Honor of Henri Tajfel." In *Social Groups and Identities: Developing the Legacy of Henri Tajfel,* edited by W. Peter Robinson, 191–214. Oxford: Butterworth-Heinemann.

Nibley, Hugh W. 1950. *Lehi in the Desert.* Salt Lake City: Bookcraft.

———. 1951. *The World of the Jaredites.* Salt Lake City: Bookcraft.

———. 1957. *An Approach to the Book of Mormon.* Salt Lake City: Church of Jesus Christ of Latter-day Saints.

———. 1967. *Since Cumorah.* Salt Lake City: Deseret Book.

———. 1975. *The Message of the Joseph Smith Papyri: An Egyptian Endowment.* Salt Lake City: Deseret Book.

———. 1985–95. *The Collected Works of Hugh W. Nibley.* 13 vols. Salt Lake City: Deseret Book and Foundation for Ancient Research and Mormon Studies.

Nielsen, François. 1985. "Toward a Theory of Ethnic Solidarity in Modern Societies." *American Sociological Review* 50 (2): 133–49.

Nielson, Reid L. 2001. *The Japanese Missionary Journals of Elder Alma O. Taylor, 1901–1910.* Provo, Utah: BYU Studies.

Norman, Keith E. 1983. "How Long, O Lord: The Delay of the Parousia in Mormonism." *Sunstone,* January–March, 48–58.

———. 1999. "The Use and Abuse of Anti-Semitism in the Scriptures." *Dialogue* 32 (4): 167–79.

Novick, Peter. 1999. *The Holocaust in American Life.* Boston: Houghton Mifflin.

Nuttall, Shea. 1995. "Activities to Promote Understanding." *Daily Universe* (Brigham Young University), February 13, 2.

Oakes, Keith R. 1971. "Church Elementary and Secondary Education." Letterhead of the Church Educational System, March 8. Copy in personal files.

O'Dea, Thomas F. 1954. "Mormonism and the Avoidance of Sectarian Stagnation: A Study in Church, Sect, and Incipient Nationality." *American Journal of Sociology* 60 (3): 285–93.

———. 1957. *The Mormons.* Chicago: University of Chicago Press.

———. 1972. "Sources of Strain and Conflict Reconsidered." In *Mormonism and American Culture,* edited by Marvin S. Hill and James B. Allen, 147–61. New York: Harper and Row.

Ogden, D. Kelly, and David B. Galbraith. 1993. "I Have a Question." *Ensign,* September, 53.

Ogilvie, Matthew C. 2001. "Children of a White God: A Study of Racist 'Christian Theologies.'" *Human Nature Review* 1 (1): 1–27.

Oliver, David H. 1963. *A Negro on Mormonism.* Salt Lake City: Privately published.

Olsen, Peggy. 1980. "Ruffin Bridgeforth, Leader and Father to Mormon Blacks." *This People* 1 (4): 11–17.

Olzak, Susan. 1983. "Contemporary Ethnic Mobilization." In *Annual Review of Sociology,* edited by Ralph H. Turner and James F. Short Jr., 355–74. Palo Alto, Calif.: Annual Reviews.

———. 1992. *The Dynamics of Ethnic Competition and Conflict.* Stanford, Calif.: Stanford University Press.

O'Neil, Floyd A. 1985. "The Mormons, the Indians, and George Washington Bean." In *Churchmen and the Western Indians, 1820–1920,* edited by Clyde A. Milner II and Floyd A. O'Neil, 77–107. Norman: University of Oklahoma Press.

Orton, Chad M. 1987. *More Faith than Fear: The Los Angeles Stake Story.* Salt Lake City: Bookcraft.

Osborne, V. Con. 1975. "An Appraisal of the Education Program for Native Americans at Brigham Young University, 1966–1974, with Curricular Recommendations." Ph.D. diss., University of Utah.

———. 1981. Interview by author, Provo, Utah, June 2.

———. 1986. Interview by author, Provo, Utah, August 20.

———. 1993. "Indian Education at Brigham Young University, 1965–1985." Report prepared for the Dean of Student Life, June. Archives and Special Collections, Harold B. Lee Library, Brigham Young University, Provo, Utah.

———. 1999. Interview by author, Provo, Utah, July 12.

———. 2000. Letter to author, December 2.

Oshley, Navajo. 2000. *The Journey of Navajo Oshley: An Autobiography and Life History.* Edited by Robert S. McPherson. Logan: Utah State University Press.

Ostergar, Allen C., Jr. 1992. "Seed of Abraham." In *Encyclopedia of Mormonism,* edited by Daniel H. Ludlow, 1292. New York: Macmillan.

Ostler, Blake. 1982. "The Idea of Preexistence in the Development of Mormon Thought." *Dialogue* 15 (1): 59–78.

Ostling, Richard N., and Joan K. Ostling. 1999. *Mormon America: The Power and the Promise.* San Francisco: HarperCollins.

Packer, Boyd K. 1962. "Manual of Policies and Procedures for the Administration of Indian Seminaries of the Church of Jesus Christ of Latter-day Saints." Ed.D. diss., Brigham Young University.

———. 1979. Untitled address to Indian student assembly during BYU Indian Week, February. Draft in personal files. (Very similar published version in *Eagle's Eye* 11 [3]: 2–3.)

Pagán, Eduardo O. 1989a. Letter to author, October 1.

———. 1989b. Letter to author, October 21.

———. 1989c. "Patriarchs and Power: The Struggle over Voting Rights in Apache County, Arizona, 1960–1976." Paper presented at the Sunstone Symposium, Salt Lake City, August.

———. 1990. "The Stumbling Block." *Dialogue* 23 (1): 5–6.

Pagden, Anthony. 1993. *European Encounters with the New World: From Renaissance to Romanticism.* New Haven, Conn.: Yale University Press.

Pagels, Elaine. 1995. *The Origin of Satan.* New York: Random House.

Palmer, A. Delbert, and Mark L. Grover. 1999. "Hoping to Establish a Presence: Parley P. Pratt's 1851 Mission to Chile." *BYU Studies* 38 (4): 115–38.

Palmer, Spencer J., ed. 1983. *Mormons and Muslims: Spiritual Foundations and Modern Manifestations.* Provo, Utah: Religious Studies Center, Brigham Young University.

Parkes, James. 1963. *Anti-Semitism: A Concise World History.* Chicago: Quadrangle Books.

Parry, Keith. 1972. "'To Raise These People Up': An Examination of a Mormon Mission to an Indian Community as an Agent of Social Change." Ph.D. diss., University of Rochester.

———. 1985. "Joseph Smith and the Clash of Sacred Cultures." *Dialogue* 18 (4): 65–80.

Paul, Erich R. 1982. "Joseph Smith and the Manchester (New York) Library." *BYU Studies* 22 (3): 333–56.

Pavlik, Steve. 1992. "Of Saints and Lamanites: An Analysis of Navajo Mormonism." *Wicazo Sa Review* 8 (1): 21–30.

Penrose, Charles W. 1922. Address. In *Conference Report,* October, 21–31. Salt Lake City: Deseret News.

Perlmutter, Nathan, and Ruth Ann Perlmutter. 1982. "The Real Anti-Semitism." *Face-to-Face: An Interreligious Bulletin* 9 (Fall): 30–34.

Petersen, Mark E. 1981. *Children of Promise: The Lamanites Yesterday and Today.* Salt Lake City: Bookcraft.

Peterson, Charles S. 1973. *Take Up Your Mission: Mormon Colonizing along the Little Colorado, 1870–1900.* Tucson: University of Arizona Press.

———. 1975. "Jacob Hamblin, Apostle to the Indians, and the Indian Mission." *Journal of Mormon History* 2: 21–34.

Peterson, Daniel C. 1992. *Abraham Divided: An LDS Perspective on the Middle East.* Salt Lake City: Aspen Books.

Peterson, F. Ross. 1999. "'Do Not Lecture the Brethren': Stewart L. Udall's Pro-Civil Rights Stance, 1967." *Journal of Mormon History* 25 (1): 272–87.

Peterson, H. Donl. 1992. "Book of Mormon Commentaries." In *Encyclopedia of Mormonism,* edited by Daniel H. Ludlow, 171–72. New York: Macmillan.

Peterson, John A. 1998. *Utah's Black Hawk War.* Salt Lake City: University of Utah Press.

Phayer, Michael. 2001. *The Catholic Church and the Holocaust, 1930–1965.* Bloomington: Indiana University Press.

Phelps, William W. 1833. "The Times." *Evening and Morning Star* 1 (10): 76–77.

———. 1834. "Letter No. 2." *Messenger and Advocate* 1 (3): 33–34.

———. 1835. "Letter No. 11." *Messenger and Advocate* 2 (1): 193–95.

———. 1836. "The Indians." *Messenger and Advocate* 2 (4): 245–48.

Philp, Kenneth R., ed. 1995. *Indian Self-Rule: First Hand Accounts of Indian-White Relationships from Roosevelt to Reagan.* Logan: Utah State University Press.

———. 1999. *Termination Revisited: American Indians on the Trail to Self-Determination, 1933–1953.* Lincoln: University of Nebraska Press.

Pratt, Alf. 1986. "LDS Neutrality Urged in Mideast." *Salt Lake Tribune,* August 23, 2B

Pratt, Nephi L. 1906. Address. In *Conference Report,* October, 103–5. Salt Lake City: Deseret News.

Pratt, Orson. 1852. Discourse, August 29, 1852. In *Journal of Discourses,* 1:62–63. London: Latter-day Saints Book Depot, 1854–86.

———. 1855a. Discourse, January 7, 1855. In *Journal of Discourses,* 2:284–98. London: Latter-day Saints Book Depot, 1854–86.

———. 1855b. Discourse, July 15, 1855. In *Journal of Discourses,* 9:174–79. London: Latter-day Saints Book Depot, 1854–86.

———. 1872. Discourse, September 22, 1872. In *Journal of Discourses,* 15:178–91. London: Latter-day Saints Book Depot, 1854–86.

———. 1874. Discourse, January 25, 1874. In *Journal of Discourses,* 16:339–53. London: Latter-day Saints Book Depot, 1854–86.

———. 1875. Discourse, February 7, 1875. In *Journal of Discourses,* 17:289–306. London: Latter-day Saints Book Depot, 1854–86.

Pratt, Parley P. 1836. Letter to the Editor, May 1, 1836. *Messenger and Advocate* 2 (8): 318.

———. 1853. Discourse, April 10, 1853. In *Journal of Discourses,* 1:256–63. London: Latter-day Saints Book Depot, 1854–86.

Pratt, Rey L. 1916a. Address. In *Conference Report,* April, 120–23. Salt Lake City: Deseret News.

———. 1916b. Address. In *Conference Report,* October, 144–48. Salt Lake City: Deseret News.

———. 1918. Address. In *Conference Report,* October, 80–83. Salt Lake City: Deseret News.

———. 1924. Address. In *Conference Report,* October, 142–45. Salt Lake City: Deseret News.

———. 1925. Address. In *Conference Report,* October, 169–74. Salt Lake City: Deseret News.

———. 1928. Address. In *Conference Report,* April, 20–23. Salt Lake City: Deseret News.

Preece, E. Bruce. 1967. "A Course of Study for the LDS Indian Seminary Program of North America for the Junior High Students." M.Ed. thesis, Brigham Young University.

"The Problematic Role of DNA Testing in Unraveling Human History." 2000. *Journal of Book of Mormon Studies* 9 (2): 66–74.

Proclamation of the Twelve Apostles of the Church of Jesus Christ of Latter-day Saints. . . . 1845. New York and Liverpool: Privately published.

Quinley, Harold E., and Charles Y. Glock. 1979. *Anti-Semitism in America.* New York: Free Press.

Quinn, D. Michael. 1993. "Ezra Taft Benson and Mormon Political Conflicts." *Dialogue* 26 (2): 1–87.

———. 1997. *The Mormon Hierarchy: Extensions of Power.* Salt Lake City: Signature Books.

Rainer, Howard. 1976. "An Analysis of Attitudes Navajo Community Leaders Have toward a Religion Sponsored Program Based upon Membership of That Faith and Amount of Information Attained." M.S. thesis, Brigham Young University.

Rainer, John C., Jr. 1976. "Comments at a Meeting of the Lamanite Committee," December 2, 1969. In "Lamanite Quotes," compiled by Richard L. Brimhall, n.p., 1976. Personal files.

Rasmussen, Dennis. 1981. "An Elder among the Rabbis." *BYU Studies* 21 (3): 343–56.

Rasmussen, Ellis T. 1971. "Judaism." *Ensign,* March, 40–47.

———. 1992. "Abrahamic Covenant." In *Encyclopedia of Mormonism,* edited by Daniel H. Ludlow, 9–10. New York: Macmillan.

Reicher, Stephen. 1996. "Social Identity and Social Change: Rethinking the Context of Social Psychology." In *Social Groups and Identities: Developing the Legacy of Henri Tajfel,* edited by W. Peter Robinson, 315–30. Oxford: Butterworth-Heinemann.

Reid, Rose Marie. 1958. *Suggested Plan for Teaching the Gospel to the Jewish People.* Salt Lake City: Church of Jesus Christ of Latter-day Saints.

———. 1973. Oral history interview by William G. Hartley, August 30. James M. Moyle Oral History Collection, LDS Church Archives, Salt Lake City.

Reines, Alvin J. 1989. "Ontology, Demography, and the Silent Holocaust." *Judaism* 38 (Fall): 478–87.

Reynolds, George. [1883] ca. 1950. *Are We of Israel?* Salt Lake City: Perry.

Reynolds, Noel B. 1998. "Shedding New Light on Ancient Origins: Scholars Illuminate Book of Mormon Authorship." *Brigham Young University Magazine,* Spring, 38–45.

———. 1999. "The Coming Forth of the Book of Mormon in the Twentieth Century." *BYU Studies* 38 (2): 7–47.

Richards, Franklin D. 1898. Address. In *Conference Report,* October, 27–34. Salt Lake City: Deseret News.

Richards, LeGrand. 1954a. *The Dawning of Israel's Day.* Provo, Utah: BYU Extension Publications.

———. 1954b. *Israel! Do You Know?* Salt Lake City: Deseret Book.

———. 1956. Address. In *Conference Report,* October, 22–26. Salt Lake City: Deseret News.

———. 1969. Address. In *Conference Report,* October, 29–33. Salt Lake City: Deseret News.

Ricks, Stephen D. 1992. "Book of Mormon Studies." In *Encyclopedia of Mormonism,* edited by Daniel H. Ludlow, 208. New York: Macmillan.

Rigdon, Sidney. 1835. "The Gospel, No. V, cont." *Messenger and Advocate* 1 (5): 71–74.

———. 1840. "The Gospel, IV." *Times and Seasons* 2 (4): 243–47.

Ritner, Robert K. 2000. "The 'Breathing Permit of Hôr' Thirty-Four Years Later." *Dialogue* 33 (4): 97–119.

Rivera, Orlando A. 1978. "Mormonism and the Chicano." In *Mormonism: A Faith for All Cultures,* edited by F. Lamond Tullis, Arthur H. King, Spencer J. Palmer, and Douglas F. Tobler, 115–25. Provo, Utah: Brigham Young University Press.

Roberts, B. H. 1907–12. *In Defense of the Faith and the Saints.* Salt Lake City: Deseret News.

———. 1909. *New Witnesses for God.* 3 vols. Salt Lake City: Deseret News.

———. 1930. *A Comprehensive History of the Church of Jesus Christ of Latter-day Saints,* 6 volumes. Salt Lake City: Deseret News.

Robinson, W. Peter, ed. 1996. *Social Groups and Identities: Developing the Legacy of Henri Tajfel.* Oxford: Butterworth-Heinemann.

Rokeah, David. 1989. "Behind the Appearances: 'Appreciation' of the Jews in the Writings of the Church Fathers." *Explorations* 3 (2): 3–4.

Romney, Gordon M. 1957. Address. In *Conference Report,* April, 80–83. Salt Lake City: Deseret News.

Roof, Wade Clark. 1974. "Religious Orthodoxy and Minority Prejudice: Causal Relation or Reflection of Localistic World View?" *American Journal of Sociology* 80 (3): 643–64.

Roof, Wade Clark, and William McKinney. 1987. *American Mainline Religion: Its Changing Shape and Future.* New Brunswik, N.J.: Rutgers University Press.

Roosens, Eugeen E. 1989. *Creating Ethnicity: The Process of Ethnogenesis.* Newbury Park, Calif.: Sage Publications.

Rose, Peter I. 1974. *They and We: Racial and Ethnic Relations in the United States.* 2d ed. New York: Random House.

Rosenberg, Morris. 1979. *Conceiving the Self.* New York: Basic Books.

Rothman, Norman. 1986. *So How Come a Nice Jewish Boy Became a Mormon?* Santa Ana, Calif.: Parca.

Royce, A. P. 1982. *Ethnic Identity: Strategies of Diversity.* Bloomington: Indiana University Press.

Russell, William D. 1979. "A Priestly Role for a Prophetic Church: The RLDS Church and Black Americans." *Dialogue* 12 (2): 37–49.

Salmon, Douglas F. 2000. "Parallelomania and the Study of Latter-day Scripture: Confirmation, Coincidence, or the Collective Unconscious?" *Dialogue* 33 (2): 129–56.

Salmon, Rusty, and Robert S. McPherson. 2001. "Cowboys, Indians, and Conflict: The Pinhook Draw Fight, 1881." *Utah Historical Quarterly* 69 (1): 4–28.

Sandberg, Karl C. 1989. "Knowing Brother Joseph Again: The Book of Abraham and Joseph Smith as Translator." *Dialogue* 22 (4): 17–37.

Sandeen, Ernest R. 1970. *The Roots of Fundamentalism: British and American Millenarianism, 1800–1930.* Chicago: University of Chicago Press.

Sanders, David L. 1985. Interview by author, Tustin, Calif., Summer.

Sanders, E. P. 1985. *Jesus and Judaism.* Philadelphia: Fortress.

Sanders, Ronald. 1978. *Lost Tribes and Promised Lands: The Origins of American Racism.* Boston: Little, Brown.

Sandmel, David F. 1997. "The Ultra-Orthodox and 'Who is a Jew?'" *Explorations* 11 (2): 7.

Schimmelpfennig, Dorothy J. 1971. "A Study of Cross-Cultural Problems in the LDS Indian Student Placement Program in Davis County, Utah." Ph.D. diss., University of Utah.

Schmidl, Thira. 1995. "Y Student Teachers in D.C. Learn Tolerance, Love." *Daily Universe* (Brigham Young University), February 21, 1.

Schnibbe, Karl-Heinz. 1984. *The Price: The True Story of a Mormon Who Defied Hitler.* Salt Lake City: Bookcraft.

Schwalbe, Michael. 1996. *Unlocking the Iron Cage: The Men's Movement, Gender Politics, and American Culture.* New York: Oxford University Press.

Scott, Mark. 1994–95. "Reflections on Howard W. Hunter in Jerusalem: An Interview with Teddy Kollek." *BYU Studies* 34 (4): 6–15.

Searle, Don L. 1985. "Quezaltenango's Saints." *Ensign,* October, 23–24.

Segal, A. F. 1986. *Rebecca's Children: Judaism and Christianity in the Roman World.* Cambridge, Mass.: Harvard University Press.

Selznick, Gertrude J., and Stephen Steinberg. 1969. *The Tenacity of Prejudice: Anti-Semitism in Contemporary America.* New York: Harper and Row.

Shepherd, R. Gordon, and Gary Shepherd. 1984. *A Kingdom Transformed: Themes in the Development of Mormonism.* Salt Lake City: University of Utah Press.

———. 1996. "Membership Growth, Church Activity, and Missionary Recruitment." *Dialogue* 29 (1): 33–57.

Shipp, Royal. 1968. "Black Images and White Images: The Combustibility of Common Misconceptions." *Dialogue* 3 (4): 77–91.

Shipps, Jan. 1998. "Difference and Otherness: Mormonism and the American Religious Mainstream." In *Minority Faiths and the American Protestant Mainstream,* edited by Jonathan Sarna, 81–109. Urbana: University of Illinois Press.

———. 2001. "Surveying the Mormon Image since 1960." *Sunstone,* April, 58–72.

Shipps, Jan, and John W. Welch, eds. 1994. *The Journals of William E. McLellin, 1831–1836.* Provo, Utah, and Urbana: *BYU Studies* and University of Illinois Press.

Shumway, Eric B. 1992. "Polynesians." In *Encyclopedia of Mormonism,* edited by Daniel H. Ludlow, 1110–12. New York: Macmillan.

Singer, David, and Lawrence Grossman, eds. 2001. *American Jewish Yearbook 2000.* New York: American Jewish Committee.

Siporin, Steve. 1991. "A Jew among Mormons." *Dialogue* 24 (4): 113–22.

Skinner, Andrew. 1997. "The Book of Abraham: A Most Remarkable Book." *Ensign,* March, 16–23.

Smith, A. D. 1986. *The Ethnic Origins of Nations.* Oxford: Blackwell.

Smith, Brent L. 1992. "Ephraim." In *Encyclopedia of Mormonism,* edited by Daniel H. Ludlow, 461–62. New York: Macmillan.

Smith, Eldred G. 1952. Address. In *Conference Report,* April, 37–41. Salt Lake City: Deseret News.

———. 1960. Address. In *Conference Report,* April, 65–67. Salt Lake City: Deseret News.

Smith, Ethan. [1825] 1996. *View of the Hebrews; or, The Tribes of Israel in America. . . .* Reprint, Provo, Utah: Religious Studies Center, Brigham Young University.

Smith, H. Shelton. 1972. *In His Image, But . . . Racism in Southern Religion, 1780–1910.* Durham: University of North Carolina Press.

Smith, Hyrum G. 1927. Address. In *Conference Report,* October, 78–80. Salt Lake City: Deseret News.

———. 1929. Address. In *Conference Report,* April, 122–25. Salt Lake City: Deseret News.

Smith, John M., and Elnora V. Smith. 1985. Interview by author, Riverside, Calif., November 23.

Smith, Joseph. 1902–32. *History of the Church of Jesus Christ of Latter-day Saints.* 7 vols. Edited by B. H. Roberts. Salt Lake City: Deseret News.

———. 1989. *The Papers of Joseph Smith,* vol. 1, *Autobiographical and Historical Writings.* Edited by Dean C. Jessee. Salt Lake City: Deseret Book.

Smith, Joseph F. 1919. *Gospel Doctrine.* Salt Lake City: Deseret News.

Smith, Joseph Fielding. [1931] 1951. *The Way to Perfection.* Reprint, Salt Lake City: Deseret Book.

———. 1954–56. *Doctrines of Salvation.* 3 vols. Compiled by Bruce R. McConkie. Salt Lake City: Bookcraft.

———. 1957–66. *Answers to Gospel Questions.* 5 vols. Salt Lake City: Deseret Book.

———, comp. and ed. 1938. *Teachings of the Prophet Joseph Smith.* Salt Lake City: Deseret News.

Smith, Julina. 1932. "A Discussion of the Inter-Relations of the Latter Day Saints and the American Indians." M.A. thesis, Brigham Young University.

Smith, Lynn C. 1962. "An Investigation of the Social Adjustment of LDS Graduates from Intermountain Indian School." M.S. thesis, Brigham Young University.

Smith, Robert D. 1968. "Relationships between Foster Home Placement and Later Acculturation Patterns of Selected American Indians." M.S. thesis, Utah State University.

Smith, Sherry L. 2000. *Reimagining Indians: Native Americans through Anglo Eyes, 1880–1940.* New York: Oxford University Press.

Smoak, Gregory E. 1986. "Mormons and the Ghost Dance of 1890." *South Dakota History* 16 (3): 269–94.

Smoot, David. 1968. "They've Said It with Music." *Improvement Era,* August, 41.

Snow, Erastus. 1882. Discourse, May 6, 1882. In *Journal of Discourses,* 23:181–89. London: Latter-day Saints Book Depot, 1854–86.

Snyder, Louis L. 1962. *The Idea of Racialism: Its Meaning and History.* Princeton, N.J.: Van Nostrand.

Sobel, B. Z. 1966. "Protestant Evangelists and the Formulation of a Jewish Racial Mystique: The Missionary Discovery of Sociology." *Journal for the Scientific Study of Religion* 3 (3): 343–56.

"Social Work Awarded $1 Million—Five Agencies OK Indian Program." 1971. *University of Utah Review* 4 (8): 1.

Sorenson, John L. 1984. "Digging into the Book of Mormon: Our Changing Understanding of Ancient America and its Scripture." *Ensign,* September, 27–37 (Part 1); October, 12–24 (Part 2).

———. 1985. *An Ancient American Setting for the Book of Mormon.* Salt Lake City: Deseret Book and Foundation for Ancient Research and Mormon Studies.

———. 1990. *The Geography of Book of Mormon Events: A Sourcebook.* Provo, Utah: Foundation for Ancient Research and Mormon Studies.

———. 1998. *Images of Ancient America: Visualizing Book of Mormon Life.* Provo, Utah: Research Press.

Sorenson, John L., and Martin H. Raish. 1990. *Pre-Columbian Contact with the Americas across the Oceans: An Annotated Bibliography.* 2 vols. Provo, Utah: Research Press.

Stack, Peggy Fletcher. 1998a. "'Black Curse' Is Problematic LDS Legacy." *Salt Lake Tribune,* June 6, C-1.

———. 1998b. "Church Leaders Haven't Discussed Racial Issue." *Salt Lake Tribune,* May 19, A-1.

———. 1998c. "Revelation of Twenty Years Ago Cause for LDS Celebration." *Salt Lake Tribune,* June 6, C-1.

Stammer, Larry B. 1998a. "Mormon Leader Defends Race Relations." *Los Angeles Times,* September 12, B-10, B-11.

———. 1998b. "Mormons May Disavow Old View on Blacks." *Los Angeles Times,* May 18, A-1, 20–21.

———. 1998c. "Mormon Plan to Disavow Racist Teachings Jeopardized by Publicity." *Los Angeles Times,* May 24, A-1.

Stapley, Delbert L. 1956. "Responsibilities to the Lamanites." *Improvement Era,* June, 416–18.

Stark, Rodney. 1996. "Why Religious Movements Succeed or Fail: A Revised General Model." *Journal of Contemporary Religion* 11 (2): 133–46.

Stark, Rodney, Bruce D. Foster, Charles Y. Glock, and Harold E. Quinley. 1971. *Wayward Shepherds: Prejudice and the Protestant Clergy.* New York: Harper and Row.

Stathis, Stephen W., and Dennis L. Lythgoe. 1977. "Mormonism in the Nineteen Seventies." *Dialogue* 10 (1): 95–113.

Steele, Carolyn S. 1968. "The Relationship of Cultural Background to the Academic Success of American Indian Students at Brigham Young University." M.A. thesis, Brigham Young University.

Stendahl, John. 1995. "With Luther/Against Luther." *Explorations* 9 (3): 7.

Stephens, John L. 1842. "Extracts from Stephens's 'Incidents of Travel in Central America.'" *Times and Seasons* 3 (2): 911–15.

Stoof, Reinhold. 1936. Address. In *Conference Report*, April, 87–89. Salt Lake City: Deseret News.

Stubbs, Brian. 2000. "Was There Hebrew Language in Ancient America? An Interview with Brian Stubbs." *Journal of Book of Mormon Studies* 9 (2): 54–63.

Sturlaugson, Mary Frances. 1980. *A Soul So Rebellious.* Salt Lake City: Deseret Book.

———. 1982. *He Restoreth My Soul.* Salt Lake City: Deseret Book.

"Summary: Meeting of Sioux Tribal Leaders with President Tanner and Elder Stapley." 1967. Summary of a meeting in Pierre, S.D., June 2. Archives and Special Collections, Harold B. Lee Library, Brigham Young University, Provo, Utah.

Swanson, Vern. 2001. "The Book of Mormon Art of Arnold Friberg, Painter of Scripture." *Journal of Book of Mormon Studies* 10 (1): 26–35.

Swenson, Paul. 2001. "Gladys and Thurl: The Changing Face of Mormon Diversity." *Sunstone*, July, 14–16.

Swinton, Heidi. 1988. "Without Regard to Race." *This People* 9 (2): 19–23.

Taggart, Stephen G. 1970. *Mormonism's Negro Policy: Social and Historical Origins.* Salt Lake City: University of Utah Press.

Tajfel, Henri. 1981. *Human Groups and Social Categories.* Cambridge: Cambridge University Press.

Taylor, Grant H. 1981. "A Comparative Study of Former LDS Placement and Non-Placement Navajo Students at Brigham Young University." Ph.D. diss., Brigham Young University.

Taylor, John. 1882. "Words of Good Cheer from President John Taylor." *Millennial Star* 44 (November 13): 732–33.

Taylor, Samuel W. 1978. *Rocky Mountain Empire: The Latter-day Saints Today.* New York: Macmillan.

The Testaments of One Fold and One Shepherd. 2000. Salt Lake City: Church of Jesus Christ of Latter-day Saints. Film.

Thernstrom, Stephen, ed. 1980. *Harvard Encyclopedia of American Ethnic Groups.* Cambridge, Mass.: Harvard University Press.

Thomas, M. Catherine. 1996. "Alma's Dynamic Life. . . ." *Church News*, July 20, 11.

Thorp, Malcolm R. 1975. "'The Mormon Peril': The Crusade against the Saints in Britain." *Journal of Mormon History* 2: 69–88.

Tinker, George E. 1993. *Missionary Conquest: The Gospel and Native American Cultural Genocide.* Minneapolis: Fortress.

Tobler, Douglas F. 1992. "The Jews, the Mormons, and the Holocaust." *Journal of Mormon History* 18 (1): 59–92.

Todd, Jay M. 1968. "Egyptian Papyri Rediscovered." *Improvement Era*, January, 12–16.

———. 1969. *The Saga of the Book of Abraham.* Salt Lake City: Deseret Book.

Toon, Peter, ed. 1970. *Puritans, the Millennium, and the Future of Israel.* Cambridge, Mass.: Clark.

Top, Brent L. 1992. "Foreordination." In *Encyclopedia of Mormonism,* edited by Daniel H. Ludlow, 522–23. New York: Macmillan.

Topper, Martin D. 1979. "Mormon Placement: The Effects of Missionary Foster Families on Navajo Adolescents." *Ethos* 7 (2): 142–60.

Toronto, James A., ed. 2001. *BYU Studies,* special issue on Islam, 40 (4).

Toscano, Paul J. 1975a. "Attack on Illiteracy." *Ensign,* December, 16–18.

———. 1975b. "Helping Lamanites Achieve Economic Independence. *Ensign,* December, 18–19.

———. 1975c. "Toppling the College Barricade." *Ensign,* December, 25

Treat, James, ed. 1996. *Native and Christian: Indigenous Voices on Religious Identity in the United States and Canada.* New York: Routledge.

Tullis, F. LaMond. 1987. *Mormons in Mexico: The Dynamics of Faith and Culture.* Logan: Utah State University Press.

———. 1997. *Los Mormones en México: La dinámica de la fe y la cultura/Mormons in Mexico: The Dynamics of Faith and Culture.* 2d ed. Translated by the Museum of Mormon History in Mexico. Salt Lake City: Deseret Book.

———. 1997–98. "A Shepherd to Mexico's Saints: Arwell L. Pierce and the Third Convention." *BYU Studies* 37 (1): 127–57.

Turner, Frederick J. 1911. "Social Forces in American History." *American Historical Review* 16 (January): 217–33.

Turner, John C. 1996. "Henri Tajfel: An Introduction." In *Social Groups and Identities: Developing the Legacy of Henri Tajfel,* edited by W. Peter Robinson, 1–23. Oxford: Butterworth-Heinemann.

Turner, Rodney. 1987. "The Lamanite Mark." Paper presented at the Third Book of Mormon Symposium, Brigham Young University, October. (Summarized in *Newsletter* [BYU Religious Studies Center] 2 [January 1988]: 2.)

Turner, Sharon (Shearon). 1799–1805. *The History of the Anglo-Saxons from their First Appearance above the Elbe to the Conquest of Egbert.* 4 vols. London: Longman.

Tuveson, Ernest L. 1968. *Redeemer Nation: The Idea of America's Millennial Role.* Chicago: University of Chicago Press.

Udall, Louise., ed. 1969. *Me and Mine: The Life Story of Helen Sekaquaptewa.* Tucson: University of Arizona Press.

Underwood, Grant. 1982. "Millenarianism and the Early Mormon Mind." *Journal of Mormon History* 9: 41–51.

———. 1984. "Book of Mormon Usage in Early LDS Theology." *Dialogue* 17 (3): 35–74.

———. 1993. *The Millenarian World of Early Mormonism.* Urbana: University of Illinois Press.

———. 1994–95. "The Jews and Their Future in Early LDS Doctrine." *BYU Studies* 34 (1): 111–24.

———. 2000. "Mormonism, the Maori, and Cultural Authenticity." *Journal of Pacific History* 35 (2): 133–46.

Urrutia, Benjamin. 1969. "The Joseph Smith Papyri." *Dialogue* 4 (2): 129–34.

Utley, Robert M. 1984. *The Indian Frontier of the American West, 1846–1890.* Albuquerque: University of New Mexico Press.

Van Hoak, Stephen P. 1999. "Waccara's Utes: Native American Equestrian Adaptations in the Eastern Great Basin, 1776–1876." *Utah Historical Quarterly* 67 (4): 309–30.

Van Orden, Bruce A. 1981. "Anglo Israelism and the Mormon Church." Paper presented at the annual meeting of the Mormon History Association, Rexburg, Idaho, May.

Van Seters, J. 1983. *In Search of History: Historiography in the Ancient World and the Origins of Biblical History.* New Haven, Conn.: Yale University Press.

Van Wagoner, Richard S. 1994. *Sidney Rigdon: A Portrait of Religious Excess.* Salt Lake City: Signature Books.

Vasconcelos, José. 1979. *La Raza Cosmica: The Mission of the Ibero-American Race.* Translated by Didier T. Jaen from the original 1925 Spanish edition. Los Angeles: CSU Centro de Publicaciones.

Vickers, Scott B. 1998. *Native American Identities: From Stereotype to Archetype in Art and Literature.* Albuquerque: University of New Mexico Press, 1998.

Vogel, Dan. 1986. *Indian Origins and the Book of Mormon: Religious Solutions from Columbus to Joseph Smith.* Salt Lake City: Signature Books.

Vogt, Evan Z. 1966. "Intercultural Relations." In *People of Rimrock: A Study of Values in Five Cultures,* 2d ed., edited by Evan Z. Vogt and Ethel M. Albert, 46–82. New York: Atheneum.

Vogt, Evan Z., and Ethel M. Albert, eds. 1966. *People of Rimrock: A Study of Values in Five Cultures.* 2d ed. New York: Atheneum.

Wade, Alton J., and John S. Tanner. 1995. "A Report of the BYU Multicultural/International Student Issues Committee." Report prepared for the Dean of Student Life, June. Archives and Special Collections, Harold B. Lee Library, Brigham Young University, Provo, Utah.

Walker, Ronald W. 1989. "Toward a Reconstruction of Mormon and Indian Relations, 1847–1877." *BYU Studies* 29 (1): 23–42.

———. 1993. "Seeking the 'Remnant': The Native American during the Joseph Smith Period." *Journal of Mormon History* 19 (1): 1–33.

Walker, Ronald W., David J. Whittaker, and James B. Allen. 2001. *Mormon History.* Urbana: University of Illinois Press.

Walsh, Andrew. 2000. "Two Cheers for the Pilgrimage." *Religion in the News* 3 (2): 4–9.

Walton, Michael T. 1981. "Professor Seixas, the Hebrew Bible, and the Book of Abraham." *Sunstone,* March–April, 41–43.

Warner, Terry. 1975. *For the Independence of a People: Indian Education, Brigham Young University.* Provo, Utah: Institute of American Indian Services and Research, Brigham Young University.

Waters, Mary. 1990. *Ethnic Options: Choosing Identities in America.* Berkeley: University of California Press.

Watrous, Steven B. 1985. "Blood Brothers." *Ensign,* October, 47–48.

Waxman, Chaim. 1989. "The Emancipation, the Enlightenment, and the Demography of American Judaism." *Judaism* 38 (Fall): 488–501.

Weaver, Jace. 1998a. "From I-Hermeneutics to We-Hermeneutics." In *Native American Religious Identity: Unforgotten Gods,* edited by Jace Weaver, 1–25. Maryknoll, N.Y.: Orbis Books.

———. 1998b. "Losing My Religion: Native American Religious Traditions and American Religious Freedom." In *Native American Religious Identity: Unforgotten Gods,* edited by Jace Weaver, 217–29. Maryknoll, N.Y. Orbis Books.

————, ed. 1998c. *Native American Religious Identity: Unforgotten Gods.* Maryknoll, N.Y.: Orbis Books.

Webb, L. Robert. 1972. "An Examination of Certain Aspects of the American Indian Education Program at Brigham Young University." Report prepared for the university president, February. Archives and Special Collections, Harold B. Lee Library, Brigham Young University, Provo, Utah.

Weber, Max. 1930. *The Protestant Ethic and the Spirit of Capitalism.* Translated by Talcott Parsons. London: Allen and Unwin.

————. 1963. *The Sociology of Religion.* Translated by Ephraim Fischoff. Boston: Beacon.

Welker, Roy A. 1937. Address. In *Conference Report,* October, 58–60. Salt Lake City: Deseret News.

Wells, Rulon S. 1924. Address. In *Conference Report,* October, 40–43. Salt Lake City: Deseret News.

Wetherell, Margaret. 1996. "Constructing Social Identities: The Individual/Social Binary in Henri Tajfel's Social Psychology." In *Social Groups and Identities: Developing the Legacy of Henri Tajfel,* edited by W. Peter Robinson, 269–84. Oxford: Butterworth-Heinemann.

White, Daryl, and O. Kendall White Jr. 1992. "African American Mormons in the South." In *African Americans in the South: Issues of Race, Class, and Gender,* edited by Hans A. Baer and Yvonne Jones, 139–53. Athens: University of Georgia Press.

White, O. Kendall, Jr., and Daryl White. 1980. "Abandoning an Unpopular Policy: An Analysis of the Decision Granting the Mormon Priesthood to Blacks." *Sociological Analysis* 41 (Fall): 231–45.

————. 1995. "Integrating Religious and Racial Identities: An Analysis of LDS African-American Explanations of the Priesthood Ban." *Review of Religious Research* 36 (March): 295–311.

————. 2000. "Negotiating Social and Cultural Contradictions: Interracial Dating and Marriage among African American Mormons." *Virginia Social Science Journal* 35: 85–98.

White, Richard. 1991. *The Middle Ground: Indians, Empires, and Republics in the Great Lakes Region, 1615–1815.* New York: Cambridge University Press.

Whitney, Orson F. 1905. Address. In *Conference Report,* October, 89–93. Salt Lake City: Deseret News.

Whittaker, David J. 1985. "Mormons and Native Americans: Historical and Bibliographic Introduction." *Dialogue* 18 (4): 33–64.

————, ed. 1995. *Mormon Americana: A Guide to Sources and Collections in the United States.* Provo, Utah: BYU Studies.

Why I Joined the Mormon Church. 1972. Pamphlet. Salt Lake City: Church of Jesus Christ of Latter-day Saints. Personal files.

Widtsoe, John A. 1950. Address. In *Conference Report,* October, 34–38. Salt Lake City: Deseret News.

————. 1960. *Evidences and Reconciliations.* Compiled by G. Homer Durham. Salt Lake City: Bookcraft.

Wilcox, S. Michael. 1998. "The Abraham Covenant." *Ensign,* January, 42–48.

Wilkins, David E. 1997. *American Indian Sovereignty and the U.S. Supreme Court: The Masking of Justice.* Austin: University of Texas Press.

Wilkinson, Ernest L., and Leonard J. Arrington. 1976. *Brigham Young University: The First One Hundred Years.* Provo, Utah: BYU Press.

Williams, Frederick S., and Frederick G. Williams. 1987. *From Acorn to Oak Tree.* Fullerton, Calif.: Et Cetera, Et Cetera Graphics.

Willson, Linda O. 1973. "Changes in Scholastic Achievement and Intelligence of Indian Children Enrolled in a Foster Placement Program." M.S. thesis, Brigham Young University.

Wilson, John F. [1840] 1844. *Our Israelitish Origin: Lectures on Ancient Israel and the Israelitish Origin of the Modern Nations of Europe.* London: Nisbet.

Wilson, Marvin R. 2000. *Our Father Abraham: Jewish Roots of the Christian Faith.* Grand Rapids, Mich.: Eerdmans.

Wilson, William A. 1978. "Mormon Folk Belief and the Arab-Israeli Wars." Paper presented at the Seventh World Congress of Jewish Studies, Jerusalem, August 10. Copy in personal files.

———. 1988. "Freeways, Parking Lots, and Ice Cream Stands: The Three Nephites in Contemporary Society." *Dialogue* 21 (3): 13–26.

Wilson, William A., and Richard C. Poulsen. 1980. "The Curse of Cain and Other Stories." *Sunstone,* November–December, 9–13.

Wood, Forrest G. 1990. *The Arrogance of Faith: Christianity and Race in America from the Colonial Era to the Twentieth Century.* Boston: Northeastern University Press.

Woodruff, Wilford. 1863. Discourse, June 12, 1863. In *Journal of Discourses,* 10:214–20. London: Latter-day Saints Book Depot, 1854–86.

———. 1880. Discourse, July 3, 1880. In *Journal of Discourses,* 21:189–96. London: Latter-day Saints Book Depot, 1854–86.

———. [1909] 1986. *Wilford Woodruff, Fourth President of the Church of Jesus Christ of Latter-day Saints, History of His Life and Labors as Recorded in His Daily Journals.* Compiled by Matthias F. Cowley. Reprint, Salt Lake City: Bookcraft.

———. 1985. *Wilford Woodruff's Journals.* 9 vols. Edited by Scott G. Kenney. Salt Lake City: Signature Book.

Woodward, C. Vann. 1955. *The Strange Career of Jim Crow.* New York: Oxford University Press.

Wright, Geneva E. 1981. *The Adventures of Amos Wright: Mormon Frontiersman.* Provo, Utah: Utah Council Press.

Wright, Sally. 1970. "The Mormon Issue: Plain as Black and White." *Concord Transcript* (Concord, Calif.), March 11, 10, and March 12, 3 (two parts).

Xi, Lian. 1997. *The Conversion of Missionaries: Liberalism in American Protestant Missions in China, 1907–1932.* University Park: Pennsylvania State University Press.

Yang, Fenggang. 1999. *Chinese Christians in America: Conversion, Assimilation, and Adhesive Identities.* University Park: Pennsylvania State University Press.

Young, Brigham. 1855. Discourse, April 8, 1855. In *Journal of Discourses,* 2:266–71. London: Latter-day Saints Book Depot, 1854–86.

———. 1857. Discourse, June 28, 1857. In *Journal of Discourses,* 4:367–74. London: Latter-day Saints Book Depot, 1854–86.

———. 1863a. Discourse, May 31, 1863. In *Journal of Discourses,* 10:187–95. London: Latter-day Saints Book Depot, 1854–86.

———. 1863b. Discourse, July 8, 1963. In *Journal of Discourses,* 10:229–32. London: Latter-day Saints Book Depot, 1854–86.

———. 1866a. Discourse, July 28, 1866. In *Journal of Discourses,* 11:263–66. London: Latter-day Saints Book Depot, 1854–86.

————. 1866b. Remarks, December 23, 1866. In *Journal of Discourses,* 11:279. London: Latter-day Saints Book Depot, 1854–86.

————. 1868a. Discourse, August 13, 1868. In *Journal of Discourses,* 12:269–74. London: Latter-day Saints Book Depot, 1854–86.

————. 1868b. Discourse, November 29, 1868. In *Journal of Discourses,* 12:308–16. London: Latter-day Saints Book Depot, 1854–86.

Young, Margaret Blair, and Darius A. Gray. 2000–2003. *Standing on the Promises* (a trilogy): book 1, *One More River to Cross* (2000); book 2, *Bound for Canaan* (2002). Salt Lake City: Bookcraft.

Young, Seymour B. 1906. Address. In *Conference Report,* October, 89–94. Salt Lake City: Deseret News.

Zucker, Louis C. 1968. "Joseph Smith as a Student of Hebrew." *Dialogue* 3 (2): 41–55.

————. 1981. "A Jew in Zion." *Sunstone,* September–October, 35–44.

Index

Abel, Elijah, 214–16

Abraham, Book of. *See* Book of Abraham

Abraham, lineage of: adoption into, 3, 23, 30, 32, 50, 104, 134, 147, 255; Arabs and, 183–84, 187–88; Christian ties to, 207; definition of, 2, 4, 23, 32, 36, 272, 276; favored lineages and, 2–3, 10, 30, 276; Lamanites from, 115, 120, 134–35; lineage of Ham and, 238; Mormons from, 10, 23, 25–26, 120, 174–75, 179; patriarchal blessings and, 35

Abrahamic covenant: Christian superses-sion of, 160, 162–63; favored lineages and, 3, 10; Jews and, 158–59, 205–7; Mormon fulfillment of, 30, 165; universal applica-bility of, 3, 30, 36, 166

affinity (religious): anti-Semitism and, 197–201, 204, 208, 287, 290–92, 295. *See also* particularism; philo-Semitism

Africa: LDS members in, 115, 237, 250, 259; McKay tour to, 232; Mormon missionar-ies from, 237; Mormon missionary work in, 115, 184, 212, 219, 236–37, 245, 274; myths about blacks in, 256; native music and Mormon church in, 113n25. *See also* Ghana; Nigeria

African Americans. *See* black Mormons; blacks

African lineage: "inferiority" of, 20, 214, 221, 256; Mormon definition of, 255, 274–75; Mormon identity boundaries and, 10–11; preexistence and, 217; priesthood restric-tions for, 30–31, 36, 213, 232, 235–36, 238, 240–41. *See also* blacks; Cain; Mormon church: racial policies of

Afro-American Oral History Project, 243, 256

Afro-American Symposium (LDS), 245

Aho, James A.: on Christian Patriotism movement, 203–4

AIM. *See* American Indian Movement

Ainsworth, Charles, 282

allotment policy: of U.S. government for Indians, 46–48, 62, 68, 75, 79, 80, 84

AME church. *See* First African Methodist Episcopal Church

American Indian Movement (AIM), 78, 101, 129, 132

Anderson, James H., 28–29

Anglo-Ephraimites, 13, 34, 275

Anglo-Israel Federation of America, 28–29

Anglo-Israelism: among Mormons, 164, 204. *See also* Anglo-Saxon triumphalism; Brit-ish Israelism

Anglo-Saxon triumphalism, 14n7, 19–21; Mormons and, 22–23, 26–29, 35–36, 135, 151, 216–17, 268–69; Nordic racialism and, 19, 20, 24–28, 30, 32. *See also* British Is-raelism

anomia: anti-Semitism and, 202, 290–93; and discrimination against blacks, 295

Anti-Defamation League, 161, 181, 194

anti-Semitism: in America, 27–29, 159, 186, 194–95; among Christians, 4, 158–63, 169, 191, 194–96, 198, 296n4; in Europe, 158–61, 186–87, 194, 206; among Mormons, 28, 167, 173, 184–85, 191–93, 195–208, 210n16, 273, 287, 290–92, 295; prejudice and, 195, 197, 272–73; proselyting as, 163, 186–87;

Armand L. Mauss, a professor emeritus of sociology and religious studies at Washington State University, has published widely on Mormon studies and other religious movements. His previous book was *The Angel and the Beehive: The Mormon Struggle with Assimilation* (1994). He is past editor of the *Journal for the Scientific Study of Religion* and past president of the Mormon History Association.

The University of Illinois Press
is a founding member of the
Association of American University Presses.

———————————————————————

Composed in 10.5/13 Minion
with Minion display
by Jim Proefrock
at the University of Illinois Press
Manufactured by Thomson-Shore, Inc.

University of Illinois Press
1325 South Oak Street
Champaign, IL 61820-6903
www.press.uillinois.edu